Global Justice and Neoliberal Environmental Governance

This book is an ethical critique of existing approaches to sustainable development and international environmental co-operation. It provides a detailed and structured account of the tensions, normative shifts and contradictions that currently characterize global environmental co-operation as a result of the existing attempt to contain the demands for global environmental justice within institutional boundaries.

With specific focus on three environmental regimes, the book explores the way that various notions of justice feature both implicitly and explicitly in the design of global environmental policies. In so doing, the dominant conceptions of justice that underpin these policies are identified and, in turn, criticized on the basis of their compatibility with the normative essence of global sustainable development. The book demonstrates that, although moral norms have a far greater impact on regime development than is currently acknowledged by orthodox approaches to regime analysis, the core policies for the most part remain rooted in two neoliberal interpretations of justice, both of which, in practice, undermine the ability to achieve sustainable development and international justice.

This text will be of particular interest to those researching and studying in the fields of sustainable development, environmental ethics and environmental politics.

Chukwumerije Okereke is a Senior Research Associate at the Tyndall Centre for Climate Change Research at the University of East Anglia, UK.

Global Justice and Neoliberal Environmental Governance

Ethics, sustainable development and international co-operation

Chukwumerije Okereke

LONDON AND NEW YORK

First published 2008 by Routledge
2 Park Square, Milton Park, Abingdon, Oxon OX14 4RN

Simultaneously published in the USA and Canada by Routledge
270 Madison Avenue, New York, NY 10016
Routledge is an imprint of the Taylor & Francis Group, an informa business.

Transferred to Digital Printing 2010

© 2008 Chukwumerije Okereke

Typeset in Times New Roman by Prepress Projects Ltd, Perth, UK

All rights reserved. No part of this book may be reprinted or reproduced or utilized in any form or by any electronic, mechanical, or other means, now known or hereafter invented, including photocopying and recording, or in any information storage or retrieval system, without permission in writing from the publishers.

British Library Cataloguing in Publication Data
A catalogue record for this book is available from the British Library

Library of Congress Cataloging in Publication Data
Okereke, Chukwumerije.
Global justice and neoliberal environmental governance: ethics, sustainable development and international co-operation / Chukwumerije Okereke.
p. cm. – (Routledge research in postcolonial literatures; 115)
Includes bibliographical references.
ISBN-13: 978-0-415-41230-8 (hardback: alk. paper)
ISBN-13: 978-0-203-94074-7 (e-book: alk. paper) 1. Environmental justice.
2. Sustainable development – Moral and ethical aspects. I. Title.
GE220.O34 2007
363.7'0526–dc22
2007006404

ISBN 10: 0-415-41230-7 (hbk)
ISBN 10: 0-415-59946-6 (pbk)
ISBN 10: 0-203-94074-1 (ebk)

ISBN 13: 978-0-415-41230-8 (hbk)
ISBN 13: 978-0-415-59946-7 (pbk)
ISBN 13: 978-0-203-94074-7 (ebk)

Contents

Acknowledgements vii

PART I
Setting the scene 1

1 Introduction 3

2 Regimes as a medium for international distributive justice 14

3 Towards a theory of global environmental justice 32

PART II
Empirical analysis of three regime texts 55

4 Managing a global commons: The United Nations Conference on the Law of the Sea 57

5 The global waste management regime: The Basel Convention 80

6 Protecting the global atmosphere: The UNFCCC 99

PART III
Normative critique 123

7 Establishing the core ideas of justice in eco-regimes 125

8 Ethics of global sustainability and neoliberal ideas of justice 146

9 Global justice and neoliberal environmental governance   168

10 Conclusions   187

Notes   194
Bibliography   202
Index   227

Acknowledgements

This book adds to the list of many others that started their lives as a PhD thesis. It was completed at the University of Keele between 2002 and 2005. As such, I would like to, first, acknowledge the invaluable assistance of those who guided me through the challenging and yet exciting period that is doing a PhD. Topmost on the list is Matthew Paterson, my original lead supervisor. He sacrificed plenty of his valuable time to read my work (including taking a certain draft copy with him on his holidays). He made insightful comments and gave me lots of encouragement and practical tips on how to complete the work. Even when he could not supervise the project to the end, he maintained correspondence with me, read through draft copies and offered particularly useful comments. Next, I would like to thank John Vogler who moved from being my second to my lead supervisor. He was exceedingly generous with his time when it came to reading and discussing my work. He also provided me with plenty of enlightening comments and suggestions. I have often said in many informal settings that these two scholars are my greatest source of inspiration.

I also want to thank Prof. John Horton for his interest in my research and career development. Although juggling many tasks as the Head of the School of Politics, Internationals Relations and Philosophy at Keele University, he nonetheless agreed to read some chapters of an earlier version of this thesis and offered very constructive comments. I would also like to thank Hugh Dyer, my external examiner, who provided me with plenty of positive and constructive feedback. Parts of the argument developed further here appeared first in 'Global Environmental Sustainability: Intragenerational Equity and Conceptions of Justice in Multilateral Environmental Regimes', *Geoforum* 37, 725–738, and are reproduced with permission from Elsevier. In this process, I have benefited immensely from the guidance of Harriet Bulkeley, Gordon Walker and Paul Robins and from the comments of two anonymous reviewers, which forced me to rethink some aspects of my argument.

A reasonable portion of this book was either written or revised after I was appointed as a Research Associate in the Tyndall Centre for Climate Change Research. As such, I would like to extend my sincere appreciation to Alex Haxeltine and Diana Liverman, my immediate supervisor and lead researcher, respectively, for their encouragement and support.

I owe a great debt to numerous friends and colleagues who read portions of this work at different stages and offered valuable comments. These include Mark Charlesworth, Tim Rayner, Jacky Pett, Fariborz Zelli, Darrell Whitman and Chima Mordi.

I am also indebted to many friends, family and Church members for their wonderful care, encouragement, prayers and support. The list is long but I would like to mention my parents, Sylvester and Patricia, and my siblings, Nneka, Uzoigwe, Ikpo, Ifeyinwa and Amauche, and my extremely supportive wife Boma. They all believed in me, prayed for me and made huge financial sacrifices to enable me to complete this project. Others include Benneth (the Boss), Robert, Oluwatoyin, Jennifer Bruce-Nanka, Tonbara, Pastor David Williams and his wife Sue, Bill and Doreen Evans, Doris and John Owens, Sai and Nirupa Singaram, John and Kath Fallows, Stewart and Jean Galloway, Chinyere and Martins Ajah and Brenda Procter. Also included in this list are Gabriel, Austin, Yasmin, Bola, Cosmas, Delphine and Donald.

Finally, it is to all those in the Third World countries whose opportunities and potential are limited by circumstances of birth and conditions of global injustice that this book is dedicated. May the Lord help us never to accept the manmade as the divine.

Part I
Setting the scene

1 Introduction

This book is about the politics of justice in institutions for global environmental governance. It explores the way various notions of justice feature both implicitly and explicitly in the design of global environmental policies based on the analysis of three global environmental regimes. The three regimes chosen are the ones established by: (i) the Third United Nations Conference on the Law of the Sea (UNCLOS III); (ii) the Basel Convention on the Transboundary Movements of Hazardous Wastes and their Disposal; and (iii) the United Nations Framework Convention on Climate Change (UNFCCC) and the related Kyoto Protocol. By paying close and detailed attention to the primary texts of regimes and, in some cases, the associated negotiation processes, I seek to capture the shifts and tensions that occur both in policy and discursive terms as a result of the increasing contestations for equity and distributive justice in the operation of multilateral environmental regimes. In practice, this is conceived as a way of extrapolating the dominant conceptions of justice that underpin key global environmental policies, with a view, in turn, to assessing the suitability of such approaches. At the same time, the analysis serves as a means of highlighting the prospects and limitations of aspirations for distributive equity in environmental regimes, especially within the context of North–South equity.

The book addresses two distinct but closely related arguments. First, I argue that, although current international environmental regimes reflect a variety of (often contradictory) notions of justice, they are very much determined by conceptions of justice that are consistent with the neoliberal political economic agenda. These take one, or both, of two forms: justice as property rights, associated with Robert Nozick, and justice as mutual advantage, as defended by David Gauthier. I further argue that these neoliberal ideas of justice do not offer a promising base for the pursuit of global sustainable development, particularly as articulated by the Brundtland Report, as they are incapable of delivering on the promise of distributive justice, which is embedded in the idea. It follows from this premise that dominant approaches to environmental sustainability fail because they do not take sufficiently seriously the role of international equity or justice understood in more redistributive terms. Hence, although it is widely asserted that equity and justice are important elements of international environmental regimes, on looking closer,

4 *Setting the scene*

it appears that a great deal of the concern for distributional justice in these institutions has been largely co-opted for neoliberal ends, much to the disadvantage of the already marginalized sections of the global community.

The second argument, which follows on from the first, is that conventional approaches to regime analysis are seriously defective to the extent that they are unable to represent and account for the contestations for distributional justice that so glaringly characterize the development of regimes. I argue that standard international relations approaches to regime analysis are dominated by positivist assumptions that fail to take due account of normative concerns. Indeed, I seek to demonstrate that a significant aspect of the processes of regime development can be explained *only* by focusing on the complex interplay between moral norms – mainly ideas of international distributive equity and neoliberal economic values.

Before proceeding any further it is important to make three conceptual clarifications. The first is that this book is concerned chiefly with intragenerational justice, which addresses the need for the equitable distribution of resources, risks and responsibilities among the states and/or peoples of the present generation (Rawls 1971, 1999; Beitz 1979; Pogge 1992; Brown 1992, 2004). Other dimensions of justice (not given much attention in this work) include intergenerational equity, which addresses issues of justice between present and future generations (Dobson 1998; Barry B 1999), and interspecies justice, which focuses on justice between human and non-human natural beings (Low and Gleeson 1998; Attfield 2003, 2005; Soper 2005). The second is that the analysis in this book focuses mainly on the conception of sustainable development as articulated by the World Commission on Environment and Development (Brundtland Report). At the same time, whereas some authors argue that there is a difference between sustainable development and environmental sustainability, I take the view (an equally popular one) that environmental protection is inherent in the concept of sustainable development and therefore use the two terms interchangeably throughout this book. Third, the term 'equity' is used, following the traditions of Aristotle and Aquinas, to refer to more specific 'forms of judgement that remedies the injustice of positive law at the point of application by attending to particular features of the persons and circumstances involved . . . so that equity is not generically different from justice' (Tasioulas 1989: 148). Justice is thus the key term in this book and equity is used mainly as a means of avoiding monotony.

Notions of intragenerational equity have in recent years pushed into the frontline of global environmental sustainability discourse with a clamour for environmental justice featuring increasingly in 'contemporary concerns with the issues of risk, sustainability and political ecology' (Bulkeley *et al.* 2003: 1). Contrary to the hitherto prevailing notion that sustainability simply entails conservation and the effort to bequeath subsequent generations with a wholesome earth (cf. Pinchot 1910; Leopold 1968; Naess 1973), it is now widely held that sustainable development requires, indeed is only realisable via, a just, fair and equitable distribution of available resources both within and between generations (World Commission on Environment and Development 1987; Guha and Martinez-Alier 1997; Redclift 2000; Low and Gleeson 2001: 3; Spangenberg 2001: 29–32; Attfield 2003; Schlosberg 2005: 102; Walker and Bulkeley 2006: 657). This awareness has, in turn, made questions of distributive justice a vital aspect in the negotiation of multilateral environmental agreements and the operation of institutions for international environmental governance (Grubb *et al.* 1992; Paterson 1996a; Agarwal *et al.* 2001; Tol *et al.* 2004; Paavola 2005: 143; Adger *et al.* 2006).

Indeed, the ethical dimensions of global environmental change and relevant institutions are fast becoming central to the discourse on sustainability (IPCC 1995, 2001). This development is closely tied to the fact that institutions for global environmental governance have metamorphosed from the traditional role of preservation of endangered non-human species to the high-profile and more sensitive roles of resource allocation, as in the case of the United Nations Convention on the Law of the Sea; burden sharing, as in the case of the climate change regime; and regulation of trade, as in the case of the Basel Convention on the Transboundary Movements of Hazardous Wastes and their Disposal. In general, regimes now play vital roles in granting access to and control over natural resources between states and people within the global community.

Hence, in assuming these regulative and distributive roles within the context of a heightened awareness of disparities, ecological interdependence and a earth's limited 'carrying capacity' (Meadows *et al.* 1972), environmental regimes have become sites for intense hegemonic struggles and the subject of vitriolic debates. At one level are those who debate the 'internal design features and exogenous issue-area factors' (Hall 1998: 86) that constrain or boost the effectiveness of regimes (cf. Young 1989a; Susskind and Ozawa 1992; Keohane and Levy 1996). But becoming equally important is the issue of how policies organized with respect to a 'singular grand narrative' (Low and Gleeson 2001: 2) may possibly reflect the priorities of cultures and states that not only heed disparate value systems but also occupy different positions in the international political economy (cf. Kelly 1990; Dyer 1993; Chatterjee and Finger 1994; Sachs 1999; McCarthy 2004). Laferriere and Stoett (1999: 107–108), in their book *International Relations Theory and Ecological Thought*, capture this concern very well when they state that:

> Though the prospect of increased co-operation on environmental issues through institutional design and growth may please many environmentalists, it may be coming as part of a package deal that in fact decreases heterogeneity, increases extractive activity, and emphasises technocratic problem solving to what are in essence political and even, philosophical dilemmas.

This concern is also implicit in Achterberg's assertion that the existence of global environmental problems not only raises 'ethical issues of first importance for global environmental governance' but also creates a condition that demands that 'the ethical basis and forms of global governance' be held up for scrutiny and questions (Achterberg 2001: 183; cf. Low and Gleeson 2001: 3–7; Bernstein 2001; Meyer 2005). Attfield (2003: 159) is equally of the view that the global nature of many environmental problems makes the need for a 'global, cosmopolitan normative ethic, and its [more explicit] recognition on the part of agents' fundamental on the road to a just and sustainable global society. Low and Gleeson (2001: 2) insist that the 'creation of new institutions for environmental governance must be accompanied by the development of human values'. They point out that institutions are yoked with ethical concerns in ways that make the two concepts inseparable, and therefore argue for the development of what they call 'an ethical "polyphonic" narrative of a new level and the institutions which will allow such politics to flourish' (ibid.: 2). However, for Spangenberg (2001), the entire clamour for a 'polyphonic ethic' in institutions for global environmental governance comes together in the quest for international distributive justice. He argues that, insofar as the concept of sustainable development rests squarely on two notions of equity (intragenerational and intergenerational), 'distributional justice will need to be constantly demonstrated and contested in every step in the process of change' on the road to global sustainability (ibid.: 41).

Spangenberg's argument echoes the position of the developing countries in the run-up meetings to the United Nations Conference on the Human Environment (Stockholm 1972). In preparation for this conference, which later marked the successful institutionalization of the environmental problematique in the international agenda, a panel of 27 experts, mainly from the developing countries, predicted that one of the major issues that would confront the international community in its search for more sustainable pathways to development would be the question of global distributive equity. The group, which articulated its view in what later became known as the Founex Report, noted that, although increased attention to global environmental protection would inevitably impose some constraints on all states alike, 'one of the major questions which would arise' as nations began to co-operate to grapple with diverse environmental problems would be 'how the higher cost of future development would be shared as between developed and developing nations' (Founex Report 1971: 7). Further, the group expressed the concern that, given the extreme disparity in the political and economic strength between the developed and the developing countries, it was not improbable that the poor developing countries could be made to 'bear the extra burden of global environmental protection without reaping any benefits that may arise'.

> Clearly there is a scope for a better allocation of the presently available resources. . . . If the concern for human environment reinforces the commitment to development, it must also reinforce the commitment to international aid. It should provide a stimulus for augmenting the flow of resources from the advanced to the developing countries. Unless appropriate economic action is taken, there are a number of ways in which the developing countries could suffer rather than profit from the new emphasis on the environment.
> (Ibid.: 3)

This view later found expression in much of the text of the Stockholm declaration. It was reflected in general admissions, such as 'the industrialized countries should make efforts to reduce the gap between themselves and the developing countries', as well as more specific statements, such as 'substantial quantities of financial and technological assistance as a supplement to the domestic effort of the developing countries and such timely assistance as may be required' are crucial measures in the pursuit of a decent global human environment [United Nations Conference on the Human Environment (UNCHE) 1972: Principles 7, 9, 14].

Apparently inspired by the eloquent articulation of the need to integrate an emphasis on environmental protection and the need for global distributive justice in the Founex Report, the World Commission on Environment and Development (WCED) later asserted that global distributive equity is a central element in the quest for global environmental sustainability and in the international co-operative arrangements that might be designed to achieved this goal. The Brundtland Report states in unmistakable terms that 'inequality is the planet's main environmental problem' and, hence, that 'it is futile to attempt to deal with environmental problems without a broader perspective that encompasses the factors underlying world poverty and international inequality' (WCED 1987: 3, 6, *passim*). The report, accordingly, recommends considerable international redistribution of wealth from the North to the South, insisting that such a step is fundamental to the search for global sustainable development. Subsequently, from the United Nations Conference on Environment and Development (UNCED) conference in Rio de Janeiro (1992) to the World Summit on Sustainable Development in Johannesburg (2002), issues of North–South equity and distributional justice have become one the most contentious elements in the global sustainable development discourse. Maurice Strong (the former Chairman of the Rio Earth Summit) could very well have been reflecting on this situation when he said:

> [N]ever more could the environment issue be considered only in the narrow context of the pollution problems of the rich. It could only be considered as inextricably linked with the development needs and aspirations of developing countries and the imperatives for new dimensions of co-operation and equity in north south relationship.
>
> (Strong 1999: 1)

Similarly, Rowlands (1991: 267) identifies four key preconditions for the success of global environmental agreements and says of equity that:[1]

> a second major precondition for co-operation is the presence of fairness, in a system wide sense . . . . Such equity will not only be based on a comparative analysis of costs and benefits, but it will also be based on the less tangible factors, such as history and ideology. This issue of fairness will continue to play a significant role in the pursuit of co-operative agreements on issues of global environmental change.

In general, the consensus is that international distributive equity is a crucial factor both as a rationale for regimes but also for their acceptability and effectiveness (Young 1989b: 368; Hurrell and Kingsbury 1992; Conca *et al.* 1995a;

Low and Gleeson 2001; Paterson 1996a; Toth 1999; Athanasiou and Baer 2002; Paavola and Lowe 2005; Adger *et al.* 2006).

But despite, or perhaps as a result of, the commonplace assertions that justice is central to the operation of, and the rationale for, regimes and despite the widespread knowledge that 'there are a number of different viewpoints on what an equitable arrangement looks like' (Paterson 1996a: 181), the general implications of equity notions and justice aspirations in regime policies remain grossly understudied. There is a burgeoning literature concerned with various aspects of environmental justice at the international level; however, the focus of most of these studies usually takes one, or both, of two forms: to assert the need for justice and equity in the development of a particular environmental regime (Shue 1992; Humphreys 1996; Shukla 1999; Adger *et al.* 2006) or to show that specific regime policies impact unfairly on certain sections of the global community (Leggett 2000; Agarwal *et al.* 2001; Tol *et al.* 2004; Bachram 2005). There are also, especially with the case of climate change, several discussions concerning how different policy proposals map onto particular conceptions of justice (Grubb *et al.* 1992; Banuri *et al.* 1996; Young 1992; Adger *et al.* 2006). Therefore, although there are many elaborate discussions focusing on the importance of equity in regimes, there is not as much scholarship devoted to showing the conceptions of justice that actually prevail in existing international regimes. At the same time, rigorous exercises dedicated to accounting for these ethical contestations and the policy shifts they engender are quite sparse. As such, terms such as 'equity', 'equitable', 'justice' and 'fairness' are frequently used in academic and policy circles but are very poorly articulated. The result is that their exact content, the processes they describe and the policy prescriptions they elicit are rarely documented in the literature. This lapse is curious for several reasons.

First, as noted, although justice has maintained its position as the principal virtue of social institutions (Aristotle 1847/1998; Rawls 1971: 3; Mill 1973; Barry and Matravers 1997: 141), the concept remains incredibly malleable and thus open to different interpretations. For utilitarians, justice is about finding and maximizing welfare utility to achieve the greatest happiness for the greatest number of people (Bentham 1789/1948; Mill 1973). For others, it is about providing all with equal opportunities and balancing in favour of the least advantaged in society (Rawls 1971). Other ideas of justice include: (i) demanding from each according to his ability and giving to each according to his need (Marx 1969); (ii) dividing equally across the board; (iii) the idea of enhancing the capability of all individuals to lead meaningful lives (Sen 1999); (iv) giving to each according to what he could hope to get in a real bargaining situation (Gauthier 1986); and (v) apportioning to each according to the market forces of demand and supply (Nozick 1974).

In the midst of such a variety of notions of justice it seems quite superficial to assert that justice should be a rationale or precondition for international institutions without attempting to specify what this means exactly. Yet, this is the approach adopted by most scholars engaging in the analysis of international environmental institutions. Beckerman and Pasek (2001: 167) addressed this point directly when they observed that, although the way 'in which the costs and benefits of any policy should be shared out between the rich and poor countries remains theoretically contentious, most discussions of global environmental agreements seem to assume that there already exists a guiding principle'.

Following on from this, the second reason why this lapse is curious is that, even when differences in the ideas of justice are noted in the process of regime development, it is not the case, nor is it necessarily desirable, that practical efforts to frame and respond to global environmental problems are suspended until such differences are resolved. In other words, despite differences in viewpoints over what constitutes justice, international environmental institutions continue to function. Therefore, because it is impossible for institutions, as social artefacts, to be morally neutral (Hoffmann 1987: 37; Tooze 1990; Ostrom 1990; Vogler 2003), it follows that, at any given time, international institutions are both functioning on the basis of, and promoting, a given set of norms and values. This means that, although international institutions may be created to promote co-operation among states, it is also the case that these institutions both promote and function on the basis of some values and norms that, in most cases, privilege the interests of some over and above those of others.

The key problem these two scenarios present is that, in an international setting characterized by immense asymmetry in economic, political and technological capabilities, it is ever so easy for institutions to become mere instruments of domination and oppression in the hands of the more powerful while on the surface creating the impression that they are functioning for the mutual benefit of all. Moreover, unlike national politics, in which those who lack the power to set policies can still make their views well known in policy-making circles, international institutional politics tend to be elitist, technocratic and undemocratic. The processes of regime formation tend to occur at a distance, which grossly limits public participation. Accordingly, there is a marked tendency for the legitimate aspirations of a vast majority of people whose lives are affected by the actions of institutions to be inadequately considered. What is more, historically, the international system is not characterized by the strong sense of community that is found in national political systems. Despite growing interdependencies and the unique sense of oneness or common destiny that environmental issues often evoke, sovereignty remains the major organizing principle of international politics. The result is that normative arguments which often form the main aspects of national political processes somehow get lost at national borders. Consequently, there are hardly any explicit debates on the norms and values on which international actions are, or ought to be, predicated. The foregoing discussion provides much of the context for the apprehension often expressed by Third World scholars and politicians towards current approaches to international co-operation for global sustainability.

Furthermore, although it is widely accepted that environmentalism poses a series of new challenges to conventional approaches to the study of international relations (IR) (Hurrell and Kingsbury 1992: 6; Vogler 1996: 2; Dyer 2001: 106), as well as the assumptions and abiding concerns of political philosophy (Eckersley 1992; Barry B. 1995, 1999; Hayward 1998; Beckerman and Pasek 2001), theories of justice that take a detailed look at the peculiar nature of environmental concerns and ethical dimensions of international institutions for co-operation towards sustainability are still in short supply. Accordingly, there remains much to be fleshed out both in terms of how justice and sustainability intertwine and the exact role of concerns for justice in global institutions for environmental governance – a situation that mostly leads to the popular but erroneous assumption that the prevalence of global environmental regimes translates to equitable co-operation between the political North and South (cf. Young 1989b: 199; Benedick 1991; Keohane *et al*. 1993).

At the same time, dominant approaches to regime analysis do a lot of disservice to the role of shared underlying values in the development and operation of institutions for global environmental governance. Because of their obsession with 'state actors' and their reliance on the rational choice analytical model, neither the neorealist nor the neoliberal institutionalist approach to regime analysis can account for, let alone promote the understanding of, the dialectic of notions of justice in particular and the functions of norms and 'discursive practices' (Litfin 1994) in general, in the construction of socio-political realities and response strategies to global environmental change (cf. Cox 1983, 1992, Kratochwil and Ruggie 1986; Wendt 1987, 1995). In accordance with the rational choice hypothesis (RCH), for example, the dynamics of international co-operation via regimes – including the process of elaboration of the rules and principles – would have to be accounted for solely in terms of power and self-interested calculations by state actors. But although this may be true for a number of policies and programmes, the rational choice model cannot account for a multitude of other principles that have now become regular features of global environmental treaties. Such principles and concepts include the common heritage of mankind (CHM) (UNCLOS III), the common but differentiated responsibility (CDR) principle (UNFCCC), the Global Facility Fund, the duty to re-import waste (Basel) and the notion of individual environmental rights (Basel), among other numerous equity principles and programmes associated with global environmental politics (GEP).

A number of scholars from the academic disciplines of both IR and political philosophy have agonized over this lacuna. In one of the first of such lamentations, Shue (1992) decried the prevalence of what he called the 'two-track' approach to environmental regime analysis. According to Shue the two-track approach refers to the situation in which some regime analysts argue that emphasizing questions of justice and the gap between the North and South during the negotiation of multilateral environmental agreements 'constitute impediments for concerted action' (ibid.: 373). In his more recent article, 'The IR/relevance of environmental ethics', David Johns (2003) has equally lamented this gap, calling for works that seek to uncover the role of ethics and underlying social assumptions in the design of national and international environmental policies. Similarly, Eugene Hangrove (2003) in 'What is wrong? Who is to blame?' has equally invited reflections on why ethical discourses at large are neglected in international institutions for environmental governance.

In response, Brown (2004) identified the general marginalization of values in international policy circles as one of the major causes. He argued that the preoccupation of policy-makers with economic prosperity and instrumental rationality ensures that 'the only priests allowed into the temple of environmental decision-making are scientists, engineers, economists and lawyers' (ibid.: 111). But at the same time, Brown equally pointed to the fact that most of the environmental ethics literature does not seek to practically connect with specific environmental issues or to address the questions that directly affect the well-being of the majority of the world's population:

> Now occasionally environmental ethics literature has acknowledged problems with this narrow instrumental rationality employed in decision making; yet this literature is rarely tied to specific environmental controversies. Therefore the second reason why environmental ethics has not penetrated day to day environmental policy making is that most environmental ethics literature is either too much abstract to engage in real environmental decisions or completely irrelevant to the kinds of ethical issues that usually come up in environmental controversies
>
> (Ibid.: 111)

Brown's argument resonates with a point made by John Vogler with respect to conventional approaches to regime analysis. Vogler (2000: 22) argues that mainstream approaches to regime analysis have arisen as a result of an 'obsession with the preservation of order at the expense of questions of justice'. As a second issue of discomfort he also notes the fact that these approaches 'have tended to neglect analysis and description in favour of large-scale theoretical debates about hegemonic decline and regime creation and change'. Of course, with the US antitoxic dump campaigns and the climate change problem, there has been a certain flourishing of issue-specific analyses on distributive justice and sustainability. For instance, a lot of work has been devoted to the moral foundations and ethical rationale of possible emission allocation approaches with respect to the climate change issue (e.g. Grubb *et al*. 1992; Toth 1999). But here again, emphasis is usually on scenarios rather than on the final product of relevant regimes.

This book is an attempt to fill some of these gaps that have been identified in the literature in the approach to regime analysis. Accordingly, I have focused on specific and contemporary environmental issues and engage first with empirical investigations before moving on to conceptual analysis. To clarify, however, it is not my aim to show that one conception of justice is superior to the others. Rather, the focus is to draw attention to the nature of the contestations for justice in environmental regimes and to indicate the prospects and limitations of these contestations. This naturally leads to the questions of why certain ideas of justice should predominate over contending interpretations, how compatible these prevailing ideas of justice are with the core ideals of sustainable development as established in the WCED Report, and why popular approaches to regime analysis should ignore these contestations. Therefore, this book is, first, an analysis of *'what is'* in contrast to *'what could be',* and, second, a critique of *'what is'* in relation *to 'what should be'*. It is this combination of empirical inquiry with an ethical critique of the dominant approaches, as well as an explanation of why they prevail in the midst of contending ideas, that constitute, I think, the main input of this work.

The rest of this work is organized as follows. Chapter 2 presents an essentially descriptive account of the ways in which environmental regimes serve as a medium for the distribution of benefits and burdens among peoples and states in the global community. In the process, I also trace the trajectory of the awareness and development of the idea of justice and intragenerational equity in the operation of multilateral environmental regimes. Chapter 3 provides an account of the different ideas of justice from which parties to international environmental conventions draw at one point or another, and indicates how each idea of justice might intertwine with the notion of global environmental sustainability. Chapters 2 and 3 form Part I of the text and set the stage for the textual analysis that is undertaken in Part II.

In Part II (Chapters 4–6) the primary texts of three environmental agreements are studied, with the aim of seeing how, where and in what ways justice, equity or related terms feature in the convention documents. This is carried out with particular reference to the core policies of the regimes and to existing interpretations of justice. The overall aim is to identify how ideas of justice inflict upon regime policies and which idea(s) of justice has the greatest command of global environmental regimes, as well as the forces and 'discursive practices' through which these are constructed and legitimized. Indeed, a key theme running throughout all three chapters is how the attachment of the North, particularly the USA, to market-based solutions to environmental problems has continually undermined alternative strategies.

Part III is also made up of three chapters but these are concerned with advancing a normative critique of the dominant approaches to sustainable development and regime analysis. In Chapter 7, the aim is to tie the three cases together and to establish the basic point that the dominant conceptions of justice in the three environmental regimes are neoliberal in the way that I suggest. These interpretations are justice as property rights, derived mainly from the work of Robert Nozick, and justice as mutual advantage, which derives in contemporary terms mainly from the works of David Gauthier and Gilbert Harman. Chapter 8 presents the core ethical requirements of global sustainable development, especially with respect to the issue of global justice, using the Brundtland Report as the main reference. The basic lineaments of the two ideas of justice (developed in Chapter 7) are then confronted with the ethical requirements of global sustainable development based on the WCED Report. The aim is to reveal the key areas of incompatibility and to show that the dominant conceptions of justice in regimes do not provide a promising base for the pursuit of sustainability and global environmental justice. The process reveals four key major areas of incompatibility between the neoliberal ideas of justice and the ethical content of sustainability. These include: the conception of the good life, the role of the state in the pursuit of sustainability, the defensibility of aspects of enclosure and the place of politics of need and welfare in the pursuit of global sustainability. Having established that regimes are indeed characterized by various notions of justice, and having shown that the main ideas of justice are not such that they are consistent with the project of global sustainability, Chapter 9 is devoted to exploring the implications of the commitment to neoliberal modes of environmental governance on global distributive equity and global sustainability. It is argued that the general commitment to neoliberal environmental governance has led to a situation where distributional justice is effectively equated with market rationality. Accordingly, international justice has come to be seen not so much as redistributing wealth among nations but as creating more opportunities for growth. It is shown that the general philosophy of neoliberal patterns of governance and the key narratives with which this philosophy is advanced remain irreconcilable with the idea of global environmental justice and North–South equity.

An immediate concern arising from what has been said so far relates to the credibility, given the existence of diverse international environmental treaties, of making generalizations concerning international justice and global environmental policies by looking only at three regimes. This objection is valid but not significant. This is because the cases selected are three very important ones taken from across the broad spectrum of the distinct (although not separable) areas of environmental issues.[2] UNCLOS III (which deals mainly with access to environmental resources) effectively sets the parameters for issues of distributional justice in global environmental regimes. The Basel Convention is central in highlighting the role of socio-economic globalization in transboundary pollution and the distribution of environmental risks. And the climate change regime is arguably the most challenging in the discourse of global environmental politics (GEP). In addition, evidence is drawn from other cases during the course of the analysis to justify the conclusions. But even with these safeguards, it must be admitted that the nature of the issue-area does play a part in determining the exact form of policies (justice) that is agreed, such that there is still a case to be made for expanding the analysis to other issue-areas. However, the emphasis here is not so much on identity as on commonality and discernible trends.

2 Regimes as a medium for international distributive justice

This chapter begins with a brief account of the development and awareness of the ideas of international justice and equity in the operation of multilateral environmental agreements. It shows that initial interest in the environment was based mainly on the aesthetic and recreational concerns of Western middle-class populations as well as the conservation concerns of ecological scientists often with aristocratic backgrounds. At the international level, co-operation for environmental protection is seen to be mainly concerned with the exchange of technical information and scientific ideas designed to conserve various aspects of the non-human environment. This, together with the customary minimalist nature of interstate relations, made questions of justice a marginal concern in the development of international environmental discourse. Subsequently, the chapter proceeds to highlight the significance of environmental regimes as a medium through which states and other autonomous actors in the international community share the benefits and burdens of global social co-operation. The distributional functions of regimes that are discussed include: (i) granting access to common property resources and the global commons; (ii) allocating property rights to contending users; (iii) determining the terms and rules of international commerce; (iv) burden sharing; and (v) the affirmation of basic environmental rights and privileges. The chapter ends by making the point that, whereas distributive equity is now widely regarded as both a precondition and a rationale for regimes, little is generally said about the actual impact of justice in regime development and which conceptions of justice underpin key regime policies.

From conservation to distribution

Mainstream environmentalism did not develop with adequate concern for distributional justice (Pepper 1984, 1993; Bowler 1992). The primary focus of early international environmental agreements (as we shall see below) was on the conservation of a range of non-human species of flora and fauna (cf. Pinchot 1910; Naess 1973; Lee 2000: 31–48). This focus reflects the trajectory of the development of environmentalism in Western democracies as well as the nature of the dominant mode of co-operation between states which, as Hurrell and Kingsbury put it, 'were largely concerned with elaborating minimal rules of co-existence built around the mutual recognition of sovereignty and the corollary norm of non-intervention' (Hurrell and Kingsbury 1992: 6).

The institutionalization of nature reserve committees in Britain and the popularization of ecological science in the west as a whole largely resulted from the works of a number of eminent scientists, most of whom enjoyed great influence in the corridors of power in their respective countries (Pepper 1984, 1993; Bowler 1992). In the USA these included scholars like Henry Thoreau, the American diplomat George Perkins Marsh (1801–82), Aldo Leopold and Gifford Pinchot – a close confidant and advisor to President Theodore Roosevelt. In Europe, scientists like Henry Huxley, Patrick Geddes (1854–1932), A.G. Tansley and the German biologist Ernst Haeckel were among the most influential. Together, albeit with varying emphasis and, at times, on the basis of conflicting ontological premises, these scholars expressed the need for the establishment of nature reserves in the USA and Europe, mainly out of a concern to boost ecological studies (Worster 1982; Bowler 1992). They also advocated for strong governmental efforts to ensure that various species of plants and animals were protected from overexploitation and possible extinction.

This view received a measure of support from aristocratic game hunters whose major preoccupation was to safeguard their favourite pastimes. But perhaps more importantly, the works of these conservationists were well received by a large portion of the Western middle-class population in Europe and the USA who had, in the wake of rapid industrialization, begun to identify the need for recreational facilities in the increasingly urbanized states and counties (Pepper 1984; Guha and Martinez-Alier 1997). In addition to urban recreational facilities, many also desired the establishment of nature areas in the countryside to provide a place away from the busy urban cities where, as Bowler puts it, 'city-dwellers could be revitalized through contact with Nature' (Bowler 1992: 320). These interests eventually crystallized into massive public pressure on the governments of the day to pursue conservation policies including the establishment of national parks and nature reserves in various parts of these countries. In the USA, public pressure of this type was responsible for the establishment of many of the great national parks in America including Yosemite Valley in California and Yellowstone Park in Wyoming (Bowler 1992: 510). It was also these campaigns that provided the momentum for the formation of some of the present-day influential environmental organizations such as the Sierra Club (1892), the Royal Society for the Protection of Birds (1880) and the International Union for the Conservation of Nature and Natural Resources (IUCN).

The point, in sum, is that modern environmentalism in Western democracies did not emerge on the platform of contentions of how environmental resources might be shared or who would bear the burden of efforts to respond to harmful environmental change. Rather, it has its roots, on the one hand, in the ideas of elitist, Promethean scientists concerned with the detailed study of organic structures and evolutionary biology, and, on the other hand, in the aesthetic concerns of a large population of Western middle classes interested in reconnecting with Nature while enjoying the economic benefits of wide-scale industrialization and, in some cases, colonial domination (Guha and Martinez-Alier 1997). This point is worthy of emphasis because it is at the root of the frequent conflict in the perspectives of the developed and the developing countries on how best to conceptualize and/or tackle modern-day global environmental challenges. Wolfgang Sachs is only one of many scholars who have argued that the starting point in analysing global political ecology should be an appreciation of the differences in what is conceived as 'the environmental' and how these differences stem from variations in the historical, material and cultural contexts of states and other autonomous actors (Sachs 1993, 1999; Guha and Martinez-Alier 1997; Low and Glesson 1998; Paterson 2000; Paterson *et al.* 2003: 2; Shiva 2006). For example, von Weizsäcker (1994: 4–5) argues that the difficulties experienced in the United Nations Conference on Environment and Development (UNCED) negotiations can be summarized in terms of the inherent discrepancies in the way that the developed and the developing countries conceptualized 'the environmental':

> The summit was devoted to the environment and its links to development, or at least that is how the Northern media presented it. [But] from the Southern perspective, the United Nations Conference on Environment and Development (UNCED) was devoted to development, global inequalities and their links with the environment. [. . .] The South has tended to define the UNCED agenda as a strategy for overcoming poverty and reversing global economic inequalities. Environmental questions would in this interpretation be subordinated to global economic issues.

The second factor that limited the scope of first-generation environmental regimes to issues of conservation and exchange of scientific information was the dominant character of the international system, with its emphasis on autonomy and state sovereignty (Hurrell and Kingsbury 1992; Vogler and Imber 1996; Humphreys 1996; Falk 2001). The 'international' as a political system has always been characterized by conflict and violence. With the absence of a central authority comparable to that which is present in the national system, anarchy is usually seen as the defining feature of the international system (Bull 1977; Waltz 1979; Hurrell and Woods 1999). Accordingly, in general, the primary purpose of early international co-operative efforts was on the prevention of war and conflict management. In relation to the environment, the focus was mainly on conservation and the exchange of scientific information. In this frame, 'co-operation was built around the rights of states to independence and autonomy and the creation of certain minimalist understandings designed to limit the degree of conflict that naturally occurred within such a pluralist and fragmented system' (Hurrell and Kingsbury 1992: 6).

The Migratory Bird Treaty between the USA and Great Britain (for Canada) is an example of this type of accord. This treaty, signed in 1916, was designed to adopt a uniform protection for certain species of birds that migrate between the USA and Canada. It simply sets certain dates for closed seasons on migratory birds and prohibits the hunting of certain categories of birds. Another example is the Western Hemisphere Convention on Nature and Wildlife Preservation – a 1940 treaty that provides a policy framework for the USA and 17 other American republics to 'protect and preserve in their natural habitat representatives of all species and genera of their native flora and fauna, including migratory birds'. It was also designed to afford the nations an opportunity to co-operate in the 'protection and preservation of the natural scenery, striking geological formations, and regions and natural objects of aesthetic interest or historic or scientific value'. Nothing in this Convention recognizes the social consequences of such ambition or the fact that different communities might have different perspectives on these areas of 'aesthetic interest', depending on their respective levels of development and material prosperity. Other examples that demonstrate the exclusive focus of these early international agreements on conservation include: the Antarctic Treaty of 1959, which was designed to 'foster scientific co-operation among Consultative members and to adopt measures for the protection of the native birds, mammals, and plants of the Antarctic'; the first-generation treaties on the climate, which had as their sole concern a desire to foster international collaboration and coordination of research in the standardization of meteorological observations (Weiss 1975); and the 1973 Polar Bear Treaty between the governments of Canada, Denmark, Norway, the USSR and the USA, which simply aims to help the respective governments coordinate their efforts in the preservation of polar bears on the 'basis of best available scientific evidence'.

The distributional functions of environmental regimes

It was noted in the introductory chapter that the remit of global environmental regimes has since widened to include issues that touch on the fundamental political economic structure of states and that have the ability to either increase or decrease existing patterns of inequality both within and between states (Paterson and Grubb 1992; Paterson 1996b: 13; Bulkeley 2003; Tol et al. 2004; Baer 2006; Williams and Mawdsley 2006: 660–670). Indeed, many commentators on international environmental politics now concede that the question of global distributional justice, that is, how the global resources as well as the benefits and responsibilities arising from interstate relations may be equitably shared between states, has become one of the 'main controversies surrounding the paradigm of sustainable development' (Conca et al. 1995b: 279; cf. Schlosberg 2006: 103). At the moment, though, the literature devoted to a detailed examination of how regimes fulfil this expectation remains extremely limited. Indeed, although it is self-evident that virtually all aspects of the human environment (from the deep seabed outside the jurisdiction of nation states through to the atmosphere and to outer space) have come under one type of international regime or another and, although most of these regimes have been the subject of several scholarly discussions, especially with the new emphasis on sustainable development, they are not commonly presented in the literature as instruments for global resource (re)distribution. Rather, the focus of much of the writings about international regimes has been concentrated on issues of measuring performance and increasing the effectiveness of regimes (Krasner 1983a; Young 1989b, 2001; Keohane *et al.* 1993; Susskind and Ozawa 1992; Susskind 1994; cf. Lemos and Agarwal 2006: 35). When looking at the distributional functions of regimes, it is, therefore, not particularly helpful to consider them in terms of the various categories of 'issue-areas', as is commonly the case in much of the literature. Instead, it is preferable to consider them in terms of the more specific ways in which the remits of regimes enable them to serve as vehicles for exacerbating or correcting existing social and economic inequalities between nations. In doing this, I have grouped the distributional functions of international environmental regimes into five broad categories, with the caveat that there are broad areas of overlap. These functions include: (i) granting access to shared resources and the global commons; (ii) allocation of property rights to states and non-state entities; (iii) determination of terms of trade and international commerce; (iv) burden sharing; and (v) affirmation of basic rights and obligations. I will consider each of these functions in more detail and, in the process, indicate how contestations for environmental justice within the context of the North–South divide arise on the basis of these distributive functions.

Granting access to shared resources and the global commons

The first distributional function of international environmental regimes is that they grant states and non-state actors access to shared resources and the global commons. Virtually all nation states have areas or resources over which they have untrammelled control. This category of resources is called national resources. Under international customary law, each nation state has near unlimited powers to use the resources that are located within the confines of its boundary as it chooses.[1] The United Nations General Assembly (UNGA), for example, through resolution 1803 of 1962 reiterates 'the rights of peoples and nations to permanent sovereignty over their natural resources' and the sovereign right of each state to dispose of its natural wealth and resources as it deems fit according to its national interests (UNGA 1962 XVII).

In another category are resources or areas such as the oceans, the deep seabed, Antarctica, outer space and the atmosphere 'that do not or cannot by their very nature fall under sovereign jurisdiction' (Vogler 2000: 1). These resources are called common property resources or, more specifically, global commons. Their distinguishing feature is that no single user or decision-making unit holds exclusive title over them (Wijkman 1982: 512). Access, use and conservation of this category of resources have been the subject of different types of multilateral environmental regimes for a long time. The purpose of these regimes, in general, is to prevent conflict arising from differing claims of ownership and to regulate the use of these resources on the basis of equitable access and utilization (Vogler 2000: 46; Birnie and Boyle 2002: 140). Several principles of international law declare that the main rationale of shared and common property resource regimes is to secure the balance of interests of the parties concerned, based on the concept of sustainable development and equitable utilization. Among these are resolution 3129 (XXVIII) of the UNGA, Article 3 of the 1974 Charter of the Economic Rights and Duties of States and the 1978 United Nations Environment Programme (UNEP) Principles of Conduct in the Harmonious Utilization of Natural Resources Shared by Two or More States, as well as decisions by the International Court of Justice (ICJ).[2]

The 1958 Geneva Convention on the Conservation of the Living Resources of the High Sea is an example of a common property resource regime. This regime, together with many other international fishery commissions such as the 1995 Agreement on Straddling and Highly Migratory Fish Stock, attempts to forestall conflict between coastal and fishing states by regulating the access of both parties to marine resources and conferring jurisdiction over various aspects of the sea to states. Another example is the International Whaling Commission (IWC), which, in the more than 50 years that it has been in existence, has presided over the allocation of several millions of whales among member states through a quota system (Stoett 1997: 73). Other examples include the seabed regime articulated under the Third United Nations Conference on the Law of the Sea (UNCLOS III) and the Antarctica Treaty, both of which embody highly intricate regulations designed to mediate the access of states and non-state actors to vast portions of global resources.

The main justice questions surrounding these regimes relate, first, to their role in determining the legal status of these resources. Given recent technological advancements and the general commitment to free-market philosophy, developed countries, in most cases, tend to favour policies that legitimize one form or another of property right regime with respect to these resources whereas developing countries, in most cases, tend to favour collective management approaches that guarantee equitable sharing of the resources in these issue-areas. Second, developing countries tend to argue that previous patterns of exploitation of these resources have tended to benefit the industrialized countries disproportionately. Accordingly, they argue for some form of compensatory justice contending that relevant regimes should legislate in favour of resource transfers from the rich North to the poor South (Sanger 1986). For example, during the elaboration of UNCLOS III, some Southern countries insisted that the developed nations had accounted for over 82 per cent of all of the previous abstraction of fish and other marine resources from the world's oceans. As a consequence they argued that, in keeping with the principles of justice, the international community should enact rules to compensate the South for this historical use and give the South equal power in the management of the world's oceans (Sanger 1986). This argument has also been replicated to differing degrees and dimensions with respect to whaling. However, the developed countries often tend to argue that it is hardly in keeping with justice to enact rules that propose to 'punish the children for the "sins" of their fathers' especially when the North did not at any time physically exclude the South from appropriating these resources (Friedheim 1993).

Other equity issues that arise in the course of the development of shared property regimes relate to the design and functions of decision-making bodies. Developing countries usually argue that the decision-making bodies of most common property regimes are either exclusionary or heavily weighted in favour of the developed countries of the North. They argue that the ideal of international environmental justice requires that the constitution and membership of such decision-making bodies be revised to reflect the interests of the poor countries of the South. An example of a common property regime in which this type of argument has been used is the Antarctica regime. The Antarctica Treaty regulates access to an area that constitutes nearly 10 per cent of the earth's land and water areas (Vogler 2000: 73). At present, this resource-area is governed by the Antarctic Treaty Consultative Party (ATCP), which comprises 38 states, mostly from the industrialized countries. The general understanding is that Antarctica contains significant amounts of precious metal reserves, including ores of uranium, gold and silver, as well as oil and natural gas, the pattern of exploitation of which is expected to greatly affect both the fortunes of nation states and corporate investors (Porter and Brown 1995: 88). At the same time, there has been much speculation among states as to how the exploitation of these resources might serve to cushion the effect of rising oil prices and provide for accelerated international economic development. However, both scholars and policy-makers from developing countries point out that before this issue can be addressed there is a need to reorganize the ATCP to make it more inclusive. The position usually taken is that the ATCP should be scrapped and replaced with a UN-constituted authority, which would ensure the equitable management of the mineral resources of Antarctica (cf. Sands 1992a; Scully and Kimball 1989).

Allocation of property rights

Another important distributional function of international environmental regimes is the allocation of property rights over natural resources among states (Lipschutz and Mayer 1993; Rayner *et al*. 1999; Tol *et al*. 1999). Shared and common property resources play vital roles in the social and economic well-being of most of the states and communities that they connect (Elliott 1998: 221–224; Homer-Dixon 2001). But these types of resources do not often lend themselves to effective legislation given their extensive and transboundary character (Birnie and Boyle 2002: 306–309). Additionally, the cost of asserting and defending exclusive rights over them are usually unprofitably high. For these reasons, this category of resource-area is often unregulated. However, the lack of regulation, coupled with the fact that these resources are often deemed to be inexhaustible, means that they usually become subject to inappropriate and imprudent utilization. In some cases, the very fact that the resources are shared by many users creates a condition in which no one is particularly interested in pursuing effective management policies (Ostrom 1990). Indeed, in some instances, the very users that should have an interest in sustainable use of a resource might feel that their immediate needs are better served by overexploitation, the rationale being that if they do not exploit others will. When many feel the need to exploit and no one has the incentive to conserve, the tendency is usually towards imprudent exploitation, which could lead to the rapid depletion of resources or even the complete degradation of the ecosystem.

Garrett Hardin (1968) described this scenario as the tragedy of the commons and contended that such is the ultimate fate of every resource where no single user or decision-making unit holds exclusive title. He argued that the only way to prevent the tragedy of the commons was for a single user to enclose and secure legal property rights over the resource-area.

On the international scene, claims and counterclaims by states of property rights over portions of transboundary or common-pool resources are very common. Mostly, these claims arise once it has become apparent that a hitherto 'superabundant' resource has become subject to depletion because of imprudent use (Ostrom 1990; Buck 1998; Birnie and Boyle 2002). Once the condition of scarcity becomes apparent, claims and counterclaims of rights of ownership, quite often with the potential to degenerate into violent conflict, arise (Homer-Dixon 1994, 1999, 2001). Hence, a number of shared/common property resource regimes are concerned with adjudicating over conflicting claims of ownership or property rights. Depending on the economic importance of the resource-area in question, the policies of such regimes will have the effect of either narrowing or increasing social inequality, both between and within states.

Some good examples of such regimes are those of the territorial sea (TS) and continental shelf (CS), negotiated under UNCLOS III (Chapter 4). The USA had, through the Truman Declaration of 1945, claimed exclusive property rights over all of the mineral resources in its continental shelf. It argued that the continental shelf is a natural extension of the land and, therefore, subject to the laws of permanent sovereignty, which apply to national resources (Friedheim 1993). This claim, as well as claims for the extension of the breadth of the territorial sea, was eventually validated after much debate by the regime of the continental shelf under UNCLOS III (1982), although, as we shall see later in Chapter 4, coastal states must provide compensation *to the rest of the world* for economic development extending up to 200 nautical miles beyond their shorelines on the basis of equity and global justice (UNCLOS III: Article 76, Article 82, Annex II).[3]

Similarly, the Convention on Biodiversity (CBD) is heavily characterized by debates on property rights and global justice. The principal issue in this instance is how to balance between the property rights claims of host countries and those of developed countries, who most often possess the scientific expertise to convert plant genetic materials into commercially viable products (Yamin 1995). The CBD is interesting because, although it recognizes the permanent sovereignty of states over national resources, it nonetheless legitimizes international interest in the conservation of resources (Birnie and Boyle 2002). The Convention also seeks, in practice, to secure limited rights for these interests in terms of the utilization of such resources, provided that the benefits arising from such endeavours are shared on the basis of equity and justice. To this end, the Convention proclaims that the conservation and sustainable utilization of these resources is the 'common concern of mankind' and, in so doing, secures limited internationalization of the plant generic resources in the developing countries.[4] This provision has subsequently provided the basis for recent calls by some in the developed countries that the

22 Setting the scene

Brazilian Amazon should be regarded as the common heritage of mankind – a call that has been soundly rejected by scholars and policy-makers from the developing countries (Rosendal 1995; Baslar 1998; Mgbeoji 2004: 821–837).

Finally, a lot of the debates that are witnessed in the development of the different international forestry regimes (Forest Principles 1992; ITTA 1994) are concerned with the issue of property rights. Here, the core issue is that most host nations prefer to grant timber rights to rich and influential concessionaries, partly in a bid to meet the demands of debt repayment, while neglecting the survival interests of the communities that live and depend on the forested areas. Gale (1998: 76), for example, observes that most forestry regimes are generally fashioned in ways that privilege the interests and ownership claims of states over the 'customary land rights of indigenous people inhabiting forested areas from the earliest periods of recorded history'. Similarly, Humphreys (1996: 226) asserts that 'the rights to timber, as asserted by the timber traders and consumer and producer delegations, and the rights to land, as asserted by the alliance between indigenous peoples' groups and NGOs, have been one of the most acute points of conflict within' most forestry regimes.

Determination of terms and rules of international commerce

The third distributional function of environmental regimes lies in their roles in the regulation of international commercial activities. The bulk of the regulation of international economic activities is currently undertaken by international economic institutions such as the General Agreement on Tariffs and Trade (GATT) and the World Trade Organization (WTO), but environmental regimes are increasingly playing an important part in this regard, both directly and indirectly. In both cases, questions of justice are usually one of the major issues of concern. Some of the environmental conventions that bear directly on the rules of international commerce include the Basel Convention on the Transboundary Movements of Hazardous Wastes and their Disposal, the Convention on International Trade in Endangered Species of Wild Fauna and Flora (CITES) and the Convention on Long-Range Transboundary Air Pollution (LRTAP). Others include the Vienna Convention on the Protection of the Ozone Layer and the Montreal Protocol on Substances that Deplete the Ozone Layer. As for indirect impact, it is probably correct to say that almost all environmental agreements have some effect on international commerce in one way or another.

The Basel Convention acts as an umbrella for the global waste management regime and regulates the movement and trade of hazardous wastes across the borders of the over 168 countries that are signatories to this treaty. It is estimated that the worth of the global waste management industry was about US$90 billion in 1991 and US$500 billion in 2000 (Coll 1994: 7). UNEP estimates that there was an annual production of around 440 million metric tonnes of toxic waste in the 1990s and between 300 and 400 million metric tonnes in the 1980s. Within the same period, it has also been estimated that up to 50 per cent of the volume of toxic waste produced annually was transported across borders, with about

10–15 per cent going to developing countries (Hilz 1992: 20–21; Krueger 1999: 14; Clapp 2001: 24–27).

During the negotiation of the Basel Convention the poor developing countries regularly invoked the concept of environmental justice (Chapter 5). They argued that unregulated trade in hazardous wastes amounts to a violation of environmental justice because it enables the rich to externalize the environmental cost of their production and consumption processes while forcing the poor residents of the world to bear a disproportionate burden of toxic waste (Kummer 1995; Weissman 2005: 28). Developed countries, on the other hand, wanted a waste regime that would regulate waste trade in line with the neoliberal free-market philosophy (Clapp 2001). In the end developing countries got their way, as the Basel Convention eventually banned the export of different categories of hazardous wastes from Organization for Economic Co-operation and Development (OECD) countries to non-OECD countries.

CITES controls international trade in about 28,000 species of plants and 5,000 species of animals. This list extends from aloes to pine trees and from mussels to lions, although charismatic creatures such as African elephants, rhinos, bears and whales remain the more prominent examples of animals whose trade is controlled by CITES. The Convention works through a system of import–export permits issued by a management authority under the control of a scientific authority. It also enforces trade regulations on a wide array of products, including food products, exotic leather goods, wooden musical instruments, timber, tourist curios and medicines derived from these listed species. It is estimated that the global trade in species and their derivative products controlled under CITES amounts to billions of dollars annually (Roe et al. 2002; van Korten and Bulte 2000). For example, before the 1989 CITES ban, up to 770 metric tonnes of African elephant ivory, corresponding to about 75,000 elephants, were exported both legally and illegally per annum. This trade amounted to between US$60 and 75 million per year. The main equity issue in CITES is that some see the blanket ban imposed by CITES as being basically designed to satisfy the conservation and aesthetic fancies of Western non-governmental organizations (NGOs) while seriously neglecting the economic implications for national and local communities (Roe *et al.* 2002; Swanson 1992). These authors argue that imposing a trade ban on elephant products, for example, without making provision for adequate resources to pursue conservation policies ultimately means that national and local communities are deprived of valuable land/water resources for agriculture and livestock production (as they compete for the same scarce resources with an ever-increasing elephant population) (Roe *et al.* 2002; Khanna and Harford 1996). Consequently, they maintain that a more equitable policy would be one that seeks to involve local people in wildlife management, to strike a balance between 'consumptive utilization and non-consumptive income' (Heltberg 1998) in addition to ensuring that a considerable part of the income generated trickles down to local and land-use decision makers (Roe *et al.* 2002; Heltberg 2002). The merit of this argument has been recently recognized by some in developed countries, who, in turn, have started a number of schemes such as the 'debt for nature swap' to compensate national and local communities for conservation programmes that impact negatively on their revenue and livelihood. The key policies of CITES, however, are not yet consistent with this philosophy.

The Vienna Convention on the Protection of the Ozone Layer, including the Montreal Protocol on Substances that Deplete the Ozone Layer, is another environmental regime that has a direct impact on international commerce. This multilateral environmental agreement places an import ban on various categories of ozone-depleting substances (ODS) such as methylbromide and bromochloromethane, which is worth billions of dollars. It also bans the export of ODS to any country that does not comply with the production control of the Convention. In addition, it has established a worldwide licensing system to track the import and export of ODS across the globe. The equity issues arising from this agreement have been the subject of much attention in the literature and policy circles (Benedick 1989; Rowlands 1991; Litfin 1994; Agarwal *et al.* 2001). The major issue here is that the developed countries wanted to impose a global ban on the use of low-cost ODS based on calculations that are completely insensitive to the economic and developmental needs of less industrialized countries. However, some developing countries, notably China and India, insisted that they would not be bound by such a convention, which seeks to outlaw a practice that aided Western economic growth for decades, after which adequate incentives were provided to enable these countries to switch to more costly technologies (Benedick 1989, 1991; Soroos 1997). In a gesture of international equity, contracting parties eventually established a 10-year grace period before developing countries were obligated to follow the agreed reduction schedule for the controlled substances. On the same basis of equity they also made allowances for the so-called basic need production, which allows limited production for use in refrigeration and air conditioning. The Convention also established a special fund to promote the participation of the developing countries, with an initial budget of US$160 million. As of the end of 2002, the total amount committed to the fund was around US$1.6 billion (Stokke and Thommessen 2003: 106).

As stated above, virtually all environmental regimes have implications for international commerce in one way or another. Consider, for example, the relatively 'innocuous' Convention on the Prevention of Marine Pollution by Dumping of Wastes and Other Matter, which aims to 'prevent indiscriminate disposal at sea of wastes liable to create hazards to human health or harm living resources and marine life'. Although the focus of this regime is on the environmental quality of the marine environment rather than international trade, the Convention has nonetheless regulated business and commerce involving up to 17 million tonnes of industrial waste, 20 million tons of sewage sludge and 400 million tonnes of dredged materials.[5] Clearly, by these regulations, the Convention imposes a significant financial burden on states that have been using the sea as a major sink for waste disposal for several decades. In North–South equity terms this means that most developed countries are able to enjoy reasonable periods of 'free ride' with respect to using the sea as a global dumping ground whereas most developing countries are deprived of a similar opportunity.[6] A similar condition of inequity in the use of global sink exists in many other environmental regimes, including the Convention for the Prevention of Pollution from Ships (MARPOL) and the Convention on Climate Change.

Burden sharing

This section discusses the distributional function of regimes that has come to be generally known as 'burden sharing' (Grubb et al. 1992; Young 1991; Shue 1993; Hayes 1993; Tóth 1999). Under this unique category is the climate change regime and, to a lesser extent, LRTAP. Burden sharing in the sense used here is a relatively new dimension of the distributive functions of multilateral environmental regimes. The characteristic feature of these environmental regimes is that they provide the framework for states to share responsibilities, which requires profound changes to be made in the economic and political structures of states and even involves tough choices at individual and household levels (Paterson and Grubb 1992; Auer 2000; Rayner and Malone 1998; IPCC 2001). However, it should be noted that the terminology 'burden sharing' is somewhat misleading in at least two ways. The first is that the other distributional functions of regimes, as much of the discussion in the previous sections has shown, also involve the sharing of responsibilities among nations in one way or another. And insofar as these responsibilities require some form of economic sacrifice, they also qualify to be seen as performing the function of burden sharing. The second is that the term 'burden sharing' tends to hide the fact that there are some nations, regions and private organizations who tend to benefit from the climate change problem and/or the international effort to mitigate climate change (Kasperson and Dow 1991; Rayner and Malone 1998: 306; Bachram 2005). Nevertheless, the term continues to be relevant in distinguishing these regimes from other resource regimes where the main emphasis is on trade regulation or granting access to shared or common property resources.

Climate change has at least three main distributional aspects and the equity function of the international regime for climate change mitigation closely follows these. The first is that the impact of climate change in the various countries and regions of the world is, and will continue to be, highly differentiated. Although producing net benefits for some (at least in the short term), climate change will produce extremely negative and, in some cases, intolerable conditions for others (Godrej 2001; Adger et al. 2006). For example, changes in weather patterns would mean that 'growing seasons in high latitudes could be extended while lower latitudes experience drought' (Rayner and Malone 1998: 306). The implication is that climate change would lead to an abundance of food production in the middle and high latitudes while causing famine and starvation in regions in the lower latitudes (Royal Society 2006: 9). At the same time, changes in mean climate conditions would lead to changes in patterns of river flow – a situation likely to open new routes for navigation and shipping while leading to a loss of jobs and investment as old familiar routes become less accessible (Rayner et al. 1998: 306). Overall, immense perturbations in accustomed patterns of living and interactions between states will be introduced as changes are witnessed in the biogeophysical conditions of coastal zones, forests, water resources and biodiversity (Pearce *et al.* 1996; IPCC 1995, 2001, 2007a,b).

Moreover, the available scenarios and models that integrate forecasts of patterns of climate change with other relevant economic and social dimensions which interact with it predict that the severest impact of global climate change will be felt within countries and regions already suffering from low income and harsh socio-economic conditions (IPCC 2007b; Stern 2007). For example, climate change would produce additional pressure in central Asian, Mediterranean and African countries that already suffer high level water stress; the livelihoods of most islanders who depend on fishing on the highly temperature-sensitive coral reefs for their daily survival would be seriously threatened and a minimal amount of sea-level rise would spell unimaginable disaster for several low-lying countries where the populations are already living in conditions of abject poverty (Dow *et al.* 2006; Royal Society 2006: 9; IPCC 2007b). At the same time, climate change will have differential impacts along age, sex and ethnic lines. Again, in most cases, it is those who are more vulnerable who will suffer the greatest impact.

The second dimension, which relates to the first, is that the cost of mitigating climate change in different countries and regions is highly varied. Differentials in the costs of mitigation are, in part, related to differences in the type and extent of impact, but are also related to differences in economic and technological capabilities and structures. Hence, even if the impact of climate change were to be equal across the board, the question of whether all nations should be made to contribute equally to its mitigation would still be valid. The validity of the question increases when, in addition to differences in economic and technological capabilities, differences in the emission profiles and contributions of different countries and regions to global climate change are factored in. Mitigating global climate change entails a reduction, or at least stabilization, of greenhouse gas emissions. This, in turn, requires a range of actions, from profound changes in the political, social and economic structure of countries to changes in lifestyles and daily choices (IPCC 1995, 2001). However, whereas some countries are well placed to make the sorts of commitments and investments that could produce significant reductions in emissions without much stress, the socio-economic conditions of many other countries would be hugely affected in the event of a commitment even to a minimal amount of emission reduction. It follows that the emission reduction scenarios or other policies aimed at mitigation, as adopted by an international climate regime, will have enormous implications for economic inequalities between countries (IPCC 2001: 118, 123, 253, *passim*).

The third distributional dimension of climate change is the differences in the costs of adapting to climate change. Initial efforts to respond to climate change focused mainly on mitigation via various emission reduction and stabilization projects. However, more recently, attention has also turned to efforts geared towards adapting to the economic and 'social consequences of the global warming that will not in fact be avoided' (Shue 1994: 121). The context for distributional implications of climate change adaptation closely follows what has been discussed in the previous sections: differences in impact, differences in degrees of vulnerability, differences in capabilities and differences in contributions. Generally, it is expected that rich countries are better placed to adapt to climate change than poor countries (Paavola 2006; Adger *et al.* 2006; IPCC 2007a,b; Stern 2007). Indeed, most developing countries have barely enough resources to maintain a basic infrastructure and social services let alone having reserves to devote to adaptation schemes. Agricultural and other income-producing activities are often undertaken under precarious conditions meaning that slight changes in physical or material conditions bring about huge losses of lives and income (Paavola 2006; Thomas and Twyman 2006). For example, Mozambique's annual growth rate was drastically reduced from 8 per cent to 2.1 per cent because of the floods and cyclones that hit some parts of the country in 2000 (World Bank 2001). Similarly, the same wave of drought and cyclones drastically reduced Kenyan hydroelectric power output forcing the country to appeal to the World Bank for a US$72 million emergency loan in the same year (World Bank 2000). Again, the distributional effect of an international burden-sharing regime lies in its sensitivity to these variations in the imperatives of adapting to the negative consequences of climate change and the wide differences in the circumstances of different countries and regions, both in terms of capabilities and contribution. To some extent, parties to the Convention on Climate Change recognize all of the three dimensions discussed above. Yet, as we shall see in Chapter 6, serious disagreements remain over how these equity concerns should be addressed. But what can be said at this stage, in line with what has been discussed in previous sections, is that international regimes play a vital role in either intensifying or altering existing disparities of power and wealth between countries.

Affirmation of basic rights and the allocation of liability for damage

The last, but by no means the least, distributional function of global environmental regimes is their role in the allocation of liability for damage in connection with the use of the environment and the affirmation of basic rights to environmental resources (Sands 1992b; Kummer 1995; Hayward 2000). There are a growing number of environmental regimes that aim to ensure adequate liability and effective compensation for damages suffered in connection with the use of the environment. Two such examples are the International Convention on Civil Liability for Oil Pollution Damage (CLC) (Brussels 1969, 1976 and 1984) and the Convention on Civil Liability for Damage Caused during Carriage of Dangerous Goods by Road, Rail and Inland Navigation Vessels (CRTD) (Geneva 1989). Other examples include the International Convention on Liability and Compensation for Damage in Connection with the Carriage of Hazardous and Noxious Substances by Sea (HNS) (London 1992), the International Convention on Civil Liability for Bunker Oil Pollution Damage (Bunkers Convention) (London 2001) and the Basel Protocol on Liability and Compensation for Damage Resulting from the Transboundary Movements of Hazardous Wastes and their Disposal (see Chapter 4).

What these conventions have in common is that that they seek to ensure justice, usually in the form of full and adequate compensation for victims of various kinds of pollution or accidents that involve individuals from different nationalities. Some of the conventions set both minimum and maximum limits on the amount of compensation that can be paid to an accident victim whereas others set a maximum time frame for the completion of cases. In all, they mimic national judicial systems in trying to ensure that justice is done, taking into consideration the relevant facts of any particular case. The significance of this category of environmental regimes lies, first, in the fact that they frequently authorize judicial actions and compensations across national boundaries. Second, they sometimes recognize not only states but also individuals as legal entities subject to claim or to be sued in the event of transboundary environmental accidents or accidents that occur in areas beyond the jurisdiction of states, such as the high sea. Third, these regimes are also important in enabling ordinary citizens to secure compensation from very powerful transnational corporations and organizations. This is not to say that these regimes are always effective or perfect, but that they remain significant as a means of actualizing some of the basic rights contained in mega-environmental declarations and, by so doing, serve as a means of distributing economic burdens internationally.

At the same time, there are dozens of international charters proclaiming different sorts of human rights in direct relation to the environment. Although the exact legal status of these proclamations continues to be the subject of much speculation, it remains both legally and politically significant that most of them are admitted in high-profile documents, some of which are generally regarded as landmarks in the evolution of international environmental law and policy (Hayward 2000, 2005). Principle 1 of the United Nations Conference on the Human Environment (UNCHE; Stockholm Declaration) condemns colonialism, apartheid, racial discrimination and other forms of unjust political systems and, in the same breath, declares that all individuals have 'the fundamental right to freedom, equality and adequate conditions of life, in an environment of a quality that permits a life of dignity and well-being' (UNCHE 1972: Principle 1). The Rio Declaration on Environment and Development endorses the view that everyone is 'entitled to a healthy and productive life in harmony with nature' (ibid.: Principle 1) and that the rights to development of states must be 'fulfilled so as to equitably meet developmental and environmental needs of present and future generations' (ibid.: Principle 3).[7] It also allows that 'the special situation and needs of developing countries, particularly the least developed and those most environmentally vulnerable, shall be given special priority [and that] international actions in the field of environment and development should also address the interests and needs of all countries' (ibid.: Principle 6). Subsequently, many other conventions dealing with specific global environmental problems have proceeded to recognize and incorporate portions and aspects of these proclamations in their texts.

However, by far the most elaborate document on the rights of individuals and groups as they relate to the environment is the Draft Principles on Human Rights and the Environment (E/CN.4/Sub.2/1994/9), compiled on 16 May 1994 by an international group of experts on human rights and environmental protection under the guidance of the United Nations in Geneva. The key argument upon which this text builds is that 'sustainable development, an ecologically sound environment and other human rights, including civil, cultural, economic, political and social rights, are universal, interdependent and indivisible' (Parts 1 and 2). Following from this, the document proceeds to enunciate various kinds of environmental rights including the right to freedom from pollution and environmental degradation, the right to safe and healthy food and the right to clean water adequate to well-being, as well as the right to adequate housing. Other rights proclaimed in the document include the right to land and the right to a secure, healthy and ecologically sound environment. It is clear that, in articulating these principles, the expectation is that states functioning independently and jointly by way of international organizations should work to secure these rights for the human population in ways that promote international justice. However, as indicated earlier, most of these declarations have not been backed up by concrete actions by the international community.

Equity concerns in international regime texts

It is equally significant, from the viewpoint of an ethical analysis of institutions, to note that most multilateral environmental agreements now contain explicit references to international justice. In other words, it is possible to argue that the notion that regimes have important distributive functions, and that justice is a vital precondition for their operation, is gradually being institutionalized. Finnemore and Sikkink (1998: 888) have suggested that international norms go through a 'life cycle'. They suggest that the first stage is the point of 'conception', when some 'moral entrepreneurs push a candidate norm' (Friedheim 2000: 191). Next, a norm may reach a 'tipping point' – a term they use to mean that the concept has become frequently adopted in the vocabulary of states, policy-makers and relevant international organizations. This is followed by the stage of norm 'cascade', which means that such a norm has been formally adopted in the practice of institutions. The stage of 'internalization' is reached when a norm commands habitual obedience from international actors.

It is not always easy to tell exactly the precise stage of a norm on the basis of Finnemore and Sikkink's model. But what is generally acknowledged is that it is a mark of progression when a norm moves from being verbally articulated to being explicitly incorporated in the text of international agreements (Bernstein 2001; Friedheim 200)). On this basis it is interesting to note that almost all of the global environmental agreements articulated since 1972 contain at least one reference to international justice and equity in the convention's text (see also Kokott 1999: 179). For example, the 1972 Convention on the Prevention of Marine Pollution by Dumping of Wastes and Other Matter pledges in its preamble due recognition 'of the interests and capacities of the developing countries' in the design of its policies. UNCLOS III states as one of its main objectives the promotion of 'equitable and efficient utilization of the resources of the sea in ways that will promote international economic justice'. The phrase 'taking into account the needs of the developing countries' is used eight times in the 1989 Basel Convention on the Transboundary Movements of Hazardous Wastes and their Disposal. The Montreal Protocol on Substances that Deplete the Ozone Layer acknowledges that 'special provision is required to meet the needs of developing countries, including the provision of additional financial resources'.

Similarly, all of the conventions articled during the 1992 UNCED in Rio equally embody some commitment to international justice. In the United Nations Framework Convention on Climate Change (UNFCCC), parties pledge to tackle the problem of climate change 'in an equitable manner and in line with the common and differentiated responsibilities principle' (Article 3). Article 1 of the Convention on Biodiversity (CBD) declares its objective as being to seek the 'sustainable use and equitable sharing of the benefits arising from the utilization of genetic resources'. The term 'equitable sharing' is also used in three other places in the Convention text (Articles 5; 8 (j); 19). The Forest Principles recognize the 'rights of indigenous peoples and of forest dwellers' and, also, the need to share 'the profits from biotechnology products and genetic materials taken from forests on mutually agreed terms'. Indeed, the singular stated goal of the Rio conference was the 'establishment of a new and *equitable* global partnership through the creation of new levels of co-operation among states, key sectors of societies and people'.

In sum, it is clear that environmental regimes perform significant distributional functions at the international level. What is interesting, however, is that, given, as noted, that there are different interpretations of justice, all of which produce different outcomes, little scholarship is devoted to studying which notions of justice underpin the main regime policies or, more generally, the exact impact of these moral commitments on the operation of regime policies. The general impression one gets is the belief that the demands of justice have been satisfied simply because parties have inserted a few clauses in regime texts purporting to pursue justice in dealing with a given environmental issue. By far the most common approach has been to focus on regime effectiveness based simply on the liberal institutionalist thinking that regimes are effective when they 'alter states' behaviour' (Young 1998: 269) or 'meet set objectives' (Keohane *et al.* 1993: 3; Young 1999). Neglecting the fact that the objectives of regimes might well be conditioned by norms and interests that are power determined, it is concluded plainly that setting targets and signing agreements equals justice for all state parties. Accordingly, as far as I know, there is no single convention text in which parties attempt to give explicit meaning to the notion of justice, at least as it applies to the environmental issue-area in consideration. For example, Article 2 of the CBD is devoted to the definition of the key terms used in the convention text. In this Article, 17 operating phrases, including what parties mean by 'sustainable use', 'biodiversity', 'habitat' and 'ecosystem', are all defined, supposedly for the sake of clarity. However, complete silence is maintained with respect to their understanding of 'equitable share of resources'. Yet, the main objective of the Convention (Article 1) remains:

[t]he conservation of biological diversity, the sustainable use of its components and the fair and equitable sharing of the benefits arising out of the utilization of genetic resources, including by appropriate access to genetic resources.

Perhaps this oversight represents a broader pattern within the domain of international relations, in which many attempts to make sense of international co-operative efforts proceed from positivist assumptions and a framework that marginalizes the role of ideas and values and proceeds without due recognition of what Hugh Dyer calls 'the normative essence of political relations' (Dyer 1989: 178; cf. Thompson 1992; Holland 2000).

Conclusion

Although the international development of environmental consciousness did not follow a path that recognized the intimate connection between environmental conservation and distributional justice, issues of distribution have become a very prominent aspect of regime operation. International environmental regimes now have very significant distributional functions including granting access to shared common resources or the global commons, allocating property rights among states, determining and shaping the rules of some aspects of international commerce, distributing the responsibilities and burdens of responses to global climate change and enabling the institutionalization of transboundary environmental rights. Furthermore, most regime texts now contain explicit (if contradictory) references to international justice. Although it is noted that this practice on its own does not tell us much about the specific content of regimes or whom such rules privilege, it nonetheless signifies a certain amount of progression in the institutionalization of equity norms in international environmental co-operation. Dominant approaches to regime analysis remain firmly rooted in rational choice analytical models although an increasing body of work seeks to highlight the importance of questions of justice in global environmental regimes. What is largely missing from this body of work, however, are more empirical accounts to study or demonstrate which notions of justice underpin specific regime policies or, more broadly, the impact of justice aspirations in multilateral environmental agreements. This task will be undertaken in the later chapters of this book. However, in the next chapter, more of the groundwork for this empirical analysis is set out by briefly discussing the various conceptions of justice from which parties tend to draw in their contestations for justice in the course of regime development.

3 Towards a theory of global environmental justice

The previous chapter provides a broad picture of the roles of environmental regimes as a medium for distributive justice in the international arena. It was noted that the need for distributive equity in international regimes is now widely appreciated. At the same time it was observed that, although there are contending interpretations of what justice entails in practice, little is said about the actual notions of justice that underpin core global environmental policies.

The function of this chapter is to provide a concise overview of the main conceptions of justice from which parties to international environmental conventions draw at one point or another, and to indicate how such ideas of justice intertwine with the notion of global environmental sustainability. This account enables us to see how the arguments and positions of states and other autonomous actors reveal important differences in their political philosophy and normative value systems. The theories discussed include justice as: (i) utilitarianism; (ii) liberal egalitarianism; (iii) property rights; (iv) mutual advantage; (v) communitarianism; and (vi) meeting needs.

After discussing these six different conceptions of justice, a brief review of the conceptual arguments for and against the idea of global justice is given. Hence, in addition to providing background knowledge that will facilitate the empirical analysis undertaken in subsequent chapters, this chapter also aims to provide some initial insights into how the notion of global environmental justice may be conceptualized. The idea is not, of course, to suggest that one conception of justice is superior to another, but simply to show what kind of environmental policies or programmes might be expected to result following the consistent application of a particular notion of justice.[1] Before proceeding it is important to clarify that these theories of justice were not originally formulated with the purpose of guiding politics between states. Rather, they were originally developed for dealing with questions of justice within national territories. As Caney (2001: 974) puts it, political philosophers 'have traditionally assumed that ideals of distributive justice should operate, if they operate at all, within countries'. Nevertheless, in the absence of an overarching theory of global justice, they remain the starting point for any meaningful discussion on the conceptions of justice in international institutions.[2]

The concept of justice

An extremely rich and diverse debate exists on the concept of justice in Anglo-American political philosophy. In fact, some scholars would claim that moral political philosophy originated around debates about justice (cf. Plant 1991: 1; Kymlicka 2002: viii). The richness of this debate can be seen as an advantage for anyone wishing to conduct a critical inquiry into the subject, as there is no scarcity of materials touching on any aspect of the concept. However, the diversity and the enduring nature of some of the controversies can so confuse or cause such despair that many have 'given up, in effect, the possibility of a nonarbitrary resolution of disputes about justice' (Sterba 1980: 4).

In spite of this controversy, the concept of justice retains a unique position as the ultimate moral guide to political actions and a potent tool for socio-political mobilization. In the everyday ordinary lives of individuals, both at national and subnational levels, people tend to assign special weight to arguments that are based on claims for justice. Aristotle distinguishes between universal and particular justice. In the former sense, justice is coextensive with virtue and, therefore, can be considered to be the greatest of all virtues. 'In justice', he says, 'is every virtue comprehended' (Aristotle 1847/1998). Part of the justification Aristotle offers is that, whereas most other forms of virtue, such as, for example, temperance, concern man's relation to himself, 'justice, alone of all virtues is thought to be "another's good" because it is related to our neighbors; for it does what is advantageous to another, either a ruler or a co-partner' (ibid.: 108).

Many other philosophers share Aristotle's sentiment. Barry and Matravers (1997: 141) describe justice as a 'necessary virtue of individuals in their interactions with others and the principal virtue of social institutions'. For Hume (1975), justice is the most important virtue of political institutions. He describes institutional injustice as the 'greatest public wrong' (p. 50) and contends that personal injustice is the vice that is the most apt to cause men 'to entertain the strongest ill will' against others (p. 49). John Stuart Mill referred to justice as 'the chief part, and incomparably the most binding part of all morality' (Mill 1973: 465). St Augustine considered that the very legitimacy of a state rests upon its claim to do justice. In the absence of justice, he says, a state is nothing but 'a large robber band' (1984: 139). Rawls (1971) considered that 'justice is the first virtue of social institutions' (p. 3). He argues that any institution, no matter how effective, deserves to be abolished if found to be unjust, because 'the rights secured by justice are not subject to political bargaining or the calculus of social interests' (pp. 5, 28). Rawls insists that individuals cannot be expected to accept social regulations or engage in social co-operation unless the terms by which society operates are seen as reasonably just. He says:

> Each person possesses an inviolability founded on justice that even the welfare of the society as a whole cannot override. For this reason justice denies that the loss of freedom for some is made right by a greater good shared by others. It does not allow that the sacrifices imposed on a few are outweighed by the larger sum of advantages enjoyed by others.
>
> (Ibid.: 3–4)

What emerges from the discussion above is that, despite the lack of agreement on a common conception of justice, there remain, as Sterba puts it, some 'assumptions and distinctions regarding justice that we do hold in common even when our conceptions of justice differ'. Sterba argues that these basic assumptions and distinctions are what, in fact, constitute the 'very "concept of justice"'. It is the presence of these shared intuitions that 'makes alternative conceptions of justice alternative conceptions of justice' (Sterba 1980: 2). Rawls endorses this distinction between the concept and the conceptions of justice. For Rawls, justice remains at the heart of moral political philosophy even though there are disagreements over the various conceptions, that is, how the concept may be interpreted in practice (Rawls 1971: 5, 1993: 14). It is easy, for instance, to agree with Aristotle that justice is all about giving individuals their dues or treating individuals concerned as equally deserving. The disagreement starts, however, once we begin to consider what it is that people deserve.

The above point is important because it suggests that, disagreements over conceptions of justice notwithstanding, it is not the case, as cynics sometime argue, that disagreements over conceptions of justice imply that the concept is meaningless and at best serves as a mere cover for raw interests or underlying power relations in regime development. Of course, there are many actions, both in national and international domains, that are motivated by greed and the selfish interests of political actors. But there are also many events and international programmes 'in which self-interest does not seem to have been a force; which drove out of considerations of justice, and even in which awareness of philosophical thinking about justice was of value' (Brighouse 2004: 5). At the same time, many would admit that, although moral concepts are particularly notorious for their 'malleability', it does not imply, as Walzer (1977: 9–12) argues, that these concepts can be regarded as subject to limitless manipulation or as words of 'inconstant signification'. As he says, 'When we charge a man with treason, we have to tell a very special kind of story about him, and we have to provide concrete evidence that the story is true. If we call him a traitor when we cannot tell that story, we are not using words inconstantly, we are simply lying.'

Franck (1995: 17–20), in a similar vein, argues that, although the concept of fairness is both 'relative and subjective', it does not lend itself to unlimited choices but rather remains circumscribed within the ambit of shared basic assumptions that govern the discourse. Henry Shue could also have had this argument in mind when, commenting on what he calls the 'unavoidability of justice' between rich and poor nations in the climate change regime, he stressed that 'whatever justice may positively require, it does not permit that poor nations be told to sell their blankets in order that rich nations may keep their jewellery' (Shue 1992: 397). The point, then, is, first, that the notion of global environmental justice does not become morally or politically insignificant simply because there are different viewpoints on what justice entails in practice. Second, the fact that parties commit to pursue justice in an international environmental agreement does not immediately tell us the kind of policies that will emerge or whose interests such programmes will privilege. It is precisely for these two reasons that the kind of analysis undertaken later in this book is required to assess the core policies of regimes not only in relation to the interests of the various blocs but also in relation to some of the basic goals associated with the concept of global environmental sustainability.

Main conceptions of justice

The following is a brief discussion of the six main conceptions of justice and how they intertwine with the idea of global sustainability. Dobson (1998) provides a very extensive and elaborate way of thinking about principles of justice with respect to environmental sustainability. Basically, he argues that principles of environmental justice can be distinguished on the basis of four different questions. The first question is whether the conception of justice includes or excludes non-humans as rightful dispensers and recipients of justice. The second question concerns the basic structure of the conception of justice. By basic structure Dobson means 'a combination of answers to questions regarding partiality, proceduralism, and universalism' (p. 69). The first (partiality) questions whether a theory of justice 'is impartial with respect of the good' or the prescribed formula depends on the nature of the notion of the good. The second (proceduralism) asks whether a conception of justice focuses on procedure or on outcomes. The third (universalism) asks whether a principle of justice is applicable globally or it is tied to particular communities. The third main question is what is to be distributed – whether it be environmental goods or bad. The final question is what the principle of distribution is.

Although Dobson's taxonomy is very useful, it is not adopted in the following discussion. Rather, my account is based around the principles of distribution that each conception of justice prescribes. Apart from being complicated, the practical use of Dobson's categorization in understanding the contestations of justice from a North–South equity context is doubtful. Besides, the stuff of any theory of justice resides in the principle of distribution it recommends, and questions about procedure are relevant only as a means to establish the morality of the outcome or combination of outcomes envisaged.[3] As Rawls (1971: 30) puts it, 'All ethical doctrines worth our attention take consequences into account in judging rightness. One which did not would simply be irrational, crazy.'

Justice as utilitarianism

Utilitarianism as a moral political theory has a long and distinguished ancestry. Developed by eminent scholars such as Jeremy Bentham, Richard Hare and John Stuart Mill, it provides, as Will Kymlicka puts it, 'a kind of tacit background against which other theories have to assert and defend themselves' (Kymlicka 2002: 10). A utilitarian conception of justice derives the requirements of justice from 'considerations of social utility in such a way that following these requirements will result in the maximization of total happiness or satisfaction in the society' (Sterba 1980: 8). Utilitarians claim that the morally right acts or policies are those that produce the greatest happiness for the members of the society. Hence, in utilitarian terms, justice is about designing political institutions and rule structures of such institutions to promote the greatest possible amount of happiness for the greatest number of people (Bentham 1970; Mill 1973; Hare 1981).

The utilitarian philosophy arose in Britain mainly as a radical critique of feudal superstition and the then elitist social structure wherein inequality was defended and justified 'in terms of some ideologically biased conception of tradition, nature, or religion' (Kymlicka 2002: 47). The main objective was, therefore, to provide a robust and coherent moral philosophical justification for the restructuring of the society in favour of the 'historically oppressed and against the privileged elite' (ibid.: 47). Utilitarianism is, therefore, avowedly consequentialist. It focuses solely on the outcome or the end result rather than on history or procedure. The key question is whether and to what degree people's lives are made better or worse by the consistent application of a given policy or course of action. The focus on consequences means that utilitarianism provides a fairly straightforward way of resolving moral questions. Given a choice of policies, utilitarians would simply seek to determine the impact of each choice or set of choices on human welfare. The option or set of options that is considered to produce the greatest maximum utility (greatest happiness for the greatest number of people) is regarded, on this doctrine, as the most just course of action. 'After all', says Mill, 'utility is the ultimate appeal on all ethical questions' (Mill 1973: 485).

The attraction of utilitarianism is the emphasis it places on human welfare as well as its rejection of moral elitism. Equally attractive is the focus on end results, which provides an easy reading of the consequences of the application of a given policy on the population. Thus, rather than focus on a set of rules or procedures, it insists that the rightness or justice of a given set of institutional principles can only be measured in terms of its ultimate consequences on human beings. Utilitarianism has also been considered progressive in that it does not seek to derive the rightness of actions from the defence of particular cultural traditions or by the appeal to a higher transcendental moral being (Barry and Matravers 1997: 143). Adherents therefore take pride in the fact that this theory of justice has a global application and is defensible against the charge of moral ethnocentrism. Ethnocentrism relates to the notion that the principles of justice are ultimately localized and, therefore, incapable of being applied across cultures and social systems without violating the moral preferences of these systems (see the discussion on communitarianism below).

However, this idea of justice and morality does have important drawbacks. There are problems with how to define utility. There are also problems with how, and even whether, utility, whichever way it is defined, ought to be maximized. And there are problems with how to aggregate utility within and across borders and what to do when the utilities of different people conflict. All of these have important implications for discussions on environmental sustainability and global distributive equity.

Taking the first concern, many utilitarians define utility in terms of the experience or sensation of pleasure. But this is hardly consistent with the way that most people see life in the real world. As Robert Nozick has famously argued, not many people would opt to be hooked continually to a wonder machine even with the promise that such a machine would produce in them a stream of unending, most pleasurable sensations for the rest of their lives (Nozick 1974: 41–45). People often think of a meaningful life as consisting of doing a range of things and working towards different types of goals, some of which might not be considered particularly pleasurable. In embracing the concept of sustainable development, there is a tacit acknowledgement that human welfare does not necessarily entail seeking the greatest experience or sensation of pleasure that can be obtained. As a matter of fact, the concept of sustainability urges a prudent lifestyle that includes the need to preserve resources for the benefit of future generations even when this entails some form of self-denial on the part of existing generations (World Commission on Environment and Development 1987; United Nations Conference on Environment and Development 1992). Hence, a hedonistic definition of welfare or utility sits uneasily with the concept of global sustainable development.

Some of those attracted to the utilitarian doctrine have sought to avoid this objection by defining utility in terms of preference satisfaction. According to this view, the idea of utility as pleasure is abandoned and welfare is rather conceived in terms of satisfying preferences, whatever these might be. Justice, therefore, entails not trying to maximize pleasure but trying to optimize people's preferences, whatever they are. But this approach hardly avoids the conflict posed by the notion of sustainability. The simple reason is that utilitarianism as maximization of preference clearly implies that preferences which are decidedly unsustainable must be weighted equally with those that are more sustainable and environmentally friendly. Added to this is the problem that satisfying people's preferences does not necessarily contribute to their well-being. It might seem all right initially to let the whole population relish the pleasure of using big gas-guzzling cars, but preference satisfaction might not ultimately contribute to welfare if it turns out that such an indulgence leads directly to changes in weather patterns with catastrophic consequences. The idea of the precautionary principle as a socio-legal concept is precisely the notion that it is more ethical to avoid satisfying a given preference if there are grounds to believe that the consequences of such preference satisfaction might be potentially severe. Authors such as Epstein (1980), Arrow and Fischer (1974), O'Riordan and Cameron (1994) and Gollier et al. (2000) show that a risk-neutral society will favour policy options and decisions that allow for more flexibility in the future over options that are certain to produce irreversible consequences. It seems that simply having a preference for something does not, in general, make it valuable. Rather, there are occasions, such as the examples of cycling, eating a healthy diet, etc., when the value of an exercise suffices as a reason for preferring it.

However, there are still deeper problems. Once it is conceded that human welfare consists of a range of preferences rather than simply seeking pleasurable feeling, it means that maximizing utility entails having a 'utility function', which results from the aggregation of the long list of factors affecting human welfare in the real world. But it is horrendously complicated to arrive at this function for a single individual given that many of the preferences might be incommensurable (Kymlicka 2002: 27–29). Even if it were possible to arrive at a neat utility function for an individual, it would be virtually impossible to aggregate preferences across societies and between countries. This problem is often encountered in different forms in the development of regimes. For instance, differences in views over imposing a moratorium on whaling, mining in Antarctica or the conservation of African elephants and rhinos reflect, in part, differences over utility functions and which preferences ought to be maximized. Indeed, one of the criticisms often levelled against regimes is that the approach is undemocratic and not preference neutral. Ruggie (1993), Cox (1983), Tooze (1990) and Bernstein (2001) among others have all forwarded the argument that current regimes emphasize a global collective utility welfare rooted in the hegemonic liberal pluralist framework (Tooze 1990: 211–212). Many other scholars have made the point that the implication of utilitarian politics even at the national level is that legitimate moral claims and aspirations of individuals may be endlessly sacrificed in a bid to achieve overall maximum well-being (Rawls 1971: 27; Nozick 1974: 155; Williams 1981: 51–53).

Justice as liberal egalitarianism

The main distinguishing feature of liberal egalitarianism as an idea of justice is that it 'attempts to combine both liberty and social equality – especially in the form of economic liberty and political equality – into one ultimate moral ideal' (Sterba 1980: 5). There are many formulations of liberal egalitarianism but their differences are merely in the ways that they try to weave and allow trade-offs between liberty and other social goods (Rawls 1971; Dworkin 1985; Barry 1989). In its most famous formulation, however, liberal egalitarianism springs from the works of philosopher John Rawls, especially as expounded in *A Theory of Justice* (1971). Accordingly, this discussion of liberal egalitarianism will focus mainly on Rawls' formulation of justice.

Rawls sets his theory of justice as a counterpoint to utilitarianism, which he accuses of not taking 'the distinction between persons seriously' (1971: 27). Rawls is concerned with social justice, that is, the justice of the 'basic structure of the society'. His focus is the justice of political and social institutions, the structure of which, he says, greatly affects the life chances of citizens and their ability to lead meaningful lives (Rawls 1971: 4, 1993: 68). In formulating his theory of justice Rawls draws upon social contract theories well established by philosophers such as Kant, Locke and Rousseau. These distinguished seventeenth-century philosophers sought to determine the right functions of state authorities as well as the correct moral and political obligations of citizens. Their key epistemological approach was to contemplate what sorts of agreement might be formulated in a hypothetical original state of nature between essentially free and rational people desirous to form a society that would regulate their co-operation. Thus, social contract theories attempt to specify the sorts of liberties and protection that free agents would require of the state in return for their obligations and obedience

(Dworkin 1977: 151–153; Kymlicka 2002: 60–62). Rawls similarly models his theory of justice in the form of a contract between free and rational agents operating from a pre-societal initial position. Rawls' initial position, however, differs from those of the social contract theories in that Rawls believes that to derive a sound conception of justice it is not sufficient that these agents are free and rational but that an original position of equality must be assumed (Rawls 1971: 12–15). It is this belief that leads him to formulate the 'veil of ignorance' – a metaphor for an original bargaining position in which moral agents are shielded from knowledge of their socio-political identities.

> Among the essential features of this situation is that no one knows his place in the society, his class position or social status, nor does any one know his fortune in the distribution of natural assets and abilities, his intelligence, strength and the like. I shall even assume that the parties do not know their conception of the good or their special psychological propensities. The principles of justice are chosen behind a veil of ignorance.
>
> (Ibid.: 12)

Working on the basis of these assumptions, Rawls formulates a theory of justice that is expressed in two key principles. The first principle is that *each person is to have an equal right to the most extensive total system of equal basic liberties compatible with a system of liberties for all.* The second principle is that *social and economic inequalities are to be arranged so that they are both to the greatest benefit of the least advantaged and attached to offices and positions open to all under conditions of fair equality of opportunity* (ibid.: 302).

The key idea, to oversimplify, is that, in an original position of equality, people would choose a principle of justice which guarantees that nobody is denied the very basic social or primary goods that enable people to lead a meaningful life. By basic social goods, Rawls means such things as 'liberty and opportunity, income and wealth, and the basis for self respect' (ibid.: 303). These 'are things which it is supposed that a rational man wants whatever else he wants' (ibid.: 92). Actually, Rawls suggests that people would choose equality as the basis for the distribution of all goods except in conditions in which unequal distribution would work to the advantage of the least well-off in the society. The reason is that, when people are effectively shielded from the knowledge of their personal attributes (that is under the veil), each person would be inclined to identify with the possible needs of others and would seek to endorse principles that would be most suitable irrespective of his 'natural chance or the contingency of social circumstances' (ibid.: 12). Justice as fairness, as Rawls fondly calls this formulation, is thus the theory of justice that 'best matches our most basic intuitions and firmest convictions on justice' (ibid.: 20).

Rawls hails his formulation of justice as an important corrective to utilitarianism. Justice as fairness, he says, recognizes the appeal in the root idea of utilitarianism, that is, the moral equality of all men, but goes on to address the fault associated with utilitarianism. First, by taking the separateness of persons seriously,

Rawls says that it becomes impossible to 'justify institutions on the grounds that the hardship of some are offset by a greater good of the aggregate' (ibid.:15). Justice as fairness thus recognizes the rights of people to live their lives according to the conception of the good that appeals to them as individuals. Second, by justifying inequality on the basis of the improved condition of the least well-off, Rawls argues that our initial intuitive aversion to societal inequities can be appeased. This way, Rawls seeks to combine the value of individual liberty, which is at the heart of liberal political ideology, with the idea of civic fraternity and social solidarity, which 'makes inequalities acceptable both to the more advantaged and the less advantaged individual' in the society (ibid.: 104).

Interestingly, Rawls clearly denies that this formulation of justice should be applied at the international level. He cites the absence of a robust global public political culture and the plurality of socio-political systems that characterize the international system as his reasons (Rawls 1999: 24–36). For Rawls, international justice should be limited to keeping the rules of non-intervention and just war, respecting human rights and assisting nations that are burdened so that they can meet their international obligations and establish 'decent political or social regimes' (ibid.: 37). Despite Rawls' objection, however, many continue to flesh out how his theory of justice might be applied in international institutions (Pogge 1998; Wingenbach 1999; Langhelle 2000; Wenar 2001; Hurrell 2001; Brown 2004). These scholars argue that a measure of global culture subsists because of the degree of political and socio-economic interdependence among peoples and states and that 'international law constitutes a unified normative order' (Hurrell 2001: 43; cf. Dupuy 1999). For instance, Pogge (1998), on the basis of Rawls' difference principle, argues for the adoption of a 'global resource dividend' scheme under which nations that have used more than their fair share of global commons ('resource deficit groups') are made to compensate those who have been disadvantaged because of such past excess usage (see Chapter 1).

And yet, although these endeavours to simulate Rawls' theory of justice on a global level are well meaning, it has to be noted that liberal egalitarianism, just like the two 'neoliberal' ideas of justice sketched below, does contain aspects that would seem to be irreconcilable with the notion of sustainability. The problem is not just Rawls' denial that his theory provides justification for moral cosmopolitanism: it is also that, in embracing perfect heterogeneity in the conception of the good life as well as the concept of the neutrality of the state, liberal egalitarianism denies environmentalists the warrant to ground most of the demands and affirmative actions often required to achieve sustainability (see Chapter 8).

Justice as property rights

The notion of justice as property rights is historically associated with the eighteenth-century discourses on the social contract, particularly John Locke's 'labour principle' in the *Two Treatises of Government* (1690/1924). Locke's overall aim was to refute the then prevailing doctrine of the divine right of the monarchy. He conceived of all men as being equally rational and collectively subject to the morality of God's law and regarded natural rights as being 'derivative' (Freeden 1991: 15) from natural law. Locke's submission was that, as all men are equally rational, it is an important moral duty of man to accord sovereignty to others such as he himself would have whereas seeking his own preservation. According to Freeden, Locke in the final analysis 'extended the notion of property to include the ownership of one's life and sovereignty over one's actions as well as the possession of goods' (ibid.: 15–16). That is, for Locke, the right to property is derived from the application of the labour of those who work it, such that, as 'labour' is naturally 'owned' by the person in whom it is embodied, it is a logical consequence that anything (hitherto unowned) to which labour is applied becomes similarly 'owned' by the labourer (Locke 1690/1924).

The idea of justice as property rights has many notable adherents. The list includes Fredrick von Hayek, Milton Friedman and John Gray. But the most elaborate attempt to construct a comprehensive theory of justice that is based on the 'sacredness' of property rights and individual liberty is Robert Nozick's *Anarchy, State and Utopia* (1974). In this work Nozick builds on Locke's notion of property and combines it with the self-ownership thesis to articulate his theory of 'justice as entitlement'. Locke argues that we are all ultimately answerable to God, who has given the fruits of nature to us all for a purpose. However, Nozick, instead, extends his theory to argue in favour of free market capitalism as well as a minimal state. A minimal state, according to Nozick, is one whose role is limited to the provision of the framework under which the pursuit of property acquisition may be effectively maintained together with protection against force, fraud and theft.

In general, proponents of justice as property rights completely reject both utilitarianism and the liberal conception of justice as outlined by Rawls. They regard both notions of justice as being quite simply incompatible with the most basic ideal of liberal society, which they hold to be individual liberty. In other words, most of the scholars that defend justice as property rights proceed on the basis that its principles are more consistent with the fundamental elements of political liberalism. Nonetheless, these scholars are better known as libertarians – a term that reflects their belief that individual liberty (which they use to include the negative rights to life and the right to property) 'trumps' all other social and political ideals. For libertarians, therefore, the 'ultimate moral foundation for a conception of justice is an ideal of individual liberty' (Sterba 1980: 10). So, whereas Rawls accuses utilitarianism of not taking the separateness of individuals seriously, the libertarians accuse Rawls of not going far enough in his formulation of justice to secure the liberty of individuals.

Libertarians insist that the real essence of liberal democratic institutions is their foundational appeal to individual freedom and liberty. According to this view, for institutions of political co-operation to be considered just, such institutions must guarantee the freedom of individuals to exploit their natural advantages (in talents, physical strength and social placements) as they would do in an original state of nature. This position is held to be inviolable regardless of the massive inequalities that might be clearly expected to result from its application. For

Hayek (1960), social inequities are inevitable consequences of liberty and to seek to correct such inequities, in the way, for example, that Rawls proposes, would destroy the very basic ideal of liberty to which democratic societies are ultimately committed. Hence, for Hayek, the only kind of equality that states are permitted to enforce is equality before the law.

> Equality of the general rules of law and conduct, however, is the only kind of equality conducive to liberty and the only equality which we can secure without destroying liberty. Not only has liberty nothing to do with any other sort of equality, but it is even bound to produce inequality in many respects. This is the necessary result and part of the justification of individual liberty: if the result of individual liberty did not demonstrate that some manners of living are more successful than others, much of the case for it would vanish.
> (Ibid.: 85)

Nozick in his entitlement theory endorses these arguments. He argues that, irrespective of the principle of justice that is chosen, inequality will arise as long as people are given the freedom to expend or deploy their original share in ways that suit them. It follows, he says, that the chief concern of any theory of justice is not to determine the end-time distribution principle but rather to specify the procedures that might be legitimately followed to acquire and expend resources (see Chapter 7). Once it is determined that one has come to acquire one's wealth through legitimate means there is no reason or moral logic compelling enough to provide a basis for asking for any other form of redistribution. Whatever arises from a just situation by just steps is in itself just and, thus, no further action by a political authority to ensure an ever-elusive equality can be morally justified.

Thus, as Beckerman and Pasek (2001: 170) put it, the central idea of Nozick's theory of justice as entitlement is that 'inequality of wealth between individuals within any country does not provide, by itself, a compelling ethical basis for the redistribution of wealth between them, unless the inequality has been the result of illegitimate procedure'. Once a rich man has acquired his wealth legally and on the basis of free transactions, he is 'entitled' to his wealth and has the ultimate freedom to withhold, enjoy, trade or give away all or part of it as he deems fit. The fact that some around him are lacking the basic necessities of life is *not*, therefore, enough reason to compel him to part with his wealth as doing so would violate his liberty and make him a slave unto others (cf. Cohen 1986; Kymlicka 2002).

Nozick, Hayek and other libertarians insist that the ultimate merit of libertarianism is that it prevents unequals from being treated as equals. Libertarians, therefore, object vehemently to differences in treatment by the state or any other agent acting with the intention of deliberately minimizing material inequality among freely acting persons. Accordingly, Milton Friedman argues that the only distributive principle that would guarantee real equality in a society committed to liberty as the ultimate ideal is 'to each according to what he and the instruments he owns produces' (Friedman 1962: 161). Friedman insists that, even if two individuals were to start from an equal position both in terms of ability and resources, the choices of the individuals, including their taste for leisure and other marketable goods, their shrewdness in investment or their attitude to hard work among other factors would soon create a condition of inequality between the two. According to Friedman, to seek a return to a condition of equality between these two individuals would result in a more fundamental sense of injustice. I will argue that a combination of this theory of justice and the following one constitute the dominant theories of justice in international environmental regimes.

Justice as mutual advantage

Justice as mutual advantage (sometimes called justice as self-interested reciprocity) proposes that the rules of justice can be derived from the rational agreement of agents to co-operate with one another in order to further their self-interest. It takes as its foundation the notion that everybody has his or her own conception of the good and that justice is best conceived as that thin framework which provides the chances and opportunities for individual utility maximization in the maximally non-conflictual environment. In the words of Barry and Matravers (1997: 144), 'Justice is thus the terms of a modus vivendi [which] gives everyone the best chance of achieving their good that they can reasonably expect, given that others are simultaneously trying to achieve their (different) good.'

Justice as mutual advantage in its contemporary form can be viewed as an alternative to a utilitarian conception of justice. Utilitarianism, as noted, takes the pursuit of aggregate utility as the ultimate political goal and seeks to formulate justice in a way that is directed towards promoting the greatest happiness for the greatest number of people (Williams 1995: 554). Justice as mutual advantage, on the other hand, proposes that the rules of justice should be those which give reason to each agent, according to his or her own conception of the good life, to seek its maximum attainment under minimum constraints. Such a co-operative framework helps us, they say, to avoid dissipating our energies fighting one another, as would be the case under the 'state of nature'. Instead, our energies are used in the pursuit of further acquisitions in a manner that reflects plural conceptions of the good.

If co-operative arrangements must be ordered to take account of the plurality of conceptions of the good, then such arrangements must reflect differences in individual talents and resources (Freeden 1991). Because resources and talents are both instruments of power it would be correct, then, to say that such arrangements should recognize and, indeed, reflect any power asymmetry that may exist among the members of the co-operative venture (Barry 1989; Buchanan 1990). Proponents of justice as self-interested reciprocity have no problem with this. Indeed, their main claim is that such a view is in itself pertinent to the success and survival of co-operative ventures. They argue that any arrangement derived from principles that do not recognize these differences, that is, one that seeks to shield the influence of resources and power in the bargaining setting (like Rawls' difference principle) cannot be rightly taken as valid (Nozick 1974; Harman 1983; Gauthier 1986). Gilbert Harman, for instance, describes as 'actual and relevant' the principles reflecting these differences and as 'hypothetical and conditional' the principles that seek to exclude them (Harman 1983: 122).

Arguments seeking to ascribe a purely instrumental value to justice and, indeed, to all morality are by no means new. In Plato's *Republic* (Knox 1938), Socrates faced in Thrasymachus an opponent who conceived of justice as being nothing other than the societal rules established for the advantage of the politically powerful – the nature of such rules varying from place to place and from time to time, depending on the composition, aim and type of the ruling bloc. In his later writings, Epicurus (341–270 BC) sought to develop a purely contractarian theory of justice. His philosophy of moral subjectivism essentially indicated that we regard actions as just only insofar as they elicit certain good feelings in us, not that such actions, independent of our feelings, are worth anything. For Epicurus (1987), justice is simply an agreement neither to harm nor to be harmed, such that what we regard as justice is merely what is useful in mutual associations. He argued that it would have been rational and logical to include animals in the community of justice if it was not for the fact that justice is solely founded on mutual gain.

This idea has received qualified support from various philosophers and political theorists including the nineteenth-century German philosopher Friedrich Nietzsche; however, the 'locus classicus' (Barry and Matravers 1997: 144) of justice as mutual advantage is definitively *Leviathan* (1968) by Thomas Hobbes. Hobbes dwelt on the conscious appreciation of the various lineaments of power and the 'justice' of their utilization in a bargaining environment. He considered the entirety of his political theory as being the 'infallible rules of nature and the true science of equity and justice' and asserted that his theory, if followed, would solve the entire political problem in a way that 'opposeth no man's profit and no man's pleasure' (Hobbes 1968: Ch. 15). To achieve this he argued that justice must be framed in terms that empower each man 'to use his own power as he will himself to the preservation of his own Nature; that is to say his own Life' (ibid.). For Hobbes, a man's power is his ultimate means of seeking more power and greater happiness. His entire life can be said to depend on its prudential use in a predominantly competitive and anarchic nature. Michael Freedman (1991: 14) describes this conception as an:

> asocial view of human organisation which embodies the unbounded egocentric drive for survival as the only minimalist valuable aspect of rationality. It firmly locates the source of that value in individuals themselves, there being no alternative fulcrum from which to asses the good and the desirable and there being no external basis for the value of life itself.

The key elements of these assumptions by Hobbes are still maintained by contemporary theorists of justice, such as Gauthier and Harman, as mutual advantage. Equally, the assumptions form important building blocks in certain mainstream theories in international relations, according to which the entire notion of justice is a matter of convention and consists of nothing that can be grounded in any inherent notion of morality. According to this view, international relations are basically anarchic and the sole concern of states is with survival, increasing their power and making gains relative to other states (cf. Morgenthau 1956, 1965; Bull 1977, esp. Part 3; Waltz 1979). Both Harman and Gauthier hold that justice in a given society, as well as international justice if it exists, must consist purely of conventions, which translate in the ordering of relevant institutions in such a way that will enable individuals (and nation states) to pursue and maximize their gains under the constraints of an agreed legal framework. Harman (1983: 121) summarizes this idea in the following way:

> In my view justice is entirely conventional. It seems extremely unlikely that there is any substantive moral demand, which all rational agents have sufficient reasons to accept. There is no single set of moral principles everyone has reasons to follow. From this I infer that there are no basic moral principles that apply to every one. So, if, as it seems to me, that there is no basic moral principle which everyone has sufficient reasons to follow, then there can be no single morality that applies to every one, no single basic set of values, no uniquely correct principles of justice.

It is at once clear that theorists of justice as mutual advantage do not believe that individuals (let alone states) can have an overarching notion of morality or idea of the good life to which agents might appeal, independent of what they can gain on the platform of rational egoistic bargaining. It is precisely in denying that individuals have inherent morality that the theory of mutual advantage differs from the theory of justice as property rights. Nevertheless, the two theories relate to each other in their endorsement of perfect heterogeneity in the conceptions of the good life and in their complete rejection of the rights to welfare of any kind. In later chapters of this book the term 'neoliberal conceptions of justice' is used to refer to these two common ideas of justice. This term is not one that is in general use in the language of political philosophy but it is used to highlight the strong ethical connection between these ideas of justice and neoliberal economic ideology. It will be shown in later chapters of this work that it is these two neoliberal ideas of justice that provide the ethical underpinnings for many of the key policies in global environmental regimes.

Communitarianism as an idea of justice

Communitarianism is not so much a principle of justice in terms of prescriptions on how the benefits and burdens of social co-operation might be distributed. Rather, it takes the form of an argument that the right principles of justice can only be determined on the basis of cultural context and the specific understanding or values associated with the good in question (McIntyre 1981; Sandel 1982; Miller 1995). Although this view was originally developed as a criticism against the atomistic and individualist approaches to moral political theory, it has also often been deployed as an argument against cosmopolitanism (Miller 1999: 188–191, 2000), the thrust of the argument being that justice cannot apply at the international level given the diversity of values and the absence of shared meanings and traditions.

Communitarians consider that the squabble between liberals and libertarians over where to draw the line between individual liberty and social equality is slightly beside the point. They believe that liberal theories of justice as a whole (that is both liberal egalitarianism and libertarianism) err to the extent that none of them give serious attention to the value of community in the formulation of their theories of justice. Communitarians insist that the idea of justice is inextricably bound with shared nationality, shared social understandings, religion or the public culture of societies. According to this view it follows that any meaningful theorization of justice must take as its starting point a detailed account of these elements. Indeed, it is these elements that provide the context within which human action can be meaningfully interpreted. Some communitarians do not necessary fault the idea of justice as liberal equality, but they believe that there needs to be a comprehensive statement on community and shared understandings to validate the liberal theory of egalitarianism. They insist, in addition, that such a comprehensive statement would require some modifications of liberal egalitarianism. Michael Sandel (1984), for instance, argues that, without an account of, indeed an emphasis on, community, liberal egalitarianism would lack the justification to treat natural talent as undeserved or to enlist the natural advantages of some towards the common good of all. According to Sandel:

> [o]n the co-operative vision of community alone, it is unclear what the moral basis for this sharing could be. Short of constitutive conception, deploying an individual's assets for the sake of the common good would seem an offence against the 'plurality and distinctness' of individuals this liberalism seeks above all to secure.
>
> (Sandel 1984: 89)

As noted, all liberal theories of justice model their formulation on the basis of 'a universal conception of human needs or human rationality and then invoke this ahistorical conception of the human being to evaluate existing social and political arrangements' (Kymlicka 2002: 209). This approach largely conceives the individual in socially abstract terms and as standing 'as an entity unto herself' (Avineri and de-Shalit 1992: 2). Communitarians, however, reject this ontological approach. They argue that it is not possible to understand people's actions and motivations outside of their socio-cultural milieu and, consequently, that much of the effort dedicated to the search for the universal conception of human rationality by liberal theorists is somewhat misguided. Communitarians argue that it is not possible to have an a priori distributive principle regarding all social goods. They insist that the appropriate distributive principle relating to a given social good can only be determined in relation to how that good is understood by society (MacIntyre 1981: 227–230). This position implies, as Kymlicka puts it, that 'the community should be seen as the source of justice' (Kymlicka 2002: 210).

Communitarians are also generally uncomfortable with the degree of priority that liberal theories accord the right over the good. They consider that this 'premises on individualism and gives rise to unsatisfactory consequences' (Avineri and de-Shalit 1992: 2). For communitarians, the two most important consequences of this normative premise are: (i) the loss of the community; and (ii) the neglect of some ideas of the good that should have been sustained by the state. These two objections to liberal approaches to justice are mostly welcomed by environmentalists in the sense that an important aspect of green political philosophy and, indeed, the concept of sustainability (as we shall see in later chapters) ascribes important places to community, citizenship and the notion of an involved rather than a neutral state (Dobson 1990, 2004; Eckersley 1992; Sagoff 1995; Attfield 2003; Barry and Eckersley 2005). In general, environmentalists suggest, or at least imply, that the state should deploy its apparatus for the mobilization of its citizens in the pursuit of environmentally sustainable development.

The problem, though, is that communitarianism, as noted, denies that principles of distributional justice can apply independently of the sort of shared social understandings that can only be found in the community. The inclination towards moral relativism leads many communitarians to reject the notion of global distributional justice on the grounds that there aren't enough networks of relationships, shared understandings or a sense of community on the global scale. It is in one such criticism of the notion of global justice that McIntyre avers 'that in making peoples citizens of everywhere it makes them citizens of nowhere' (cited in Dower 1994: 144). In the same vein, Miller (1999: 190) insists that the multitude of international environmental agreements (and other similar international treaties) 'do not by themselves create either a shared sense of identity or a common ethos', which is required to ground claims of international distributive equity.

But environmentalists continue to insist that the concepts of global community and global justice are by no means misnomers (see below). Although they concede that the belief in the value of community is creditable, they insist that the conclusion by communitarians that all moral rights and obligations depend on relations and community ties is without warrant and ultimately 'dubious' (Attfield 1999: 30). Cosmopolitans, instead, argue that 'the international world itself is or could be a community – with its own relationships, traditions and standards' (Thompson 1992: 20; cf. Franck 1995: 10).[4] In addition, they also argue that there is scarcely any state that can be conceived of as being homogenous or a moral community in ways that communitarians are wont to suggest (Barry and Matravers 1997: 154). In *The Ethics of the Global Environment* (1999) Attfield concludes that belief in universal moral responsibility does not necessarily entail a disregard of the value of community any more than a belief in community should lead to the rejection of moral obligations between communities and across community boundaries.

Justice as meeting needs

The final conception discussed in this section is justice as meeting needs. This approach to justice is often associated with scholars such as Onora O'Neill, Amartya Sen, John O'Neill and Martha Nussbaum. Although the term 'justice as meeting needs' might first strike one as being a very simple and straightforward formulation, it is quite difficult, in practice, to provide a good interpretation of this idea of justice. The reason is mainly because most of the writing that expresses sympathy with this interpretation usually takes the form of a critique of other dominant approaches rather than the more positive preoccupation of fleshing out a coherent doctrine of justice. Hence, although these accounts often present an impressive and intuitively appealing argument against prevailing conceptions, they do not provide comprehensive materials on a number of the important questions often associated with a theorization on distributional justice. Furthermore, it is not always possible to be categorical about its intellectual ancestry or its exact relationship with some of the other ideas of justice discussed earlier.

Notwithstanding these drawbacks, these scholars provide very compelling arguments against mainstream conceptions of justice. In this approach, the obligation of justice is derived from the moral equality of human beings irrespective of their race, creed and nationality (O'Neill 1991; Brown 1992: 169; Beitz 1979; Sen 1999). The emphasis is on the positive rights of citizens – that is the kinds of rights that require state authorities to do something in order to provide citizens with the opportunities and abilities to act to fulfil their own potential – as opposed to negative rights/liberty, which refers to freedom from coercion and non-interference. The notion of justice as meeting needs, as seen in Chapter 2, figures very prominently in quite a number of the influencing materials that form the starting point for the discourse on global sustainable development. It has been suggested, in general, that this idea of justice is 'increasingly influential on non-governmental organizations and the community of international policy makers' (Brighouse 2004: 67).

In general, proponents of justice as need criticize liberal ideas of justice for concentrating on political equality (equal right to speech, vote, etc.) without addressing the problem of material equality – especially in the form of equal access to resources. They also claim that the ability to own property as well as the ability to exercise political rights (say the right to vote) depends first and foremost on the ability of citizens to function effectively. When the basic human needs of citizens, for example food, are not being met, other rights become merely 'hypothetical and empty' (Sen 1999: 75). Following on from this basic reasoning, the rights approach to justice is rejected and, in its place, human basic need is seen as the correct basis of political morality and the right benchmark for the determination of political judgment (Plant 1991: 185).

In previous sections we saw that libertarian notions of justice sanction unlimited material inequality between citizens, provided that each person has obtained their possessions through legitimate means. All that matters is that the state should ensure fair rules of transitions and equality before the law. We saw also that liberal accounts of justice, especially Rawls' liberal egalitarianism, reject this formulation of justice because it does not secure the welfare of the less able in society. On the contrary, Rawls recommends that political institutions should be structured in ways that protect the interests of the least advantaged individuals in society. Accordingly, he sanctions societal inequities provided that such inequities work to the advantage of the least well-off. On closer reading, however, it turns out that Rawls difference principle (that inequities should work in favour of the least well-off) does not contain any explicit demand relating to the basic needs of the poor. As such, it is possible for Rawls' proviso to be met even when the least well-off in the society are denied their basic needs. For example, a distribution that changes from 20:10:2 to 100:30:4 satisfies Rawls difference principle but tells us nothing about the actual well-being of the least well-off. So, whereas some (mainly libertarians) criticize Rawls for not specifying the extent to which other people's liberty can be sacrificed for the sake of the least well-off, others (proponents of justice as meeting need) criticize Rawls for leaving the fate of the least well-off unprotected. Many scholars in the latter group sometimes argue along Marxian lines that as long as the means of production remain in the hands of the 'haves' there is no guarantee that inequities will benefit the least well-off.

Maslow (1968), Bradshaw (1972) and Forder (1974) have all consequently argued that only the theory of need provides, as Maslow (1968: 4) puts it, 'the ultimate appeal for the determination of the good, bad, right and wrong' in a political community. Without the theory of need, they say, it would be impossible to justify the welfare state in capitalist Western democracies. On the other hand, the co-existence of welfare and capitalism confirms the place of need as the criterion of moral political judgment. O'Neill (1991), Sen (1999) and Nussbaum (2000) have all extended versions of this argument to the international domain. O'Neill (1980, 1991) argues that adherence to the Kantian categorical imperative entails that the global community must act to remove the aching poverty and famine that threaten the existence of millions of people in developing countries. Sen (1999), for his part, calls for the strengthening of international institutions to make them able to assist the least well in the global society to achieve the measure of actual living that is required for the basic function and well-being of citizens. For Sen, as for O'Neill, all forms of liberty and rights are meaningful only when people have the substantive 'freedom to achieve actual living' (Sen 1999: 73; cf. O'Neill 1989: 288; 1986). Thomas Pogge also places emphasis on human basic need and starts his well-known book *World Poverty and Human Rights* with the rhetorical question: 'How can severe poverty of half of humankind continue despite enormous economic and technological progress and despite the enlightened moral norms and values of our heavily dominant Western civilization?' (Pogge 2002: 3).

Many environmentalists believe that this is the conception of justice most consistent with the Brundtland version of sustainable development (Dobson 1998; Benton 1999: 201; Langhelle 2000: 299). This assertion is not difficult to sustain because the Brundtland Report contains several explicit arguments that firmly link the concept of sustainability with meeting the needs of the global population. It says, for example:

> The satisfaction of human needs and aspirations is the major objective of sustainable development. The essential needs of vast numbers in the developing countries – for food, clothing, shelter, jobs – are not being met, and beyond their basic needs, these people have legitimate aspirations for improved

quality of life .... Sustainable development requires meeting basic needs of all and extending to all the opportunity to satisfy their aspirations for a better life.

(WCED 1987: 43)

It is undoubtedly the view of the Brundtland Commission, says Dobson, 'that policies for greater material equality are the most important ingredient in any recipe of measures aimed at environmental sustainability' (Dobson 1998: 14). Similarly, many other international bodies and projects regularly employ, and sometimes are explicitly based on, the discourse of need. For example, to various extents the United Nations Development Programme (UNDP) and the Millennium Development Goals (MDG) work on the basis of the desire to meet the basic needs of the global population. The difficulty with justice as meeting needs, as with utilitarianism, is in defining what counts as need. But unlike utilitarianism, proponents are mostly able to show (as is outlined in the quote from the Report above) that there are basic life requirements which even the fiercest critics of justice as meeting need are not able to deny.

Arguments against global justice

In the next two sections the main arguments that are often deployed by those opposed to the notion of global justice as well as the standard responses that are offered by those in favour of the concept are briefly reviewed. We have, of course, encountered some of these arguments in one form or another in the preceding sections but the aim here is to try and disentangle the nature of these arguments in a more concise and direct way to assist those who might want a quick summary of the state of the debate. The summary draws upon the work of Frost (2001), who, as far as I know, presents the most comprehensive conceptual arguments for and against the notion of international distributional justice.[5] I shall follow Frost in calling those opposed to global justice 'statists' and those in favour 'globalists'.

The first argument by statists is that the degree of institutionalization in the global system is neither strong nor dense enough to warrant a discourse on global justice. Statists argue that 'the global' is not a primary context of justice because it lacks the kind of institutionalization that characterizes national political systems. They argue that 'the national' is a context of justice only because of the extent of the political, legal, social, economic and cultural ties that are achieved within this domain, and that insofar as the global system lacks such a degree of cohesiveness and mutuality it does not qualify to be regarded as a legitimate context of justice. Outside of the context of reciprocity obtainable only in the national political system, justice, they say, becomes depoliticized and pales to an 'impersonal distributive arrangement' involving some production slaves and perpetual recipients linked by a largely 'anonymous global distributive agency' (Kersting 1996: 201, cited in Forst 2001: 162; cf. Miller 1999).

The second argument by statists is that 'the national contexts of justice are already normatively structured in their own ways and that global principles would violate those structures (of property) for example' (Frost 2001: 161–162). Here, statists draw upon Nozick's argument that things don't just appear from nowhere and then wait to be distributed according to one principle or another but that, in most cases, the goods which claimants of social justice argue should be distributed already belong to people who acquired these goods through a legitimate pre-existing process of distribution (normally inherent in national political and economic systems). It follows, according to this view, that any attempt to redistribute these goods would violate the rights of those who legitimately own them. To this end, statists argue that production and distribution are not two separate processes but rather form a progression, which would be inevitably undermined if the appeals for global (and national, in some cases) redistribution are heeded (Nozick 1974: 153–160).

The third argument against global justice advanced by statists is that it is impossible to achieve or to aspire to conceptions of global distributional justice without committing to the notion of a world government. They insist that the 'political logic of nationalism' (Falk 1971: 37) as well as the anarchical nature of the international domain generates a normative structure whereby only the state can serve as a credible centre of gravity for distributional justice. According to this view, the architecture of the international system is adjudged as being far too weak, fragmented and competitive to permit meaningful efforts at distributional justice. Statists, therefore, argue that only a global superstate would have the kind of coercive powers needed to surmount this problem and organize production and wealth distribution at a global level. And because such a global superstate is neither possible nor desirable, it follows that the concept of global justice must remain mere wishful thinking.

Fourth, statists argue that the ideal of global justice, as far as it goes, is liable to the charge of ethnocentrism. Following on from the communitarian view that justice is only meaningful within a context of shared social, cultural and political understanding, some of those opposed to the notion of international justice argue that the search for justice in the international domain must entail the imposition of some (typically liberal democratic) culture on the entire globe.

The final argument is that statists reject the idea that poverty and international inequities are largely caused by unjust global political economic structures. Rather, they blame the conditions of poverty and underdevelopment in poor countries on the undemocratic systems, wasteful cultures and political traditions of these societies. Following Rawls, they argue that what these societies need, at most, is measured assistance by the international community to help them change their systems to ones that enhance democracy and material prosperity (Rawls 1999: 27).

Justifications for global justice: the cosmopolitan response

Proponents of global justice do not consider the objections summarized above as decisive at all. Rather, they press a series of arguments that 'either directly refute or weaken the critiques' (Frost 2001: 163) advanced by the statists.[6]

The first line of response by globalists is to directly deny that the extent of interdependence and institutional linkages in the international arena does not afford a sufficient condition for questions of distributional justice. Globalists maintain that 'there is now a denser and more integrated network of shared institutions and practices within which social expectations of global justice and injustice have become more securely established' (Hurrell 2001: 35; cf. Vogler 2000: 212). Globalists identify several distinct but closely interwoven areas of global co-operation where 'globalized interdependence has reached a point where it is impossible not to speak' in the context of justice (Frost 2001: 165). This list includes the context of global trade, labour and production; the global ecological context, especially taken together with the problems of scarcity and pollution; the global context of institutions such as the UN and the International Monetary Fund (IMF); the global context of legal treaties; and the global context of cultural production, consumption and communication. Indeed, for some globalists, the rejection of global justice on the basis that international institutions are not dense enough is, at best, an 'old philosophical wangle which appears quaint in the context of' today's realities (Jameson 1994: 102). Yet, for others, the obligations that generate mutual reciprocity and the circumstances for justice need not rest on 'a skein of actual reciprocity for mutual advantage but rather on a broadly Kantian conception of moral equality in which justice requires that we all treat each other as equals' (Nielsen 1995: 39–40). According to this view, the question is not whether the degree of co-operation is as dense as those found in nation states (for clearly international co-operation is not designed to be so). Rather, the question is whether these co-operative arrangements do have the ability to produce winners and losers. Framed in this way there are very few who would be able to produce a convincing argument to the effect that neither the international system nor international institutions are significant in the context of global economic inequities (see Korten 1996; O'Neill 2001; Pogge 2001).

Next is the charge that appeals to global justice are ahistorical and prone to upset shares which have been acquired through legitimate means within a national political setting. The response of the globalists to this charge is that insofar as the global domain is a legitimate scope of justice 'the question of domestic justice cannot take priority to, or be settled in advance of, the question as to what principles of global justice require' (Frost 2001: 163; cf Shue 1983: 602–603). In other words, advocates of global justice insist that questions of national and global justice are inextricably interwoven and, therefore, cannot be settled independently. For example, globalists point out that a good number of the developed countries achieved their prosperity, at least in part, through the domination and exploitation of the poor developing countries by means of the slave trade, colonialism or uneven terms of international trade. Accordingly, it would amount to a kind of 'compound injustice', says Shue, for rich nations that have 'benefited from exploitation to insist that poor nations that have suffered from exploitation must cope with unsolved problems using "their own resources"' (Shue 1992: 388).

But even if it is conceded that global distributive mechanisms should violate existing legitimate holdings in national political communities it would still not be the case that questions of global justice would immediately become irrelevant. This is because there still exists a vast portion of the planet that does not, and by its very nature cannot, fall under national jurisdictions. Globalists argue that areas such as the world's oceans and high seas and the seabed beyond the jurisdiction of states, as well as other resources such as the atmosphere, Antarctica, the geostationary orbit and outer space, all constitute legitimate domains for global justice discourses (Sachs 1999; Vogler 2000; Attfield 2003).

Globalists address the charge of the inevitability of a world government and ethnocentrism with the same argument. As a starting point, globalists highlight the fact that the common dependence of all mankind on a singular planet does not immediately obscure the sense of the more immediate relationships (at national, state or even family levels). Further, they point out that the dense network of interactions and international institutions have, so far, existed side by side with national political institutions. On these grounds globalists argue that it is spurious to tie the fulfilment of global distributional justice to the condition of a world government. They also, following a similar logic, deny the charge of ethnocentrism arguing rather that there is a distinction between 'moral cosmopolitanism', which insists that 'every human being has a global stature as ultimate unit of moral concern' (Pogge 1992: 49), and legal or institutional cosmopolitanism, which 'implies the necessity of an overarching political authority or world government' (Frost 2001: 164; cf. Beitz 1999: 199). Hence, so long as, in practice, the equity-significant international institutions coexist with national political systems, globalists insist that there is no reason to assume that 'institutional conceptions' (Pogge 1992) of justice are inherently incompatible with the pursuit of justice in national political systems.

At the same time globalists claim that the charge of ethnocentrism is somewhat misguided because, insofar as the phenomenological reality of the international domain is one of a dense institutional network and complex interdependence, there already exists a global 'cross-cultural discourse' (Pogge 1989: 271), the normative features of which can only be justified in universal terms. The urgent task, therefore, as Barry (1995: 156) following Thomas Scanlon (1982) says, is to make sure that these co-operations can be justified both reciprocally and generally or, in other words, that the underlying power structures are fair and that the agreements are established 'on terms that nobody could reasonably reject'.

Conclusion

In this chapter we have undertaken a review of the concept, as well as the main conceptions, of justice in Anglo-American political philosophy. The intended outcome is a better understanding of the ways in which different ideas of justice intertwine with the notion of global sustainability. Familiarity with the different conceptions of justice is also desirable in the bid to study the ways in which various ideas of justice feature and underpin respective regime policies (Part II). It was firstly demonstrated that, despite the disagreements over what justice entails in practice, that is, over conceptions of justice, there remains a wide consensus that

Setting the scene

the concept of justice occupies an important position both in terms of justificatory purposes and for the stability of political institutions. This chapter also reviewed the main conceptual arguments against global justice. It finds that these arguments are mostly misguided, especially as it is evident that international institutions as currently constituted form a central element in the normative structure of the international society and, by their very operation, serve to narrow and/or exacerbate inequities both within and between countries. The urgent task identified is that of making the roles and general discussions of justice in international institutions more explicit. This includes identifying how various ideas feature both implicitly and explicitly in international policies as well as identifying the dominant conceptions of justice that underwrite key institutional policies and programmes. It is to this task that the next part of the book is dedicated.

Part II
Empirical analysis of three regime texts

General introduction

Part I presents an account of the roles of international environmental regimes as a medium for international distributional justice. It also provides an account of the various conceptions of distributive justice indicating how each intertwines with the notion of global environmental sustainability. It was noted that, although there has been a general acceptance that distributive equity is important in the operation of multilateral environmental regimes, much still remains to be learnt in terms of which conceptions of justice underpin major global environmental policies or, more broadly, how the general contestations for justice affect global environmental management options and strategies. These are the questions that are addressed in the second part of the book.

Chapter 4 examines the principles and policies guiding the use and exploitation of the resources of the sea as codified in the Third United Nations Conference on the Law of the Sea (UNCLOS III). Chapter 5 examines the Basel Convention on the Transboundary Movements of Hazardous Wastes and their Disposal, which is regarded as the umbrella institution for the global waste management regime. Chapter 6 takes up the international effort aimed at combating global warming by focusing on the United Nations Framework Convention on Climate Change (UNFCCC).

In all of these cases the central aim is to analyse the primary texts of the regimes to determine the roles of various ideas of justice in the development of each regime and to identify the notions of justice that best provide conceptual explanations for both the core and peripheral policies of each regime. The approach is discursive in that attempts are repeatedly made to place the texts and policies in the broader political and historical context under which they were articulated. The aim is to gain a deeper understanding of the forces that guide the evolution of most of the important norms under which global sustainability is pursued. It is also the aim to reveal the winners and losers in these processes, which are otherwise portrayed as symbols of collective efforts and evidence of a joint commitment towards the achievement of sustainable development by the international community. Some scholars often point to the prevalence of regimes as a sign that mutually beneficial co-operation between the rich and poor countries of the world is taking place. But little is done to show the extent to which regime policies have actually resulted in a narrowing of the economic gap between the rich North and the poor South.

UNCLOS III is dealt with first because it not only precedes the Basel Convention and the UNFCCC in time but also it was the very first global environmental conference where contestations for international justice played a major role in shaping discussions, texts and policies. The Basel Convention, which is analysed next, centres on aspects of international trade as well as the relationship between globalization and industrial practices and how these impinge on global environmental integrity. Finally, the Convention on Climate Change enables us to examine the impact of lifestyles and aspects of the economic and political structures of states on the global environment.

4 Managing a global commons
The United Nations Conference on the Law of the Sea

This chapter looks at the role of equity contestations in one of the most prominent environmental regimes in existence. It highlights the role of the common heritage of mankind (CHM), which inheres within an egalitarian conception of justice in shaping the discussions and policies of this regime. But it also goes on to show that, although the CHM and related equity concepts had some impact on the normative structure of the regime, it was policies that 'fit' market-based interpretation of justice that eventually prevailed in the design of the core rules of the regime.

A global 'constitution for the oceans'[1]

By many standards the Third United Nations Conference on the Law of the Sea (UNCLOS III) should provide the starting point for any analysis seeking to capture the ethical challenges confronting institutions for international environmental governance and the import of equity aspirations in the construction of response strategies to global environmental problems. In terms of chronology it precedes most other international environmental regimes, such as the ozone depletion, climate change and biodiversity agreements, which now tend to dominate mainstream discussions on global environmental governance (GEG). In terms of scope it remains the widest and most comprehensive environmental agreement ever attempted by the international community (Song 2005: 263). In fact, the conference has been described in some quarters as the 'single most important diplomatic event since after the creation of the United Nations' (Koh 1983: xxxiv). And in terms of approach and content, the conference is innovative in several important respects and has been described as establishing important signals for the development of sustainable global environmental governance (UNCED 1992; Friedheim 1993: 290; Song 2005: 263).

UNCLOS III was opened for signature in Montego Bay, Jamaica, in 1982 after almost 8 years of arduous negotiations by over 150 countries (Zuleta 1983: 6).[2] It set out to elaborate on the rules, norms and standards of practice that should govern international relations in an area that constitutes about 70 per cent of the earth's surface (Song 2005: 263) and is described by Vogler (1995: 47) as the 'original global commons'. Specific aspects of the conference focused on: (i) delimitations of boundaries between opposite and adjacent states and setting the limits of the territorial sea and the contiguous zone; (ii) the extent and nature of coastal states' jurisdiction in areas beyond the territorial sea; (iii) the nature of rights and conditions for explorations in respect of the continental shelf; (iv) the rights of landlocked and geographically disadvantaged states; (v) protection of the marine environment and conservation of the living resources of the high seas; (vi) exploration and exploitation of the minerals and other resources in the deep seabed; and (viii) peaceful settlement of disputes (O'Connell 1984; Sanger 1986; Churchill and Lowe 1988).[3]

With such a list of topics (and this is by no means exhaustive) it is not surprising that the conference commanded the attention of states with diverse histories and interests in the use of the sea. Neither is it surprising that negotiations were tough, lengthy and, in some places, quite complex and difficult to follow. The result was a Convention with 320 articles and 9 annexes (some of which themselves have up to 40 articles). The Convention entered into force on 16 November 1994, 12 months after the deposition of the sixtieth instrument of ratification by Guyana on 16 November 1993 (Vogler 2000: 47; Duff 2004: 199). As of 18 October 2006, a total of 150 states and entities (such as the EU) are parties to the Convention. The United States is the only member of the United Nations Security Council and NATO that is yet to ratify the Convention.[4]

The political context of UNCLOS III[5]

In keeping with traditional thinking in international relations, the dealings among states with respect to the use and appropriation of the resources in the oceans and high seas have been highly anarchical, lacking any sustained considerations of equity, justice and fairness among states (Anand 1982; Kiss 1985; Kwiatkowska 1988). Although there has never been a unified position, patterns of appropriation closely followed the writings of the Dutch lawyer and scholar of international relations, Hugo Grotius. Grotius mostly comes across as an advocate of peace and order in international relations, but his original writings were actually dedicated to defending the forceful seizure of a Portuguese ship (*Catharina*) by the Dutch East India Company in the straits of Malacca (Sanger 1986: 9). Grotius advocated the doctrine of *mare liberum*, which stands for complete freedom in the use of the high seas for navigation purposes and in the appropriation of the natural resources therein. Under the Grotian view the sea was regarded as a *res nullius*, meaning that its resources belonged to no man and, as such, were open to everyone on a first come, first served basis. Grotius was only mindful of the needs of the European countries who used the sea mainly for trade routes, including for the purpose of slave trade (Djalal 1980). This freedom relied essentially on the presumption that every state had an equal opportunity to appropriate the resources of the sea. It was freedom advocated in total disregard for the welfare of the weaker, poorer and technologically undeveloped countries (Djalal 1980, 1985).

The major alternative position from that of Grotius came from the English lawyer, John Selden, who advocated, under the doctrine of *mare clausum*, that states should have control over the waters adjacent to their coasts. Selden wrote in defence of the British seizure of some Dutch ships that were returning from Greenland waters with a heavy catch of walrus (Sanger 1986: 10). He disagreed with the view of Grotius that the resources of the sea were inexhaustible and argued that it was both politically and economically expedient for states to exercise control over their coastal waters (Churchill and Lowe 1983: 5; Sanger 1986: 10). But Selden's view, similarly to that of the Crown, which he defended, also proceeded purely out of rational egoistic calculations and had nothing to do with international justice in the use and appropriation of the resources of the sea. Indeed, the view of the British government oscillated quite regularly in keeping with their military might and envisaged gains. As Sanger (1986: 11) puts it:

> The England of Queen Elizabeth I emphasized the freedom of the sea against the claims of sovereignty of Spain; but within two generations the policy was reversed. For Spanish threat had faded by then, and the greater concerns for Britain during the Stuart period were to assert jurisdiction over coastal fisheries and to profit from the import trade.

One can say, in general, that neither of the leading authors nor the economic powers that dominated the early debates explicitly took the notion of international justice into account in their proposals. And in particular, that the development of the international customary law of the sea followed a path that neglected the welfare of the developing countries, most of which were clearly unable to take part in the debates or to harness the resources of the sea in any appreciable degree (Ramakrishna 1990: 439). The marginalization of the developing countries and the resultant inequity in the international customary law of the sea was a dominant theme during the negotiations of UNCLOS III. For example, Hasjim Djalal, who led the Indonesian delegation, stated that:

> The conquest of what have now become independent developing countries was to a large extent facilitated by the principles of the freedom of the sea as practiced at that time. The freedom of the sea in the past, in effect, meant the freedom of those who had the navy to control the oceans, thus controlling the world.
>
> (Djalal 1980: 22)

Many delegates from the developing countries shared the sentiment expressed by Djalal. In general, they argued that the pattern of evolution of the international customary law of the sea was symptomatic of the wider trends in international law, which were mostly dedicated to the service of the economic and strategic interests of the imperial West. As a result, they insisted that UNCLOS III must be seen as an opportunity to rewrite and to entrench equity and global justice as the hallmark of the new law of the sea (Pardo 1975). This view is clearly reflected in the statement credited to Mr Joseph Warioba, a Tanzanian delegate to UNCLOS III:

> Freedom of the sea has ceased to serve the interest of international justice. It has become a catchword and an excuse for a few countries to exploit ruthlessly the resources of the sea, to terrorise the world and to destroy the marine environment. That type of freedom belonged to the old order and has outlived its time.
>
> (Cited in Ramakrishna 1990: 439)

On the other hand, the developed countries seemed largely determined to salvage whatever was left of the customary law of the sea with all the rights and privileges it accorded them. It was these mindsets from both sections that, in the words of Friedheim (1993: 290), 'turned the Conference into the arena for the acting out of one major episode of the North–South quarrel that has shaped the outcome of many issues in multinational organisations in the late twentieth century'.

Conceptions of justice in UNCLOS III

There is copious use of the terms 'justice' and 'equity' in UNCLOS III (perhaps more than in any other existing, issue-specific, international environmental treaty). The commitments to justice, mutual co-operation and compromise were repeated in several pre-conference speeches on the floor of the United Nations Assembly.[6] These commitments were also frequently reiterated during the preparatory sessions by several of the delegates taking part in the conference (UNCLOS III *Official Records: Summary Records of Meetings*, 1975–82). In the preambular section alone (comprising eight short paragraphs), the commitment to international distributive justice is repeated in at least six places. In paragraph 1, parties promptly declared that their engagements in the overall activity of elaborating a new law of the sea were 'prompted by the desire to settle, in a spirit of mutual understanding and co-operation, all issues relating to the law of the sea', bearing in mind the need to ensure that the Convention should contribute 'to the maintenance of peace, *justice* and progress for all peoples of the world' (authors' italics). Paragraphs 3 and 4 express the parties' understanding of the ecological unity of the ocean space and the commitment to ensure 'the *equitable* and efficient utilization of their resources'. In paragraph 5 of the preamble, parties expressed the hope that the conference:

> will contribute to the realization of a just and *equitable* international economic order which takes into account the interests and needs of mankind as a whole and, in particular the special interests and needs of developing countries, whether coastal or land-locked (author's italics).

Parties also explicitly expressed the hope that UNCLOS III would set a precedent in the overall approach of states to international co-operation in conformity '*with the principles of justice and equal rights*'. The preambular section ended with the expression of the will to 'promote the economic and social advancement

Managing a global commons 61

of all peoples of the world' (Preamble para. 7). There is no section for the definition of concepts, neither is there any other place in the Convention text where parties attempt to define their understanding of justice and equity. However, some authors (e.g. Zuleta 1983: xx) suggest that the unique procedures adopted during negotiations at the conference offer some insight on how parties meant to achieve the stated aim of achieving international justice in the law of the sea.

Procedure

The procedure adopted during the negotiations of UNCLOS III has been described by some as both a sign of international justice in itself as well as a major factor in accounting for the successful negotiation of equitable policies during the conference (Zuleta 1983; Koh 1983; Perez de Cuellar 1983; Vogler 1995). In most of these accounts, the concepts of 'package deal' and the maximal pursuit of consensus, as well as the 'balanced' geographical representations in committees, are the 'innovations' most frequently mentioned.[7] For the Undersecretary-General, Bernardo Zuleta, it was the package-deal arrangement that served as the most important safeguard in ensuring that the aspirations for justice, which triggered the effort to elaborate a new law of the sea, eventuated.

The notion of a package deal refers to the proposal that the whole of the Convention with its 320 articles (covering sometimes divergent issues) be regarded by parties as a single document. The package-deal approach, according to Djalal (1985: 50), was aimed at preventing states from adopting a 'pick and choose' tactic towards the Convention. It meant, according to Vogler (1995: 50), that 'nothing will be finally decided until everything was decided'. For Koh (1983: 60), the reason for the package-deal approach was to promote 'the spirit of negotiation and compromise'. However, this approach was also intended as a means to discourage the powerful states from pouring their energies into securing their narrow interests while refusing to make concessions on matters of wider global equity. In other words, the package deal was a procedural means of ensuring that the multitude of interests and needs of states, particularly of those with rather low bargaining chips, were taken into account, because it allowed such states to exert a greater influence in the determination of the final structure of the document. As the former Secretary-General of the UN himself puts it, the idea was 'devised in recognition of the indivisibility of the single whole which the law of the sea must constitute, [and conceived as] the only way of reconciling divergent interests and promoting compromise, thereby ensuring as full participation as possible in the final agreement' (Perez de Cuellar 1983: xxx; cf. Attard 1987: 33–34).

The second and equally important issue in terms of procedure was the 'gentleman's agreement' appended to the rules of procedure (A/CONF.62/30/Rev.3) wherein parties agreed to work on the basis of consensus. The agreement on consensus 'required parties to decide that it had exhausted all efforts to reach consensus before any voting on questions of substance can take place' (Zuleta 1983: xxi). Again, this provision is usually defended on the basis of the need for fairness and, in particular, of the desire to carry everybody along in the negotiation process.

It was thought that the sensitivity of the matters for legislation called for a determined effort by states to achieve agreement. In particular, there was the need to avoid sweeping dissension under the carpet by means of a simple majority or two-thirds majority vote, by which most issues were resolved in the UN General Assembly meetings (ibid.: xxii). Anand (1985) further describes the adoption of the rule on consensus as an expression of the wish of the conference organizers to achieve fairness by encouraging a spirit of give and take. It was a means, he says, of asking 'all delegations to make good-faith efforts to accommodate the interests of others' (Anand 1985: 74). Consensus was also desirable as a means of ensuring that the Convention, when it finally emerged, would be universally acceptable by state parties. This was all the more important given the strategic nature of some of the issues involved and the massive changes pre-empted in the international customary law of the sea of which the common heritage concept and its practical implications were the most prominent (Stavropoulos 1985).

A follow-through of the proceedings of the conference reveals that parties did make reasonable efforts to abide by this gentleman's agreement. One after the other, many of the proposals, which in the beginning seemed to be diametrically opposed, were eventually 'reconciled' through the process of listening, exchange of ideas and other bargaining tactics. According to Tommy B. Koh, the last chairman of the conference, this achievement was made possible because the procedure 'allows various deferments and "cooling-off" periods before the actual voting may begin' (Koh 1985: 18). This approach contrasts sharply with the 'negotiation through exhaustion' and the gavelling through of clauses, which have been a regular feature in post-Rio environmental conferences (see Mintzer and Leonard 1994; Leggett 2000; Grubb and Yamin 2001).

The final point of interest under procedure relates to the appointment of committee officers during the treaty-making process. Here, it is the opinion of some close observers that the composition of the key committees and their chairmanship both reflected and promoted the pursuit of international justice within the context of UNCLOS III. Borgese (1986), for example, stresses the positive input of equitable regional representation in the Preparatory Commission of the Seabed Authority and the International Tribunal for the Law of the Sea. Zuleta (1983) places emphasis on the fact that, by organizing the informal negotiating groups on the basis of interest in specific issues rather than by the use of regional bloc membership, a more than average chance was provided for each state to articulate, canvass and defend its interests in the various subject matters. Sanger (1986) equally observes that an air of commonality and co-operation was promoted because the industrialized countries conceded the chairmanship positions to the developing countries and did not seek to exert pressure on them until towards the last years of the conference.[8]

The foregoing discussion largely establishes intent on the part of state agents to adhere to notions of distributive equity. But although the ideas of a package deal and decision by consensus may be intuitively appealing, there is nothing in them that necessarily guarantees that the policies which emerge in this way will be fair and equitable. On the contrary, bargaining and philosophical literature grants that power relations can still play a role in a bargaining situation where consensus is adopted as the ground rule (Zartman and Berman 1982). Here, it is understood that there are still a number of avenues – including subtle threats – through which the more influential actors may be able to induce consent to their advantage (cf. Raiffa 1982; Oye 1986; Barry 1989). Hobbes (1968: esp. in Ch. 15 of *Leviathan*) clearly maintained that the outcomes of agreements entered into out of fear – including the fear that is deliberately created by the other party – represent a fair and just outcome. The reason for this is that Hobbes believed that justice is nothing other than the carrying out of the contract to which one enters into. The terms and conditions under which the contract was made do not matter. Rawls, however, argues that an understanding of justice that relies for its elaboration on simply saying that a decision was arrived at mutually is too simple and incapable of telling much about the inherent quality of such a decision (Rawls 1971: 17–19).

Further, in the context of UN conferences, the term 'consensus' can be very deceptive, for it does not always mean absence of disagreement or active consent to a final decision. Neither does it mean that any country which chooses to stand in disagreement has a power to veto the decision in question. All that consensus means in the UN context is simply an agreement to 'proceed without formal objection' (Stavropoulos 1985: lxiv). Moreover, although important on its own merit, it would be erroneous to assume that poor developing countries could secure equitable international policies by simply supplying the chairmanship of a few important committees. The reason is that international injustices are often deeply embedded in existing power structures and economic relations in ways that cannot be easily revoked merely by acting as the chairman of a given committee (cf. Cox 1983, 1992). Indeed, more sophisticated accounts of power tell us that power resides more in the 'enduring capacity to act' rather than in the occupation of functional positions (Isaac 1987: 74). Power, according to this view, derives from the social identity of participants and is 'implicated in the constitutions of the conditions of interaction' (ibid.: 75), being, as it were, 'intrinsic to a social context' (Lee 1995: 148) rather than in titles or procedural functions.

All this should serve as an important reminder that the substantive policies of international regimes still require ethical scrutiny irrespective of the negotiation procedure or the amount of rhetoric that might have been admitted in the preparatory stages. Indeed, there is ample evidence that, despite the positive noises that were made with respect to the need for equity in UNCLOS III, a majority of the participating countries knew deep down that their success in the conference would ultimately depend on the extent to which they were able to strategically maximize whatever bargaining chips were available to them. The effects of these approaches can be seen by looking at the debates surrounding the negotiation of some the substantive policies of the Convention.

The seabed regime and the common heritage of mankind

It was basically Dr Arvid Pardo, the then Permanent Representative of Malta to the UN, who set the pace for the elaboration of a new law of the sea through his speech on the need for international justice in the management of the resources of the seabed beyond national jurisdictions (Ogley 1984; Sanger 1986; Friedheim 1993; Vogler 1995). In his speech, at the United Nations Assembly in December 1967, Ambassador Pardo drew attention to the 'unity' of the sea as an ecosystem and to the imperatives of a holistic management approach entailed by this perspective. He called for the need to protect the oceans from serving as a dumping ground for the increasingly diverse and dangerous wastes from industrial processes. And most significantly, he called for the recognition of the deep seabed beyond the jurisdiction of states as the 'common heritage of mankind'.

Pardo explicitly based his proposals on the principles of peace, *equity and international justice*. He argued that the resources of the seabed belonged to all mankind equally and, therefore, ought to be managed in ways that served the interests of the most needy and the least advantaged groups (Duff 2004: 196). Pardo's vision thus transcended the Grotian idea of freedom of the sea and Selden's notion of enclosure, both of which, rightly or wrongly, favoured the idea of justice as 'to each according to his power'. Pardo drew attention to what he called the 'vast resource potential that lay beneath the ocean floors' and the huge disparity in wealth that would occur if the area were managed in ways that allowed those with advanced technology to gain exclusive access, saying that the consequences of inaction by the international community would result in conditions of 'intolerable injustice'.

> The resources of the seabed and of the ocean floor are as great as the resources on dry land. The seabed and the ocean floor are also of vital and increasing strategic importance. Present and clearly foreseeable technology permits the effective exploitation of virtually all this area for military or economic purposes. Some countries will therefore be tempted to use their technical competence to achieve near unbreakable world dominance through predominant control over the seabed and the ocean floor. [...] The process has already started and may lead to a competitive scramble for sovereign rights over the land underlying the world's seas and oceans, surpassing in magnitude and in its implications last century's colonial scramble for territory in Asia and Africa. The consequences will be very grave – at the very least a dramatic escalation of the arms race and sharply increasing world tensions, caused also by the intolerable injustice that would reserve the plurality of the world's resources for the exclusive benefit of less than a handful of nations. The strong would get stronger, the rich richer.

Following Pardo's speech, the United Nations General Assembly passed a resolution declaring the seabed and ocean floor beyond the jurisdiction of states as the CHM [UNGA resolution 2749 (XXV) 1970]. The General Assembly also set up a Committee for the Peaceful Uses of the Ocean Floor and High Sea Beyond National Jurisdictions, which eventually acted as the Preparatory Commission for UNCLOS III (UN Doc. SEA/MB/2). Indeed, most of the nearly 11 years of negotiation was devoted to the task of defining and refining the concept of the CHM, which had become a rallying point of a sort for the G-77 nations and other forces that nursed the idea that the time had come to establish questions of distributive justice firmly within international politics and the law of nations (Zuleta 1983: xxiii; cf. Kiss 1985; Dupuy 1983: 313). Vogler (1995: 49) spoke of the situation in the following way:

> Although the developed maritime states would have preferred a limited negotiation on navigation rights and the new limits of territorial seas, the very different requirements of the G-77, stressing national economic sovereignty and issues of North–South equity, could not be ignored. The politically necessary conjunction of the two provided the essential basis of the Third Law of the Sea Conference (UNCLOS III) and its extraordinarily broad and inclusive agenda.

To a large extent, therefore, it is plausible to claim that the entire process of articulating a new law of the sea was galvanized by the concept of the CHM and the general search for justice and equity in the international order. For Mr P. Engo, who acted as the Chairman of the Seabed Committee, the appeal of the common heritage concept resided in the fact that it 'transcends the inherent opposition between the doctrines of *res nullius* and *res communes*' and embodies an all together different resource management option (UNCLOS III *Official Records: Summary Records of Meetings*, 1975: 2). The way that this opposition is overcome, according to Borgese (1986), is that the concept demands positive action on the part of agents such that the notion of the commons ceases to be associated merely with the fact that 'a legally defined user can not be excluded' (Buck 1998: 5. cf. Wijkman 1982: 512). Instead, the situation becomes one in which emphasis is given to the overall economic standing of the 'owners' in mapping what constitutes the equitable distribution or usage of the resources. In this sense, the notion of the CHM is not merely a resource management option but firmly incorporates the 'ideological and philosophical setting required for the application of the concept' (Borgese 1986: 125). We see in the emphasis on positive action rather than negative rights – rights to non-interference – a close philosophical association between the concept of the common heritage of mankind and the interpretation of justice along the lines of meeting needs and providing the capacity for 'functioning' (Sen 1999: 74–75; see Chapter 3).

Divergence and reconciliation of views

It was obvious that the notion of CHM and the other equity issues involved in the management of the seabed were not only novel with respect to the existing laws of the sea but also that they held the prospect of transforming the entire landscape of international relations (Sanger 1986: 158; Friedheim 1993: 230). Parties were more or less aware, as Borgese (1986: 99) puts it, that the CHM had 'significant value as a model for future relations among states'. And, perhaps as a result of this, neither the developed nor the developing countries were willing to move from their positions on most of the issues involved.

At the heart of the issue was the prospect that there were billions of tonnes of manganese nodules on the seabed, the extraction of which would lead to cheap and alternative sources of a number of economically important metals including copper, cobalt and nickel (Ogley 1984). Much of the global demand for these minerals is met by land-based production in African countries and almost all industrialized countries (except Australia and Canada) are net importers (Sanger 1986: 158). From the developed country perspective, therefore, seabed mining was envisioned as an end to dependence on African minerals. For most in the developed countries, the CHM was intuitively appealing, but, in practice, it meant no more than the payment of a couple of thousands in royalties to the UN. There are, of course, some in the US Senate who insisted that that the CHM was 'nothing more than declaring a right to steal'.[9] From the developing country perspective, however, deep seabed mining was going to prove the ultimate equalizer in the international system and the means to an end to the material dominance of the industrialized west. After all, the UN General Assembly had declared that the deep seabed beyond the jurisdiction of states (later to be known simply as the 'Area') was the common heritage of mankind to be used for the benefit, especially, of less advantaged people. So, then, the chief task before the draftsmen in UNCLOS III became how to reconcile the diverse viewpoints on equity attached to the notion of the CHM and how to translate the answers into policy options acceptable to both political blocs.

First, there was contention over the exact nature and power of the authority that would be responsible for overseeing the mining activities. Second, there was disagreement on whether mining activities should be undertaken solely by such an authority, in conjunction with state and private enterprises, or solely by private corporations. There were also questions on what rules should govern state or private enterprises if they were allowed to take part in mining activities. Third, there were 'issues' concerning the criteria for sharing the profits that might accrue. Should they be based on per capita income, on land mass or on gross domestic product (GDP)? Fourth, there were concerns about the possible implications of seabed mining on the welfare of states whose economies depended on the export of land-based minerals. Whether the prices of the seabed metals should be regulated and whether the activities of the land-based industries should be subsidized are just two of the many questions that were asked under this issue. And finally, questions arose with respect to how the pioneer investors might be protected in the context of the CHM and how it would be possible to achieve a transfer of technology from the North to the South to avoid monopoly (Ogley 1984; Sanger 1986; Friedheim 1993; Vogler 2000).

In sum, the developed countries, mainly following the position of the USA, wanted a Seabed Authority whose role would be restricted to that of a clearing house and licensing office (Friedheim 1993: 230). They strongly advocated a regime that adhered closely to free market ideals, rooting, in so doing, for property rights interpretations of justice. Generally, developed countries thought that private corporations should be allowed to mine the minerals in the seabed under minimal regulation. They sought to secure freedom for private investors to explore, mine and market their products in line with the dictates of demand and supply (Sanger 1986: 186–187). The developed countries also advocated strong protection for the pioneer investors, arguing that such a protection mechanism was important to cushion the risks of exploration and stimulate the competition needed to get the metal out of the seabed in the first place (Oxman 1994: 689–693; Friedheim 1993: 250–256). Hence, here, the idea of justice approximates to the libertarian conception of justice with its emphasis on the free market and minimal state interference.

Developing countries, for their part, were not convinced that the task of getting the polymetalic nodules out of the seabed was as difficult and as remote as the industrialized countries portrayed it (Oxman 1994: 689).[10] In sketching their answers to some of the questions raised above, they favoured a more egalitarian notion of justice that operated within the framework of what Hedley Bull calls a 'solidarist conception' of the international community (Bull 1983: 168). In practice, they wanted the drilling operation to be carried out by the International Seabed Authority with an arm that would be able to refine, sell and share the bounties that would be received. The developing countries also wanted adequate safeguards to ensure the protection of the countries whose economy depended on land-based mining. In addition, they wanted to be more than observers in the decision-making bodies of all of the relevant organs in charge of the activities. There was, in effect, a determination to see a change 'from the donor–beggar relationship exemplified by the World Bank and International Monetary Fund' (Sanger 1986: 158).

After years of protracted debates characterized by frequent name-calling and stonewalling, both sides shifted from their original positions. The outcome of these intense negotiations is the voluminous and delicately worded compromise contained in 60 articles in the main body of the Convention (Part XI) and 38 articles in the annex sections. First, it is reiterated in the text that '[t]he Area and its resources are common heritage of mankind' (Article 136). '[N]o State or natural or juridical person shall claim, acquire or exercise rights with respect to the minerals recovered from the Area' except in accordance with the Convention [Article 137 (3)]. The right to the resources is vested on the whole of mankind and every activity in the Area should be aimed specifically at benefiting 'mankind as a whole . . . and taking into particular consideration the interests and needs of the developing countries' [Article 137 (2), 140 (1)]. With these articles the international community firmly endorsed a common landlord status over the Area, which meant that no amount of mining operation or years of occupation could prompt a corporation to seek claims over any portion of the seabed. This common ownership is, for Borgese (1986), the first and most important principle of the common heritage of mankind.

The Convention equally established an International Seabed Authority whose function would be to oversee the activities in the Area in 'accordance with the principle of equality of states' (Articles 156 and 157). This Authority had a business arm – the Enterprise – which would participate in mining and related economic activities alongside state and private corporations in what was popularly referred to as the 'parallel system' (Article 170). This provision represented a significant product of astute diplomacy. If it had taken off as planned, the Enterprise would have been the first of its kind in international relations. It would have been the first corporation to undertake business activities and to compete with private corporations on behalf of the international community.

It is the responsibility of the Authority to 'provide for equitable sharing of the financial and other economic benefits derived from the activities in the Area through an appropriate mechanism on the basis of non discrimination' [Article 140 (2)]. All research in the Area should be carried out exclusively for the benefit of mankind as a whole [Article 143 (1)]. Active steps should be taken as well to ensure the transfer of technology to the developing countries 'under fair and reasonable terms and conditions' [Article 144 (2.a)]. In addition, space should be provided in the Enterprise to ensure that personnel from the developing countries obtain relevant training in marine technology and participate fully in the activities of the Area [144 (2.b)].

There are also provisions for the promotion of 'just and stable prices' and the desire to ensure that activities in the Area are not monopolized by those from a single geographical location through detailed specifications on how the seats in both the Council and the Assembly may be occupied on a regional basis [Article 150 (f, g, h and i), Article 151]. In addition, parties equally sought to ensure that the principle of sovereignty and equality of states should be observed in the determination of every substantive matter relating to the operation of the Authority and the Enterprise [Article 157 (3)]. The overall goal, as specified in Article 150 of the Convention, was that:

> Activities in the Area shall be carried out in such a manner as to foster healthy development of the world economy and balanced growth in international trade and to promote international co-operation for the overall development of the countries especially developing states.

In sum, the seabed regime can be seen as a mixed regime operating under the conceptual framework proposed by the developing countries but significantly modified by market-oriented approaches to accommodate the desires of the developed countries. It emphasizes international control, equity and price regulations but it also seeks to provide adequate protection for pioneer investors. In addition, the seabed regime represents an expression of faith in common resource management and a vote against the traditional first come, first serve basis of ocean resource exploitation. It does this whilst at the same time providing for entrepreneurship through the parallel system.

However, notwithstanding these painstaking efforts to achieve a balance between the positions of the North and the South, the USA, leading a majority of other industrialized countries, considered that the international community had given in too much to the 'socialist' demands of the developing countries (Boezek 1984: 49). Accordingly, they defected, abandoning the product of 10 years of negotiation, and refused to sign the Convention. What is more, some of these countries (the USA, UK and Federal Republic of Germany) even threatened to negotiate an alternative treaty, which would permit them to mine the resources in the seabed outside of the UNCLOS III provisions.

Abandoning the common heritage: substance versus ideology

There are some who insist that the refusal of the USA to accept the seabed regime had more to do with ideology than with substance. Borgese (1986), for instance, argues that the controversy over the issue of seabed mining had far more symbolic than substantive implications. Friedheim (1993: 213–222) makes the point that, as manganese nodules did not constitute a core aspect of the economy of many of the developed countries and given the viable alternative production techniques that existed, it is easily conceivable that the technologically advanced countries could have 'made a number of concessions that would not significantly harm their economy'. The real problem, as Friedheim describes it, was that the propositions from the developing countries were more than anything a challenge to the 'general structure of the world economic system'. 'The newness', he says, 'was not merely a change in the particular or specific rules describing permissible activities or the means of managing them, But rather, a new set of rules for an entirely different political, economic and moral framework for managing human affairs' (ibid.: 220).

The developing countries, for their part, were convinced that, if the developed countries could be shown that the deep seabed could be managed in ways that truly benefited the less developed countries and offset some of the disadvantages that they suffered in the world market, an important precedent would have been set, not only with respect to showing the imperfection of the market but also in relation to the workability of a just and fairer alternative (Kiss 1985). They were also mindful that, for all intents and purposes, the deep seabed beyond national jurisdiction was the perfect place to demonstrate this conviction as, by its nature, it is difficult to enclose and, by tradition, it has been regarded as belonging to all (Friedheim 1993). For the developing countries, then, it was the seabed regime that was regarded as the real symbol of an equitable law of the sea (Sanger 1986; Friedheim 1993).

But despite the intellectual recognition that the concept had powerful intuitive appeal to the developed countries, it emerged that such recognition was not sufficiently powerful to penetrate the capitalist and free market dogma, which shapes their basic understanding of equity in the relationship among nation states. The US stance has since compelled the UN to make significant changes to the seabed regime along neoliberal free market lines. The modification document (the Agreement Relating to the Implementation of Part IX) unabashedly states in its preamble (despite insisting that justice and peace remain the key objectives of the Convention) that the changes to the original seabed regime as contained in the document were designed to reflect 'political and economic changes, including in particular a growing reliance on market principle'. Accordingly, the documents proceed to whittle down the powers of the Enterprise, remove most of the protection offered to developing countries whose economy depends on land-based mining and grant extensive rights and protection to pioneer investors. The document also provides that any transfer of technology from the North to the South must be in 'commercial terms and conditions on the open market' [Annex Section 5 (1.a)].

On 7 October 1994, having obtained virtually all of the modifications that it wanted to Part IX of the Convention, President Clinton forwarded the Agreement and the Convention to the US Senate for consent (Duff 2004: 198; Song 2005: 263). It was not, however, until October 2003 that the Senate Foreign Relations Committee began to take hearings to examine the merits of domestic ratification of the Convention. Curiously, despite the drastic amendments in the implementation agreement already noted, a minority in the USA continue to call for the rejection of the Convention for what Doug Bradlow, an aide to President Regan in the 1980s, calls 'the redistributionist bent' embodied in the seabed regime (cited in Duff 2004: 205). Moreover, individuals such as Bradlow continue to query the rationale of ratifying the Convention when the other sections of the Convention (which they claim only reflect traditional international law) do not constitute a threat to US security and commercial interests. The sorts of agreements reached in these areas are thus worth investigating.

Breadth of the territorial sea and the right of passage

The notion of the territorial sea (TS) emerged in the early centuries as the concept by which the international community negotiated the tension between proponents of complete freedom of the sea (*mare liberum*) and those who campaigned that the sea should be appropriated for individual use (*mare clausum*) (Colson 1985: 36–37). It was eventually accepted that coastal states might exercise sovereignty over 'a marginal sea adjacent to their coasts subject to the limited right of innocent passage for foreign ships' (Oxman 1985: 139). But although the concept was, in itself, accepted, the question of what delimitations represented just and equitable boundaries proved far more difficult to settle.[11] The result was that states made claims as strategic, political and economic situations warranted (Churchill and Lowe 1988: 66–67; Buck 1998).[12]

From the late seventeenth century, a 3-nautical mile limit was one of few accepted criteria regarded as defining the limit of a state's jurisdiction over their coastal waters.[13] The different claims into what constituted the TS often caused difficulties, even in the early centuries, But with developments in technology and the many possibilities that this yielded in terms of transport, resource exploitation and military operations, it became increasingly desirable to find a common agreement to the issue of the limit of territorial seas. In UNCLOS III, parties eventually granted that 'every state has the right to establish the breadth of its territorial sea up to a limit not exceeding 12 nautical miles, measured from the baselines determined in accordance with the Convention' (Article 3). The Convention also

Managing a global commons 71

established the benchmark for measuring the breadth of the territorial sea (Article 4) and gave guidelines on how two coastal states opposite or adjacent to each other might go about the business of finding a territorial boundary (Article 15).

One remarkable lesson learnt in the extension of the TS limit from 3 nautical miles to 12 nautical miles during UNCLOS III is the degree to which states can adjust their preferences and ideas of justice in response to wider changes in the norm structure of the international order. But equally, or, perhaps, even more importantly, the TS regime also reveals the way in which the norm structure of the global community itself is determined or influenced by the interests of the most powerful members. After World War II, the USA, in response to 'the reality of off shore drilling on the continental shelf' (Vogler 2000: 45), unilaterally declared that it was going to exert exclusive property rights over all of the oil and gas reserves 40 nautical miles seawards of its coast (Truman Declaration). However, not long after, other coastal states, most of which were developing countries, began, in apparent response to the Truman Declaration, to claim that they had extended their TS up to the 12-nautical mile limit to combat illegal sea trading, land-based pollution and security-related issues (Kwiatkowska 1988: 290; Friedheim 1993: 113). Friedheim, however, describes these claims as motivated by a search for economic prosperity, extended sovereignty and the desire of the developing countries to 'push the industrialised states as far away from their coasts as possible' (Friedheim 1993: 81).

Meanwhile, the USA and other great naval powers responded by saying that they were not prepared to recognize such extensions of the TS limit. Their reasons were that such extensions would affect some international straits used for navigation, trade and military operations. The USA, for one, apparently wanted to enjoy the benefits of having exclusive property rights up to 40 nautical miles off its coast but could not bear to see the international straits, some of which were less than 10 nautical miles off the coast of some states, enclosed. Indeed, US negotiators in UNCLOS III freely indicated that their main aim of attending the Conference was not so much for the seabed and the CHM as it was for the need to keep the international straits open. This statement from one of the leading US negotiators, Mr O. Colson, conveyed the sentiment:

> [T]hose straits had been open to world commerce and the world's navies for centuries. It was the US position that these straits should not be subjected to the regime of the territorial sea . . . . The United States sought to ensure that the traditional navigational rights and freedoms exercised in international straits would not be affected by the extension of the territorial sea to 12 nautical miles.
>
> (Colson 1985: 38)

In the end, the USA and the other great naval powers got what they wanted. The concepts of 'transit passage' and 'innocent passage' were both formulated to ensure that the extension of the TS limit to 12 nautical miles did not lead to the privatization or enclosure of the international straits. Article 17 states that '[s]ubject to this Convention, ships of all states, whether coastal or landlocked, enjoy the rights of innocent passage through the territorial sea', whereas Articles 37–42 secure the right of transit passage for all naval and merchant ships through all straits used for international navigation irrespective of the extent of their proximity to any given coastal state. Here, it should be remembered that most of the maritime states are, themselves, coastal states. This implies that, provided that the right of passage through the international straits was maintained, a deal which allowed the coastal states in the developing countries to extend their TS would equally benefit the powerful maritime states while preserving their security and strategic interests (Stevenson and Oxman 1974: 9–13). Accordingly, the USA, through the new TS and the accompanying exclusive economic zone (EEZ) regime, was able to both secure property rights over the oil and gas reserves off its own coast and the right of passage through the straits that should have, by the same standard, 'belonged' to other states (Anand 1982: 217; Allott 1983).

In sum, the debate on TS extension might not be characterized as a North–South issue. Although most of the developing countries were in favour of extension, having in mind the economic prospect of extended sovereignty, it has been shown that the extension of the TS was also in the economic interests of some naval powers such as the UK and the USA. Once the rights of passage are accepted as the caveats that made the extension possible, it would be plausible to suggest that the extension benefited the USA and other coastal naval powers even more than the costal states in the developing countries (see Egede 2004). Friedheim puts this point bluntly when he asserts that it was simply not possible to foresee an agreement on the 12-nautical mile extension of the TS without the successful negotiation of the right of innocent and transit passage (Friedheim 1993: 78). Hence, if the extension of the TS and the rights of passage could be conceived in terms of justice at all, it would have to be the conception of justice that appreciates the strong bargaining power of the naval states relative to those of the states who would have wished to gain control over the straits near their own coast. Such is the understanding of justice canvassed by Gauthier (1974), who proposed that rational men could not be expected to accept principles of justice or outcomes which did not reflect what they could hope to get in the absence of co-operation.

The exclusive economic zone (EEZ) and the continental shelf (CS)

The regime of the EEZ established that coastal states have jurisdiction over the resources not only within the TS but also up to 200 nautical miles from their coastal baselines (Articles 55 and 57). In Article 56, the rights, jurisdictions and duties of coastal states in the EEZ are outlined whereas the rights and duties of landlocked states and other states are contained in Articles 69 and 58 respectively. In summary, coastal states would maintain control over the minerals and living resources in this area whereas other states would have the right of transit passage, the right of overflight and the right to lay submarine cables.

As with the extension of the TS the doctrines of the EEZ and CS were closely tied to the Truman Declaration, briefly mentioned in the previous section. President Truman had, in 1945, unilaterally declared that the USA would exercise jurisdiction over the living resources and minerals in the seabed of its CS. While maintaining that this part of the sea remained open to innocent passage by ships, the President laid out plans for the exploration of the oil and gas in the seabed within a water depth of 200 meters or 40 nautical miles from the US sea baseline.[14] By this unilateral declaration the USA signalled its intention to depart from the traditional understanding that the resources of the sea belonged to every one (*res communes*) as had been understood from the times of Pax Romana. Attard (1987: 2) describes this declaration as the 'turning point in the law of the sea'. Birnie and Boyle (2002) refer to it as the clearest signal that the concept of the commons as well as the traditional notion of global resource management by international co-operation was going to be radically challenged or at least redefined by the new wave of international economic liberalism. For Djalal (1985: 51), the declaration and the resultant regimes (EEZ and CS) tell us much about the changes in the philosophy of states with respect to global natural resource management and how the changes that occurred in the 'economic and political relations among states' between World War II and 1973 impacted on the new law of the sea.

The 200 meters depth mark contained in Truman's declaration was not arbitrarily set. Rather, it was carefully calculated to cover all of the recoverable minerals in the immediate coasts off Louisiana, Texas and California (Borgese 1986: 80). Indeed, it represented the maximum depth 'confirmed by the best geological knowledge of the time from which seabed oil and gas resources could be extracted' (Friedheim 1993: 113). This declaration was clearly self-serving and provocative. But because of the nature of this period of world history, Truman's proclamation passed rather quietly, without any opposition. However, it was clear from subsequent events that the foundation had been laid for an unprecedented global scramble for oceanic resources and the most drastic limitation of the concept of *res communes* and *res nullius*.

Meanwhile, it was clear that not all coastal states shared the same geological features with respect to the CS. For instance, those whose continental shelves curved sharply into the abyssal depth would gain no major economic advantage by extending jurisdiction over 200 meters water depth (Attard 1987: 19). A number of Latin American countries who fell under this description promptly attempted to cover for this shortfall by making proclamations ascribing to themselves jurisdictions over extensive areas of the sea, with some stretching up to 300 nautical miles from their baselines. They based their claim 'on the need to meet their development requirements by obtaining access to resources and ocean space that they regarded as belonging to them' (Dupuy 1983: 315). But apart from invoking the right to development, they also used arguments based on justice and equity. In their view, the extensions were intended to correct 'both the inequalities produced by nature and those resulting from defects in the organisation of international society' (ibid.: 315). In its declaration of 1947 announcing the extension of its 'patrimonial sea' to 300 nautical miles, Peru called the extension 'a just rule and one intended to balance the advantages enjoyed by others [referring to the USA] as a result of geographical happenstance and prehistoric geological upheavals'. In its own declaration, Ecuador equally showed a determination to correct the injustice and economic inequity it perceived as arising from the Truman proclamation. Ecuador declared bluntly that 'since submarine terrace alone is not sufficient to create the equality conducive to well-being, the important thing is not the contour of the submarine areas but the maritime resources that will produce this well-being' (cited in Attard 1987: 8).

But one consequence of these extensions, among others, was the nationalization and enclosure of large portions of the high sea and virtually all of the international straits. It was understandable that the big naval powers should feel concerned. The USA, for one, did not waste time in denouncing these claims (Hollick 1981). However, in the face of the Truman Declaration, this denunciation amounted to what Friedheim describes as an 'attempt by the US to control other states' appetite without controlling its own' (Friedheim 1993: 124). Thus, the situation before UNCLOS III remained one of confusion in that most coastal states, emboldened by the claim of the USA over the oil and gas resources within its CS, continued to claim various types of rights within up to 300 nautical miles of their coasts, even though the nature of these rights were largely ill-defined.

In the early stages of negotiations, the USA and other naval powers formed an anti-EEZ coalition with the landlocked states (from both developed and developing countries) to challenge the claims of the coastal states (Friedheim 1993: 99). The concern of the landlocked states who were not naval powers was mainly that they should be allowed some share in the fish and other living resources within the EEZ of neighbouring coastal states. However, once the naval powers realized that the rights of passage and transit were going to apply within the EEZ, they quickly abandoned the alliance with the landlocked states. In so doing they were aware that the landlocked states had nothing with which they could make side payments for such support. The Organization of African Unity (OAU) showed a remarkable sense of communal justice on this issue. In their declaration on this issue (Doc. A/CONF.62/33) the OAU proposed that landlocked states be allowed access to the EEZ of neighbouring coastal states 'on an equal basis as nationals of coastal states'. This suggestion was incorporated in the draft provisions but it eventually got lost in 'transit' and was not reflected in the final draft (see Provision 195A, B, C and E of Informal Composite Negotiating Text (ICNT), U.N. Doc. A/CONF.62/WP.10 [6th Session, 1977]). In the end the landlocked states fought primarily on the basis of 'moral appeals' (Friedheim 1993: 101) and expectedly secured no single rights in the use of resources within the EEZ of neighbouring states (cf. Sanger 1986: 64). The Convention, however, contains a few appeals in Articles 59 and 61 (1) that coastal states should take into account 'the relevant economic and geographical circumstances' of their neighbours, including allowing the landlocked states limited access to the '*surplus resources*' within their EEZ and that any conflicts that may occur in the process should be resolved on 'the basis of equity'.

Another lame gesture towards international justice and new international economic order is found in Article 82 (1–4) of the Convention. Here, coastal states are asked to contribute in kind or to make an annual payment of 1 per cent of the yearly production value of profit from explorations in their CS to the international community. Article 82 (2) decrees that 'the rate shall increase by 1 per cent for each subsequent year until the twelfth year and shall remain at 7 per cent thereafter'. And in Article 84 (4), parties agreed that '[t]he payments or contributions shall be made available through the Authority which shall distribute them to state parties to this convention, on *the basis of equitable sharing criteria, taking into account the interests and needs of developing states, particularly the least developed and landlocked among them*'. No attempt is made to define what this 'basis of equity' or 'equitable sharing criteria' mean. Nor did the parties concerned attempt to explain how the 'payments in kind' might be quantified.

Again, as in the section on the breadth of the territorial sea, one sees that, the provisions of Articles 69 and 82 notwithstanding, the regime of EEZ was decided *not* on the basis of an independent or inherent notion of justice or morality but simply by practical, hard-nosed bargaining within the constraints of the prevailing neoliberal economic structure. In this instance, the drive for the establishment of the EEZ was obviously the control of the living resources in the sea and the rich oil reserves in the CS (Borgese 1986: 80–81). Justice corresponds not to attending to the interests or 'special needs' of any group of countries – developing or landlocked – but to each state carefully articulating and pursuing its economic and strategic interests through various means such as coalition forming, stonewalling, subtle threats and trade-offs. For some of the great naval powers, such as the USA, the EEZ regime corresponds to the symbolic act of having one's cake and eating it. They secured their security and commercial interests (right of passage through straits) by pretending to concede to the 200-nautical mile EEZ limit and then, quite easily, recovered enormous economic leverage by the means of the regime on the CS. This amounts, according to Borgese (1986: 80), to a 'curious twist of history and of reason' and illustrates the place of 'international oil power' in the design of international rules.[15]

Although, then, the concept of the EEZ is usually attributed to the desire of the developing countries to gain more territory, it represents, in reality, the canonization of the Truman Declaration of 1945 and the triumph of national over international approaches to ocean management (Birnie and Boyle 2002: 648). The EEZ and the CS doctrines also signpost the ascendancy of the nationalization and enclosure doctrine, and they symbolize the triumph of market-based interpretations of justice in regimes for international co-operation. Yet, there are some who point to the failure of various international common-pool resource management regimes and infer that nationalization was not only appropriate but also, in fact, necessary to ensure the sustainable utilization of oceanic resources and preservation of the marine environment. These claims merit closer investigation.

Protection and preservation of the marine environment

Protection of the marine living resources and legislation against pollution were certainly not among the traditional concerns of the law of the sea. The ocean was

76 *Empirical analysis of three regime texts*

seen as having a limitless capacity for waste absorption and oceanic resources were considered to be superabundant (Johnston 1981; Anderson 1996). Because it is the condition of scarcity that primarily creates the demand for distributive justice, the concepts of sustainable exploitation and equitable allocation of oceanic resources were virtually non-existent in the language of global ocean management. Grotius (1608) vaguely recognized the possibility that overexploitation of marine resources could occur if many people hunted down marine animals but, in general, it was the idea that the sea contained limitless resources and was capable of serving as an open-ended sink for wastes that retained dominance. It was not until the beginning of the last century that various events, some of which have been mentioned in previous sections, began to suggest that both assumptions were completely misguided. Accordingly, a push began for the establishment of some kind of global regime to ensure the conservation of marine resources and the prevention of sea pollution. The next section focuses on the regime for the conservation and distribution of the living resources in the marine environment. Attention to aspects of sea pollution is limited only to a few remarks.[16]

Equity and the conservation of the living resources of the sea

Early approaches towards the utilization of the resources of the sea were conceptually underpinned by the notion that the sea and its resources belonged to all (*res communes*), as well as the impression that these resources were inexhaustible (Birnie and Boyle 2002: 647). The notion that people were free to take as much as they wished from the sea to satisfy their wants corresponds roughly to a utilitarian conception of justice. Utilitarianism was described in Chapter 3 as being concerned with seeking the maximum happiness of the greatest number of people with respect to the distribution of 'the good'. In a situation in which the good is superabundant, as in the case of the marine resources, this would translate to equal access by all agents that have legal entitlement (Luper-Foy 1992: 48). The obvious prescription of a utilitarian in a situation in which resources are known not to be superabundant would be equal division. The EU Common Fisheries Policy (CFP), which is based on setting a total allowable catch (TAC) and dividing the figure equally among the number of fishing states, is the closest representation of this understanding of justice.

However, the policies set out in UNCLOS III for the management of the global fish stock and other marine animals are at variance with the approaches sketched out above. The policy option that prevailed in UNCLOS III was essentially the nationalization of marine resources and their conversion from common-pool resources to resources governable under private property laws (Articles 61–68). By legalizing the CS and the EEZ doctrines, 30 per cent of the ocean and high sea and 90 per cent of its resources were 'enclosed' through nationalization (Pontercorvo 1988: 229). EEZ thus represents a firm verdict against the concept of commonality, which underpinned early responses of the global community to marine resource management. Birnie and Boyle bring out this point very clearly:

The EEZ regime agreed during the UNCLOS III negotiations addressed the problems of sustainable exploitation of common property by removing living resources entirely from that status; it gives the coastal states the exclusive right to control access, exploitation, and conservation – the very opposite of high sea freedom. It relies on national self-interest, not international co-operation, to ensure rational and sustainable use [of marine resources]. [It is] a modern day version of the eighteenth century enclosure of the common land.

(Birnie and Boyle 2002: 648)

There are several factors that explained this radical shift towards the nationalization of oceanic resources, but three, according to Burke (1994: 95), stand out. The first two were the 'invariable unsuccessfulness' of various international fisheries commissions in the past and the successful positioning of the coastal states as the true custodians of the marine resources. The third factor was the general orientation towards economic liberalism and free market ideology driven by the marine policies of the USA and its Western allies.

From 1898 till the time of UNCLOS III, coastal states had engaged in various struggles to obtain some extensive property rights over the sea resources off their coasts, both on conservation and equity grounds. For example, in the Bering Sea Fur Seals Arbitration of 1898, the USA argued that it had the right of protection and property over the fur seals off its coast (International Arbitration Awards 1898: 43). It submitted that it was in line with international common law to be accorded the right of trusteeship over the organisms for the benefit of mankind. In addition, they noted that the seals had an *animus revertendi* because they returned cyclically to US waters and, thus, could be equated to domesticated animals over which exclusive property rights apply (Birnie and Boyle 2002: 649). Similarly, in the Icelandic fisheries cases of 1972, Iceland submitted to the International Court of Justice (ICJ) that it had the right to an extended fishery jurisdiction, which would curtail the fishing activities of the UK and Germany in the claimed Icelandic waters. The thrust of their argument was the need for conservation coupled with the central place of the resources in the economic well-being of the country. In essence, they were 'invoking the rights of people to development' (Dupuy 1983: 315).

The arbitration panel in 1898 and the ICJ in 1972 found against both the USA and Iceland respectively in that the rights of other countries to fish in the disputed areas were upheld. However, both bodies established the need for conservation, co-operation and equity in the management of sea resources. Coastal states were also granted 'preferential rights' (Birnie and Boyle 2002: 651) in the preservation and allocation of these resources. In other words, although these cases were decided on the basis of freedom of the sea, they also contained hints that the notion of res communes was becoming inadequate and that the international community was instead moving quickly towards enclosure. In fact, by the early 1950s, through these and similar cases, the idea was already beginning to take shape that coastal states have some kind of trustee rights over the marine resources adjacent to the waters in their territorial seas. This was recognized in the 1958 Geneva Convention on Fishing and Conservation of the Living Resources of the High Seas, articulated under UNCLOS I, through the admission that coastal states have 'special rights' (Article 6) in the management of high-sea fisheries adjacent to their territorial seas. Subsequently, the concepts of 'emergency rights', 'preferential rights', 'ad hoc rights' and 'reasonable duty' evolved as a means of accommodating this newly sought trusteeship (ibid.: 653).

Accordingly, in the run-up years to UNCLOS III, coastal states were visibly excited by the prospect of managing vast portions of their coasts. They operated under the illusion that securing property rights over resources automatically translated into wealth and greater influence within the international community. Thus, they reasoned that voting for more enclosure would set them on the path to combating poverty and closing the economic gap between them and the industrialized countries (Dupuy 1983: 316). But has the enclosure of 90 per cent of the global oceanic resources ultimately secured an equitable and sustainable exploitation of these resources?

Dupuy (1983), for one, continues to dismiss the notion of effective conservation as providing any conceptual explanation whatsoever for the EEZ. He maintains that any interest expressed by coastal states towards conservation is simply a camouflage.

> It must be noted that the claims of these states were based on the need to meet their development requirements by obtaining access and ocean space that they regarded as belonging to them. [. . .] The fact that they also invoked considerations relating to natural management resources is irrelevant here. A coastal state that issues regulations for the protection of species and the conservation of the environment is, of course, acting in an interest wider than its own national interest; but it is none the less the state which benefits first and foremost from such protection.
>
> (Dupuy 1983: 315)

Some other authors are more circumspect. Hey (1992) has argued, after noting the poor conservation records in most EEZ as agreed under UNCLOS III, that effective international co-operation, due diligence and equitable distribution remain the only way of ensuring the optimum utilization of natural resources that are shared across international boundaries. For Birnie and Boyle (2002: 660), the lesson of the dismal conservation records of the world's EEZ regimes is that they very well 'illustrate that even the best regulated national fisheries are not immune to improvident policies motivated by short term social and political concerns'. This is the conclusion equally endorsed in separate articles by Carroz (1984), Burke (1994) and Bourne (1997). Burke (1994: 91) insists that the EEZ regime must be seen as a stark sign of the degree to which the international community was willing to capitulate in the bid to accommodate US interests and its free market ideology. He maintains that 'effective international co-operation rather than gleeful nationalisation policies is the *sine qua non* for effective high sea fishery management'.

Conclusion

UNCLOS III presents a classic example of the intrigues of international relations. In particular, it also shows the extent to which traditional practices can be challenged when actors are sufficiently mobilized through a well-articulated counter-hegemonic vision. The Conference also conveys the dilemma posed by the peculiar nature of global environmental problems and the complexities involved in operationalizing the concept of international justice. It offers a vivid illustration of the struggle for world resources and how this struggle is legitimized with various kinds of rhetoric including conservation, sovereignty, efficiency and equity. In total, 36 per cent of the ocean and 90 per cent of marine resources are now enclosed by the various provisions of UNCLOS III and the Area that was designed to be commonly managed created so much controversy that major powers refused to sign the Convention. This is in spite of the fact that the resources in this area are economically less significant than the ones in the already enclosed space. The fact that many of these major powers are coastal states, which benefit from the concept of the CS and EEZ, did not alter their perceptions and position.

It is openly agreed that the Convention is a package deal, which means that decisions were reached by means of compromise and hard-nosed bargaining. It was obvious from the start that parties did not consider that there was any independent moral code or conception of justice to which they could appeal despite the fact that the commitment to equity and international justice were frequently bandied about in the text. For this reason, alliances were formed and broken at random as parties jostled to find how best to articulate and defend their interests. In the end, however, the notions of justice that can be said to underpin the core policies are the ones which favour sovereignty, property rights and rational bargaining. This is despite many of the assertions regarding the need to give attention to the circumstances of the poor and disadvantaged. In the end, those arguing for greater property rights had their way, as they were able to show that common resource management in the global setting was not working. To this extent, equity was seen mainly in terms of appropriation, enclosure and alienation. Hence, despite the influence of the CHM and other equity concepts, it might well be, as Pontecorvo (1987: 138) puts it, that it was more the developments in technology and economic philosophies of the powerful states and the underlying structure of international institutions that 'preordained the new order of the oceans'.

5 The global waste management regime
The Basel Convention

This chapter provides an account of how the various proposals from the North and the South reflect preferences for pluralist and more solidarist conceptions of the international community, respectively, in the design of the policies of the global waste management regime – the Basel Convention.[1] The chapter indicates how the policies of the Basel Convention attempt to accommodate these opposing views of international society and the conceptions of justice that support them. It demonstrates that the 'minimum justice' recorded in Basel by way of the 1994 ban was possible only to the extent that a fundamental premise of neoliberal justice was upturned in favour of justice as care and justice as need, which were originally limited to declarative portions in the original Convention.

The Basel Convention offers a good site to study the relationship between the increasingly dynamic socio-economic interactions among peoples and states and the transboundary transfer of pollution and related environmental hazards. Increase in waste generation and the ease of their circulation are both functions of industrial development and socio-economic globalization. But although development is pursued as a means of improving the standard of life, the story of Basel demonstrates that, without adequate institutional arrangements, the negative ecological and social impacts of economic globalization may be disproportionately distributed such that the co-operating agents who gain the least from economic interdependence suffer the most harm.

Elaboration of the Basel Convention[2]

Before the Basel Convention there were various on-going efforts to legislate on the issue of transboundary movements of dangerous chemicals and hazardous wastes. One such effort was the Cairo Guidelines and Principles for the Environmentally Sound Management of Hazardous Wastes, elaborated under the United Nations Environment Programme (UNEP) in 1982. However, the Basel Convention breezed onto the international environmental agenda with a speed that overshadowed most of these other efforts (Weissman 2005: 28). This is often explained by reference to the circumstances under which it emerged. If not a direct response, the Convention was greatly facilitated – but at the same time deeply politicized

The global waste management regime 81

– by the widely publicized incidences of spurious deals and outright dumping of toxic wastes in Africa, Asia and Eastern Europe by waste dealers from the more industrialized countries.

The Convention on the Control of Transboundary Movements of Hazardous Wastes and their Disposal was negotiated between 20 and 22 March 1989 in Basel, Switzerland. The original text treaty, which contains 29 articles, nine annexes and an accompanying eight resolutions, was unanimously adopted by the conference of plenipotentiaries comprising about 116 states. The official process of the elaboration of the Convention started when the UNEP Governing Council, through decision 14/30 of June 1987, authorized the Executive Director to set up a working group with the task of articulating a comprehensive text on all aspects of transboundary movements of hazardous wastes and their disposal (Rummel-Bulska 1994). In the same decision the Governing Council also mandated the Executive Director of UNEP to convene a diplomatic conference in 1989 at the latest for the purpose of adopting a global convention on the control of transboundary movements of hazardous wastes (UNEP 1982; Kummer 1995: 40)

Following this mandate, the Executive Director inaugurated an *ad hoc* working group of experts with a charge to produce a draft convention that would be considered for signing by the conference of plenipotentiaries in 1989. Utilizing the opportunity presented by the World Conference on Hazardous Wastes in Budapest in October 1987, the *ad hoc* committee met for the first time, using as the basis for their first discussion a draft copy presented to it by the UNEP Secretariat (Tolba 1990: 205–206; Strohm 1993). It subsequently met four other times between October 1987 and March 1989 to discuss various aspects of trade in hazardous wastes. Its stated objective was 'to protect humans and the environment from the risks and dangers of inappropriate and unregulated disposal of hazardous wastes'.[3]

Despite the many debates and heated arguments that characterized the sessions, the working group of experts was able to submit, at the last minute, a final draft convention upon which the diplomatic conference deliberated and agreed with some amendments (Kummer 1995: 40).[4] As stipulated in Article 25 (1) of the Convention, the Basel Convention entered into force on 5 May 1992 with the deposition of the twentieth instrument of ratification. As of 22 May 2006, there were already 168 parties to the Convention, including the EU. This number makes the Basel Convention one of the most extensively endorsed international environmental treaties. Afghanistan, Haiti and the USA have all signed but not ratified the Convention.

Conceptions of justice in the Basel Convention[5]

There are many who see the Basel Convention as a direct outcome of the campaign against the 'morally reprehensible' act of dumping hazardous wastes on the poor less-industrialized countries by their richer neighbours (Vallette and Spalding 1990; Kiss 1991; Puckett 1992). Jim Puckett, for instance, describes it as an act that 'uniquely disturbs both our physical and ethical well-being'. He also labels it as 'a poisoning by pollution and of moral principles' (Puckett 1992: 93).

For Daniel Arap Moi and several other African leaders, the events that led to the elaboration of the Basel Convention are best understood in terms of neo-imperialism and colonial domination. Moi described the series of spurious waste trade deals and outright dumping of hazardous wastes in Africa and Asia by dealers from the industrialized countries as the latest evidence of 'garbage imperialism', and the Organization of African Unity (OAU) Council of Ministers called it 'toxic colonialism' and 'a crime against Africa and African People'.[6] And, for the United Nations Commission on Human Rights, the dumping of hazardous wastes by the developed countries on their less technologically advanced neighbours represented acts of 'environmental racism'.[7]

But there are others who reject the above characterizations (e.g. OECD 1994, 1998; Hunter 1996; Alter 1997). These authors caution against the description of the circumstances surrounding the Basel Convention using emotive words like crime, imperialism and racism. Hunter (1996: 68) actually accuses the likes of Moi and other African leaders of always seeking to drag in questions of justice and equity into technical efforts to protect the global environment. For Hunter the Basel Convention might have been facilitated by the publicized waste deals but it is still better seen as a consolidation of already on-going efforts to control the transboundary movements of hazardous wastes at the international level. In other words, these authors prefer to portray the Convention as one of the many existing control mechanisms designed to manage a few side effects emanating from an otherwise beneficial process – that is, industrial development and international trade. This difference in characterization brings to mind the argument made by Laferriere and Stoett (1999; cited in the introduction) that, although institutions for international environmental co-operation entail both political and philosophical dilemmas, there are some who prefer to view them in purely managerialist and technocratic terms (Laferriere and Stoett 1999).

A striking manifestation of this technocratic approach can be seen in the more or less determined efforts to avoid the express use of moral terms and concepts in the text of the Basel Convention. For example, except in Article 20 of the main text in which parties are encouraged, among other channels, to submit their disputes to the International Court of Justice (ICJ), the word 'justice' is used nowhere in the entire Convention text.[8] In addition, not once are closely associated terms such as 'equity' or 'fairness' employed in the Convention's key texts. Curiously, even the Basel Protocol on Liability and Compensation for Damage Resulting from Transboundary Movements of Hazardous Wastes, which is directly concerned with issues of fairness for hazardous waste accident victims, does not employ much moral terminology. It is also curious that, of about 73 articles and book chapters consulted in relation to the Basel Convention in the course of writing this chapter, not one of them used the term 'justice' or 'equity' in its title. Generally, authors tell detailed stories of specific incidences of waste scandals and condemn the dumping of hazardous wastes on the poor less-industrialized countries of the world, but they do not go further to contextualize these events in terms of historical domination and the existing global economic infrastructure. As a result, very little was available to me in terms of literature in conducting the ethical analysis of this regime. Thus, I identify with Wynne (1989) and Krueger (1999: viii) who have, in service to a different set of arguments, described the Basel Convention as a 'most dynamic' and 'most significant' and yet the least understood regime in many quarters. Notwithstanding this, a careful reading reveals that the Basel Convention was influenced by different and often conflicting visions of a just global society. These conflicting visions are manifested not only in the debates surrounding the substantive policies but also in the choice of the title and scope of the treaty.

Title and scope of the Convention

Judging from its title – 'The Basel Convention on the Control of Transboundary Movements of Hazardous Wastes and their Disposal' – one can see that parties to the Basel Convention managed to set its target quite modestly. It is immediately clear from the title that the Convention did not purport to be concerned with the issue of waste generation *per se* but only with its *transboundary movements and disposal*.[9] By styling its objective in such a specific way, parties clearly declared that they were not concerned, at least centrally, with the sociology of waste generation or with the productive logic that underpins it. The primary objective of the Convention was not, for instance, to ask what the kinds of lifestyles, habits or production processes are that result in increased generation of wastes worldwide? The Convention was also not geared towards a search for a global pattern of waste production and distribution and how best to manage it. Rather, the concern was merely with already manufactured wastes, particularly the ones that the holder, for one reason or another, desired to transport across a national border.

But more than a few experts believe that an adequate approach to global waste management ought to address not only the transboundary movements and disposal of wastes but also the other stages that together constitute the 'waste cycle' (Wynne 1989: 130; Kummer 1995: 12; Birnie and Boyle 1992: 300). The waste cycle, according to these authors, comprises all of the activities that generate wastes, the movements of these wastes within and across borders, possible treatment or storage patterns, the final disposal and even the means by which the raw materials from which these wastes are generated are obtained.[10] The import of focusing only on the last stages of the waste cycle (transportation and disposal) should not be missed because, in many ways, it already sets the tone of the debates, the questions that can be asked and the policies that are permissible under a given waste management treaty. Indeed, scholars of international environmental politics generally accept that the way an environmental issue is framed greatly influences the outcome of the negotiations and the basic rules of the relevant regime (cf. Young 1994; O'Neill 1998: 141).

Actually, in taking such a narrow title, the Basel Convention differed rather surprisingly from the focus of the preceding efforts at global hazardous waste management by UNEP. Technically, the shift from the environmentally sound management of hazardous wastes (which is the title and focus of the Cairo Guidelines) to merely the control of their transboundary movements implied a change in emphasis.[11] This shift was not coincidental but intricately bound up with pre-Basel events and how they might be interpreted in the light of the dominant worldview. If, for instance, one subscribes to the 'global citizenship' view (see Chapter 3) that the peoples of the earth have an equal right to a clean environment and dignity of life, which they can claim from relevant political institutions (national or international), then the aim of the Basel Convention might be not only to outlaw spurious deals on toxic wastes but also to raise questions about the underlying international political economic structure that drives the process. But if, on the other hand, one's central concern is the preservation of people's liberty (especially along national lines) to buy and sell and to bargain from the standpoint of their respective strengths, then one might consider as appropriate a Convention that merely seeks to regulate such deals and appropriately channel its proceeds. Each approach reflects, in essence, a different weighting and understanding of what justice demands in the given circumstance, and different visions of a just and sustainable global society.

During the negotiation process, delegates from the poor South canvassed for a waste management treaty with a broad and inclusive agenda (Clapp 2001: 11; Weissman 2005: 28). They wanted a regime that would not only ban the export of toxic wastes to the poor countries but also one that would address the connection between toxic exports and 'growing levels of international debt, the globalization of production processes, increased fluidity of trade and the economic inequities between countries' (Clapp 2001: 11. cf. Wynne 1989: 121–123). But at the end of the day, it was the alternative view that was endorsed. The developed countries fought for and got a regime whose original focus was that of *control* rather than the *ban* of toxic waste trades (Wynne 1989: 122; Agarwal *et al.* 2001: 63). However, over the course of the development of the Basel Convention, parties from the developing countries have successfully pressed for the recognition of the normative dimensions of the global movement of hazardous wastes including the widening of the scope of the Convention (to deal with the environmentally sound management of waste, technology transfers and eventually a ban on waste trade). One area in which these efforts generated considerable tension within the Basel texts and policies relates to the establishment of group and individual rights to environmental protection.

Notions of cosmopolitan rights in the Basel Convention

Although the Basel Convention does not, unlike the Third United Nations Conference on the Law of the Sea (UNCLOS III), contain explicit references to commitments to international justice, it makes important contributions in terms of 'constitutional environmentalism' (Hayward 2000). A constitutional approach to environmentalism is one in which individuals and/or states are seen to have a substantive, moral and legally enforceable right to adequate environmental conditions and natural resources (Hayward 2000: 558). This approach is noticeable in the series of 'rights' to a high-quality, safe and clean environment recognized in many mega-environmental conferences (see Chapter 2). But authors within the critical school tend to argue that these 'rights' are mere declarations of good intentions, as they never quite manage to make their way into issue-specific environmental regimes (cf. Sax 1990; Lipschutz and Mayer 1993; Falk 2001: 221). The Basel Convention, however, makes some attempt to accommodate these rights. In some places, parties use words that point towards individuals rather than states as the primary focus and, to this extent, endorse certain notions of cosmopolitan environmental rights. But in quite a number of other areas, states and their economic rights are clearly privileged over the individual and the environment.

A cosmopolitan perspective can be found, for instance, in paragraph 4 of the preambular chapter in which parties profess their conviction to take the necessary measures to ensure that the disposal of waste is 'consistent with the protection of human heath and the environment *whatever the place of disposal*' (italics mine).[12] The first appearance of the word 'states' in the Convention text is further down in paragraph 4 of the preambular chapter and relates to the obligation of states to take actions required to ensure a toxic-free environment for '*all the peoples of the earth*'. In effect, the Basel Convention recognizes states as the dispensers of these individual and group rights to a toxic-free environment. It is as if the parties are expressing a determination to act in close co-operation and through relevant institutions to protect *all humans* from the risks and dangers posed by the transboundary movements of hazardous wastes and their disposal.[13] The Basel Protocol on Liability and Compensation for Damage Resulting from the Transboundary Movements of Hazardous Wastes and their Disposal equally aims, in some respects, to endorse this approach. Overall, the Convention aims 'to provide for a *comprehensive* regime for liability and for *prompt* and *adequate* compensation for damage resulting from the transboundary movement of hazardous wastes and other wastes and their disposal including illegal traffic in those wastes' (Article 1). In numerous articles in the Protocol, rights and duties are conferred upon the individual rather than states. For example:

> The Person who notifies in accordance with Article 6 of the Convention shall be liable for damage until the disposer has taken possession of the hazardous waste and other wastes. Thereafter the disposer shall be liable.
>
> [Article 4 (1)]

> If two or more persons are liable according to this Article, the claimant shall have the right to seek full compensation for the damage from any or all of the persons liable.
>
> [Article 4 (6)]

> Without prejudice to Article 4, any person shall be liable for damage caused or contributed by his lack of compliance with the provisions implementing the Convention or by his wrongful intentional, reckless or negligent acts of omissions.
>
> (Article 5)

All these, and many more, apparently represent efforts by the contracting parties to ensure that the cost of prevention and reparations due for damage caused by inadequate handling or disposal of toxic wastes are borne by the actual polluter in line with the polluter-pays principle (PPP).

Apart from making individuals rather than states the claimants and duty bearers of damage resulting from the transboundary movements of wastes and their disposal, the Basel Protocol also embodies other cosmopolitan provisions. One such is that it aims to give claimants multiple choices with regard to where they can institute legal action concerning damages resulting from transboundary movements and disposal of hazardous wastes. It also seeks to remove legal and administrative obstacles that may stand in the way of actualizing this objective. Accordingly, in the event of suffering damage arising from the transboundary movements of hazardous wastes and their disposal, claimants have the option to seek redress in one of three courts including: (i) a court in the state where the damage was suffered; (ii) a court in the state where the incident occurred; and (iii) a court in the state where the defendant has his habitual residence or principal place of business, provided that such states are parties to the Convention [Article 17 (1–2)].

The regime also attempts to ensure that related actions are not entertained concurrently in the domiciles of different parties. When related actions are brought in the courts of different parties, any court other than the first may, while the action is pending, at the first instance, stay its proceedings [Article 18 (1, 2 and 3)]. Parties also provide that 'nothing in the protocol shall be construed as limiting or derogating from any rights of persons who have suffered damage or as limiting the protection or reinstatement of the environment which may be provided by domestic law' [Article 20 (1)]. Further, the Protocol establishes that any judgement of a court having jurisdiction in accordance with relevant provisions of the Convention will be enforceable in any state that is a party to the Convention. Different formalities required in the state of each contracting party to enforce such judgements are allowed provided that such formalities 'shall not permit the merits of the case to be re-opened' [Article 21 (2)]. In addition, the provisions of the Protocol should be applied without discrimination based on nationality, domicile or residence [Article 10 (3)]. In short, by making 'comprehensive, prompt and adequate' compensation its key objective (introductory paragraph), the regime aims to simulate the national judicial systems of advanced democracies, which are often judged not only in terms of how fair (adequate) a decision is but also by how speedy (prompt) is the process.

The truncation of individual cross-border rights

However, the Basel Convention does not pursue this cosmopolitan-based individual rights approach with great consistency. In ways that can only be understood to derive from customary international law traditions, which pay overriding attention to the issue of sovereignty, parties to the Basel Convention still reserve the right to determine for themselves what constitutes hazardous waste and to place import restrictions in accordance with their definitions and individual economic needs [Articles 3 (1), 4 (1.a); paragraph 6 of preamble]. This means that there is no uniform understanding of what makes a waste hazardous – a point that can make transboundary litigation (as intended in some of the articles cited in the previous section) quite problematic, if not impossible (Kummer 1995: 50). Actually, the declaration in Article 4 (2.a), that every effort towards the reduction of the generation of wastes and their transboundary movements would be carried out with regard to the social and economic demands of states, carries the implication, as Kummer (1995: 55) puts it, that the 'obligation for reduction in hazardous waste generation is not absolute' but subject to the economic and social considerations of each party. This, in turn, implies, in technical terms, that what constitutes pollution, a clean environment or even a life of dignity is to be defined subject to the economic and social demands of each state. And, to the extent that this argument is valid, the whole concept of global environmental rights itself becomes very questionable.

Another example of the 'sovereign based approach' (Kummer 1995: 20) of the Basel Convention is the fact that the responsibility for illegal movements of waste is firmly allocated to states rather than individuals or corporations [Article 9 (2–4)]. This implies that it is not possible for victims to hold individual corporations or waste brokers accountable in cases of illegal dumping of wastes. This clause, which apparently contradicts efforts made towards the legitimization of PPP (as outlined in the previous section), represents, according to one source, 'the most important weakness of the Basel Convention' (Agarwal *et al.* 2001: 2). The authors expressed their frustration in this way:

> Direct attempts to put in place a liability mechanism, where industries take responsibilities for their products, have failed in at least two counts – under CPB and the Basel Convention's liability protocol. Whereas the North succeeded in resisting a liability protocol for the former altogether, the latter does not fix responsibility on the hazardous waste generating industry, in order to discourage them from producing the wastes in the first place.
>
> (Ibid.: 2)

In short, in seeming disregard for what would otherwise have been considered a gallant effort towards the endorsement of cosmopolitan constitutional environmentalism, parties to the Basel Convention made a complete turnaround in Article 4 and declared that:

> Nothing in this Convention shall affect in any way the sovereignty of States over their territorial sea established in accordance with international law, and the sovereign rights and the jurisdiction which States have in their exclusive economic zones and their continental shelves in accordance with international law, and the exercise by ships and aircraft of all States of navigational rights and freedoms as provided for in international law and as reflected in relevant international instruments.
>
> [Article 4 (12)]

This article is unique because it makes no reference at all to the other attempts in the Convention to establish transboundary group and individual environmental rights. Indeed, the phrase 'Nothing in this Convention' establishes, as Kummer rightly observes, that parties gave Article 4 'priority over other rules established by the Basel Convention' (Kummer 1995: 53). A similar provision exists in the Protocol on Liability and Compensation, in which parties make clear that the Protocol 'shall not affect the rights and obligations of the contracting parties under the rules of general international law with respect to state responsibility' (Article 16). In essence, there is no procedure for 'prompt' and 'adequate' compensation established by the Protocol for victims of damage of transboundary movements of waste who are not first and foremost subject to the rights of states, including, of course, the right to completely overturn these processes by reason of internal formalities or 'national interest'.

Of course, the foregoing is not to suggest that the sovereignty-based approach to international environmental policies has no appeal; given the absence of a world government there are obvious difficulties in implementing cross-border individual rights. It does, however, establish that the sovereignty-based approach has serious inadequacies especially with respect to meeting the demands of global environmental sustainability and international justice (cf. Lipschutz and Conca 1993; Hayward 2000; Falk 2001). For, in operating purely at a *meta* level, sovereign rights-based approaches are grossly unable to secure the protection and welfare of many individuals especially those in the poor developing countries whose national economies and capacities for implementing regime policies might be both weak and inefficient (Clapp 2001; Agarwal *et al.* 2001: 63). This, in fact, is the chief criticism against the principle of prior informed consent (PIC), which is the major policy instrument of the Basel Convention.

The principle of prior informed consent – PIC

Krasner (1983b) proposes that the provisions of any given international regime can be placed into one of three different categories – the principles, the norms and the rules. Norms refers to established standards or behaviour shared by members of a group to which each member is expected to conform. Principles refer to the more fundamental logic or thinking to which the norms may be indexed. They are the theoretical essence that makes the norms explicable and defensible. Rules are, then, the prescribed and verifiable methods of conduct or procedures of action (Krasner 1983b: 2–3). Using Krasner's analytical framework, Montgomery (1990) separates the key provisions of the Basel Convention into three categories. According to Montgomery, the principles of Basel are enhanced control of waste movement as a means of reducing waste generation, promotion of sound management of waste, dissemination of information and transfer of technology. The norms established or reiterated are the rights of states to exploit their own resources and protect their environments by having their own definition of wastes, and the norm that all waste disposal should, as far as possible, be environmentally sound. For the Basel Convention, the substantive rules, according to Montgomery

(1990: 319–323), are mainly PIC, the legal commitment to re-import waste and the liability and compensation regime.[14]

In simple terms, PIC aims to secure the liberty of the parties to engage in trade in hazardous waste subject to two provisos. The most important is that the exporter of waste must inform and obtain the consent of the importer before shipping waste. The second is that the wastes to be exported must not belong to certain categories of wastes, which are listed in Annex 1 of the Convention. The methods and means by which this must be done are spelt out in several provisions of the Convention text [Articles 4 (1.c), (2.f), 6 and 7]. One of the most important of these is that member countries would have to designate a 'Competent Authority', who would be responsible for receiving, assessing and authorising the import of hazardous wastes [Article 5 (1–3)].

As indicated earlier, the parties from the developing countries were vehemently opposed to PIC. They raised a number of issues regarding the appropriateness of the policy. First, they pointed out that the designation of a Competent Authority does not automatically confer competence in the management of hazardous wastes (Krueger 1998: 120). This was a way of stressing the point that they did not have enough expertise or the kind of national infrastructure needed to make informed judgements with respect to the sorts of hazardous wastes that were likely to be exported by the industrialized countries (Kummer 1995: 81). Second, and related, they noted the immense possibility for fraud in the PIC process as there is no way of independently ascertaining that the generator or exporter has not falsified documents or filled in forms with incorrect information (Strohm 1993: 141; Clapp 1994: 23–25). In general, parties from the developing countries saw PIC as a smoke screen for the legitimization of waste dumping and 'garbage imperialism' in Africa, Asia and South America by the more technologically advanced countries (Wynne 1989: 129). They expressed the fear that, once trade in toxic waste was legitimized through PIC, waste brokers from the industrialized countries would be more than willing to exploit these loopholes to dump all sorts of hazardous wastes in developing countries who would not be able to dispose of them adequately (Puckett 1994: 53). This would be relatively easy not only for the reasons mentioned above but also because many of the countries are themselves so poor and needy that they might be attracted to such morally reprehensible deals (ibid.: 56).

In 1987, for example, two Italian firms, Jelly Wax and Ecomar, managed to dump about 4,000 tonnes of highly toxic waste in the backyard of a farmer (Sunday Nana) in Koko, Nigeria, under the label of 'substances relating to the building trade' (Vallette and Spalding 1990: 93–96; Krueger 1998: 121). Although this waste was dumped as far back as August 1987, information about the dumping did not come to light until May 1988 (almost a year after). And what is more, the revelation was made only following a petition letter sent to the Nigerian government by a group of Nigerian students in Italy. Also, in 1984, Zimbabwe accepted about 200 barrels of toxic dry cleaning fluid from a US firm shipped under the guise of 'solvent' (Wynne 1989: 125).

In 1986, the Marshall Islands received a proposal from another US company to import toxic wastes; the waste was proposed as a cheap material for use in land reclamation to avoid inundation from the sea due to global warming. It was only following an alarm sounded by Greenpeace that investigation eventually showed that the wastes were heavily contaminated with toxic incinerator ash (ibid.: 126). Also, it emerged in 1988 that the government of Guinea Bissau was offered four times the value of its gross national product (GNP) to accept a waste trade deal which would have seen the country receiving up to 15 million tonnes of US and European pharmaceutical waste over a 15-year period. When the deal was exposed, the Minister of Environment's simple answer was that 'we needed the cash' (Wynne 1989: 121; Clapp 2001: 35). These are only a few of the many similar examples which show that the developing countries did not have the expertise to identify hazardous wastes and, also, that many waste brokers from the developed countries were not reluctant to exploit PIC for their own advantages. Moreover, it was not all about waste brokers as some accounts might suggest. Some of these cases, such as the Khian Sea voyage, which involved about 14,000 tonnes of incinerator ash belonging to the city of Philadelphia, clearly involved state agents (Wynne 1989: 124–126; Weissman 2005: 28–29).

But neither these incidents nor the arguments by the developing countries proved convincing to the parties from the developed countries, who continued to argue with passion in favour of PIC. The parties from the developed countries vehemently disagreed with the characterization of the waste trade between the industrialized and the non-industrialized countries as 'garbage imperialism' or as a 'crime' against anybody. Rather, they argued that waste is like any other product whose value should be determined by the market forces of supply and demand (Kummer 1995: 43; Clapp 2001: 39). They further contended that a ban would be *unfair* to the nations who might still wish to import or export toxic wastes, perhaps because of their economic, social and technological needs (Clapp 2001; O'Neill 1998; Moyers 1991). Conversely, they argued that the principle of PIC was fair and equitable in that it secured the rights and liberties of parties to choose. This right was also sometimes pointed out (cf. Montgomery 1995: 18) as being a fundamental requirement of freedom and justice. In general, the parties from the developed countries, as Wynne puts it, 'wished to see international waste trade free to develop as a commercial activity' (Wynne 1989: 122). Here, again, one is confronted with another clear example of conflicting understandings of how the international community might achieve a just, fair and, yet, effective response to a given environmental problem, with the arguments running along a familiar course. All of the parties had, in the preamble, pledged their determination to protect human health and the environment from the dangers of toxic wastes 'no matter the place of disposal'. But even in the face of such overwhelming evidence of both economic and infrastructural weakness on the part of the developing countries, the industrialized countries still insisted that international justice was all about maintaining freedom of trade with as few obstructions as possible and allowing each country the liberty to define what constitutes hazardous waste.

National definition of wastes

An important norm established in the Basel Convention, and one which is sometimes discussed in connection with equity and justice, is the right of states to set their own definitions of hazardous wastes (Montgomery 1995). Article 3 of the Basel Convention states that:

> Each Party shall within six months of becoming party to this convention, inform the Secretariat of the wastes considered or defined as hazardous under its national legislation and of any requirements concerning transboundary movement procedures applicable to such wastes.
>
> [Article 3 (I-4)]

The argument that is most often advanced in this regard is that giving each state the chance to determine or define its own wastes enables parties from the developing countries especially to enjoy the benefits of international trade and socio-economic globalization without necessarily becoming vulnerable to imports from the technologically more advanced parties (Kummer 1995: 33). The policy is deemed as being fair because nations can make their choices with reference to their perceived economic needs, social circumstances and scientific capabilities. This is basically the same as saying that states should be allowed to import toxic wastes if they feel that they have the comparative advantage to do so. The argument of comparative advantage has wide currency within the Organization for Economic Co-operation and Development (OECD) and EU circles (O'Neill 1998: 149–151; Krueger 1999). This is understandable as it is quite possible that wastes could be treated in a more environmentally sound manner by exporting to another OECD/EU state better equipped to deal with a particular type of waste. But there are some who stretch the argument and suggest, with reference to Africa and Asia, that it would be better for countries to accept hazardous wastes rather than die from the more immediate threat of hunger and starvation (cf. Hunter 1996; Alter 1997).

The argument that impoverished countries should accept hazardous wastes for the purposes of survival harbours some logic, but it is a proposal that is difficult to defend morally, except, of course, in terms of the libertarian conceptions of justice. But even then, the proposal that countries who are clearly unable to dispose of toxic wastes properly should import such wastes is contrary to established thinking about global environmental sustainability. A related point, which has been made by Clapp (2001), is that a national definition of waste policy might, in fact, prove to be oppressive in the sense that the policy makes it legal for the technologically advanced countries to export materials, the toxicity and exact nature of risks of which may be completely unknown to the developing countries. This is not merely a hypothetical proposition as is illustrated by the case of DDT. Although the use of this highly poisonous pesticide has been banned in most Western countries since the early 1970s, most of these states continue to ship the product to Africa and Asia, mostly in the form of Official Development

Assistance (ODA) loans or aid, or in return for profitable contracts awarded by African governments to Western-based industries.[15] Indeed, a recent investigation by the Food and Agriculture Organization (FAO) revealed that over 500,000 tons of this outdated pesticide are still stored in 'deteriorating and leaky containers all around Africa, the Middle East and Asia'.[16] These pesticides, according to the same report, are, at the moment, known to be affecting the health of more than one million people and causing about 20,000 deaths annually in Africa alone (Africa Recovery 2001). Hence, although, in some ways, these transactions could be said to be a reflection of the economic need of these countries, they can not be said to be consistent with the spirit of sustainability, neither can they be seen as being just on an intuitive scale of morality.

Parties to the Basel Convention are not completely oblivious to this argument. In what appears to be an attempt to placate the parties from the developing countries, the Basel Convention admits some provisions which urge the technologically advanced parties to refrain from shipping wastes to developing countries when they 'have reason(s) to believe that such wastes would not be properly managed or disposed' [Article 4 (2.e and g)]. This is an interesting obligation from an ethical point of view in that it relies solely on the *in situ* moral judgement of the exporting party. The obligation is purely normative and depends for its effective functioning on the ethical judgement of the more advanced and informed parties, rather than on the legal requirements relating to the national definition of wastes. Accordingly, the waste exporter has to judge whether the importer, irrespective of his intent (and willingness), has the facility to dispose of the wastes that he proposes to import in an environmentally sound manner. This provision would seem to tally more with what a conception of justice as fairness or justice as need would prescribe.

Further, Article 4 (8) institutes the principle of non-discrimination under which state parties are expected to ensure that wastes are transported from their country to another country only on the condition that such wastes be disposed of in a manner at least equal to or better than would have been the case were the wastes disposed of in the exporting country. This provision is an important addition to Article 4 (2.e and g) above because it means that the obligation of a state in ensuring the adequate disposal of its wastes does not stop at the legal requirements of proper labelling, information provision, etc., but extends to such a time that the wastes have been finally disposed of in an environmentally sound manner. It also means that states are required to take positive actions to ensure and, if need be, assist in the proper disposal of wastes outside their own borders. This provision may be weak in that, as Birnie and Boyle (2002: 437) point out, it 'assumes that exporting states are realistically in a position to asses the capability of importers', but, nonetheless, its moral and ethical implications remain remarkable. What is implied is that states do, after all, have the moral capacity to look beyond short-term economic interests towards the welfare of the more vulnerable and towards general ecosystemic integrity. This idea is further strengthened by looking at the duty to re-import waste as established in Article 8 of the Convention.

The duty to re-import wastes

The duty to re-import wastes constitutes yet another strong ethical concept introduced into international environmental policy-making through the Basel Convention. It seeks to establish what Semmens (2001: 84) would call 'minimal justice' for the vulnerable on the basis of shared moral values. The main objective is to ensure that risks are squarely borne by those who are responsible for their creation by preventing the move by the rich to buy their way out of the risks that they create.

Article 8 of the Basel Convention establishes that exporters have the legal responsibility to re-import their wastes when such wastes cannot be disposed of in ways that are considered environmentally sound. This responsibility holds irrespective of whether or not such wastes had been exported following due regulations and procedures as established in the Basel Convention. Article 8 reads:

> When a transboundary movement of hazardous wastes or other wastes to which the consent of the States concerned has been given, subject to the provisions of this Convention, cannot be completed in accordance with the terms of the contract, the State of export shall ensure that the wastes in question are taken back into the State of export, by the exporter, if alternative arrangements cannot be made for their disposal in an environmentally sound manner, within 90 days from the time that the importing State informed the State of export and the Secretariat, or such other period of time as the States concerned may agree. To this end the State of export and any Party of Transit shall not oppose, hinder or prevent the return of those wastes to the State of export.

This provision brings out clearly the notion that waste producers are obligatorily tied to their waste until it is evidently disposed of in a proper way. This obligation extends across national boundaries and 'trumps' claims that the export was conducted following the due process of the Convention. Thus, Article 8 aims to establish beyond doubt that, until the state of import is completely satisfied that a given waste has been properly disposed of, the fate of the waste remains the responsibility of the exporter and the state of export, even when money has changed hands. This can be seen as a major achievement on the part of the states who wanted to go the full mile to protect the weaker members of the Convention, even when such actions involve going back on pre-established conceptions of sovereignty.

The duty to re-import wastes relates closely to the duty of care (Birnie and Boyle 2002: 113). The duty of care derives from the conviction that the action of people should be guided by a moral and ethical code – what Aristotle (1847/1998) calls the spirit instead of the letter of the law. This duty of care rests on three main requirements – reasonableness, responsibility and practicability – and is traditionally associated with the protection of the vulnerable (Alder and Wilkinson 1999: 284, 356). The concept is mostly applied to the protection of children in a school environment and in the health-care profession, and relates to the responsibility that carers have to protect those under their care even when such actions of care are not explicitly spelt out in the contract of employment (ibid.: 356). Hence, the concept relies on good judgement and works to place within the realm of litigation actions or inactions that are not necessarily covered in the written terms of a contract (Kummer 1995: 16–20; Birnie and Boyle 2002: 113–114).

In a similar fashion, the duty of care demands that wastes should be handled with extreme caution at every stage – from cradle to grave. This is expected to involve discretion, the consideration of other people's interests, and the honest and justifiable application of correct principles. It places a demand on waste handlers to act with foresight and to exercise good judgement in all their dealings, even in cases in which they are not expressly regulated by legislation. The principle of justice involved is one that is rooted in care and prudence rather than in economic rationality and the maximization of financial gains. The reliance on the three requirements of reasonableness, practicality and responsibility as opposed to hard-wired legal rules in the preservation of nature and the human environment from toxic wastes stems from the inability to capture the multiplicity of situations and scenarios that may possibly arise in the process of waste handling or disposal.

The duty of care has been a legal responsibility in the waste management policy of the UK since 1992. Introduced under the Environmental Protection Regulations 1991 (as amended), and in Northern Ireland under the Controlled Waste Regulations 2002, it places a timeless limit of responsibility upon waste manufacturers, handlers, carriers and disposers.[17] This means that a waste handler is still responsible for his waste even after it has passed to another party. It obliges one to take the utmost care in the handling of one's wastes including making sure that wastes are transferred to those who are provably qualified to deal with them. The legislation spells out clearly that it is the responsibility of waste handlers, as part of their duty of care, to verify the qualifications and licences (legal authority) of waste dealers before contracting them to remove wastes from their premises. This is, in principle, the idea that parties to the Basel Convention sought to simulate in enacting the duty to re-import (Article 8). It is also the idea that underpins the principle of producer liability established in Chapter 20 of *Agenda 21* (United Nations Conference on Environment and Development 1992).

A care approach to justice, either between or among nations, is traditionally associated with the feminist ethic (Dobson 1998; Kymlicka 2002). In the main this ethic is collectivist in that it emphasizes relationships and the group rather than the individual. The care ethic does not deny autonomy as a fundamental value, but it claims that autonomy need not, as Grace Clement puts it, 'be understood individualistically or allowed to threaten our sense of community' (Clement 1996: 13). The contention, rather, is that the individual is best understood as a part of a larger whole and that pure justice requires people to be guided not only by legal codes but also by empathy and selfless consideration of others. This is not the same as saying that people should be tolerant, as neoliberals are inclined to argue, but that they should take all reasonably practical actions to help those in need and offer assistance to fellow humans regardless of whether or not the letter of the law commits them to do so.[18]

Duty to co-operate

Parties are explicit in admitting that a determined effort at mutual assistance and co-operation among states and international economic and/or political organizations is needed to achieve the aims of the Basel Convention [Article 10 (I-4)]. There are several provisions in the Convention that stress the importance of co-operation in the bid to achieve effective and efficient global waste management schemes [Article 10 (I-4)]. The whole of the Ministerial Declaration on Environmentally Sound Management is awash with the need to co-operate on all fronts and 'to make all possible efforts to ensure the universality' and success of the Convention. In this document, parties commit themselves to co-operating in a large number of areas including: (i) information sharing and harmonization of technical standards and practices; (ii) research and monitoring of the effects of wastes on humans and the environment; (iii) research into technical improvements and transfer of technology; (iv) capacity building; and (v) the development of common codes of practice in the area of waste management.

Article 10 (2.d, 3 and 4) recognizes differences in the needs and abilities of the parties and indicates the desire to co-operate to develop capacity among members, 'especially those, which may need and request technical assistance in this field' [Article 10 (2.d)]. The Strategic Plan for Implementation declares that 'the Parties shall take into account the principle of common but differentiated responsibility in seeking effective involvement and co-ordination of all concerned stakeholders'.[19] In general, therefore, parties recognize that co-operation ought to be styled with the needs and capabilities of those in the developing countries in mind [Article 10 (3 and 4)]. In Article 14 (1) parties establish a provision for regional and sub-regional centres for the promotion of training and technology transfer, which must be 'according to the specific need of different regions'. And finally, Article 11 allows for bilateral and multilateral agreements under the Convention according to the interests and needs of the parties, especially those from the developing countries.[20] This article is very significant because it eventually provided the ground for the articulation of the Bamako Convention banning the import of hazardous wastes into Africa and many of the other regional conventions on hazardous wastes, which effectively altered the context of debate in the Conferences of the Parties (COPs) to the Basel Convention and, in the end, paved the way for the Basel ban of 1994 in COP-2.

The international political economy of hazardous wastes and the 1994 Basel ban

Despite several gestures made towards the endorsement of cosmopolitan individual rights, the duty of care, the principle of non-discrimination and the recognition of the special needs of the developing countries, the Basel Convention that was adopted in March 1989 upheld free trade through PIC as its main policy instrument. The attempt to endorse these ethical principles while at the same time upholding the principle of free trade was the main reason why the Basel Convention had a very weak start (Wynne 1989; Kummer 1995; O'Neill 1998). The developing countries rejected the Convention because, for them, it did not go far enough to uphold the principles of international justice by completely banning the export of wastes from the developed countries (Wynne 1989: 129). The developed countries, on the other hand, rejected the Convention for going too far in the direction of establishing anti-free trade policies (Kummer 1995: 46; Krueger 1999).

Meanwhile, even though the number of proposals for the export of toxic wastes to developing countries fell dramatically after the adoption of the Basel agreement, a new dimension of toxic waste trade quickly blossomed. Following the provision of the Basel Convention allowing for the export of hazardous wastes destined for recycling, over 90 per cent of the hazardous waste trade between the developed and the developing countries immediately shifted from that destined for disposal to that intended for recycling or as raw materials (Greenpeace International 1994). At the same time, cases of mislabelling and incidences of insufficient or inadequate information being given about certain cargoes of wastes also became rampant. Apparently, the weak position of African countries in the international political economy, in particular, their high levels of indebtedness and their drive for foreign currencies, continued to make them ready prey in the hands of waste brokers from the industrialized countries who had no qualms exploiting these vulnerabilities through the multiple avenues offered by the highly fluid global economy (Clapp 2001: 10–11).

The various regional bans on the importation of hazardous wastes sent clear signals to the parties from the developed countries but they were not sufficient as they did not impose any legal requirements on the industrialized states. Against this background, the developing countries, backed fervently by environmental non-governmental organizations (NGOs), especially Greenpeace, continued to press for a complete ban on the import of hazardous wastes from the developed countries within the context of the Basel Convention. In canvassing for this complete ban, the developing countries and Greenpeace relied essentially on moral arguments. They continued to expose the negative health impacts of the numerous waste deals and 'waste recycling' plants that had surged in Africa following the adoption of the Basel Convention and to embarrass the companies involved in such deals (Greenpeace International 1994). In so doing they relied mainly on the underlying shared values and solidarity of ordinary people, including those in the industrialized countries. Eventually, despite strong opposition from the USA and some other Western states, the developing countries mustered enough support in COP-3 to secure a complete ban on the export of hazardous wastes from the industrialized countries irrespective of whether such wastes are destined for disposal or for recycling.

But what exactly are the ethical implications of this ban? Well, apart from the fact that it relied on the ability of Greenpeace and the developing countries to show that the export of wastes from the industrial countries to the less developed countries contravenes the principle of non-discrimination and the commitment to environmentally sound management of hazardous wastes as agreed by the parties, the wide support for the ban, even from ordinary citizens across Europe and America, lends a certain measure of credence to the global citizenship arguments. The support also indicates the willingness of 'ordinary citizens' to act upon shared moral values in defiance of national boundaries and the preferences of some state agents and corporations. The argument of Greenpeace, similarly to that of many of the developing countries, was that a complete ban was the only means of securing the protection of the vulnerable, of imposing grater responsibilities on the waste manufacturers themselves and of securing justice in the context of the global waste management regime (Greenpeace International 1994; Agarwal et al. 2001: 64–73).

But although the Basel ban can be regarded as an obvious improvement on PIC, it must be pointed out that its approval as an instrument of justice depends greatly on the fact that parties had, in the very beginning, managed to shape the Basel Convention as being concerned only with the last stage of the waste cycle, that is, the disposal stage. Hence, the ban can be judged as sufficient only on the condition that parties were right in largely ignoring what happens in the earlier stages of the waste cycle. But if, on the other hand, one accepts the argument that the rules of international trade and the other multitude of co-operative activities among states already produce winners and losers, which the pattern of waste movements across the globe merely serves to highlight, then the rating of the Basel ban as a tool of international justice is automatically weakened. From this latter perspective, it would seem that a waste management regime that truly seeks to be equitable must consider the fairness of all of the stages involved in the waste cycle, ranging from the securing of the raw materials, through the production processes to disposal. But not many will doubt that neither the Basel Convention nor any other convention for that matter, operating under the prevailing economic and political climate, can afford to probe deeply into these areas.

Conclusion

The balance of evidence indicates that the parties' approach to the problem of hazardous wastes follows a managerialist understanding of global environmental problems. This understanding is also evident in the majority of the literature devoted to this issue-area, much of which simply focuses on the 'end of the pipe' stage of the waste management process. By conceiving of the escalation of waste dumping in the less industrialized countries in the early 1980s as arising because of the coincidental interaction of 'push' and 'pull' factors, and by judging that these incidences were the handiwork of a 'few unscrupulous' waste brokers bent on exploiting the opportunity to make a quick profit, the parties from the developed countries sought to downplay the effect of the underlying inequitable global economic structure in stimulating the waste crisis.

Consequently, and as a result of the ideological commitment to the notion of free trade, prior informed consent (PIC) emerged as the central principle upon which global waste management was based, particularly before the Basel ban of 1994. PIC emerged as the core policy because of the successful move by powerful interests to frame the scandalous waste deals not as 'toxic imperialism' or 'environmental racism' but as the natural fallout of the otherwise mutually beneficial activities relating to industrial development and international trade. PIC was thus conceived as a way of respecting the sovereignty of the individual states to protect themselves whilst engaging in trade and economic activities in ways that reflected their respective needs and comparative advantages. It was pointed out, however, that PIC did not truly reflect freedom of choice as the developing countries, most of whom are under the weight of a strangulating debt burden, are rather too weak and vulnerable and incapable of making rational choices.

However, because of the enormous pressure exerted by the developing countries and their environmental NGO allies, especially Greenpeace, the original treaty still managed to accommodate other, arguably more intuitive, notions of justice. The Convention sought to establish some form of cross-border liability on waste exporters – it sought to grant groups and individuals access to compensation for damages resulting from the transboundary movements of toxic wastes. The Convention also established or reiterated the non-discrimination principle, the duty to re-import waste, and the common but differentiated responsibility principle – all of which pull against the dominant sovereign and market-based approaches to international environmental policies. The Basel ban was further seen as the product of a counter-hegemonic resistance, which fed upon the underlying shared value that some activities are simply unjust no matter the economic rationale behind them, and that this judgement of unfairness holds irrespective of the states of origin of either the beneficiaries or those at the receiving end. Hence, it was shown that moral arguments increasingly form an effective platform for either the legitimization or the de-legitimization of certain economic practices, even at the global level.

Nonetheless, it was pointed out that even the Basel ban, although in some ways inspiring, could not be taken as satisfying the aspirations of international justice as it does not and cannot address issues of inequities endemic in the contemporary patterns of globalized trade, inadequate pricing of primary export goods and the internationalization of production processes – all of which sit deeper and serve to produce the noticeable patterns of the transboundary movements of toxic wastes. Yet, it bears emphasis that the 'minimum justice' recorded in Basel by way of the 1994 ban was only possible to the extent that a fundamental premise of neoliberal justice was upturned in favour of justice as care and justice as need, which were originally limited to the declarative portions in the original Convention.

6 Protecting the global atmosphere
The UNFCCC

In this chapter the highly significant United Nations Framework Convention on Climate Change (UNFCCC) is used to further highlight some more of the tensions and complex interplays between moral norms and political economic ideas that characterize the development of environmental regimes at the global level. The following discussion also reveals a great deal of the complexities that arise at the interface between philosophical understandings and practical implementation of notions of international distributive equity in regimes. The chapter indicates the role of moral concepts such as per capita emission and the common but differentiated responsibility (CDR) principle in the policies of the climate change regime. But, as in the case of the Third United Nations Conference on the Law of the Sea (UNCLOS III), this chapter demonstrates that it is the conceptions of justice that have a close fit with the dominant neoliberal economic system which actually underwrite the core policies of this all-important regime. It emerges that even equity programmes such as the clean development mechanism (CDM), which allows the developed countries to assist in the development of poor countries while winning emission reduction units (ERUs) in line with the Kyoto agreement, have been turned into profit-making avenues by state and corporate actors in the developed countries with the effect that most investments are made in regions and locations that can guarantee quick financial returns rather than in areas that are the most vulnerable to the threat of climate change.

Because there is a mountain of literature already available on the subject of justice and equity in the global climate change regime, I feel the need to reiterate how this work relates to and differs from existing ones. Unlike many works on this subject, I do not engage in abstract speculation on what a just emission allocation scheme could look like. My analysis (as in the two previous chapters) is primarily based on the Convention's key texts. I seek mainly to highlight the ethical tensions that characterize the regime and the interpretations of justice that underwrite the core policies and programmes as they currently exist (see the introductory chapter).

Facing up to the ultimate environmental threat

The two words that unite all commentaries on the global climate change problem are 'significance' and 'complexity'. Academics, policy-makers and lobby groups from virtually the whole ideological and political spectrum seem to agree that climate change poses a very significant and complicated problem for global environmental diplomacy, if not international relations in general. Sands (1995: 273) suggests that 'it is difficult to identify any type of human activity which will over time fall outside its scope'. Grubb (1995: 465) observes that 'climate change raises international questions that are quite unprecedented [and that] addressing these questions may emerge as a central feature of international relations in the next century'. The Prime Minster of Japan, Ryutaro Hashimoto, described it as a problem that is of 'direct threat to the future of humankind' (quoted in Leggett 2000: 307). For French (1998: 227), climate change remains the greatest challenge to the international community and one to which the nature of response will determine the type of world that future generations will inherit. Bodansky (1993: 476) believes that the climate change agreement has a 'much more profound effect' than any other international agreement, whereas Paterson and Grubb (1992: 293) describe it simply as the 'acid test' of whether or not countries are serious to act collectively over global environmental problems.

Concern with global climate change is not an entirely new phenomenon. Civilizations, states and sovereigns have always expressed measures of interest in both atmospheric and climatic changes (Erickson 1990; McCorriston and Hole 1991; Luterbacher and Sprinz 2001). This is because climatic variations can have an enormous impact on a wide range of economic, recreational and socio-political activities. For example, knowledge of weather patterns can affect decisions relating to war, navigation, trade, agriculture, tourism, etc. As a result, efforts to better understand worldwide patterns of weather variations were among the first areas of known scientific and intergovernmental co-operation on environmental issues.[1] It was not until the 1980s, however, that questions of global climate change assumed a deeply political dimension to the extent that they became the hotbed of controversies in the international effort at environmental governance and sustainable development (Paterson 1996b). Yet, more than a decade after the UNFCCC was signed (in Rio 1992) and after more than 11 subsequent meetings of the Conference of Parties (COP), little agreement exists on how the thorny questions thrown up by the issue may be equitably resolved.

Justice implications of climate change

Although it was the issue of hazardous waste dumping that more squarely introduced 'environmental justice' into the vocabulary of modern environmental discourse, it is the problem of climate change that has encouraged the most widespread ethical analysis of environmental issues and regimes at the global level. Paterson (1996a: 182), in fact, contends that 'virtually any general overview of the prospects of successful responses to global warming will have a paragraph on international equity'. This arguably stems from the fact that the climate change problem clearly highlights virtually all of the key issues (discussed in Chapter 2) around which the wider discourse of international distributive justice revolves. The constraints imposed by natural limits, the reality of pollution (harm) transfer on a global scale, the overuse of the global commons by a select few and the controversial role of knowledge (science) in international environmental management are all significant elements of the climate change regime. In addition to all these, the climate change problem has its peculiar attributes. For instance, it brings to the fore questions on compensatory justice with respect to liability in the destruction of other nations' ecosystems and the loss of human lives. It also highlights the prospects of and difficulties in attempting to hold states responsible for the harm that might have been caused by past generations. All of these factors combine, in the words of Michael Grubb, to make the climate change problem one 'that relates centrally to the nature and ethical basis of international economic and political relationship . . . in ways that have never been faced' (Grubb 1995: 464).

Conceptions of justice in the UNFCCC

As in the Basel Convention, the word 'justice' appears in the UNFCCC text only in the context of dispute settlement through the International Court of Justice (ICJ) (Article 14). However, unlike in the Basel Convention, there is a significant use of a number of other terms and concepts that relate directly to international distributive justice in the text of the UNFCCC. These include a direct reference that parties are determined to approach the problem of climate change on the *'basis of equity'* [Article 3 (1)] and *'taking the need for equitable and appropriate contributions by each party'* [Article 4(2)]. But just as it was with UNCLOS III, the explicit commitment by parties to the UNFCCC to pursue equity did little to make the negotiation of the climate change agreement any less acrimonious. For nearly 24 months (1990–1992) the attempt to negotiate an effective and equitable climate change regime brought about a replay of almost all of the melodrama that characterized the negotiation of UNCLOS III roughly two decades earlier.

But despite its normative significance, it is still extremely difficult to pin down what exactly constitutes the policies of the climate change agreement. The nature of the problem is such that, apart from the declarations of broad principles (Article 3), parties mainly had to resort to national policies (difficult to verify) to deal with the issues. This approach has led some (e.g. Borione and Ripert 1994: 91) to describe the UNFCCC as dealing merely with matters of procedure and 'contractual obligations'. At the same time, despite the significant moral concepts accommodated in the text of the UNFCCC and the international equity embodied in the Kyoto agreement, neither of these instruments says anything explicit on the notion of justice that underlies these aspirations and programmes. For example, apart from dividing broadly between the developed and the developing countries and the more or less arbitrary choice of a 1990 baseline date, there is nothing else in the texts that tell us the criteria by which the specific emission reduction quotas were allocated. This gap has prompted plenty of discussions, both in the literature and in policy circles, about what concept of justice might offer the most promising basis of explaining the Kyoto targets or, more comprehensively, for sharing the burden involved in dealing with the problem of global climate change. To this end, many criteria, including status quo rights, grandfathering, comparative burden, polluter pays principle, willingness to pay, allocation by landmass, capacity to pay, rewarding efficiency and equal entitlement schemes, have all been suggested (Young 1991; Grubb *et al.* 1992; Butraw and Toman 1992; Shue 1993, 1994; Fermann 1993; Banuri *et al.* 1996; IPCC 1996, 2001; Rowlands 1995; Rayner and Malone *et al.* 1998; Paterson 2001). However, in keeping with the focus of this book, I do not discuss the merits or demerits of any of these criteria. Instead, the following sections concentrate on the principles and concepts that are explicitly mentioned or alluded to in the Convention text.

Justice in participation and procedure

The first contention in the negotiation of the UNFCCC related to the issue of procedure and equitable participation (Paterson 1996b: 51). Basically, the developing countries wanted the climate change negotiation to be under the auspices of the UN (Bodansky 2001: 30). Two reasons are often proffered in defence of this choice. One relates to the widespread expectation that the climate change agreement would serve as an opportunity to address background issues of injustice in the international system and, as such, that both the commitments and the institutional arrangements that would be eventually needed to secure an effective and equitable climate change agreement would likely go beyond what an average multilateral environmental treaty could offer (Pachauri 1992: 15; Borione and Ripert 1994: 81–82; Rowlands 1995: 196). It was envisaged, as Dasgupta (1994: 131) puts it, that 'the sharing of costs and benefits implied in the convention could significantly alter the economic destinies of individual countries'. Such alterations were deemed manageable only within a system that guaranteed justice and security for the developing countries – the UN system (Bodansky 1993: 477; Borione and Ripert 1994: 82).

The second and related point is that developing countries thought that the UN system offered them a better forum for effective participation in the negotiation process (Bodansky 1993: 474, 2001: 30; Birnie and Boyle 2002: 523). All along, they viewed with serious suspicion the scientific approach of the World Metereological Organization (WMO) and the United Nations Environment Programme (UNEP) in their effort to organize a global response to the climate change problem (Bodansky 2001: 28). The two bodies initially concentrated on understanding the science of global climate change at the expense of the socio-economic and political dimensions (Rowlands 1995: 198). This approach meant that only little space existed for any form of meaningful participation by the developing countries, many of whom had neither the resources nor the expertise to make critical inputs (Rowlands 1995: 189; Thompson and Rayner 1998: 308). However, developing countries were not unaware of the extent to which claims to knowledge had become a political tool in the context of international environmental management (Dyer 2001). The controversies that surround the role of science in the whaling, ozone, and Antarctica regimes are only a few of many examples that show how science can be used as a proxy in the pursuit of a deeper material and political agenda (Hawkins 1993; Litfin 1994; Jasanoff and Wynne 1998). Against this background it is understandable that the developing countries insisted that negotiation take place in a forum that could secure what Habermas (1981) calls an 'ideal speech situation'. The following is the way that the head of the Pakistan delegation to the Intergovernmental Negotiation Committee, Tariq Osman Hyder, attempted to justify this move:

> In the UN process as a whole, the medium is often more important than the message. The UN system permits all sides to express their opinions from a position of sovereign equality and therefore to maintain self-respect. Countries acknowledged to have dominant economic, political and military power are forced to take into account the contrasting views of many other countries, however weak those countries may be. This balance promotes a more equitable dialogue.
>
> (Hyder 1994: 203)

In the end, the developing countries got most of what they wanted. In relation to representation and effective participation, the UN established a special voluntary fund that financed the attendance of the representatives of the developing countries. The aim was to enable the developing countries to 'participate fully and effectively in the negotiation process' (UNGA resolution 45/212). The developing countries further secured a resolution (INC/1992/1) assuring that all of the Intergovernmental Negotiation Committee (INC) participants would be specifically invited and enabled to attend the meeting of the first COP. These gestures helped to create a sense of fairness, universality and an atmosphere of solidarity, which many delegates, especially those from the developing countries, accept, with hindsight, contributed greatly to the success of the negotiations (Djoghlaf 1994; Hyder 1994; Dasgupta 1994). In terms of procedure, it was accepted (in favour of the position of G-77) that the Committee should adopt the rules of the UN General Assembly (that is voting) to resolve any substantive issue when 'no agreement appears to be attainable' (INC A/AC.237/5). The developed countries had favoured a consensus approach, which, according to Dasgupta (1994: 132), 'tend in practice to confer something approaching a veto only on the most influential states'. Further, the G-77 secured a UN General Assembly directive, which approved that the negotiations should be open not only to members of the UN but also to members of the UN specialized agencies. This recommendation made it possible for a number of the small island states to take an active part in the negotiation process (ibid.: 132). Finally, in terms of participation, UN involvement made it possible to involve non-governmental organizations (NGOs) in the early stages of the negotiations in an open, sincere and transparent manner (Rahman and Rocerel 1994: 240–267; Djoghlaf 1994: 106–107). As Elizabeth Dowdeswell, the leader of the Canadian delegation, and Richard Kinley put it:

> The climate change negotiations were in the forefront of opening UN processes to participation by non-governmental representatives. Virtually all the sessions, including those of the working group were open. . . . This was an important element of the negotiations – it meant that the non-government sector was fully informed of developments, had a better understanding of the negotiation process, had an opportunity to interact with delegations, and could serve as a mechanism to ensure accountability and a source of public pressure.
>
> (Dowdeswell and Kinley 1994: 119–120)

In sum, then, one can say that the initial 'procedural wrangling' (Paterson 1996b: 51) produced results that were meant to promote a fair, balanced and equitable negotiation. But it is doubtful how far these 'procedural victories' by the South contributed to the negotiation of a just climate change regime. What can be said for sure is that the desire for the radical restructuring of the international economic order, as hoped for by the developing countries, did not eventuate. In fact, after many months of torturous negotiations, they could not get the parties from the developed countries, who account for over 60 per cent of the global greenhouse gas emissions, to cut their emission levels within a specified time or to any specific level.[2]

The Convention's objective

Unlike in many conventions, in which the aims and objectives form part of the preamble, parties to the UNFCCC devoted one whole article to stating the objective of this treaty. Indeed, the contention over the wording of the objective was so intense that some commentators consider the eventual compromise as 'one of the most important achievements of the Convention process' (Hyder 1994: 204) and as 'one of its most important elements' (Mintzer and Leonard 1994: 17).

Article 2 of the Convention deals solely with the objective and states:

> The ultimate objective of this Convention and any related legal instrument that the Conference of Parties may adopt is to achieve, in accordance with the relevant provisions of the Convention, stabilisation of greenhouse gas concentrations in the atmosphere at a level that would prevent dangerous anthropogenic interference with the climate system. Such a level should be achieved within a time frame sufficient to allow ecosystem to adapt naturally to climate change, to ensure that food production is not threatened and to enable economic development to proceed in a sustainable manner.

At first, it is not immediately clear what to make of this long and complicated statement. Panjabi (1993: 507), for example, expresses his frustration over its complexity, calling it an objective 'so ambiguous as to be almost meaningless'. On a closer look, though, it emerges that the Convention objective is a classic formulation, which embodies both the parallels and the tensions, or what Diana

Liverman (2006) calls the 'core narratives', of the global climate change discourse.

The first of these is that the parties clearly endorsed the view that mitigation rather than adaptation was their main focus in dealing with the problem of climate change (cf. Adger *et al.* 2006: 1; Baer 2006: 131). This was contrary to the position of some [e.g. the Association of Small Island States (AOSIS)] who had wanted the Convention to give equal attention to adaptation on the grounds that they had already begun to suffer the effects of global climate change. However, although the focus on mitigation was largely in keeping with the preference of the USA and other developed countries, it nonetheless entailed a certain legitimization of the precautionary principle in international environmental management. For, irrespective of the initial US references to scientific uncertainty regarding the extent and effects of climate change, parties to the Convention still managed to establish their preparedness to take steps to mitigate global climate change in the absence of 'hard' and conclusive scientific findings. The ethical and distributive implications of the precautionary principle have been discussed in Chapter 3. Accepting that there is a need to take care to prevent irreversible damage to the global environment in the absence of 'hard' scientific evidence is an ethical position that sits better with the notion of sustainable development and global distributive equity than the neoliberal conceptions of justice (see Chapter 8). Adger *et al* (2006: 3) make this point well when they assert that 'climate justice requires the consideration of principles such as precaution and the protection of the most vulnerable because of the uncertainties and irreversibilities inherent in the climate system and climate science'.

The second narrative, following on from the above, is that the Convention's objective endorses the narrative of global environmental sustainability. This is implicit in the attempt to balance environmental protection interests with those of food production and sustainable economic development. This point assimilates in two different directions. On the one hand, for scholars such as Rahman and Roncerel (1994), it signifies a verdict against untrammelled economic growth and the elevation of environmental protection to the same status as money and profit-making. And, on the other hand, for commentators such as Hyder (1994: 204–205) and Djoghlaf (1994: 97–99), it connotes the successful attempt by the G-77 to marry the need for environmental protection – which was the main focus of the North – with the need for economic development –which was the priority of the G-77 and China.

The third narrative implicit in the framing of the Convention's objective is the primacy accorded to neoliberal economic growth and the policy mechanisms conducive to this philosophy over all other narratives of climate change and global environmental sustainability. The first point here, as Mintzer and Leonard (1994: 17) cleverly observe, is that the 'language of the objective is framed in terms of stabilizing concentrations and not emissions'. This framing, as Mr William A. Nitze, the former head of the US delegation to the INC, openly admits, is mainly to maintain flexibility, especially with respect to where and how emission reductions might be achieved (Nitze 1994: 189). Of course, the word flexibility has long been a code for options that do not impede neoliberal economic globalization. Flexibility in this case, as we shall see, later translated into a range of policy recommendations such as tree planting, sequestration, emission trading and anything at all that avoided direct confrontation with free market economic growth and related monetarist political economic policies. It is according to this mindset that the Convention objective ducked the question of what level of concentration of greenhouse gases was needed to achieve stabilization, as well as what might be considered the 'sufficient time frame' that was needed to achieve stabilization. This was in keeping with US opposition to any attempt to establish a form of target or binding commitment. It did transpire, however, that despite these US oppositions (what Leggett 2000: 291 calls the 'White House effect'), parties to the Convention eventually made reference in Article 4.2 (b) to the aim of 'returning individually or jointly to 1990 levels of anthropogenic gas emissions of carbon dioxide and other greenhouse gasses'. Let us examine these three narratives in detail.

Mitigation, adaptation and the ethics of valuation

During the preparatory meetings the developing countries, and especially AOSIS, wanted adaptation to be the main focus or to at least be assigned the same weight as mitigation in the Convention. They argued that many in the developing countries were already suffering from the impact of climate change resulting from the industrial activities of the developed countries. The AOSIS argued that many of the severe droughts, floods and hurricanes that swept across Africa, Asia and the Caribbean in the late 1980s were mostly a result of the industrial activities of the developed countries (cf. Huq 2001; Adger *et al.* 2006: 2). They presented detailed proposals on different kinds of international insurance schemes including a certain 'green fund scheme', which they believed should prove effective and equitable in dealing with the issue of adaptation (AOSIS 1992).[3] The USA and most other Western countries, however, refused to be drawn into discussing these proposals. The USA insisted, as Borione and Ripert (1994: 82) put it, that 'there was an overriding need for further scientific research and a better assessment of the economic costs and benefits of the different possible options before they could discuss the proposals'. In reality, though, it was all too apparent that the much more important point of discomfort for the USA and the other Organization for Economic Co-operation and Development (OECD) countries was the prospect of setting up a strong international financial body or distributional schemes, which many of the AOSIS proposals entailed. The parties from the developed countries apparently considered that such a body, which might have ended up resembling the International Seabed Authority (ISA) negotiated under the seabed regime (Chapter 4), was inconsistent with the dominant neoliberal economic ideology.[4]

Furthermore, developed countries decided to concentrate on mitigation because they feared that an emphasis on adaptation would greatly provoke questions of responsibility, liability and the polluter pays principle – all of which they were anxious to avoid during the negotiation process. By their nature, efforts on mitigation, within the context of the CDR principle, can be undertaken by developed countries independently of agreements on degrees of responsibility, historical contributions and liability. Actually, in most cases, these efforts can be promoted in developed countries on the basis of instrumental arguments. Here, the most persuasive is emphasizing the profit dimensions of investing in low-carbon development projects in developing countries. Adaptation projects, in contrast, are mostly needed in vulnerable communities and, moreover, are of the sort that hardly yield profits to external investors. In other words, arguments for adaptation projects would have to rely much more explicitly on ethical and moral justifications than those of mitigation. Besides, parties from developed countries were well aware that discussions on liability for funding adaptation projects in developing countries would only be a prelude to actual demands for compensation resulting from climate change damages. Baer (2006: 132) captures this point well when he says:

> It seems likely that Northern governments are resistant to explicit claims for 'polluter pays' liability for adaptation investments because there is a clear link between current responsibility for adaptation and eventual liability for compensation for actual climate damages. Northern governments might reasonably fear that acknowledging such claims would obligate Northern countries to the largest share of a potentially enormously financial labiality.

Baer's observation leads on well to another important equity issue related to adaptation and climate damages in the international setting. This has to do with the valuation of property and life. Pearce (1995), Fankhauser (1995), Grubb (1995) and Fankhauser and Tol (1996) are among the many who have written about the enormous ethical complexities that confront attempts to assign internationally acceptable values to lives and property lost as a result of climate change in different parts of the world. The questions are multifaceted but at the core is how (assuming an international insurance body is created) one human life or a piece of property in, for example, Bangladesh may be valued in relation to another life or similar property in, for example, the Netherlands if citizens in both countries suffer damages from sea level rise caused by the industrial activities of the North. Since the signing of the UNFCCC this kind of debate has become topical in the work of the Intergovernmental Panel on Climate Change (IPCC) (cf. IPCC 1995, 1996, 2001).

At present, there is a tendency for some Western economists to adopt a method that values life in proportion to the national per capita gross national product (GNP) (Fankhauser and Tol 1996, 1997; Cline 1992; Nordhaus 1991). But this approach, which suggests different values of life for people in different regions of the world, has been vehemently opposed by the developing countries. The Indian Environment Minister, Kamal Nath, could barely suppress his anger when he wrote to other heads of delegations to an IPCC working group at which these sorts of proposals were tabled for discussion. He completely rejected:

108 *Empirical analysis of three regime texts*

> The absurd and discriminatory global cost/benefit analysis procedures propounded by the economists in the work of IPCC WG-III . . . we unequivocally reject the theory that the monetary value of people's lives around the world is different because the value imputed should be proportional to the disparate income levels of the potential victims . . . it is impossible for us to accept that which is not ethically justifiable, technically accurate or politically conducive to the interests of poor people as well as the global common good.
>
> (Cited in Grubb 1995: 471)

Such calculations have also provoked fierce opposition from transnational non-governmental bodies, an example of which is the Global Commons Institute. This Indian-based group has also launched a campaign to protest against an approach that they say 'values one European as equal to ten Chinamen' (Global Commons Institute 1994).

The point here is that, although these questions were not expressly discussed in the main Convention text, they are quite likely to become more urgent with the rise in catastrophic climatic changes in the developing countries that can be traced to global warming. Baer (2006: 133), for one, predicts that these questions will assume great urgency 'when legitimate claims for adaptation funding or for residual impacts of climate change exceed the magnitude of about $1 billion per year'. The UNFCCC has recently created a number of mechanisms for funding adaptation in the developing countries. These include the National Adaptation Plan of Action (NAPA), the Least Developed Country Fund (LDCF) and the Special Climate Change Fund (SCCF). However, in all these schemes, contributions remain purely voluntary rather than being tied to any notion of justice or responsibility. The point of emphasis here is not that these questions should be resolved in any particular way. Rather, the point is that their discussion, like the other equity issues that have been touched upon, represents an important (and largely unaccounted for) shift in the frontiers of international politics and in the conceptual parameters within the discipline of international relations in the twenty-first century (cf. Kjellen 2006: viii).

Balancing environmental protection with economic development

The second narrative identified in the ambiguous wording of the objective is the effort to strike a balance between the goal of environmental protection, expressed in the desire to 'stabilise greenhouse gas concentrations in the atmosphere', and the protection of industrial and material interests, expressed in the language of sustainable economic development. As I indicated above, this approach has been interpreted both as a sign of the elevation of the goal of environmental protection to an equal status with economic development and as a representation of the recognition of the importance of marrying the need for economic development (especially in the South) with the environmental protection need of the North (Rahman and Roncerel 1994; Hyder 1994: 204–206). Mintzer and Leonard (1994:

21) endorse the view that 'the convention sets an ambitious two-part goal for international co-operation: atmospheric stabilisation of greenhouse gas concentrations and the promotion of sustainable development'. In so doing, they say, 'the Climate Change Convention simultaneously endorses ... and emphasizes the essential connection between environmental protection and economic development, giving each equal importance'.

Now, the popular characterization in the literature usually frames the debate in simple dualistic terms – ascribing to the developed countries a passion for stronger environmental protection and to the developing countries an obsession with more economic development. But this characterization is somewhat dubious because there is no reason to believe that the developed countries are any less interested in continuous economic growth. Rather, the argument for linking environmental protection and economic development is, at its core, an argument for distributive justice (Chapter 1; cf. Ramakrishna 1990: 428–432; George 1990: 441–445). Its main pillar has been reviewed in Chapter 1 and includes the contention that most of the urgent global environmental problems have arisen as a result of the developmental/economic activities of the North, such that it amounts to gross injustice to ask the developing countries to mortgage their own developmental needs in support of efforts at environmental protection without making allowance for the extra cost of such involvement (cf. Founex Report 1971: 3–5). It is basically a contestation over 'how countries that have not yet benefitted from a century and a half of carbon emissions can have an equitable chance of development' (Adger *et al.* 2006: 10).

The pursuit of international climate justice was, thus, the primary reason why the developing countries insisted throughout the negotiation process that the concept of equity should be the touchstone of the Convention. In particular, they insisted that the developed countries should: (i) 'take the lead' in efforts to combat global warming including making specific commitments to reduce emissions; and (ii) transfer technology at concessionary terms and equally 'provide new and additional financial resources to the developing countries to enable them to cover the cost of action taken to achieve the objectives of the Convention' (Article 4.3). It was the articles that dealt with these equity arguments which constituted the main bone of contention throughout the negotiation processes. The eventual compromise came in the form of a renewed emphasis on the concept of the CDR principle. However, we will see from the following sections that the key programmes of international climate action have not been moulded to reflect the dimensions of liability and the degree of North–South responsibility clearly implied by the CDR principle.

The common but differentiated responsibility principle

The CDR principle as described by Sands (1995: 217) arose 'from the application of equity in general international law and the recognition that the special needs of developing countries must be taken into account in the application and interpretation of international environmental laws'. The CDR can be said to have begun its journey in Principle 23 of the 1972 Stockholm Declaration, where it emerged as a simple recognition that national environmental standards adopted by the advanced countries may be 'inappropriate, of unwarranted social cost and therefore inapplicable for the developing countries'. This clause is repeated verbatim in paragraph 10 of the preambular chapter in the Climate Change Convention but has appeared in various forms in nearly every other global environmental treaty since 1972.[5]

Typically, though, the CDR comes not in the form of assigning different burdens on states but merely as a statement expressing the need to bear in mind the different economic situations and capabilities of the parties from the developing countries. In this sense, therefore, it is possible to claim that the different emission stabilization targets agreed for different countries in the Convention provides the most pronounced example of the application of the CDR in any international environmental agreement.[6] All together, the CDR is mentioned five times in the Convention text and three times in the Kyoto Protocol[7] in a way that would seem to suggest that the contracting parties regard it as the equity principle that underwrites the equity-based policies of the international climate regime.[8]

Article 4 (1) expressly endorses the principle of CDR [which was also mentioned in Article 3 (1)]. It states that all efforts to combat the global climate change problem shall proceed on the basis of CDR and the 'specific national and regional development priorities, objectives and circumstances' of the parties. In the same manner, Article 4 (2.a) expressly states that parties should protect the climate system '*on the basis of equity*' according to which the '*developed country parties should take the lead in combating climate change and the adverse effects thereof* [cf. Article 3 (1)]. Article 4 (2.a) states, *inter alia*:

> The developed country Parties and other Parties included in annex 1 commit themselves specifically as provided for in the following: (a) Each of these Parties shall adopt national policies and take corresponding measures on the mitigation of climate change, by limiting its anthropogenic emissions of greenhouse gases .... These policies and measures will demonstrate that developed countries are taking the lead in modifying long-term trends in anthropogenic emissions consistent with the objective of the Convention ... and taking into account the differences in these Parties' starting points and approaches, ... as well as the need for equitable and appropriate contributions by each of these Parties to the global effort regarding that objective.

The wordings of these articles is significant in at least three ways. The first is that they represent an admission, the first express admission of culpability (to the best of my knowledge) on the part of the developed country parties regarding a differentiated contribution to global environmental degradation in any issue-specific environmental treaty. This admission of responsibility contrasts with the popular approach of the developed countries, which is usually to berate the developing countries for 'pointing accusing fingers' and to stress the need for collective action without expressly admitting responsibility for damage (Hyder 1994; Dasgupta 1994). This admission is all the more significant in that it embodies a recognition that present generations can be held accountable for the activities of past generations.

The second point, following on from the wording of Article 4 (2.a), is that the international community once again concedes, as was the case in UNCLOS III (Chapter 4), that international justice should be the central basis of all collective efforts aimed at combating global environmental degradation. By expressly stating that parties should be guided by considerations of equity and by endorsing the notion of CDR, parties underscore the point that approaches which tend to stress effectiveness to the exclusion of justice, or what Shue (1992) describes as the 'two track approach' to global environmental management, are no longer acceptable to the international community. The third point is that the wording of Article 4 reinforces the pattern already established in the Basel Convention (and partly also in the Montreal Protocol), which divides the community of nations into two and thus sets a simple, albeit unclear, formula for apportioning tasks and responsibilities in global institutions for environmental governance.[9]

But it must be noted that the CDR remains a very ambiguous concept – one that is extremely difficult to unravel in terms of its conceptual relationship with equity and international distributive justice. This is evident not least in the fact that both the developed and the developing country parties are largely able to hide behind the concept to push for disparate policies in the context of the climate regime. For example, some tend to interpret the CDR as meaning that the burden imposed by climate change should be shared according to the proportion to which each state has contributed to the problem. In this instance responsibility is used in the sense of causality, and justice simply requires that the one who has caused the problem should directly bear the burden. This is the form in which authors like Agarwal and Narain (1991) and Hayes (1993) tend to use the concept. Indeed, most of those who take the causality-based view of the CDR always tend to conflate it with the polluter pays principle. Kokott (1999: 187) is representative of this group when she writes that the 'differentiated responsibilities correspond to differentiated contributions to atmospheric pollution in the past and, thus, harmonize with the principle of causation or with the polluter pays principle'.

In general, the causality-based interpretation of the CDR has significant resonance among diplomats and policy-makers from the Third World countries. Sections of the proposals from both China and India illustrate this point. The Chinese proposal included a paragraph stating that 'emissions of greenhouse gases affecting the atmosphere has hitherto originated from the developed countries which should therefore have the main responsibility in addressing the problem' (cited in Dasgupta, 1994: 133). The Indian proposal was even more forceful, stating that:

> In these negotiations, the principle of equity should be the touchstone for judging proposal. Those responsible for environmental degradation should also be responsible for taking corrective measures. Since the developed countries with high per capita emissions of greenhouse gases are responsible for incremental global warming, it follows that they have a corresponding obligation to take corrective action.
>
> (Cited in Dasgupta 1994: 133)

Indeed, many proposals tabled by the developing countries during the negotiation process contained references to the concept of the polluter pays principle. However, not one of them survived up to the final document. But despite the complete deletion of this concept, it continues to feature freely in academic commentaries as a possible means of grounding the differential targets and general burden-sharing involved in saving the global atmosphere (Grubb et al. 1992, Fermann 1993; Smith and Ahuja 1993; Paterson 1996b; Thompson and Rayner 1998).

On the other hand, developed countries tend to interpret the CDR as meaning that the international burden imposed by climate change should be shared on the basis of capacity and the ability to shoulder the responsibilities involved (Bodansky 1993: 478–480; Sands 1995: 217–220; Baer 2006: 133). Responsibility in this instance is used in the sense of duty or care (see Chapter 5) and a communist or communitarian understanding of justice is implied. During the negotiation of the Climate Change Convention, Northern governments refused to accept any wording that clearly linked the obligation that they 'should take the lead in combating climate change' [Article 4 (2)] with the responsibility for causing the climate change (Bodansky 1993: 478; Dasgupta 1994: 135; Paterson 1996b: 75). The closest that they came was in accepting the wording of the objectives of Working Group I (INC 1991 Annex II), which state that the committee should discus, *inter alia*:

> Appropriate commitments, beyond those required for existing agreements [apparent reference to the Montreal Protocol] for limiting and reducing net emissions of carbon dioxide and other greenhouse gases . . . *taking into account* that contributions should be *equitably differentiated according to countries' responsibilities and their levels of development.*

But subsequently, as the drafting of the final text entered into the advanced stages, the developed countries resisted any move by the developing countries to document that their leadership role in tackling climate change was based directly on the notion of justice as bearing responsibility for past action. It was according to this logic that the industrialized countries insisted on the use of the phrase 'according to respective capabilities' almost any time that the CDR was used in the Convention text.

Based on the foregoing, it cannot be said without equivocation which notion of justice underwrites the differentiated emission reduction quotas. But what can be said, the posturing of the developed country parties not withstanding, is that the separation of states into Annex I and non-Annex I countries does have a direct relationship with the causality-based interpretation of the CDR. This is evidenced not only in the fact that the Convention made explicit provision for the growth of the per capita emissions in developing countries (preamble) but also in the fact that the developed country parties ultimately agreed to bear the extra cost of compliance by the developing country parties [Article 4 (3); Mintzer and Leonard 1994: 19–20; Baer 2006: 132).

The concept of per capita emissions

The Convention text accordingly admits that, although 'change in the Earth's climate and its adverse affects thereof are the common concern of human kind', the 'per capita emissions in the developing countries are still relatively low' and, therefore, 'the share of global emissions originating from the developing countries will grow to meet their social and development needs' (preamble).

It was the opinion of a number of developing country parties that the burden of combating climate change should be viewed along the lines of per capita emissions. Per capita emission means the annual emission per person per state and is obtained by dividing the cumulative emission of a state by its population so that every individual has an equal entitlement or equal pollution right. In their respective proposals both India and China considered it a matter of the 'first principle of justice' (cited in Panjabi 1993: 518) that the objective of the Convention should contain a commitment stating that parties would work towards achieving equal per capita emissions across various countries of the globe (cf. Bodansky 1993; Paterson 1996b: 75).

This proposal to strive for equal per capita emissions in the long term was vehemently opposed and defeated by the developed countries (Grubb 1995; Paterson 1996b). As a result, the phrase 'per capita' makes only a single and brief appearance in paragraph 3 of the preambular chapter where it is noted, as described above, that 'the per capita emissions in developing countries are still low and that the share of global emissions originating in developing countries will grow to meet their social and development needs'. Notwithstanding this, a great deal of the calculations in the literature, as well as discussions in policy circles, continue to include explicit reference to the per capita index. This involves calculations aimed at determining historical emissions of countries and regions (Grubler and Nankicenovic 1991), the net contributions of states in purely contemporary terms (Banuri *et al.* 1996) or as the basis for the allocation of future emissions, or emission reduction quotas (Grubb, 1989; Agarwal and Narain 1991). In addition, the per capita criterion is equally utilized in more official circles; the three regularly cited emission scenarios proposed by the IPCC – IS92a, IS92b and IS92c – are all based on the per capita criterion.

As a concept in moral philosophy, per capita signifies, first and foremost, the equality of all human beings. But it can also be conceived of as an approach that lends greater emphasis to individuals than states as the focus of international laws and policies. Its clear mention in the Climate Change Convention is surely an important boost to idealist notions of international relations and a significant indication of the normative shift that has taken place in this subject discipline – a landscape that has, until recently, been virtually obsessed with state-centric thinking and rhetoric.

The concept of equality of humans does not require much introduction. It features in many international documents including, perhaps most prominently, the UN Universal Declaration of Human Rights (1948). It is equally the key condition upon which Kant relies to derive his 'categorical imperative', which in turn forms the basis of many theories of justice (Rawls 1971; Nozick 1974; Scanlon 1982; Thompson 1992). The most important assumption that is built into calculations utilizing the concept of per capita is simply that all human beings have equal rights to the global resources, in this case, the atmosphere (Birnie and Boyle 2002: 143–144). Per capita, therefore, can be seen as the moral tool that effectively translates the concept of common concern into common and equal ownership. Although it does not resolve all equity concerns in the context of climate change, it does suggest that all human beings have *ipso facto* equal entitlements to clean environments and equal emission rights. This is in harmony with the concept of global environmental citizenship, which tends to confer some degree of environmental and welfare rights to individuals. Another way to ground the per capita and equal entitlement rights is in the form of justice as need. This could involve a statement saying that no one who has an equal right to the environment should be allowed to live without the basic needs of life. In other words, global per capita entitlement can translate to an overriding commitment to meeting the basic needs of 'equal owners' of global resources (Barry B. 1999; cf. Pogge 1998; O'Neill 2000; Attfield 2003), after which the rest of the pollution rights might be shared out along the lines of any other equity criteria.

Notwithstanding what has been said so far, the per capita index cannot be regarded as an explicit criterion of any major policy in the context of the Climate Change Convention. As indicated before, it was mentioned only once in the preamble section. But just as in the case of the value of life, discussed in the previous section, there is no reason to believe that notions of climate justice as per capita emission will go away. As soon as resource-rich and populous developing countries such as China and India come under pressure to take on quantified emission reduction in the post-2012 climate change negotiations, it can be expected that the debates surrounding per capita emission will be seriously revived.

New and additional funds and technology transfers

The debates over funding and the transfer of technology were about the most protracted and vitriolic sessions during the climate change negotiations (Paterson and Grubb 1992; Bodansky 1993, 2001; Rowlands 1995; Paterson 1996b). In summary, the developing countries made it clear that their co-operation and participation in the Climate Change Convention were conditional on the fact that no new financial burdens were imposed upon them (Dasgupta 1994; Hyder 1994). The understanding was strong that, because the bulk of emissions about which the international community was now concerned originated from the economic activities of the North, it was only just and fair that the burden of solution be distributed in such a way that the economic development of the South not be jeopardized (Bodansky 2001: 32). Accordingly, the developing countries insisted that any financial commitment from the South would have to be written off by the North and that such 'cheques' would have to be different and 'additional' to any transfers that currently took place under existing agreements. Many of the forward-looking industrialized states, on the other hand, suggested that 'all signatories should accept binding commitments, while acknowledging their need to "assist" developing countries to fulfil their commitments' (Dasgupta, 1994: 134). Borione and Ripert (1994: 81–82) captured the situation succinctly:

> The developing countries were unanimous in putting forward the 'historical' responsibility of the industrialized nations for exacerbating the greenhouse effect and refused to envisage any specific commitment to emission reductions on their own. Nevertheless on the basis of 'common but differentiated responsibility' they agreed to participate in the negotiation process on the condition that their development priorities were recognized and that they received guarantees of financial and technological aids. [. . .] In the absence of financial support, they would be bound only by 'moral' commitments.

The unanimity and resolve shown by the developing countries on this issue was eventually rewarded. Accordingly, the Convention states [Article 4 (3)] that:

> The developed country Parties and other developed Parties included in Annex II of the Convention shall provide *new and additional financial resources to meet the agreed full costs incurred by developing country Parties* in complying with their obligations under Article 12, paragraph *1*. They shall also provide such financial resources including for the transfer of technology needed by the developing country Parties to meet the agreed full incremental costs of implementing measures that are covered by Paragraph 1 of this Article [that is Article (4.1)].

And, apparently to avoid any ambiguity, Article 4 (7) makes it very clear that:

> The extent to which developing country Parties will effectively implement their commitments under the Convention will depend on the effective implementation by developed country Parties of their commitments under the Convention related to financial resources and transfer of technology and will take fully into account that economic and social development and poverty eradication are the first and overriding priorities of the developing country Parties.

The Global Environmental Facility (GEF) fund is the mechanism that was negotiated to provide the means for fulfilling these provisions. As constituted, the GEF is a compromise arrangement reflecting the equity aspirations of the developed and the developing countries. The developing countries initially rooted for the establishment of a brand new funding body, which would, as Tariq Hyder (1994: 216) puts it, 'avoid the inherent inequities of the weighted voting system associated with the World Bank and related Bretton Woods institutions'. The developed countries, on the other hand, expressed a preference for a World Bank-supervised GEF, citing efficiency and experience as their reasons. In the end, the developing countries were made to accept the GEF but won the concession that the fund would 'function under the guidance of the Conference of parties, which shall define its policies, programme priorities and eligibility criteria related to the Convention' [Article 11 (1)]. In striking this compromise, both parties sought to 'marry the (traditional) GEF's strength of efficiency, higher resource flow and cross-linkages with the COP's expertise on climate change policy and its commitments to action' (Dowdeswell and Kinley 1994: 124). This desire is made clear in Article 11 (2), which states that 'the financial mechanism shall have an equitable and balanced representation of all parties within a transparent system of governance'.

Again, it is evident that all of these are important provisions that result from the aspirations of the developing countries for a more solidarist conception of the international society. As noted, the provisions recognize differences in the priorities and capabilities of state parties; they acknowledge the need for resource transfer from the North to the South; and they make the implementation of any commitment by the developing countries contingent upon these resource transfers. Nonetheless, a closer observation reveals that these provisions are quite deceptive. For, although they might seem, in the first instance, to offer the prospects of massive transfers of resources from the rich to the poor countries, the clauses of 'agreed full cost' and 'agreed full incremental costs' imply, in technical terms, that the rich countries might choose not to transfer any resources if there are disagreements on what actually represents the full cost or full incremental cost of implementing such measures. Not surprisingly, discussion over what constitutes additional funds has proved very contentious and divisive since the negotiation of the climate regime.

In addition, the Convention text is completely silent on the rationale of these transfers. The reader receives no help whatsoever with respect to questions on whether these provisions on 'new and additional resource transfers' should be taken as: (i) instruments of reification of justice or simply as help from a stronger (benevolent) party to a weaker party; (ii) arising from the rights to development of developing countries or based solely on charity; (iii) connected to past injustices or merely forward looking; or (iv) emanating from a set of obligations in the relations of states or purely voluntary.

Shue (1992, 1993) is one of the few who bothers to consider the moral implications of the absence of a clear rationale for these proposed transfers. He argues that it is possible for the South (if they act as a single coalition or if the most populous countries act together) to secure resource transfers from the North, both through rational bargaining and on the basis of international justice. He argues, however, that the basis upon which financial and technology transfers are secured will have remarkable effects on the terms of transfer (who transfers what and who gets what) as well as the level of commitment and the means of administration (cf. Baer 2006: 132–134). Shue's conclusion is that no amount of transfer can be deemed as either just or unjust without a prior debate on the justice of the current holdings.

Paterson (2000) makes a similar point when he observes that the argument for the transfer of resources, although significant in its own right, does not give any definitive indication of what notion of justice obtains in the international system. He points out that there are other ways – including long-term loans, help and strategic welfare-oriented foreign investments – through which resource transfer may be secured without addressing the question of justice. But perhaps the most striking thing about these provisions for resource transfer is found in the comments of Bodansky (2001: 212) when he notes that 'while the developing countries obtained a commitment from the OECD countries to fully finance their required national reports on climate change, the Convention does not require any particular country to contribute any particular amount'.

Hayes (1993: 150) has calculated that developed countries owe the developing countries a natural debt of about US$529 billion, payable by an annuity of about US$34 billion over a 30-year period. Grubb (1990, cited in Paterson 2001: 124) estimates that an annual North-to-South transfer of about US$100 billion is required as just compensation for the burden imposed on them as a result of climate change. It is instructive, however, that, despite the elaborate arguments over the provisions on financial transfers as well as the huge figures bandied about in the literature, 'Northern countries have in practice refused to provide anything more than nominal sums' (Paterson 2001: 124). Instead, attention has since shifted to market mechanisms, such as emissions trading and the clean development mechanism (CDM), as the key ways to solve climate change problems and respond to the equity implications involved.

The supremacy of market-based approaches

The literature is almost unanimous that, apart from the issue of providing new and additional financial assistance to the developing countries, the other issue that attracted a great deal of debate during the INC meetings was that of quantified emission reduction commitments by the industrialized countries (Grubb 1992; Pachauri 1992; Bodansky 1993; Mintzer and Leonard 1994; Paterson 1996b; Toth 1999; Luterbacher and Sprinz 2001). Basically, there were three positions. In one camp was the USA, who vehemently opposed the inclusion of any form of quantified emission reduction targets or deadlines in the Convention. The USA also favoured the so-called 'comprehensive approach', which 'looked at all greenhouse gases together and allowed trade-offs of reductions in one gas for increases in another' (Paterson 1996b: 54).

In the second camp were the other industrialized countries led by the EU. The EU-led coalition wanted the Convention to contain quantified emission reduction targets. They were also opposed to the comprehensive approach of the USA and preferred the Convention to make a distinction between CO_2 and other greenhouse gases already covered in the Montreal Protocol (Bodansky 1993: 136, 2001: 27). The third position was that of the G-77. The G-77 supported the idea that the Convention should make provision for reduction commitments strictly for the industrialized countries. They were also concerned to see that the Convention should make it clear that such extra commitments were being imposed on the industrialized countries solely on the basis of responsibility and social justice

118 *Empirical analysis of three regime texts*

(Pachauri 1992: 15). Eventually, most of the debates on the issue centred on what Paterson (1996b: 62) describes as attempts 'to work around the US position in order to achieve as strongly worded a Convention as possible'. The result of these efforts was Article 4, which expressed the need for action but did not contain any specific emission reduction targets for the developed countries.

The Kyoto Protocol was essentially an attempt to consolidate and build on the minimal commitments that were extracted from the developed country parties just before the signing of the Climate Change Convention at the Rio Conference (United Nations Conference on Environment and Development; UNCED) in 1992 (Bodansky 2001: 34). After a period of grim negotiation, the parties eventually committed themselves to a set of different stabilization targets for each Annex I country, subject to their 1990 greenhouse gas emission levels. The commitment period was set at between 2008 and 2012, with a minimum aggregate percentage reduction of 5.2 per cent as the target. This agreement entered into force on 16 February 2005 at the instance of the ratification of the Protocol by Russia.

Environmentalists have mostly concentrated their critique of the Kyoto Protocol on the fact that the cumulative aggregate percentage reduction as agreed by parties to the Protocol is a far cry from the 50–60 per cent reduction recommended by the IPCC (Legett 2000; Athanasiou and Baer 2002; Anand 2004). But although this is an important dimension that deserves to be highlighted, global equity discourses need to concentrate on the means provided for achieving the nominal targets set at Kyoto and what this means for the power and economic disparities between the rich and poor countries.

The literature records that parties had protracted periods of debate on the exact nature of the policies that might be adopted by states in the bid to achieve the objective of stabilizing anthropogenic greenhouse emissions (Leggett 2000; Grubb and Yamin 2001; Metz *et al.* 2002). The ideas that competed for supremacy were, on the one hand, traditional command and control strategies involving setting targets and caps and, on the other hand, market and economic mechanisms involving especially tradeable permits, international tax schemes and/or 'joint implementation' (Cooper 1998). A number of proposals that featured in pre-negotiation summits include a climate change stamp, a climate fund based on a percentage of a country's GNP (Tolba 1990) and a 'planet protection fund' under UN control, proposed by the late Indian Prime Minster, Rajiv Ghandi. In general, those from the developing countries favoured these routes whereas the developed country parties camped around the more flexible market-based mechanisms.

None of these suggestions was explicitly mentioned in the UNFCCC but the text contains a number of veiled references to the tension that existed in this regard. A couple of clauses were inserted randomly on the need to allow the developed country parties some flexibility in achieving their Article 4 (2) commitments. Article 3 (3) contains a clause saying that parties would have to 'take account that policies and measures to deal with climate change should be cost effective'. And Article 3 (4) contains the view that 'economic development is essential for adopting measures to address climate change'. Other insertions are contained in the preamble chapter, in which parties recognized that the actions of the developed countries would have to be based on 'a flexible manner on the basis of clear priorities'.

In the final analysis, though, parties to the Kyoto Protocol agreed on a number of policy instruments including bubbles, joint implementation, emissions trading and the CDM (collectively called the flexible mechanisms), all of which were designed to enable them to enter into different kinds of special economic ventures with the aim of meeting the Convention's objectives. It is these market-based programmes that ultimately constitute the core policies of the Climate Change Convention (Paterson 1996b; French 1998; Cooper 1998: 67, 1996: 184; Bodansky 2001: 209; Liverman 2006). However, given the focus of this book, my commentary is limited to the CDM, which is designed as an instrument of North–South equity.

The clean development mechanism

The chief market mechanisms agreed under Kyoto are 'joint implementation', which allows Annex I parties to transfer or acquire emission reduction units from one another by investing in projects that are aimed at reducing anthropogenic emissions by sources or sinks (Article 6); 'emissions trading', which permits those that have been assigned quantified emission reduction targets under the Protocol (Annex B) to trade the assigned emissions among themselves for the purpose of fulfilling their commitments; and the 'clean development mechanism', which allows parties from developed countries to invest in pollution reduction schemes in non-Annex I (developing) countries. The purpose of this instrument is to allow Annex I countries to win emission reduction units (ERUs) while at the same time helping the non-Annex I countries to develop and contribute to the achievement of the Convention's double objective, that is sustainable development and environmental protection (see Section above). The CDM is, therefore, mostly presented as the ultimate instrument of North–South climate justice.

However, more than a few have raised questions over the equity implications of this market instrument. The first concern is that the mechanism for the allocation of emission quotas seems to reward rather than punish heavy industrial polluters (Lunde 1991: 21–22; Epstein and Gupta 1990). The second concern is that, in the development of the mechanism, adequate effort might not be given to monitoring – a situation that makes it difficult to verify the figures claimed by the investors (Bachram 2005). A third and related concern is that, in the absence of robust monitoring and given the penchant of corporate actors for quick profits, it would be difficult to ensure that schemes which are validated as CDM projects do actually have long-lasting and meaningful impacts on the lives of those in the developing countries (Loske and Oberthur 1994; Lunde 1991: 21; Markandya 1991).

Unfortunately, it would seem, speaking with the benefit of hindsight, that the worst fears of those who expressed these concerns have come to pass. In the last few years, the CDM has become an extremely popular climate policy instrument, especially among business investors, partly because it provides an opportunity to make large economic profits while at the same allowing such investors to present themselves as helping the developing countries and doing their bit to save the planet. At present, ERUs are awarded to investors on the basis of the volume of carbon that is saved compared with the volume that would be saved using a hypothetical alternative path of development or a no-action scenario. However, the poorly understood nature of science in this area and the hypothetical calculations employed mean that investors are able to claim enormous carbon credits which they are able to sell on the open market with huge profits. Moreover, there have been many indications that a number of CDM projects are not benefiting the local communities but are actually leading to an increasing commodification of nature, the dispossession of indigenous communities and the intensification of existing patterns of social injustice.

In Uganda, for example, a carbon sink project sponsored by the Norwegian government with the intention of passing it off as a CDM scheme led to the forcible eviction of about 8,000 people from 13 villages. In both Brazil and India, there has been a series of CDM projects that have been shown to be ecologically destructive and prone to lead to greater suffering by the local communities. One such project is the World Bank-funded eucalyptus plantation in Brazil, which has been shown to lead to heavy pollution of the local rivers, a rapid decrease in the ground water table and the loss of extremely rich biodiversity. What is more, some CDM projects have led to the enclosure of vast portions of land in the South, which were previously owned and managed in common. Acts of enclosure bring these valuable lands under the ownership of foreign investors, leaving the local population with extensive areas of monoculture plantations that serve no function to improve the well-being of these communities.

All of this has led some to argue that the CDM is far from being an instrument of North–South equity. If anything, these authors claim that the scheme is purely a clever instrument which is enabling a different kind of colonialism by the developed countries (Bachram 2005: 3). Bachram (2005: 5–6) puts it succinctly:

> The Kyoto Protocol allows industrialized countries access to a parcel of land that is roughly the size of one small Southern nation – or upwards of 10 million hectares – every year for the regeneration of CDM carbon sink credits. Responsibility for over-consumptive lifestyles of those in richer nations is pushed unto the poor, as the South becomes a carbon dump for the industrialized world. On a local level, long standing exploitative relationships are being reinvigorated by emission trading. [. . .] The ruination caused by the trafficking in pollution credits serves only to place the cloak of ecological respectability over local and global unequal power relations.

Although some of these issues form part of the discussions in the UNFCCC COP meetings and other important conferences, the developed country parties show no sign of entertaining any suggestions to shift away from these market mechanisms. Incidentally, even the environmental NGOs, who were very critical of the market-based mechanism during the negotiation of the UNFCCC and the Kyoto Protocol, have all backtracked, with many declaring their support for this mechanism and even forming partnerships with corporate actors to exploit the South. Suggestions that include references to the establishment of a strong international monitoring and control mechanism (Wettestad *et al.* 1991) have been mooted but will not be touched by the industrialized countries for the fear that such an approach will violate their commitments to the free market ideology. Indeed, the industrialized countries have never hidden their obsession for market rationality, even in their attempts to solve the problem of climate change. In Article 3 (4) parties reaffirm that 'economic development is essential for adopting measures to address climate change'. Altogether, the need to pay heed to economic considerations appears nine times in the preamble and about 17 times in the main text[10] without any single reference to the fact that the problem of climate change itself has been largely a result of untrammelled industrial pollution in the bid by states for economic prosperity. This scenario has indeed triggered the fear that states and corporations who are pushing for the market-based mechanism may actually be doing so with the aim of turning it into yet another weapon with which they can literally dictate the pace of development in the South.

Conclusion

The climate change problem brings to the fore a large number of justice issues in global environmental co-operation and international relations in general. But it also holds some opportunities through which they may be tackled. Unfortunately, it seems that even the threat of the complete extermination of societies and cultures has not provided enough impetus for an ideological shift away from the neoliberal political economic philosophy. At first sight it would appear that the UNFCCC gives adequate attention to intragenerational equity. The treaty expressly mentions the need to adopt equitable policies and the need to pay heed to per capita emissions as well as containing profuse references to the concept of the common but differentiated responsibility principle. Equally remarkable is the effort by the UN to encourage the effective participation of the developing country parties; the confinement of a commitment to quantified emission reduction targets to the developed country parties in the Kyoto Protocol; the fact that the commitments of the developing country parties are expressly tied to the transfer of new and additional funds by the developed country parties; and the structural adjustments introduced in the workings of the GEF.

In reality, though, the situation is different. The analysis shows that the admittance of the numerous equity concepts in the Convention text arose mainly from the determination of the developing countries to secure greater procedural and substantive justice in the management of the global resources. However, it has been shown that these efforts seem to have been effectively co-opted for neoliberal ends in that, although the developing countries are excluded from quantified emissions limitations, the core polices remain rooted in market-based mechanisms, which not only have the potential of allowing developed countries to increase actual emissions but also the opportunity to strategically increase their capital base while creating the impression that they are helping the developing countries.

Further, it is important to appreciate that only two provisions constitute an obligation on the part of contracting parties to the UNFCCC. These are the obligation to produce national reports on mitigation programmes and the obligation of financial assistance from OECD countries. However, neither of these obligations is substantive but merely procedural, intending to encourage rather than require specific national actions (Bodansky 2001: 204). There is no real provision in the Convention requiring any state to commit any specific amount. Further, even if some transfers do in fact take place, these would not be enough to conclude that equity or distributional justice has been achieved. As long as the justice of current holdings is not discussed it is difficult to determine how just and equitable any given transfer truly is. It is clear that the CDM is based on the philosophy of North–South environmental justice, but indications are strong that this equity policy has again been co-opted not only for corporate gains but also as an instrument of dispossession and pauperization of many in the South.

Part III
Normative critique

General introduction

The analysis conducted in Chapters 4, 5 and 6 establishes the concept that ideas of international justice are now a regular and important feature in the operation of multilateral environment regimes. The analysis also demonstrates the relationship between most of the concepts, policies and programmes of the environmental regimes studied with various conceptions of justice in the Anglo-American tradition of political philosophy while at the same time indicating that many of the core policies of these regimes are underpinned by conceptions of justice that are consistent with the neoliberal political economic ideology. In this last and final section, the aim is to establish the basic point that the dominant conceptions of justice in the three regimes are justice as property rights and justice as self-interested reciprocity (Chapter 7). Collectively, I call them neoliberal ideas of justice to indicate their link with the prevailing neoliberal economic ideology.

The aim in Chapter 8 is to show that these versions of justice, their predominance notwithstanding, do not offer a promising base for the pursuit of global sustainable development or the actualization of the aspirations for distributive justice by the political South. This is achieved by highlighting the areas of incompatibility (I call them fault lines) between these ideas of justice and the basic ethical lineaments of global sustainability based on the Brundtland Report. And finally, in Chapter 9, the findings of all of the previous chapters are interpreted in terms of their implications for global justice and global sustainability. Dominant theoretical frameworks in international relations are criticized on the basis of their insensitivity and underappreciation of the normative dimensions of regime development. I argue that the compromise over the neoliberal political economic doctrine has led to aspirations of global environmental justice being downgraded and co-opted for neoliberal ends much to the disadvantage of the South and in negation to the original vision of global sustainability.

7 Establishing the core ideas of justice in eco-regimes

This chapter is intended to tie together the three cases assessed in Chapters 4–6. Many of the arguments presented in this chapter will have been encountered in one form or another in the preceding chapters but the aim here is to bring them together in a more concise form. I start by reviewing the two neoliberal ideas of justice that I claim predominate in international environmental management circles. I then go on to show that the core policies in the three studied regimes are indeed underpinned by these two ideas of justice as claimed. Subsequently, I highlight how much of the vagueness and contradictions that characterize regime texts and policies arise from the resistance against these two ideas of justice and the compromises that are secured as a result. As in Chapter 3, my discussion on justice as property rights will centre on Robert Nozick's theory of 'justice as entitlement', especially as articulated in his book *Anarchy, State and Utopia* (1974). For justice as self-interested reciprocity I focus on the works of two leading contemporary theorists, David Gauthier's *Morals by Agreement* (1986) and Gilbert Harman's *Justice and Moral Bargaining (*1983). The chapter critically examines these two neoliberal conceptions of justice to reveal the difficulties that they engender as the ethical basis of the core policies of most international environmental regimes that bid to secure a more equitable distribution of global resources within the context of North–South equity and sustainable development.

Neoliberalism and neoliberal justice

It is important to emphasize that the term 'neoliberal' is not normally utilized by philosophers in mainstream discussions of conceptions of justice. Instead, the phrase 'liberal justice' is normally used to refer to the Rawlsian formulation of justice, which has its emphasis on liberal democratic principles, especially those of equal opportunity (see Chapter 3). Some philosophers (e.g. Kymlicka 2002) refer to both justice as property rights and justice as mutual advantage as 'libertarian conceptions of justice'. I, however, adopt the term 'neoliberal' not only because a number of political theorists continue to assert that libertarianism is, after all, a line in liberalism (see Plant 1997) but also because important aspects of the critique I offer in the later parts of this chapter and the next chapter are also relevant for almost all versions of liberal ideas of justice, including that of Rawls. In this sense, the term 'neoliberal' relates to the fact that, in both formulations, the 'principles' of justice are derived from an essentially reductionist and atomistic perspective (cf. Goodwin 1987; Williams 1995; Plant 1991). Reductionism concerns the belief that explanations of social and political theory should begin with the behaviour of individual actors rather than the structure of a society (Walker 1989: 175). And by atomism, I mean that both perspectives hold that the framework of justice must be such that it promotes, as Sagoff (1995: 171) puts it, 'the interests of individuals, independent of social interests and preferences'.

I also adopt the term 'neoliberal' to highlight strongly the relationship between these two ideas of justice and the prevailing neoliberal political and economic ideology, which has at its core 'the norm that trade should be free and open' (Humphreys 1996: 216) or, as Holifield (2004: 286) puts it, 'a commitment to extending the competitive relations of the market as far as possible [while] keeping state intervention to a minimum'.[1] So, I will use the term 'neoliberal' with reference to these two key aspects while reserving the term 'libertarian' for the times when I refer to aspects that are specific features of the two ideas of justice under focus.

Another point of clarification relates to the use of the terminology 'contractarian justice'. In some of the literature, Rawlsian justice is referred to as contractarian justice, in which case it falls into the group I reserve here for Gauthier and Harman. But even though Rawlsian justice is in some sense contractarian, it nevertheless differs significantly from justice as mutual advantage and justice as entitlement such as to make any conflation (none of which is intended here) inapposite. Rawls attempted to derive a theory of social justice by modelling socio-political co-operation, indeed entire morality, on a 'contract between parties who are already committed to some shared moral life' (Williams 1995: 556). Rawls' main argument is that it is possible, indeed predictable, that rational men, who all have a capacity for and sense of justice, will agree to a given formulation of justice as long as they are shielded from the knowledge of such personal attributes, which, although extraneous to justice, often work to prompt people to skew or want to skew the principles of justice to their own advantage. Hence, Rawls' formulation of justice, although contractual like those of Gauthier and Harman, has a different emphasis, principally because it assumes that the individuals wishing to co-operate are themselves imbued with self-originating moral claims which are not merely conferred upon them at the instance of the co-operative arrangement, hence their claim for fair treatment, irrespective of their talents and abilities (see Chapter 3). For Rawls then, the contract device serves only to give content to what these natural duties of justice are, whereas Gauthier denies that such inherent moral status (residing in) can be attributed to any man who is unable to benefit or harm us. In sum, it is important to stress that the terms and classification adopted here are based mainly on methodological convenience. I do not seek as my main aim to deny or establish a relationship between these conceptions of justice.

Nozick's theory of justice as 'entitlement'

Although adherents of justice as entitlement are divided over the kind of state (minimal or nightwatchman) that would be ideal, they are 'united in their support for a right to private property and their rejection of a right to welfare' (Sterba 1986: 1). Thus, this version of the neoliberal conception of justice holds that the right of property – which they use to include the negative rights to life and the right to freedom – 'trumps' any other kind of right that people may lay claim to in a given society. Proponents of justice as property rights insist that individuals, in their pursuit and acquisition of private property, have rights that may not be violated, unless, perhaps, adequate compensation is paid to the 'victims' (Nozick 1974: ix). 'This particular right over things', according to Nozick, 'fills the space of rights, leaving no room for general rights to be in a certain material condition' (Nozick 1974: 238).

As already noted, Nozick drew much of his inspiration from the writings of John Locke on property rights. Locke defended the right of ordinary English citizens to own property against the then prevailing feudal laws. His argument was to show that all men had a natural right to life; that an inviolable right to property was an intimate part of this right to life; and that the essential part of property ownership was the application of labour. The starting thesis is that all natural resources were given to man freely by God and that any one man comes to own a given piece of these resources by mixing his labour with the hitherto unowned part. Once this requirement is satisfied, the person who has mixed their labour with the part comes to own it as much as they own their life. To take this property away from them without adequate compensation may not be equal in gravity to taking their life, but both acts amount to similar acts of injustice.

In his entitlement theory Nozick is concerned with three aspects of distributive justice. The first aspect is the original acquisition of the holding, that is how initially unheld things may come to be held (he calls this the principle of initial appropriation). The second is the transfer of holdings from one person to another, that is the process through which one may legitimately transfer or acquire property that has been initially appropriated. The third is the principle of rectification of justice, that is how to deal with holdings when they are unjustly transferred. Nozick outlines three definitions, which he believes exhaustively cover the subject of distributive justice in holdings (Nozick 1974: 345):

1   A person who acquires a holding in accordance with the principle of justice in acquisition is entitled to that holding.
2   A person who acquires a holding in accordance with the principle of justice in transfer from someone else entitled to the holding is entitled to that holding.
3   No one is entitled to a holding except by repeated applications of 1 and 2.

According to Nozick, if we assume that everyone is entitled to their current holding, then the complete principle of distributive justice would say simply that a distribution is just if everyone is entitled to the holdings they possess under the distribution. A distribution is just if it arises from another just distribution by legitimate means, the legitimate means of moving from one distribution to another being specified by the principle of justice in transfer. Whatever arises from a just situation by just steps is in itself just (Nozick 1974: 151).

In focusing on the history of acquisition and the legitimacy of transfers, Nozick hails his theory as being unique and superior to other theories of justice that focus *merely* on the end result of distribution. He regards all such patterned theories as being mistaken (ibid.: 155). 'Patterned theories of justice focus on structural features of a society' (Bogart 1985: 828): they operate by simulating broader social conditions via the analysis of selected relations among individuals or groups from which a suitable or combination of suitable principles of distributive justice are articulated. Thus, Rawls' difference principle is an example of a patterned theory.

Nozick points out that the general outline of his entitlement theory seeks to illuminate the nature of the defects of pattern theories of justice, which he describes as *current time-slice* or *end-result* principles of justice (Nozick 1974: 153, 155, italics in the original). The defects of these theories, he claims, lie in their erroneous conception of justice as being based on 'matrices representing only current information about distribution' (ibid.: 149). Nozick rejects these kinds of theories because they are 'overly concerned' with who gets what, without paying enough attention to the process by which the 'what' was acquired (ibid.: 154–159). To illustrate, Nozick argues that, if it makes no sense for us to speak of the sentence a prisoner is serving without referring to the nature of his offence, it would not, in the same vein, be plausible to speak about inequality of resources without an examination of the history of the distribution. He writes:

> If some persons are in prison for murder or war crimes, we do not say that to assess the justice of the distribution in the society we must look only at what this person has, and that person has, ... at the current time. We think it relevant to ask whether someone did something so that he *deserved* to be punished, deserved to have a lower share.
>
> (Ibid.: 154, both ellipsis and italics in the original)

According to Nozick, a 'historical' (ibid.: 153) account of justice enables us to escape from the temptation of merely considering what a person has in relation to another and to focus on the more relevant information, which, to him, is the process of appropriation. He says that this ought to be so because 'whatever one gets he gets from others in exchange of something or as a gift' (ibid.: 149–151). 'To think', he says, 'that the task of a theory of distributive justice is to fill in the blank in "to each according to his ___" is to be predisposed to search for a pattern' (ibid.: 159).

The main objection of Nozick to patterned theories of justice is that their application always requires some form of continuous intervention and redistribution of what has already been distributed. Because people largely acquire whatever property they have in exchange for something – time, labour, talent, services, etc.

– or as gifts, it follows, according to Nozick, that stepping in at some point or repeated points to redistribute according to, say, need or any other such criterion means doing a great injustice to members of the society who have, by the conscientious use of their time and skills under the existing legal framework, acquired more wealth or property than others. According to Nozick, people deserve to own whatever they have legitimately acquired and it cannot be taken away from them, even through tax, without violating a most basic right.

Now, Nozick accepts that there is something intuitively wrong about allowing the weak and infirm to starve to death while the rich enjoy. He denies that he is against the idea of helping people. Nor does he think, he says, that people should not be blamed when they do not help other people or give to charity. The only problem he has is if someone seeks to elevate such help to a status of right comparable to that of property ownership. He writes:

> The major objection to speaking of everyone's having right to various things such as equality of opportunity, life, and so on, and enforcing this right, is that these 'rights' require a substructure of things and materials and actions; and other people may have rights and entitlements over these. No one has the right to something whose realisation requires certain uses of things and activities that other people have rights and entitlements over.
>
> (Ibid.: 237–238)

In this statement we see an intimate connection between Nozick's idea of justice and some of the arguments that have been used by anti-cosmopolitans to reject the notion of global distributional justice (see Chapter 3). According to this view, it might be acceptable for the South and those sympathetic to their cause to make passionate appeals for more international aid or Official Development Assistance. What is not permitted, though, is for these appeals to be made on the platform of distributional justice because the Northern governments and their citizens have rights and entitlements over their resources. Moreover, this idea of justice emphasizes the central role of the market in the allocation of the benefits and burdens of social co-operation. Given that the workings of the free market are deemed inherently just, the discourse of justice, according to this view, should be limited to fleshing out the rules of market transactions and strengthening such rules up to the point that they can virtually work independently of national and international political systems.

Justice as self-interested reciprocity

David Gauthier is arguably the most forceful contemporary advocate of justice as self-interested reciprocity but he proceeds to construct a theory of justice and morality on the basis of game theoretic assumptions. To this end, Gauthier's ideas are shared intimately by the works of Robert Keohane and many other liberal institutionalists, who attempt to explain international co-operation strictly on the basis of bargaining and game theories. In his *Morals by Agreement* (1986)

130 *Normative critique*

Gauthier completely denies that there is any inherent morality in man. What is often referred to as a moral code, he says, is, in reality, a conventional construction of a social contract on the basis of mutually advantageous norms. The obvious implication is that there is no such thing as unchanging moral paradigms or principles handed unto man by a divine being. Rather, what we call morality today is nothing but a conglomerate of tiny rules designed by man to facilitate social and economic interaction in ways that will maximally enhance the mutual advantage of all those involved. Watt Forste (1986), hence, describes Gauthier's thesis as an attempt to explain 'moral constraints as a spontaneous order arising from rational utility-maximizing behavior'.

Similarly, for Harman (1983), because all morality is a matter of convention, the entire logic of justice collapses into a set of implicit and explicit bargaining norms and conventions resulting in a sort of social compromise. This compromise, he contends, has its root in mutual advantage. 'I don't push you so that you don't push me. You are nice to me so that I will be nice to you' (Harman 1983: 123). Hence, proponents of justice as self-interested reciprocity argue that the entire moral code is generated form rational constraints arising from a non-moral premise of rational choice. As Gauthier (1986: 225) puts it, they are 'strictly speaking a moral artifice in that they mimic the traditional conception of morality but actually proceed from self-interested motivations'. Gauthier appeals to results in rational decision theory and tries to show that it is in each egoistic agent's interests to become what he calls 'a constrained maximiser'– someone who limits his pursuit of self-interest for the interests of others.

Suppose that as the ruler of a coastal state, I am interested, for economic reasons, in whaling but that my neighbour, for cultural or perhaps environmental reasons, prefers that the whales be preserved. Under the reading of justice as mutual advantage it would be perfectly rational, indeed justifiable, for me, irrespective of my neighbour's objections, to continue with my whaling in as much as he can neither harm nor benefit me. As a matter of fact, there really is no independent moral code that my neighbour may invoke to appeal to me. But suppose, in the meantime, that my neighbour has some economic motivation to burn coal within his own territory to generate energy and that a cheap way of doing this deposits harmful pollutants in my backyard as well as in my own part of the river. Again, it would be rational and completely justifiable for him to use what he considers the cheapest and most profitable way of generating energy, irrespective of my complaints. The above is a state of unrestrained conflict, which, according to Hobbes, Gauthier and Hume, represents a perfect state of Nature.

However, through the process of bargaining (this can either be tacit or explicit), my neighbour and I could agree to a convention that prohibits me from whaling (serving my neighbour's interests) and to another that compels my neighbour to find a less-polluting, perhaps more expensive, source of energy generation (serving my interests). Harman and Gauthier insist that all of morality consists only of such micro-agreements and conventions. They appear as moral codes only because either the bargaining occurs more tacitly than explicitly or most of us have been brought up in a society in which such moral codes have been long practised, hence our coming to assume their independent status. 'For them, there are no natural duties or self-originating moral claims' (Kymlicka 2002: 128). Thus, concerning my neighbour and me, the abstinence from whaling and/or polluting is not tied to any independently existing morality such as it is not good to pollute the land of my neighbour or it is not good to overfish. Rather, our abstinence is purely conventional, proceeding from Gauthier's 'constrained maximiser' principle and based on the existence of what Allen Buchanan (1990) calls 'strategic capacity'.

For Allen Buchanan, strategic capacity is the ability that an agent has to offer benefit or cause harm to another agent. So, in this case, my neighbour's strategic capacity is the ability to harm me by polluting my farm. At another time, this capacity may be my desire that he votes in my favour in another international convention or that he continues to provide a market for certain of my products other than whales.

Now, intuitively speaking, one may protest that there is something wrong with such a conception of justice, which depends entirely on convention and approves the use of power in a bargaining environment. However, proponents of justice as mutual advantage are not unaware that their theory is intuitively perverse. But the validity of such intuitions is exactly what is at issue. Hence, they encourage us to do away with 'groundless feelings' and embrace rationality, for sentiments offer no basis for alternative theories to justice. As Harman puts it:

> [t]here is really nothing to worry about, as moral codes arrived at through these tacit and explicit bargaining process are no less helpful in maintaining a harmonious society than the so-called inherent ones. [. . .] If it becomes generally believed that justice rests on bargaining in which self-interest plays a major role, then the bargaining between the rich and the powerful on the one hand and the poor and weak on the other will become more explicit. I see no reason to think the result will be much different from our current moral consensus, which is the result of implicit bargaining.
> (Harman 1990: 545)

Gauthier (1986: 254) further assures us that these conventions, which are 'generated as rational constraints from non-moral premises of rational choice', are in themselves robust enough to sustain commodious living because, over time, they would, in any case, acquire the status of independent moral codes, thus 'mimicking' traditional morality.

Expressions of libertarian conceptions of justice in the three multilateral environmental agreements

Having reviewed once again the main ideas of the two neoliberal theories of justice, the next task is to demonstrate that most of the core policies of the three environmental regimes studied are underpinned by these ideas of justice. To start with, we note again the ways in which these two ideas of justice relate. The first is that they relate in their aversion to any form of welfare-based or egalitarian notions

132 *Normative critique*

of justice. Second, they relate in their emphasis on the liberty of individuals as opposed to the welfare of the community. And third, they relate in their attempt to secure minimal state interference in economic activities as well as in the weight they allocate to property rights and plural conceptions of the good (cf. Luper-Foy 1992: 47–49; Plant 1997; Kymlicka 2002: 102–163).

Furthermore, it is important to emphasize that these theories were not originally formulated with the purpose of guiding politics between states. The development of these theories and the debates around them have, for years, been undertaken within the context of national political systems. These constraints notwithstanding, contemporary scholars have continued to explore the implications of applying them at the international level (Beitz 1979; Pogge 1988, 1994; Barry 1989; Luper-Foy 1992; Palmer 1995; Dobson 1998; Beckerman and Pasek 2001; Caney 2001; Kymlicka 2002). The justification for this seems to lie in the evidence that states, either because there is no overarching theory of international justice or simply for self-seeking purposes, seek to push for policies in their dealings at the international level which bear a very close affinity with these interpretations of justice.

However, it still has to be acknowledged that, although it is possible to recast the original arguments of these principles of justice along the lines of international justice without doing great injustice to the core assumptions, there remain ways in which shifting the context from individuals to states presents some analytical difficulties. There are times when states, guided by the notion of equality, tend to treat each other as individuals on the international scene, but there are other times when the ideas of justice work more indirectly in the sense that states who adhere closely to their principles feel committed to promote certain kinds of policies or that they are unable to endorse certain programmes, irrespective of compelling reasons why they should act differently. This point will become clearer as I discuss in the following sections how these notions of justice are expressed in the regimes. The discussion is organized under five broad headings: (i) a general aversion to resource redistribution on the basis of welfare; (ii) an overriding emphasis on property rights; (iii) an emphasis on free market solutions to environmental problems; (iv) approval of the use of power and other bargaining chips in negotiating agreements; and (v) the focus on states rather than individuals as the locus of rights.

Aversion to welfare-based resource redistribution

James Bogart (1985) has submitted that every political theory has at least one 'root' idea. He defines root ideas as those which constitute fundamental moral commitments. They constitute the bedrock principles and concepts of which the more sophisticated critical theories serve as an explanation (Bogart 1985: 832). In his essay *Lockean Provisos and State of Nature Theories* (1985: 832–833), Bogart argues that the root idea which Nozick presents in the entitlement theory of justice falls under the general rubric of 'separateness of persons'. This general rubric has three offshoots: first, that no person is a resource for any other person; second, that each person owns their body and labour; and third, that what people are entitled to is a function of what they legitimately acquire by their efforts or what is freely given. The second and the third, according to Bogart, are predicated on the first, which is the basic idea.

Nozick's argument, according to Cohen (1986), seeks to show that each person is the morally rightful owner of himself. 'He possesses over himself as a matter of moral right all those rights that a slave holder has over a complete chattel slave as a matter of legal rights' (Cohen 1986: 378), and respecting these rights is a 'necessary aspect of respecting people's claim to be treated as ends in themselves, not means to others' (Kymlicka 2002: 108).[2] Nozick, therefore, shares with Locke the idea of self-sovereignty.[3] This implies that, when one mixes one's labour with unheld things, such acquired properties belong to the labourer, much as the talents or power which were used to acquire the goods. It follows, then, for Nozick that any scheme which seeks to commit one to part with one's legally acquired properties involuntarily cannot be consistent with the demands of social justice. For Luper-Foy (1992: 49), this position accords with what he calls the 'liberty maximizing principle' in which each party in the international community seeks to secure the most extensive 'scheme of liberties consistent with guaranteeing the same scheme for all'. He further suggests that, in the event that there are no explicit existing claims over a given resource, the libertarian notion of justice would favour appropriation on a first come, first served principle on the basis that it offers everybody an equal chance to appropriate natural resources.

The principal objection of Western countries, but especially the USA, to the common heritage of mankind principle (Third United Nations Conference on the Law of the Sea; UNCLOS III) relates to the fact that its application was generally regarded as likely to generate some form of resource redistribution on the basis of need, welfare and common ownership. Friedheim (1993: 229), for instance, argues that, although there was no common agreement on the definition of the 'common heritage of mankind', the concept nevertheless came to be quickly associated with 'a set of specific features of the deep seabed management that embodied a new conceptual framework which stressed an equitable international economic system and special compensatory benefits to the less advantaged within the international community'. This was why, according to Friedheim (1993: 230), it became widely supposed that the concept of the common heritage of mankind was essentially 'the ocean manifestation of a New International Economic Order (NIEO)'. Friedheim (1993: 221) identifies these specific features as: (i) the termination of the first come, first served basis of appropriation of ocean resources; (ii) the establishment of an 'Enterprise' whose function was geared towards the protection of the interests of the weaker states; (iii) the establishment of the International Seabed Authority with emphasis on equitable representation and redistribution along egalitarian lines; and (iv) ensuring production control and the transfer of technology in ways that favour the less advantaged within the international community.

In general, then, it was thought that the ocean resources could be used to counteract the economic disadvantages suffered by the developing countries (Friedheim 1993; Vogler 2000). It was for these expressed commitments to welfare-based redistribution that the USA rejected the Convention. Friedheim (1993: 221) argues that these aspirations were 'an anathema' to the developed countries because they did not adequately reflect the need to protect industry, labour and investment along the lines of justice as self-ownership described above. Hence, it was important from the perspective of ideology to ensure that a precedent was not set which would encourage pressure for a total conceptual shift in international economic relations. As he puts it:

> Ocean mining was equally symbolic for some major capitalist states. They viewed an NIEO-based minerals regime as unworkable under any set of conceivable circumstances, and insulting as well. It had to be defeated, and states brought to their senses, so that they would support a conceptual framework that provided a proper guide to operating the world economy. The larger issue of avoiding a bad precedent was more important than establishing an ocean industry.
>
> (Friedheim 1993: 230)

It was for this same reason – preserving the free market ideology – that some in the US Senate during the negotiation of UNCLOS III proceeded to dismiss the notion of a common heritage of mankind as 'nothing more or less than declaring a right to steal'. These senators considered it 'absurd' that the USA should be drawn into negotiations which, in practice, amounted to attempts to legalize international socialism (see Chapter 4). It was this and similar characterizations that largely informed the decision of the USA to eventually drop out of the negotiations into the seabed regime during the last stages of UNCLOS III.

The negative role of the US Senate in determining the posture and eventual shape of the seabed regime resonates with the more recent role of the same Senate in not only shaping the Kyoto Protocol but also ultimately stalling its successful operation. Senators Chuck Hagel and Robert Byrd had, in proposing the motion against a US commitment to a specified quantified emission reduction target, argued that such an approach to solving any perceived climate change problem which did not involve reasonable commitments from the developing countries was tantamount to the resurrection of the NIEO ideals with its commitment to endless resource redistribution at a global level. It was essentially the posture of the US Senate and their efforts to link the Kyoto Protocol with the NIEO agenda of global resource redistribution that made it politically unreasonable for President Clinton to even attempt submitting the document to the Senate for ratification. Equally, in arguing against the proposal by the developing country parties for the establishment of a separate operator of the financial mechanism of the United Nations Framework Convention on Climate Change (UNFCCC), the developed country parties made it clear that they would not back any mechanism which was not under the direct control and/or supervision of well-established international financial bodies such as the International Monetary Fund (IMF) or the World Bank. But although, as Tariq Hyder (1994: 223) argues, the developed country parties relied mainly on the arguments of efficiency and cost-effectiveness, it was really

Establishing the core ideas of justice in eco-regimes 135

a determination to avoid any form of welfare-based redistribution, he says, that underpinned this approach.

Overriding emphasis on property rights

Each of the three regimes analysed provides sufficient evidence that parties regularly employ and are highly attracted to property rights-based arguments in the design of international environmental policies. Indeed, it would appear that the core of most of the debates that take place during regime development has to do, in one way or another, with the attempts by states or corporate interests to establish and/or redefine the nature of property rights that exist with respect to the given issue-area. For example, the whole debate over the territorial sea, the contiguous zone, the exclusive economic zone (EEZ), the high sea and the seabed in UNCLOS III was in large part about the nature and degree of property rights that might be allocated to coastal states as against the maritime and the non-coastal states (Churchill and Lowe 1983: 73).

It is a sure mark of the ascendancy of property rights-based approaches to global environmental management that the limit of the territorial sea, which had customarily stood at 3 nautical miles for over half a century, was extended by over 300 per cent at UNCLOS III. This massive extension, according to Ghosh (1980: 37), was permitted mainly because states had generally bought into the arguments the imperative for enclosure. Hence, the territorial sea regime, according to Ghosh, stands on the basis of the doctrine that 'states must have control over ships within its territorial sea for fiscal and political reasons, and over resources thereof for its economic well-being' (ibid.: 37). However, this new right given to coastal states to extend their territorial sea up to 12 nautical miles (Article 3), was, as pointed out in Chapter 2, accepted subject to the adoption of a new legal regime, which again established limited property rights – in this case, the rights of innocent passage for ships and aircraft from naval and non-coastal states. Accordingly, Ghosh (1980) argues that at the heart of the tussle over the limits of the territorial sea in UNCLOS III was how to balance the claims for exclusive property rights by coastal states with the claims for inclusive property rights by the naval powers.

At the same time, the regimes of the continental shelf and the EEZ, as elaborated at UNCLOS III (Articles 55–85), clearly show the overwhelming power of property rights discourses within the context of global environmental governance. The argument during the Conference was between those who favoured a communal-based approach to the management of the resources in the oceans and high seas through international regulations and co-operative schemes and those who felt that these areas of the sea should be 'divided up' and made the 'national property of states' (Birnie and Boyle 2002: 660–661). For Tommy T. B. Koh (2001), the debate over the EEZ regime is best understood as a contestation for property rights between coastal states seeking greater control over the sea for various reasons (fiscal, security, political, etc.) and distant water fishing states seeking to maintain the fishing and navigation rights they had under the traditional law of the

136 *Normative critique*

sea. It was pointed out in Chapter 4 that a number of politico-economic developments in the global arena between the time of the First United Nation Conference on the Law of the Sea (UNCLOS I) and UNCLOS III seriously tilted the balance in favour of the coastal states. The most important of these developments was the ascendancy of the neoliberal economic ideology, especially as expressed in the Truman Declaration of 1945, under which the USA enclosed vast portions of the sea, which belonged, until that point, to the entire global community (Borgese 1986, Sanger 1986). It was the Truman Declaration of 1945 that set the stage for the various claims and counterclaims of rights over extensive portions of the oceans and high seas, the result of which is now the 'enclosure' of about 36 per cent of the sea and 90 per cent of its resources (Boezek 1984; Vogler 2000).

Similarly, the controversy that was associated with the seabed regime and the common heritage of mankind principle arose, according to Friedheim (1993: 222–223), because some of the proposals from the developing country parties presented 'a challenge to the distribution of power in world politics and economics' and an affront to the 'general structure of the world economic system'. The common heritage of mankind principle promised a wide deviation from the dominant doctrine of enclosure and, although the developing countries showed that the seabed offered a unique opportunity for innovative pluralistic management approaches, the USA and its allies, for the reason of 'ideological purity' (ibid. 1993: 247), refused to sign the Convention. Friedheim (1993: 290–291) captures the situation very well:

> Despite some softening of the Group of 77's position, its willingness to make concessions was not enough for the United States, who chose to call the question, force a vote and vote against the Convention. The United States was not alone in refusing consent to the seabed portion of the agreement. In all, 21 states voted against or abstained from approving the Convention. . . . In each, the government in power is committed to private-sector solutions to economic problems, and with the end of the Cold War, have even less incentive to make concession to socialist solutions.

Of course, libertarians contend that it is their desire that everybody be happy and fulfilled. The only problem, they say, is that they cannot see any other means of doing this except through unlimited property rights and free market liberalism (cf. Hayek 1960; Anderson and Leal 1991; Bhagwati 1993). They therefore argue that to succumb to the environmentalists' appeal for welfare and state interference in the market would amount to sacrificing others limitlessly for the welfare of the poor South (Rowlands 1997; cf. Hardin 1972; Nozick 1974: 30–31, 33). Accordingly, libertarians would advocate for international regimes that are determinedly committed to the protection of the property rights of state parties. According to this view, the main goal of co-operation would be to strengthen the institutions required to enhance free exchange, and considerations of justice would focus primarily on assessing the validity and legitimacy of claims and counterclaims of ownership. Indeed, this was in large part the disposition of many developed country parties during the articulation of UNCLOS III, the Basel Convention and the UNFCCC. It is this disposition that, in part, accounts for the frequent reiteration (in almost all global environmental regimes) of the rights of states to exploit resources within their sovereignty in accordance with standard international law (UNCHE 1972; UNCED 1992; UNFCCC preamble; UNCLOS preamble; Basel preamble). It was on the basis of this economic world view that the USA, during the negotiation of the climate change regime, rejected proposals for the transfer of technology to the developing countries on non-commercial terms, arguing that such moves would be 'incompatible with the protection of Intellectual Property Rights' (Dasgupta 1994; 135). It was also on grounds of ideology that the USA, during the negotiation of the seabed regime, insisted that the role of the 'Enterprise' should be limited to issuing licences to states and corporations who wished to exploit the resources in the seabed (Chapter 4).

The rejection of the common heritage of mankind principle in relation to the global atmosphere as proposed at the UN in 1988 by the President of Malta, as well as the opposition to the ban on the shipment of hazardous wastes into Africa, can also be seen as being underpinned by the desire for 'ideological purity' by the USA and its Western allies. When the Maltese President, following in the footsteps of his fellow countryman Arvid Pardo, proposed that the global atmosphere should be declared the common heritage of mankind, the developed countries objected to this terminology. They argued that the nature of the atmosphere was different from that of the seabed and that there are senses in which the atmosphere can be regarded as the property of states (Birnie and Boyle 2002: 516). And in the case of hazardous wastes they maintained that a ban on shipment constituted a violation of the rights of individuals and corporations to property and trade (Krueger 1999: 43; Agarwal *et al*. 2001). In advocating this approach they hoped, in each case, to steer away from policies that might encourage distributional and collectivistic approaches to global resource management.

Emphasis on free market solutions to environmental problems

A key manifestation of parties' allegiances to the neoliberal economic regime and its preferred versions of justice in the design of global environmental policies can be seen in the ever-increasing emphasis on free market- and private sector-based solutions to environmental problems. Libertarians conceive of an ideal market as an arena in which free individuals (free in the sense that there is no market regulation) deploy their resources, powers and talents in a bid to acquire more property (Hayek 1960; Nozick 1974). And, as individuals own their powers, they also own whatever comes from the exercise of those powers in the marketplace, such that whatever one acquires by mixing one's labour with becomes one's own as much as one owns one's body. Libertarians believe that the 'unseen hand' has the ability to deal to each person his rightful portion of wealth and property through the working of the forces of demand and supply. The amount that each person receives will be commensurate with the extent to which they utilize their resources, power and

138 *Normative critique*

talent in the marketplace. Proponents of international free trade also use similar arguments. They contend that states should employ their comparative advantages to gain maximally from an open international economic system, which ultimately works to the benefit of all states (Bhagwati 1991, 1993).

When pressed, libertarians admit that the working of the market may result in a sharp increase in material inequality, but they insist that even the worse-off are still better in overall terms as the wealth of the rich eventually trickles down to the poor to create an average increase in general economic well-being (Bhagwati 1993). Most developed country parties argue during environmental negotiations (e.g. United Nations Conference on Environment and Development; UNCED) that growth in the North increases the market for Southern resource exports as well as funds for aid and investment by the North in the South. They discount the opposing view that this growth makes things worse by 'pre-empting the remaining resources and ecological space needed to support Southern growth' (Daly 1994: 185 fn. 2).

Anderson and Leal (1991), for instance, seek to assure us that: 'To the extent that actions can be effectively measured and monitored, demanders and suppliers will internalize costs and benefits, profits will be made, and efficient resource allocation will be a by-product' (Anderson and Leal 1991: 10). The point, however, is that libertarians are, deep down, generally unimpressed by arguments on the limits to growth and the distributional implications of the concept of environmental sustainability. Despite occasional 'green speak', their propositions fundamentally run on the premise of a superabundance of resources and on 'the promise of perpetual material growth' (Meadows *et al.* 1992: xvi). The libertarian model equally assumes, according to Munda (1997), complete commensurability between natural and manmade resources as well as the possibility of value-neutral assessment and estimation of environmental resources. These factors combined explain the general monetization of national and international environmental policies as well as the emphasis on market and cost–benefit analysis in global environmental governance (Daly 1994; Leff 1996; Sachs 1999; Bachram 2005).

In pressing for prior informed consent (PIC) together with the national definitions of waste to become the core policies of the Basel Convention, developed country parties argued that these approaches were in keeping with the demands for international justice and equity because they allow each state party to define what constitutes hazardous waste in line with their specific needs. PIC, in particular, was presented as an opportunity for both the developed and developing country parties to employ their comparative advantages by trading in toxic wastes (Krueger 1998: 118–119). In this way, the developed country parties implied that it was perfectly in order for developing country parties, who have an advantage in land mass, to import toxic wastes from the industrialized countries (Tolba 1990: 206; Strohm 1993: 133; Clapp 2001: 23). This assertion is advanced regardless of the health hazards posed by these dangerous wastes and regardless of the fact that a cargo of toxic waste that costs about US$2.50 to dump in Africa sometimes costs about US$500 to be disposed of in the USA.

The need to respect the market was also the main reason for the adoption of the so-called flexible mechanism and the emission trading schemes as the main policies of the UNFCCC and the Kyoto Protocol. The developed country parties, especially the USA, were determined to veto any proposal that did not respect the need for the free market, capital investments, industrial competition and minimum state interference in the running of corporations. Such proposals were branded inefficient, wasteful or simply unworkable (Paterson 1996b: 54–60). Throughout the negotiation process and well beyond, the USA has been insistent on the fact that efficient and equitable climate change policies require not only the most extensive use of market instruments but also the 'reasonable' commitment of all states including the poor developing countries. And yet, the former head of the US delegation to the INC, William Nitze, who had also been the head of the US delegation to the Intergovernmental Panel on Climate Change (IPCC), now accepts that the position of the USA was not so much based on a 'rational assessment of the national interest in the light of facts [as it was] on a volatile mixture of ideology and politics' (Nitze 1994: 189). He writes:

> The internal policy debate [within the US government] was driven by the ideological preoccupations of a small circle of presidential advisors led by former Chief of Staff John Sununu. These men believed that the climate change issue was being used by environmentalists to impose their 'anti-growth agenda' on the US economy. This perception made it difficult for them to see that they could have linked increased investment in energy efficiency, renewable energy and other technologies to reduce greenhouse gas emissions with a market-oriented, pro-growth agenda.
>
> (Ibid.: 189)

Strange (1983, 1987) and Paterson (1996b) are among the many scholars who have reflected on the series of policy constraints incurred by states as a result of their commitment to the prevailing neoliberal economic regime. Strange (1987) argues that the transformation of states from distributors of wealth to rivals competing for investment in a globalized world means, for one, that economic efficiency and cost-effectiveness has become the sole criteria by which the viability of a given environmental policy is assessed. Emphasis is thus on policies that offer states and corporations greater space for economic manoeuvre and the quickest return of investments. Paterson (1996b: 169) captures the point well in the following:

> The effect of neoliberalism has been to narrow available policy options. Discussion of environmental questions in general has been severely curtailed by its dominance. . . . Also Neoliberalism has led to environmental economics being almost exclusively concerned with 'market-based solutions'. These dominate policy debate in global warming with the advantages of 'market mechanisms' over 'command and control' regulations often regurgitated, rather in the form of mantra.

The use of power and other 'chips' in the bargaining environment

Nozick, as has been pointed out in earlier sections, promotes his theory of justice because it emphasizes history and procedure in ways that he claims are not recognized by 'end-state' theories of justice, such as, say, justice as need. He believes that a given distribution (no mater how unequal the outcome) is just as long as it is in accordance with the appropriate societal rules (cf. Gauthier 1986). Libertarians generally maintain, as Bogart (1985: 828) puts it, that 'the justness of a society is marked by the conformance of the society to procedural principles'. Further, Nozick is not opposed to the use of power or other bargaining chips in the cause of negotiating an agreement, provided, he says, that such powers are not used in ways that cause direct harm to the other parties (Nozick 1974: 169).

However, for Gauthier and Harman, like Hobbes, there is no limit to how much agents might use their power to their advantage in a bargaining situation. Indeed, for these theorists, the likelihood of the success of a bargaining solution depends to a large degree on the extent to which the agreement reflects the power symmetry of the co-operating agents. 'The relevant principles', according to Harman, 'are the principles that *actually are* accepted, not those that *would be* agreed to under certain conditions of "initial equality" or "constrained neutral dialogue"' (Harman 1983: 122). Gauthier (1986: 21) brings out this point even more clearly when he insists that 'rational men' cannot be expected to acquiesce to principles of distribution that do not reflect what they would have hoped to get for themselves in the absence of social co-operation. Enduring agreement is possible, he says, only when these rational men view 'society as a means of producing and distributing an optimal social surplus. They will only accept principles of distribution if they restrict their scope to the surplus, and apportion it in accordance with the contribution each makes to its production' (Gauthier 1986: 23). Theorists of justice as mutual advantage thus propose that the mutual interests of those participating in an agreement or co-operative venture are fairly served by agreements which simulate what the agents would have hoped to get in the absence of co-operation. Bargaining solutions that deviate radically from this Pareto frontier, they say, are unrealistic as they are most likely to place an undue burden on the powerful. Such agreements would be merely hypothetical and there would be a lot of incentives to break them (Gauthier 1986; cf. Barry 1989: 52–54).

It is reasonable to infer that the great allowances often made by the developing and the majority of the other developed country parties to accommodate the position of the USA during the negotiation phases of most international environmental agreements proceed from this logic. During the elaboration process of the UNFCCC, for example, the USA maintained a hard-line stance. It put forward its position and was not willing to compromise on any of the key issues. 'The United States', as Borione and Ripert (1994: 82) well observed, 'adopted certain clear-cut positions even before the start of the negotiation and was not afraid to appear isolated'. Eventually, it was the other Organization for Economic Co-operation and Development (OECD) countries, most of whom would have wanted tough action to combat climate change, that had to beat a retreat to accommodate the position of the USA. It is not surprising, then, that the leader of the US negotiating team to the INC, Mr Nitze, should boast of the performance of his team:

> The US achieved its major negotiating goals in the final agreed text of the convention signed in Rio. It avoided a binding commitment to hold its CO_2 emissions below a specified level by a certain date, won agreement on the so-called 'comprehensive approach', and persuaded all of the world's major countries in an ongoing process for addressing the problems that is consistent with the US proposals.
>
> (Nitze 1994: 188)

But perhaps of even greater import with respect to the discussion in this section is the reason that Mr Nitze offers for this overwhelming victory. He says:

> The US success in achieving its major negotiating goals resulted from the unwillingness of either the other OECD countries or the major countries to sign an agreement without the participation of the US. These countries *determined for themselves* that an otherwise well-structured convention with non-binding language on short term targets that could be signed by the US was preferable to a similar convention with binding language that was not signed by the US. Many delegates argued that this approach was probably justified by the need for active US participation in shaping a successful international strategy for addressing climate change.
>
> (Ibid.: 188)

The USA has also relied on this logic – i.e. that countries would naturally determine for themselves the need to retreat to accommodate the USA – a couple of other times in the elaboration of international environmental regimes. During the negotiation of the Basel Convention, the USA at one point resorted to a take-it-or-leave-it approach. Specifically, they asked the developing countries to either accept PIC or risk having no Convention at all (Puckett 1992: 97). However, even though PIC was eventually accepted, the USA declined to sign the Convention. It argued that some of the other clauses, such as the duty to re-import wastes, were inconsistent with accepted notions of free trade (Krueger 1999: 56). During the latter part of the UNCLOS III negotiations, the USA also relied on this logic to get the G-77 to drop some of its most cherished proposals on how the seabed regime might be made more equitable (Sanger 1986: 187). Even though delegates had extensively discussed (for more than 6 years) many of the key points and were expecting a last-minute compromise from everybody, the USA went back to its pre-conference position and circulated in the so-called 'Green Book' a number of proposals that, in effect, demanded the complete and total surrender of the G-77 (Friedheim 1993: 262). However, although these proposals were successfully resisted to the annoyance of the USA, it has eventually managed, through the 'Boat Paper' agreement, to get the seabed regime into a shape that fits its ideology. In their analysis of the collapse of the sixth Conference of Parties (COP) to the UN-FCCC in The Hague in December 2000, Grubb and Yamin (2001) see the main problem as essentially a dilemma on the part of the other parties on whether it was better to proceed without the USA or to bend over backwards to accommodate its demands, even though some of these demands 'would simply have had the effect of rewriting the targets agreed three years earlier' (Grubb and Yamin 2001: 147).

Ridley and Low (1993) have recently come out fully to back the idea that the pursuit of sustainability through multilateral environmental agreements could be made more effective by recognizing the interests and power asymmetry in the negotiation processes. They argue that making self-interests more explicit during negotiation processes is the best way 'to avert global ecological disaster'. It is high time, they say, 'that we tapped the boundless and renewable resource: the human propensity for mainly thinking of short term interests rather than appealing to some form of rare altruistic behaviour that cost the performer and benefit someone else' (Ridley and Low 1993: 3). By being more overt about the interests and power asymmetry, Ridley and Low imagine, in line with theorists of justice as mutual advantage, that institutions for global environmental governance would be able to enact policies that parties would, in practice, wish to respect.

Focus on states as the locus of rights

The analysis undertaken in Part II confirms that states are still the main foci and actors in institutional arrangements concerned with the distribution of global environmental resources. Although there is some evidence that the roles of international civil society, indigenous groups, non-governmental organizations (NGOs) and the business community are growing, states currently remain the most influential and significant players. In most cases, it was discovered that the roles of these other actors, important as they were, consist essentially of attempts to influence states to act in ways that are in keeping with their particular visions of sustainability, usually with respect to specific issue-areas. At the same time, the analysis reveals that, in discussing the fairness of given policies and programmes, it is the picture of states as agents (recipients and givers) that dominates. Hence, although many mega-environmental conferences contain statements acknowledging individual rights (Chapters 1 and 2), it is generally assumed that it is the job of individual states to secure these rights; however, the inclusion of certain cosmopolitan individual rights terms, such as per capita emissions in the UNFCCC, was identified as an emerging counterpoint to this dominant approach.

The principle that states have the sovereign right to exploit their own resources pursuant to their own environmental and developmental policies (UNCHE 1972: Principle 21) is one of the best known and most frequently repeated in any international treaty. In endorsing the principle of PIC, for example, it was states and not those living in the localities where hazardous wastes might be dumped who were the objects of consideration. The definition of what constitutes hazardous wastes is a *national* prerogative and, as such, cannot be exercised by minority groups who might have reasons to feel that the government is unfairly using their

Establishing the core ideas of justice in eco-regimes   143

land as a dumping ground for toxic wastes. UNCLOS III contains innumerable references to various states' rights with absolutely no concern given to the lot of the (sometimes vulnerable, severely deprived and marginalized) coastal communities. Indeed, a report of the Independent World Commission on the Oceans (IWCO) published in 1998 mentioned the complete neglect of the circumstances of the indigenous people, traditional fishing communities and costal communities as one of the main weaknesses of UNCLOS III (IWCO 1998: 61–63). In a similar manner, the UNFCCC contains several references to countries prone to natural disasters, such as arid, low-lying, small island and mountainous countries; however, even though the Convention contains clear references to the need to give special assistance to these countries to enable them to cope with the threats of climate change [UNFCCC: Article 3 (2), Article 4 (8)], it is not acknowledged anywhere in the text that climate change, even within these vulnerable countries, will affect specific age groups, cultural groups and tribes very differently (Grubb 1995; Paterson 1996b: 13–15).

However, to avoid any confusion it has to be clearly acknowledged once again that the theories of justice under investigation here were not, in their original formulation, designed to offer a guide to interstate relationships. Hence, strictly speaking, it would not be right to attribute the emphasis on states' rights in international regimes to the dominance of market ideas of justice. However, it remains plausible to assume that the circumstances of indigenous peoples, local communities and individuals, rather than states, would get more attention if state parties were drawn to more egalitarian notions of justice in the institutional arrangements for global environmental management.

Resistance and contradictions

It is clear by now that the core policies of international environmental regimes are dominated by neoliberal conceptions of justice. However, it is important to reiterate the point that was made in several places in Part II that these market ideas of justice are not the only ones that can be found in regime texts and policies. Indeed, a central result from the analysis in Part II is that regime texts and policies are characterized by diverse interpretations of justice. In particular, the situation can be conceived of as one in which the poor South presses for the recognition of the ideas of justice that promote global resource redistribution along egalitarian lines, whereas the North prefers the ideas of justice that promote free market capitalism. The analysis in Part II indicates that most of the vagueness and contradictions in regime texts stem from attempts to balance these two competing preferences.

In the case of UNCLOS III (Chapter 4), this tension manifested itself in the simultaneous endorsement of the nationalization of the ocean in accordance with sovereignty and of market-based ideas of justice, as well as in the acceptance of the concept of the common heritage of mankind with agreement with the cosmopolitan interpretations of justice on the principle of need. Part IX of the Law of the Sea in its original form (that is before the 1994 Implementation Agreement) is a finely balanced, intricate piece of international legislation designed to ensure the equitable management and just distribution of the resources of the seabed. The arrangement represents an important vote for solidarist conceptions of the international society and an understanding of international justice that is sensitive to the well-being of the least advantaged members of the international community. Further, in providing for an Authority whose role includes ensuring the 'equitable sharing of financial and other economic benefits derived from the Area ... on a non-discriminatory basis' as well as an Enterprise legally capable of engaging in production and market transactions, the relevant positions of Part IX laid an important groundwork for a possible business arm of the UN, which would work to offset the disadvantages suffered by the marginalized sections of the global community in line with justice as need.

In Chapter 3 it was discovered that the tension between the market ideas of justice and the more egalitarian notions of justice expressed itself, among other ways, in the legitimization of PIC (market-based idea of justice) alongside the duty to re-import waste and undertake technology transfer (need-based idea of justice) and, later, in the ban on hazardous waste trafficking. Although there had always been some provisions in the original convention that empowered individual countries to ban the import of hazardous wastes into their territories, it was the overall ban that ultimately indicated that the international community had rejected the libertarian argument upon which the ban was previously resisted. The philosophy of the ban was simply that the conditions of free trade were not enough to secure the safety of the developing countries or to protect the special needs of the vulnerable communities in line with the objective of the Convention. To this end the Basel Convention has been hailed as a veritable piece of environmental justice legislation.

In the case of the UNFCCC, the resistance against market ideas of justice led to the endorsement of the common but differentiated responsibility principle and the need for additional resource transfer as well as the adoption of different emission stabilization targets for individual countries, all of which seem consistent with the idea of justice as assisting the vulnerable and meeting needs. Furthermore, the act of dividing parties into Annex I and non-Annex I countries and exempting the latter from specific emission reduction obligations, as is the case in the UNFCCC and Kyoto Protocol, is surely an equity-based policy directly connected with the common but differentiated responsibility principle [UNFCCC: Article 4 (1), Article 4 (2.a)]. Specifically, developed country parties are expected to take the lead in modifying their long-term emission trends and to provide financial assistance to the developing country parties [Article 4 (1–10) (5.c) (7.b)]. In this regard, the UNFCCC establishes an important precedent in that the North is required to 'take all practical steps to promote, facilitate and finance the transfer of environmentally sound technology and other resources to the developing countries' (Article 2.5) but also that 'the extent to which developing country parties will effectively implement their commitment under the Convention will depend on the effective implementation of the developed country parties of their commitment under the Convention related to financial resources and transfer of technology' (Article 2.7). In the same article the Convention further states that parties 'will take fully into account that economic and social development and poverty eradication are the first and overriding priorities of the developing country parties'. Also, by admitting the concept of 'historical emissions' into the text, parties acknowledge that the present generation have a duty to care for the environment for future generations and that the developed countries have contributed disproportionately to global emission levels. This concept of causality reinforces the common but differentiated responsibility principle in justifying the demand for industrialized countries to play a leading role in mitigating climate change. Even if one takes the view, as some scholars do, that these differentiated duties are better explained in terms of capability than responsibility, there remains an element of altruism in a situation in which a more capable party agrees to undertake a burden that could possibly have been shared between two materially unequal agents (see Weber 1946: 120).

Conclusion

After establishing the core tenets of justice as entitlement and justice as self-interested reciprocity, this chapter sought to establish a conceptual relationship between the two notions of justice and some of the most important policies in the three contemporary environmental regimes analysed in Part II. It was shown that, although these ideas of justice were not designed in their original formulations to apply between states, they are nevertheless promoted in environmental regimes, mainly because of their close 'fit' with the dominant neoliberal politico-economic ideology. The chapter demonstrates that the rich industrialized countries, who have commanding roles in the international political economy, tend to favour these ideas of justice because it not only helps them to retain their leverage over the developing countries but also ensures that global co-operation towards sustainability does not radically upset some of the core values of these societies. In the final section it was reiterated that the door has not been completely shut because mobilization for the inclusion of other versions of justice continues to create serious ethical tensions in both the language and the policies of regimes. In the next chapter I will confront the dominant neoliberal ideas of justice in regimes with the idea of sustainable development sketched out in the World Commission on Environment and Development (Brundtland Report) to show that neoliberal ideas of justice do not provide a hopeful base for the pursuit of global sustainability.

8 Ethics of global sustainability and neoliberal ideas of justice

In this chapter I confront the core ideas of the two dominant notions of justice (established in Chapter 7) with the ethical prescriptions of sustainable development based on the 1987 Report of the World Commission on Environment and Development. The main objective is to show that these two notions of justice do not offer a promising base for the pursuit of global sustainability in general and North–South environmental equity in particular. This claim is elaborated by highlighting at least four key areas of 'mismatch' (or fault lines) between the core assumptions of the two ideas of justice and the ethical content of the version of sustainable development articulated in the Brundtland Report (*Our Common Future*). These fault lines are concerned with: (i) the degree of elasticity permissible in the conceptualization of the good life; (ii) the role of states in the facilitation of social justice and the promotion of sustainability; (iii) the interdependence of the earth system and its implications for the arguments between subsistence and property rights; and (iv) the notion of limits and the defensibility or indefensibility of certain aspects of enclosure.

Because most, if not all, of these four points touch on classical debates and concepts of politics, it is important to stress from the outset that the discussions in the following sections are not designed to revive, let alone offer definitive answers to, age-old, open-ended debates in the discipline. Rather, they are designed to show only that the positions that proponents of the two ideas of justice under investigation occupy with respect to these fundamental issues will be at variance with those whose analysis starts from a perspective that takes the concept of global sustainable development seriously. For a start, let us establish the idea of justice that is endorsed in the Brundtland conception of sustainable development.

The concept and conception of sustainable development

It should be quickly conceded from the outset that the strongest feature of the concept of sustainable development is not the clarity of its meaning. But although the notion has attracted diverse interpretations, it continues to retain some core elements, which not even its fiercest critics have been able to deny. Of course, some have argued that the conflicting objectives and goals of sustainability make it a useless concept (cf. Beckerman 1994; de Geus 2001). But these kinds of arguments fail, not least because their advocates still recognize that sustainable development has objectives and goals. It seems better then that these arguments should be taken as attempting to show that some of the goals of sustainable development might be irreconcilable rather than that there are no clear objectives (cf. Redclift 1987; Daly 1995; Ozkaynak *et al.* 2004).

This point has been eloquently articulated by Michael Jacobs in two of his essays, *Reflections on the Discourse and Politics of Sustainable Development* (Jacobs 1995) and *Sustainable Development as a Contested Concept* (Dobson 1999). Jacobs draws attention to the fact that, much like other political terms such as liberty and democracy, the contested meaning of sustainable development does nothing to vitiate its core themes. The fact that there are various understandings of how a democratic society should work does not imply, he says, that there is no agreement at the normative level regarding the meaning of democracy. The reason for this, according to Jacobs, is that many of these important concepts operate on 'two-level meanings', the 'general', 'unitary' and usually vague meaning, in which the core idea resides, and the second-level meaning, in which the focus turns to how the concept my be interpreted in practice. Accordingly, Jacobs maintains that the objective of sustainable development has been accepted by the deep greens, the light green capitalists and the technocrats alike. The debate, he says, now revolves around how it should be interpreted and implemented in practice (Jacobs 1995: 4–6; 1999: 25–26).

Jacobs' formulation thus approximates Rawls' distinction between 'concepts' and 'conceptions', which was briefly mentioned in Chapter 3 of this work. For Rawls, concepts are different from conceptions in the sense that 'the concept is the meaning of *the* term while particular conceptions include as well the principles required to apply it' (Rawls 1993: 14). In making a distinction between the core themes and conceptions of sustainable development, Jacobs strengthens the claim advanced by Sharachchandra Lele (1991), who observed that much of the confusion in conceptualizing sustainable development is traceable to the frequent failure to distinguish between its goals and the means of achieving them. She terms this a mixing of 'fundamental objectives and operational ones' (Lele 1991: 611). McNeill, writing in *The Concept of Sustainable Development* (2000: 10–11), makes a similar point. He differentiates between the roles of definition and description in the discourse of sustainable development and argues that, although a final uncontested definition may never emerge, the concept continues to 'provide an excellent anchor for an analysis of the wider issues'.

Now, given the fact that the notion of sustainable development 'tries to respond to an amalgam of scientific, economic, ethical and political considerations' (Faucheux *et al.* 1998: 3), differences in approach and interpretation are more or less unavoidable; however, as an ethical concept, it goes without saying that the core objective of sustainable development is pretty well established in the Brundtland Report (WCED 1987) as well as in almost all other influential definitions (Dobson 1994: 105–109; Benton 1997: 23; Jacobs 1999: 26).

The Brundtland Report emphasizes in several places that the core objective of sustainable development is the eradication of poverty and meeting the basic needs of the global population. Its definition of sustainable development is 'development that meets the needs of the present generation without compromising the ability of future generations to meet their own needs' (WCED 1987: 43). The report proceeds to make plain that this definition 'contains two key concepts' (ibid.: 43):

- the concept of needs, in particular the essential needs of the world's poor, to which overriding priority should be given; and
- the idea of limitations imposed by the state of technology and social organization on the environment's ability to meet present and future needs.

Further, and as if to make sure that this point is not missed, the report, in the very first paragraph of Chapter 2, asserts that:

> The satisfaction of human needs and aspirations is the major objective of sustainable development. The essential needs of vast numbers in the developing countries – for food, clothing, shelter, jobs – are not being met, and beyond their basic needs, these people have legitimate aspirations for improved quality of life ... Sustainable development requires meeting basic needs of all and extending to all the opportunity to satisfy their aspirations for a better life.
>
> (Ibid.: 43)

Of course some may still argue that the Brundtland Report is equivocal, perhaps ambivalent, in its recommendations of how this goal might be achieved. For although the report adopts the basic needs approach and criticizes the reliance on growth as a means of meeting the demands of global justice, it also recommends growth in some cases as the means of achieving global equity. But even these apparent contradictions do little to affect the substantive objective of the concept as articulated in the report. Hence, Oluf Langhelle is right to insist that 'social justice is the primary development goal of sustainable development' (Langhelle 2000: 299). According to Ronald Engel the concept boils down to concern with 'the elemental moral question of what way of life human beings ought to pursue' (Engel 1990: 1), such that sustainable development is first and foremost an ethical rather than an economic, scientific or even an environmental concept (cf. Spangenberg 2001: 39–40). A major implication of this characterization is that debates over the 'hows' of sustainability derive their importance, and therefore ought to be constantly judged, primarily on how well each approach performs in terms of meeting the core demand of providing 'equal opportunity to all and meeting the basic needs of all' (WCED 1987: 43). This point is embedded in Julie Davidson's assertion that sustainable development should be understood as 'the *normative goal*, which sets the parameters of sustainable economic development' (Davidson 2000: 30). The point is also implicit in Jacobs (1995: 14) assertion that the idea is an ethical concept 'describing a new goal of economic and social (and by implication political) life'.[1]

The literature amply supports the idea that the core ethical objective of sustainable development is equal opportunity and meeting the basic needs of all in the global community (Meadows *et al.* 1992; Dobson 1998; Langhelle 2000; Calvert and Calvert 1999: 185; Jacobs 1999; Davidson 2000: 26; Walker and Bulkeley 2006: 657). Langhelle (1999, 2000), for one, has consistently argued that the provision of equal opportunity and the meeting of the basic needs and aspirations of the world's present population are 'not necessarily functional for physical sustainability, but essentially what makes up the challenge of sustainable development'. Contrasting the ethical dimension of sustainable development as embodied in the Brundtland Report with the economic approach, which tends to focus on intertemporal equity and capital accumulation, he says:

> Why bother about inter-generational equity if your own children have very poor chances of reaching adulthood? The priority given to the world's poor [in the Brundtland Report] is thus a moral constraint on possible alternative development trajectories. More precisely, it is an attempt . . . to avoid present injustices being translated into the future.
>
> (Langhelle 2000: 305)

Against this background the alarm sounded by Chatterjee and Finger back in 1994 remains as valid today. These authors argued that there was a noticeable tendency by many in the West to overstretch and thereby distort the real meaning and objectives of sustainable development (Chatterjee and Finger 1994). They cautioned that there was a need to ensure that the concept of sustainable development was *not* used as a cover for business in the income and spending patterns of the West and in their economic relations with the South. Others, such as McNeill (2000: 22–23), equally concede the importance of such intellectual awareness. McNeill argues that, even in the midst of the diversity of perspectives and interests, it must be made certain that 'the central ethical – and thereby also political – issue with the development debate is the rights of the poor as against the rights of the rich'. Jacobs (1999) is more confident. He asserts that the ultimate linguistic (rather than intellectual) meaning of sustainable development is already firmly established in favour of the commitment to 'meeting at least the basic needs of the poor of the present generation (as well as equity between generations)'. According to Jacobs, '[t]he core ideas of sustainable development are fixed and can no longer be changed by rational argument' (Jacobs 1999: 26).

Between sustainable development and the neoliberal notions of justice

In the following section I examine the 'fit' between the two dominant notions of justice in the three multilateral environmental regimes and the ethical prescriptions of sustainable development as embodied in the Brundtland Report. The focus on the Brundtland Report is informed by the fact that this report remains the most influential available in terms of articulating the nature of the concept of global sustainability and the steps (broadly speaking) that might be required to actualize the objectives. To this end the Brundtland Report is not merely a list of wishes for greater global environmental justice but contains extensive arguments and prescriptions required to actualize the vision to which it subscribes. As stated at the beginning of this chapter, the confrontation between the prevailing neo-liberal ideas of justice and the Brundtland version of sustainability reveals four fault lines (or areas of fundamental mismatch). There are, it seems, irreconcilable differences in the conception of the good life, the role of the state in the pursuit of sustainability, the conception of property rights and the defensibility of the enclosure of the global commons.

Conceptualizing the 'good life'

The first fault line between sustainable development and the two neoliberal notions of justice lies in the way in which the idea of the good life may be conceptualized. The problem resides in the fact that, although sustainability as an ideal implies an acknowledgement of the 'rightness' of a particular moral purpose and order, the two notions of justice completely reject any approach to politics that does not accept complete heterogeneity in conceptions of the good life.

Nozick, Gauthier and Harman all insist in several places in their works that the freedom of each to lead his life according to his own conception of the good is the ultimate value, the foundational basis of justice and human dignity, and one which cannot be surrendered for any other social ideal (Nozick 1974; Harman 1983; Gauthier 1986). They generally believe, as Dobson puts it, that the dispute over what the good life entails cannot be resolved by rational argument and, as such, that 'justice should not be seen as being in the service of this or that theory of the good' (Dobson 1998: 198). In fact, the idea that differences in conceptions of the good are irresolvable is at the heart of not only the two libertarian notions of justice but also all liberal ideas of justice (Rawls 1980: 544; Ackerman 1980: 361; Dworkin 1985: 156).

Proponents of justice as entitlement and justice as self-interested reciprocity take pride in the fact that their theories are purely deontological and, as such, do not seek to impose a view of the good on citizens (cf. Goodwin 1987; Kymlicka 2002). According to Nozick, the liberty to pursue one's ends in the manner one chooses is inviolate. Such freedom is an essential requirement for self-determination and is the ultimate test of self-ownership, which sits at the heart of the theory of justice as entitlement (Nozick 1974: 51). In general, liberals defend heterogeneity in conceptions of the good because they believe that it is a principle requirement for any society which aims to secure the rights of people to lead meaningful lives rather than being used as means or resources for other people's lives. They argue that life is meaningful only when it is lived from the inside, that is when it is lived 'in accordance with our beliefs about what gives value to life' (Kymlicka 2002: 216). Nozick says that such meaningful lives are possible only under the condition of his liberty principle – which he repeatedly describes as providing people with the opportunity 'to track bestness' (Nozick 1981: 314, 411, 503). Nozick makes it clear that 'treating us with respect by respecting our rights allows us individually, or with whom we choose, to choose our life and to realise our ends and our conceptions of ourselves, insofar as we can, aided by the voluntary co-operation of other individuals possessing the same dignity' (Nozick 1974: 334).

But the conception of sustainable development articulated in the Brundtland Report appears to contradict important aspects of Nozick's liberty principle. The report is explicit on the need for the adoption of some sort of common good both within societies and on a global scale. The notion of common good articulated in the report is not one that questions or challenges every single action of individuals or states. But it is nonetheless morally particular in the sense that it gives overriding weight to equity and the preservation of the natural resource base and argues that the 'rightness' of both individual and collective actions can be judged on the extent to which they 'respect' these objectives (WCED 1987: 27, 37, 44–45, 53). That is, rather than justify actions on the basis of individual liberty and freedom, as Nozick insists, the report implies that liberty can be legitimately restrained to meet other people's need, as well as to preserve the natural environment.

In arguing that the extent of liberty and freedom which individuals can either claim or enjoy is context-based, the report takes a position that is very close to that of communitarians (cf. Sandel 1984; Taylor 1989). But the stance of the report differs from the position of communitarians in that, whereas communitarians emphasize community relations and social preconditions as the most important context, the report emphasizes equity, meeting needs and ecosystemic integrity (WCED 1987: 28, 32–33).[2] The core argument that the report adduces in defence of its position is that both the liberty and freedom required to lead meaningful lives can be circumscribed by a deteriorated ecosystem. According to the report, a deteriorated ecosystem erodes the potential for development and invariably robs both present and future generations of important life-enhancing opportunities (WCED 1987: 35).[3] It is therefore important, as the report puts it, to adopt a notion of the common good that 'places the right to use public and private resources in its proper social context and [which] provides a goal for more specific measures' (WCED 1987: 63).

Accordingly, the Brundtland Report is unequivocal in proclaiming its desire that the concept of sustainable development should be elevated to the position of 'a global ethic' (WCED 1987: 308). It describes its mission as that of helping to 'define shared perceptions . . . and the appropriate efforts needed to deal successfully with the problems of protecting and enhancing the environment' (WCED 1987: ix). The report, in keeping with this common good approach, calls for 'the need for a common endeavour and *new norms* of behaviour at all levels and in the interests of all' (ibid.: xiv); changes 'in attitudes and in *social values*' (ibid.: xiv); and a 'new view of human need and well-being' (ibid.: 53). The report describes all of these aims as '*part of our moral obligations* to other living beings and future generations' (WCED 1987: 57).

152 *Normative critique*

The foregoing strongly suggests therefore that the notion of sustainable development is indeed a counterpoint to the idea of moral pluralism favoured not only by Gauthier and Nozick but also by the proponents of other liberal theories of justice. For insofar as the notion presses for a common validation of, commitment to and pursuit of a given set of values, it posits itself against the libertarian idea 'which accepts as a fact and a principle, radical and irresolvable differences over what the good for human beings is and what their ultimate nature is thought to be' (Plant 1991: 74).

But some adherents of 'liberal environmentalism' (Bernstein 2001) have proposed a form of reconciliation. They point out that the sort of moral pluralism endorsed by liberals is not inherently atavistic to resource conservation or environmental protection. They argue that the goals of sustainable development represent a set of competing ideas of the good life. There is nothing, they say, that a priori prevents these desires from being taken on board and from being allowed the chance to show in the socio-cultural marketplace why they should 'trump' competing notions of the good (cf. Barry 1995; Wissenburg 2001; Hailwood 2004). This position is implied in Marcel Wissenbug's idea that 'a sustainable society need not be one big Yellowstone Park since we could imagine', he says, 'a worldwide version of Holland stuffed with cows, grains and greenhouses, or even a global Manhattan without the Park to be sustainable' (Wissenburg 2001: 81). Barry (1995: 171) also conveys this sentiment in unmistakable terms when he says:

> I am myself quite strongly attracted to an ecocentric ethic and would favour sacrificing a good deal of human want-satisfaction (especially if the sacrifice were equitably distributed) in pursuit of ecological conception of the good ... But I do not see how its claim can be presented in such a way as to show that it would be unreasonable to adopt a different view, and I take it that any other conception of the good is subject to the same liability.

But many environmentalists are inclined to reject this overture (cf. Engel 1990; Goodin 1992; Dobson 1998; Davidson 2000; Spangenberg 2001; Soper 2006: 59). They argue that the notion of sustainable development offers a definitive answer to the 'elemental moral question of what ways of life human beings ought to pursue' (Engel 1990: 1). They further contend that the imperative of sustainability is 'universal and non-negotiable' (Goodland and Daly 1996: 1002) and therefore ought not to be surrendered, as liberals suggest, for resolution in the cultural marketplace (Bromley 1998). Proponents of this view advance three key lines of defence, all of which are well reflected in the Brundtland Report.

First, they argue that natural resources are so intricately connected that the actions of individuals, predicated as it were on their freedom and liberty, often have far-reaching consequences, including the possibility of limiting the quality of life or life chances available for other people who may be far removed from the point of the first action (WCED 1987: 27, 35; Dobson 1998; cf. Ford 2003; Smith 2003). This understanding thus implies a greater sense of responsibility towards the environment and the well-being of other people than can possibly be secured in the cultural marketplace (O'Neill 1997; Bromley 1998; Davidson 2000; Soper 2006). Second, they argue that, unlike most other choices, the way we choose to act towards the environment often has consequences that cannot be reversed (WCED 1987: 27; cf. Arrow *et al.* 1996). This implies that promoting moral pluralism or the kind of rights to individual liberty that neoliberals advocate will ultimately limit the chances that future generations have to lead meaningful lives. Kymlicka (2002: 247) captures this point succinctly:

> The interest people have in a good way of life, and the forms of life they will voluntarily provide, do not necessarily involve sustaining its existence for future generations. For example, my interest in a valuable social practice may be best promoted by depleting the resources, which the practice requires to survive beyond my lifetime. The wear and tear caused by the everyday use of (historical artefacts and sites or of natural wilderness) would prevent future generations from experiencing them, were it not for state protection. So even if the cultural marketplace can be relied on to ensure that existing people can identify valuable ways of life, it cannot be relied on to ensure that future people have a valuable range of options.

Lastly, environmentalists argue that the liberal's emphasis on the cultural marketplace is dubious in that it deliberately glosses over current inequities in both power and access over resources (Daly and Goodland 1994; Davidson 2000; Low and Gleeson 2001). Thus they argue that leaving the distributional goals of sustainable development to the marketplace ultimately means giving the rich and the powerful the opportunity to further impoverish the poor and buy their way out of the environmental hazards that they create (The Ecologist 1993: Ch. 4; Bromley 1998). The Brundtland Report clearly supports this view when it asserts that 'the search for common interest would be less difficult if all development and environmental problems had solutions that would leave every one better off'. The report however notes that 'this is seldom the case, [and that] there are usually winners and losers', which mostly arise 'from inequalities in access to resources' (WCED 1987: 48). The significance of these points in relation to issues like climate change, hazardous wastes and deforestation, as well as how they provide an important premise for the push for greater distributional justice by the developing countries in the global arena, have been highlighted in preceding chapters.

Recall again, the issue of transboundary movements of hazardous wastes discussed in Chapter 5. Part of the reason why environmentalists thought that a ban on toxic waste trade was desirable, indeed a moral obligation on the part of states, was that such trade occurs between peoples and states who occupy very different positions in the international economic structure (Galli 1987; Puckett 1992; Clapp 2001: 10–11). Given the huge disparity in wealth, access to material resources and technological advancement, proponents of a waste trade ban did not trust that spontaneous market forces would be able to secure justice for the weaker parties. They also reasoned that most of the negative consequences of the badly disposed of toxic wastes would be borne not by those directly engaged in the trade but by vulnerable people in marginal communities and by generations as yet unborn (Wynne, 1989; O'Neill 1998). It was as a result of this line of reasoning that they sought to characterize all such 'trade' and export in toxic wastes as 'morally reprehensible' (Puckett 1992: 94), 'a crime' and 'toxic colonialism' (OAU 1989).

But it was noted that most of the industrialized countries refused to accept such characterizations. Their liberty-based arguments focused essentially on securing the freedom of individuals and states to engage in trade. They contended that most of the toxic waste deals involved the consent of free and self-determined agents and therefore qualified as a fair exchange. Accordingly, they urged the other parties to see these deals as expressions of the liberties and preferences of those involved, based on their values, cognitions and comparative advantages (Hunter 1996: 68; Alter 1997: 30; cf. Kummer 1995; Clapp 2001). The developed country parties argued that, even though toxic wastes may be dangerous, they do still have a value, even if it is a negative one. They therefore considered that it was not the duty of states to stop those who wished to engage in its trade, as doing so would amount to enforcing a particular conception of the good in the face of varying opinions. It was on this view that the core policy of the Basel Convention, the principle of prior informed consent, was eventually premised.

Sagoff (1995: 167), in fact, contends that this understanding of liberal justice is the key to explaining the 'value premise upon which many economists base the cost benefit or efficiency criteria in [environmental] public policy'. Drawing from Kenesse and Bower (1979) he argues that the value premise embodies as its core the notion that 'the personal wants of individuals in the society should guide the use of resources in production, distribution and exchange and that these personal wants can most efficiently be met through the seeking of maximum profits by all producers' (Kenesse and Bower, cited in Sagoff 1995: 165). However, it is exactly the unbridled pursuit of these personal wants that the Brundtland Report blames for the impoverishment of the environment and the exacerbation of global inequalities, hence its insistence that the neoliberal kind of 'politics of rights' and moral pluralism should be abandoned for, or at least be supplemented by, a politics of the common good.

The minimal and neutral state

The second fault line between sustainable development and the two neoliberal interpretations of justice borders on what should be the correct role of the state in the politics of sustainability and redistribution. The prescription of both justice as right and justice as self-interested reciprocity is that the state should stay 'small' and 'neutral'. A small state is one that aims to protect the rights of everyone in a given territory but divests itself of the role of providing welfare or of 'prohibiting independents from taking risky ventures' (Sterba 1986: 1). A small state tries as much as possible not to interfere with the economic choices and decisions of its citizens, preferring instead to set the ground rules while allowing market forces to determine production, allocation and the redistribution of material and economic resources among its citizens (Hayek 1960: 84). A neutral state is one 'which does not justify its actions on the basis of the intrinsic superiority or inferiority of conceptions of the good life and which does not deliberately attempt to influence people's judgement of the value of these different conceptions' (Kymlicka 2002: 217). On this view, the state, as Barry (1965: 74) puts it, 'must be capable of fulfilling the same self-effacing function as a policeman on point duty, who facilitates the motorists' getting to their several destinations without bumping into one another but does not have any power to influence those destinations'.

Conceptually, the neutrality of states derives from the fact that the controversy between competing conceptions of the good cannot be rationally resolved and, insofar as this is the case, that the state has no justification to promote the pursuit of one set of good over the other. Nozick, like many other libertarians, vigorously defends a minimum state. He argues that only a minimum state is capable of preserving individual liberties and securing justice for its citizens. Libertarians, as well as most liberals, argue that giving states the approval to interfere in people's choices results in paternalism (Ackerman 1980: 11; Dworkin 1985: 222; Rawls 1993: 179ff.). A paternalistic state is one that holds a certain idea of the common good and acts in definite ways to encourage its citizens to pursue such goals and objectives. Hence, 'export restrictions on hazardous wastes may be inappropriate and condemned as paternalistic' (Galli 1987: 78). Libertarians argue that every act of paternalism, no mater how good the intention, is an act of injustice and a violation of people's liberties. Here again, one can see how this libertarian notion of justice stands in tandem with and satisfies the minimum state requirements of the neoliberal politico-economic ideology.

Of course, states are not usually neutral when it comes to deciding how a given environmental good may be distributed in the international arena, neither do they attempt to be. On the contrary, they often have strong ideas of what their interests are and seek to promote policies that secure these interests. But the ideological commitment to a minimal state as well as state neutrality by most Western countries, especially the USA, affects global environmental policies in at least three ways: (i) it severely limits the options that are considered possible with respect to how a given global environmental problem might be tackled, especially with the increasingly common thinking that the international community would do well to make efforts to design environmental policies that the USA will sign up to; (ii) the commitment to a minimum and neutral state mostly consigns adherents to a dogged pursuit of free market solutions even when it is apparent that such approaches will not satisfy the demands of distributional justice globally; and (iii) it sets a very low limit to what the state itself can do domestically to influence the action of its citizens. This in turn results in the inability of such states to obligate themselves 'internationally to measures requiring positive actions domestically' (Hatch 1993: 6). It is according to this obligation for neutrality that Western governments mostly favour (and because of their influence, often secure) international environmental policies that are consistent with *laissez-faire* politics and free market solutions.

But there are ample reasons to believe that these positions conflict with what the Brundtland Report considers to be the right approach and obligations of states in the politics of sustainability and redistribution. As we saw in the preceding section the Brundtland Report believes in the politics of common good. To this end the report expressly urges states to actively organize their institutions and policies to promote the pursuit of sustainable development and distributional justice. In its very first page the report asserts that 'the Commission's hope for the future is *conditional on decisive political action now* to begin managing environmental resources and sustainable human progress' (WCED 1987: 1). The report equally emphasizes that the challenges to a sustainable future can be overcome only if steps are taken 'to ensure that the new values [which the concept embodies] are adequately reflected in the principles and operations of political and economic structures' (ibid.: 28). Moreover, the report lays this responsibility on the doorstep of states. Hence, rather than simply aggregating different notions of the good, as adherents of neoliberal ideas of justice would wish, the report argues that states should aim specifically 'at a type of development that integrates production with resource conservation, and that links both to the provision for all of an adequate base and equitable access to resources' (ibid.: 39–40). It also calls on states to 'promote values that encourage consumption standards' (ibid.: 44) and to actively intervene in the working of the market to 'remove disabilities from the disadvantaged groups', both nationally and internationally (ibid.: 53). In short, the report contends that sustainable development requires 'changes in the legal and institutional frameworks [that will enable states] to enforce the common interest' (ibid.: 63).

Of course, all of this is not to say that the Brundtland Report advocates the establishment of 'nanny' states. On the contrary, it lauds the institutionalization of democratic practices as a viable means of achieving sustainable development (ibid.: 63). But it nevertheless insists that 'physical sustainability cannot be achieved unless development policies pay attention to such considerations as changes in access to resources and in the distribution of costs and benefits' (ibid.: 43). It further recommends that these changes in access to resources and the general pursuit of justice both within and between states should be facilitated through appropriate laws, redistributive taxes, subsidies and other methods (ibid.: 47). Clearly then, the report recommends policy options that conceptually clash with the libertarian's idea that the state should be small and neutral and that the market is inherently just, efficient and the best way of producing social wealth.

Most environmentalists generally support the view that governments should make use of the variety of policy instruments available to them in nudging the whole of society towards the path of sustainable development (Daly and Goodland 1994; Attfield 2003; Meadowcroft 2005; Barry and Eckersley 2005). Although they recognize that governments in industrial and pluralistic societies may face some challenges in doing this, they nevertheless remain resolute that being able to rise courageously to these challenges is a necessary precondition for the task of 'elevating sustainable development to a global ethic' (WCED 1987: 308; cf. Attfield 2003). Indeed, for the Brundtland Report, such commitments are part and parcel of the moral obligations of industrial societies, whose actions contribute most to global environmental degradation, in order to safeguard the rights of future generations as well as the rights of the vulnerable (states and groups) in the present generation (WCED 1987: 39–40, 48–49, 59, 227, 256, 308–309).

But the ideological commitment of some influential governments in the West to *laissez-faire* politics conflicts with this vision. Recall the account of the former leader of the US delegation to the climate change negotiations, Mr William Nitze, cited in Chapter 6. Nitze's account expressly admits that there were a multiplicity of opinions in the USA as to how and to what level it should make commitments to the international regime on global warming. But he puts the final decision down, not to any feeling of constraint on the part of the government from the civil society, but to the 'personal ignorance' of the US President and the ideological stance of a few of his cronies (Nitze 1994: 192). Nitze argues that the disengagement of the President in both the domestic and international politics of global warming meant that 'just one man [the Chief of Staff, John Sununu] was free to shape US policy to his liking' (ibid.: 193–194). At the same time he contends that the positive changes seen in the US position – as expressed in its eventual concession to stabilized emission reduction targets – followed on from the resignation of Mr Sununu as well as the input of a few environmentalists in the US administration, especially William Reilly of the Environmental Protection Agency (ibid.: 193–195). This view is sobering and casts as ultimately flawed the popular account that the ability of the US government to 'obligate itself internationally to measures requiring positive actions domestically [in relation to the climate change regime] was severely circumscribed' by a desire to live up to its own ideal of remaining neutral within a pluralistic policy process (Hatch 1993: 6).

Of course, some may wish to challenge this 'few cronies' thesis by calling to mind the overwhelming vote against a US commitment to the Kyoto Protocol by members of the US Senate. Such people would argue that the decision of the US government reflected the view of the majority of the elected senators. But such arguments automatically invoke questions as to why the US government should decide to ignore the results of the opinion polls, which expressly suggested that the majority of ordinary citizens wanted the government to commit to the Kyoto Protocol, irrespective of what populous developing countries like China and India did (opinion poll conducted by *The New York Times*, quoted in Leggett 2000: 297).

Ultimately, Nitze's account of the internal decision-making process of the USA in relation to the global warming regime actually strengths the view already canvassed by some environmentalists that there is no such thing as state neutrality in practice (Eckersley 1992, 2005) and that the concept is only invoked by the West when it helps them to defend the profligate lifestyles of their citizens and to avoid facing up to their responsibilities in the international community. John O'Neill (1997), for instance, has argued that, although in theory liberal ideas of justice pretend to ascribe neutrality to states in terms of the conception of the good, in practice they boil down to the promotion of a unitary and, for that matter, very 'narrow interpretation of the good life and the goods that it involves' (O'Neill 1997: 3, 24–25; cf. Sahlins 1996: 400). For O'Neill, therefore, the prospect of achieving sustainability lies first in deconstructing the liberal idea of the good, which presently relies essentially on 'a very limited self understanding fostered by the market preferences' (ibid.: 3). It is this idea of the good life, according to O'Neill, that is mobilized against environmental sanity and the true search for equity in the use and distribution of environmental resources both within and across national boundaries.

Davidson (2000: 25) agrees strongly with O'Neill. She argues that, starting from the eighteenth century, the state has actively promoted 'a particular set of politico-economic components in which the pursuit of individual freedom was elevated to an ethical and political ideal' such that the rhetorical claim of most Western states to neutrality is flawed. She further argues that Western democratic states, through a particular set of policies and incentives, have deliberately encouraged the definition of well-being along the narrow sense of self-interest and preference satisfaction. According to Davidson (2000: 32), '[i]ndividual well-being has come to be equated with material comfort, with the result that the good of the individual in the liberal polity is a narrowly conceived one'. 'However', she says, 'if sustainability is to be the goal of the human activity, well-being must be rethought with respect to a different set of goods for the making of human lives' (ibid.: 32). Redclift (2000: 98–100) agrees with Davidson on the need to rethink well-being but laments that, with the 'triumph of global capitalism' and its emphasis on market convergence, it has become extremely difficult for states to accommodate this and other ethical demands embodied in the concept of sustainable development. In general, the insistence of Western democracies on private sector-led solutions to global environmental problems has been responsible, according to Leff (1996), for the ascendancy of 'managerialist approaches' to environmentalism and the emphasis of technocracy over and above the ethical dimensions of sustainability (cf. Sachs 1999; Davidson 2000).

Needs, subsistence rights and neoliberal ideas of justice

At the beginning of this chapter it was asserted that the normative essence of sustainable development is social justice, expressed mainly as meeting the basic needs of all and the preservation of the global resource base to give future generations equal chances of meeting their own needs. At the same time it has already been underscored in the previous chapters that the prevailing neoliberal ideas of justice strictly prohibit the politics of redistribution both within, and by extension between, states. Nozick tells us that people have the right to keep whatever they have laboured for because in so doing (that is, labouring) they have mixed a significant part of their 'being' with whatever becomes the fruits of their labour. Hence for Nozick, as Cohen puts it, 'to deny people the proceeds of their labour might not be equal to cutting off their hands, but it is nevertheless wrong for exactly the same kind of reason' (Cohen 1986: 110). And because it is predictable that not many would find it acceptable to part with one of their limbs or to give one of their eyes to the blind for the sake of equality, it follows, in the line of Nozick's logic, that taking away from some people for the sake of feeding others or attaining equality is equally unacceptable.

Nozick also asserts that when things come to the world they do so already bearing upon them the signatures of those who worked to create such goods. He notes that, if this is so, we cannot talk about distributing according to need, welfare, desert or a combination of any such principles without violating the rights of those who owns the goods of whose distribution we now refer. So for Nozick, there really is no room for such a thing as redistribution. 'We are not', he says, 'in the position of children who have been given portions of pie by someone who now makes last minute adjustments to rectify careless cutting' (Nozick 1974: 149). In taking this stand Nozick echoes a classical libertarian view explicitly expressed by Malthus back in 1803:

> A man who is born into a world already possessed (i.e. under ownership), if he cannot get subsistence from his parents, on whom he has a just demand, and if society do not want his labour, has no claims or right to the smallest portion of food, and, in fact, has no business to be where he is. At nature's mighty feast there is no vacant cover for him. She tells him to be gone.
> (Quoted in Goodwin 1987: 57)

Proponents of justice as mutual advantage such as Gauthier and Harman equally subscribe to the above sentiment. Gauthier insists that there is nothing in justice which warrants that some should be deprived of their means so that others, no mater how disadvantaged, should be made better-off. He sees any act of state intervention designed with the aim of achieving such social equality as a violation of people's rights to freedom and liberty.

This conflict over the legitimacy of redistribution on the basis of people's needs can, therefore, be regarded as the third fault line and perhaps the clearest point of divergence between these neoliberal notions of justice and the concept of sustainable development. For the Brundtland Report, as we saw at the beginning of this chapter, is emphatic that meting the basic needs of all members of society in the global community should be the ultimate goal of sustainable development (WCED 1987: 43). Further, the report places this goal in the context of a moral obligation on the part of states and thus elevates the rights to subsistence and a qualitative environment to a comparable status with property rights. Accordingly, the report declares that 'all human beings have the fundamental right to an environment adequate for their health and well-being' (ibid.: 348). The USA has, on the other hand, continued to oppose the incorporation of the right to development and subsistence in international legal documents. It was on the basis of this ideological stance that it lodged a reservation against Principle 3 of the United Nations Conference on Environment and Development (UNCED) in Rio, which declares that 'the right to development must be fulfilled so as to equitably meet developmental and environmental needs of present and future generations'.

It is significant that, in making the meeting of basic needs its central feature, the Brundtland Report did not merely limit itself to sating a moral wish. On the contrary, it advances detailed and extensive arguments for why the poor (groups and states) within the global community qualify for considerations of justice. First, it considers the implications of our common dependence on 'one biosphere

160 *Normative critique*

for sustaining our lives' (WCED 1987: 5). Second, it gives attention to the ethical implications of 'the growth in economic interactions between nations' (ibid.: 27). Indeed, the report states clearly that 'these deepening interconnections are the central justification for the establishment of the Commission' (ibid.: 27–28). And third, the report weighs the validity and implications of ownership and property right claims by states over key transboundary environmental resources and the global commons. On each of these counts the report finds reasons enough to be convinced that there is a moral obligation to direct development and institutional policies in a manner that meets the basic needs of the global poor (ibid.: 27, 35, 45, 47, 53, 59, Chs 3, 10 and 12).

The Brundtland Report underscores the systemic nature of the biosphere and identifies that growth in economic interactions between nations further 'amplifies the wider consequences of national decisions' (ibid.: 27). It acknowledges that many of the risks associated with the productive activities of specific countries effortlessly cross national boundaries so that the risks become shared by 'those who benefit from such activities and those who do not' (ibid.: 35). The report shares the view that gains in international trade are unequally distributed such that 'the heaviest burden in international economic adjustments is carried by the world's poorest people' (WCED 1987: 36; cf. Wenar 2001; Clapp 2001). Finally, it argues that our common dependence on some of the ecosystems that fall outside national jurisdictions implies joint ownership. It is on the strength of these arguments that the report builds its recommendation that free market capitalism and inalienable property rights, the kind which the libertarians would favour, cannot be justified.

Proponents of global environmental justice in general argue that beyond the right to property emphasized by the libertarians there lies a much more fundamental right – the positive right to life and to a decent environment (Dower 1998; Drydyk 2001; Attfield 2003). Because the possibility of labouring and acquiring property is an option that is available only to the living, they argue that a discourse which neglects the right to subsistence offends against a most fundamental intuition of justice (Langhelle 2000). They point out that the neglect of the right to life in the discourse of rights in the Western world reveals a 'full belly' and a nationalistic rather than a universal approach to rights (Dower 1998; Hunt 1998).[4] This logic has been generally validated by the many important international conventions that now tend to recognize this right in their primary documents (see Chapter 2). At the same time, many of the issue-specific regimes, including the three regimes studied, equally contain references to the importance of attending to the basic needs of the poor and meeting the needs of the developing countries. But as has been shown in the previous chapters, these expressions do not ultimately influence core policies in significant ways because of the ideological commitments of most Western countries to property and the opposition to welfare rights.

Commons and the imperative of enclosure

It has been noted earlier that Nozick makes a distinction between two kinds of goods. The first are secondary goods such as mobile phones and cars, which he believes come to the world already attached to those having entitlement over them. The second are primary goods such as fish in the ocean and landed property, which he believes are generally unowned and can be acquired through the process of just appropriation. In this section I confront the arguments laid out by Nozick on how this second category of goods may be acquired with the arguments contained in the Brundtland Report (*Our Common Future*) to reveal the fourth and last fault line between the neoliberal notions of justice and the concept of sustainable development. This dimension is important because, although Nozick believes that most of the external world is generally unowned, he still supports the idea that even the parts which are very clearly owned in common, or at least have been the object of common use, can still be appropriated by individuals without the consent of co-users, provided that certain minimal conditions are met.

Nozick, drawing from Locke, explains (see Chapter 7) that such goods, which are hitherto the objects of common usage, may come to be legitimately appropriated by individuals through the principle of just initial acquisition. For Locke, a just acquisition is one that leaves 'enough and as good' for others. Hence, a local fisherman is entitled to his catch insofar as it leaves enough and as good in the river for other local fishermen. But Locke, who was writing to defend the enclosure of some previously commonly owned parcels of land in seventeenth-century England, realized that most appropriations do not leave enough and as good of the objects being appropriated. He nonetheless defends such acts of enclosure on the grounds that the people who are by such acts of enclosure denied legal titles are left as well-off or better-off overall. Nozick accepts this logic, which he calls the 'Lockean proviso'. He says that 'a process normally giving rise to a permanent bequeathable property right in a previously unowned thing will not do so if the position of others no longer at liberty to use the thing is thereby worsened' (Nozick 1974: 178). Nozick, like Locke before him, takes it as given that all common property resources are ultimately subject to complete ruin following the classical problem of the 'tragedy of the commons' (cf. Hardin 1968; Chapter 2). Together with Locke, Nozick believes that most acts of enclosure represent an improvement from a pre-appropriation common usage condition. Accordingly, for Nozick, most appropriations satisfy the Lockean proviso and are therefore legitimate.[5]

Nozick asserts that, once the world comes to be fully appropriated through various acts of enclosure, a free market for land will develop and, given that some people will have been initially excluded, a free market for labour will also develop. Over time, and because self-owning people will be free to trade, transfer and use their land and/or labour as they desire, the market force itself will ultimately ensure that everyone gets a just share in keeping with their talents, labour, hard work and free choices. As such, the intervention of governments for the purpose of redistributing things among self-owning people would be both unnecessary and undesirable (Nozick 1974: 178–182; cf. Cohen 1986; Kymlicka 2002: 115–116). Following this line of reasoning, libertarians such as Locke, Hardin and Nozick all recommend, indeed encourage, the private enclosure of common resources because it is, they argue, the only way to: (i) prevent their ultimate degradation; (ii) make the most out of such resources; and (iii) increase general social wealth.

162 *Normative critique*

Here again, as in the previous three sections, one sees a clear 'fit' between these notions of justice and the neoliberal agenda, with its emphasis on privatization and cost–benefit. Recall the discussions in the previous chapters on how state parties regularly seek to deploy this same argument of efficiency and cost-effectiveness in the defence of many environmental policies that, in practice, imply some form of enclosure or privatization of common property resources. This is most evident in the case of the territorial sea, the EEZ and the continental shelf regimes, according to which about 38 per cent of the world's oceans and 90 per cent of its living resources were 'carved up' with the ownership transferred directly to states. Indeed, with the collapse of Soviet communism and the triumph of the free market, the approach of states in virtually all environmental regimes has been to privatize and/or nationalize whatever is possible and to keep the option of joint management to the barest minimum (Benton 1997; Birnie and Boyle 2002).

Now, although it is clear that neither of the libertarian theories of justice leaves any room for common ownership of natural resources, it must be emphasized that this does not necessarily mean that they are opposed to co-operative schemes aimed at the joint gains of co-operating agents (Luper-Foy 1992; Almond 1995; Kymlicka 2002: 118). The key point is that they insist that such schemes must be freestanding. This means that one's natural membership of a community does not qualify one to claim any part of the external world over which one has not mixed one's labour or voluntarily contributed to an appropriation of (Buchanan 1990). In other words, there is no form of resource ownership that follows simply from one's natural membership of a society. It is according to this libertarian understanding of how people qualify to share in natural resources that it becomes extremely difficult to ground concepts such as the common heritage of mankind (Kiss 1985).[6] In fact, the whole controversy over the seabed regime in the Third United Nations Conference on the Law of the Sea (UNCLOS III) and the sole reason why the USA, Germany and the UK jettisoned the results of over 11 years of diplomatic effort was because they considered that the common heritage of mankind and the seabed regime that it generated fell foul of this ideological commitment to enclosure and presented an irreconcilable conflict with this dominant understanding of property ownership.

The Brundtland Report picked up on this point. After describing UNCLOS III as 'the most ambitious and advanced of international conventions ever' (WCED 1987: 261), the report, in apparent reference to the virtually abandoned seabed regime, lamented that a few countries could, for ideological reasons, decline to adhere to the provisions of the regime and in so doing block 'the implementation of some of its key aspects' (ibid.: 261). The report, therefore, not only sanctions the equity and common management approach inherent in the concept of the common heritage of mankind but also admits that the presence of life-dependent, cross-boundary resources and the global commons result in increasing challenges to dominant thinking on resource ownership and 'traditional forms of national sovereignty' (ibid.: 261). The report reiterated its conviction that these resources – outer space, the atmosphere, the oceans, Antarctica etc. – are better considered as commonly owned rather than unowned resources because they perform life-

Ethics of sustainability and neoliberal ideas 163

giving functions from which all states and peoples benefit. Following this line of reasoning the report recommends that 'sustainable development can be secured *only* through international co-operation and agreed regimes for surveillance, development and management in the common interest' (ibid.: 261). In effect, the report's position differs from the libertarian recommendation, which favours nationalization, enclosure and private management (cf. Steiner 1977, 1994; Vallentyne and Steiner 2000).[7]

Indeed, Nozick has accepted that there are a limited number of objects and tracts of nature over which his theory of justice has no purchase. He says that, for this limited number of objects, which 'appeared from nowhere, out of nothing', it should be all right to apply 'the usual conceptions of distributive justice' (Nozick 1974: 160; cf. Dobson 1998: 79). But it is important to examine whether the libertarians actually make their case with respect to the reasons for enclosing the commons that fall outside this 'limited number'. Much can be said here but I will, for reasons of scope, limit myself to just a few general lines of argument by which many environmentalists think that the libertarians' case for enclosure is flawed.

Libertarians argue that every enclosure is an improvement on the pre-appropriation common usage condition because it prevents the ultimate tragedy of the commons, results in better management of resources and leads to improved social wealth for all concerned. However, environmentalists, most of whom promote the notion of the commons at the local, international and global levels, reject the libertarians' claims on three main counts. First, they accept that, although in some cases an act of enclosure might be necessary to avert the 'tragedy of the commons', there are many other instances in which people have been able to manage the commons with a great deal of success and to the satisfaction of all beneficiaries (Illich 1983; Ostrom 1990; Vogler 2000). In fact, environmentalists argue that the libertarians' conclusion of unavoidable tragedy is a self-fulfilled prophesy that follows from assumptions such as lack of constraints on individual behaviour and the inability of users to alter rules (Ostrom 1985, 1990; Baden and Doughlas 1998).

On the other hand, environmentalists point out that the libertarians' assumption that enclosure necessarily leads to improved management and increased social wealth is false. There have been, they say, an impressive number of instances in which the act of enclosure led not only to the dispossession of people but also to the impoverishment of the given resource (Ostrom 1990; Vogler 2000). And finally, environmentalists point out that the libertarians' appeal for enclosure rests essentially on false dualism – i.e. that proponents of enclosure focus on only two alternatives and foreclose the possibility of many other options, including, say, combining ideas (Illich 1983; Baden and Doughlas 1998; Ostrom 1990).[8]

In fact, some scholars claim that the most viable prospect for averting the present ecological crisis threatening the entire globe might, after all, lie in our ability and willingness to harness the ideas embedded in the concept of the commons (Ostrom 1985, 1990; *The Ecologist* 1993; Vogler 2000). These ideas include an emphasis on equitable sharing and the consistent care of resources based on an enhanced appreciation of the intimate relationship between environmental sanity and humans' well-being (as opposed to the libertarians' rights-based approach). Other values include the devolution of power and the promotion of all-inclusive decision-making models in relation to the management of resources (Bachram 2005; Weissman 2005). Ostrom (1985: 13) speaks for this group when she contends that:

> Small-scale communities are more likely to have the formal conditions required for the successful and enduring collective management of the commons. Among these are the visibility of common resources and behaviour towards them; feedback on the rules and their rationales; the values expressed in these rules (that is, equitable treatment of all and the protection of the environment); and the backing of values by socialisation, standards, and strict enforcement.

Deeper problems

The preceding argument has been designed to show that the libertarian's reasons for endorsing enclosure fail on account of their incompatibility with the idea of global sustainable development. But there are even deeper problems with the two notions of justice – problems that arise from the inconsistency of their internal logic. The first is that, in relation to his recommendations for initial acquisitions, Nozick fails to consider the implications of these acts of enclosure for the self-ownership status of all those who might arrive in the world after all or most of it must has been 'enclosed'. He says that acts of enclosure would generate the need for labour but glosses over the inevitable fact that the owners of property would find it in their favour to design the terms of labour in ways that might lead to the continuous dominance of the latecomers. In some cases, such a situation might even result in the approval of slave labour. The concentration of property in the hands of a few would mean that the chances of equal acquisition by latecomers would be severely undermined and that the quality of their lives would no longer be determined 'on conformity to procedural principles or successful efforts [but] on the gifts and jobs others are willing to bestow on them' (Bogart 1985: 833). The implication of this is enormous, for it means that these latecomers are no longer free in the Nozickian sense of it. Their lives and the qualities thereof depend on whether the property owners want their labour and what they are willing to pay such that, at the end of the day, they are, following Nozick's logic, merely resources for others. Bogart (1985: 833–834) puts it well:

> The latecomers' prospect is severely limited by luck. They cannot alter them through any legitimate effort of their own . . . The latecomers have no reason to accept the extant pattern of holdings. They lack even the opportunity to make acquisitions. So if they are compelled to co-operate in the scheme of holdings, they are forced to benefit others. This forced compliance with the property system constitutes a form of exploitation and is inconsistent with

the most basic of the root ideas, rendering as it does the latecomers mere resources for others.

The foregoing implies that, insofar as it is admitted that natural resources are not limitless, even the most strict application of Nozick's enclosure doctrine would ultimately lead to the violation of the root idea of his theory, which is self-ownership and individual liberty.

The second internal problem for the entitlement theory of justice, or at any rate for those who seek to adopt it uncritically – I say for those who seek to adopt it uncritically because Nozick himself admits that this is a serious problem – is that it ultimately relates every claim of justice 'to the legitimate acts of original acquisition' (MacIntyre 1981: 234). History shows that the majority of those who now enjoy 'ownership' of rich islands, mineral resources, artefacts, etc., acquired them by forcefully dispossessing the original owners. Much of New England was acquired from the American Indians (Lyons 1981). The labour and material resources of many African nations were forcefully utilized through the slave trade and colonization respectively (The Ecologist 1993). Vast tracts of present-day Ireland and Germany were violently taken from the original Irish and non-German Prussian inhabitants (MacIntrye 1981: 234). Hence, following Nozick's principle of justice requires that any discussion of justice can only proceed after these resources have been restored to their rightful owners and the effects of these illegitimate acquisitions rectified. Nozick suggests that we might rectify the illegitimacy of existing titles by a one-time general redistribution of resources in accordance with Rawls's difference principle after which a libertarian conception of justice should permanently take over. Although Nozick does not contemplate how the difficulties that would arise from such an exercise might be surmounted, it does mean, again, that a strict application of Nozick's theory of justice would legitimize a great deal of the claims for the transfer of resources from the North to the South.

Contractarianism and equality of co-operators

Gauthier's own formulation of justice as self-interested reciprocity equally suffers from serious internal weaknesses. Because it completely rejects the existence of any morality outside of mutual interest, it follows that only those who are party to a co-operative venture are permitted to share in the surplus or to be accorded the gains that accrue from such ventures. This further entails that justice is possible only when each party has some powers or bargaining chips with which to secure justice. But applying this argument to society as a whole, in the way that Gauthier suggests, leads to the conclusion that newborn babies who cannot be catered for by their parents and those who as a result of their deformities cannot contribute to the running of society would have no claim to any form of justice (Buchanan 1990: 236).

Gauthier actually defends this view. He argues that the deformed and the infirm 'fall beyond the pale of justice' (Gauthier 1986: 268). It follows in Gauthier's terms that these groups of people are merely societal parasites and that the best they can hope for from the strong is mercy and not justice (cf. Lomasky 1987: 161; Buchanan 1990: 237). Barry and Matravers (1997) and Kymlicka (2002: 133–134) also argue that the implication of Gauthier's argument is that newborn babies do not qualify for considerations of justice because babies cannot contribute anything to society. The austere nature of this libertarian version of justice could not be clearer. But herein lies the contradiction of this theory, for if indeed justice is predicated on nothing other than the pursuit of utility maximization by self-interested egoists, why is it not rational for the more able to completely eliminate the weaklings of this world as this would surely mean a greater abundance of resources? Why should I share the land and the valuable fruits in it with my poor neighbour when I could just as easily eliminate him altogether without causing myself any discomfort? And why should stronger countries tolerate weaker countries when they could make themselves even richer by sacking them and taking over their lands and resources?

Proponents of the libertarian notion of justice realise that this is a serious contradiction in their theory. Their response is usually to claim that justice as self-interested reciprocity works because people are roughly of equal power. They claim that, by and large, everybody has something with which to bargain (Hobbes 1968). However, it is very doubtful whether this Hobbesian thesis of 'cumulative equality', which is so vital for the coherence of Gauthier's thesis, has ever held. If, by any chance, it did hold at the time that Hobbes wrote it, it definitely could not be said to be plausible now. With the exponential increase in the disparities of wealth within and between nations and the rise of military, technological and material superpowers, no philosopher can afford to base his or her theory of justice on the apparent or cumulative equality of persons or nations. Shue (1992: 374–379) brings out this point clearly with respect to the climate change regime when he observes that, if justice is based on rational bargaining and only intended to advance narrow interests, countries such as Haiti and Sudan may never hope to secure justice from a country such as the USA as it is clear that these countries do not have any chips with which to advance their interests. Overall, 'it is doubtful that mutual advantage theorists really believe in this assumption of a natural equality in bargaining power. Their claim in the end is not that people are equal but rather that *justice is only possible insofar as this is so*' (Kymlicka 2002: 134, italics in the original). Besides, even if we accept for the purpose of this argument that everybody does have something with which to bargain (we shall not accept this), it would still *not* be the case, for reasons already adduced above, that justice rests solely on the outcome of rational bargaining contracts.

Conclusion

The foregoing is obviously only a brief précis of what is ultimately a much longer argument, but it suffices, I think, to show that the two ideas of justice have serious internal weaknesses. On a more confident note, though, one can say that the appeal of justice as self-interested reciprocity and justice as property rights by state parties within global environmental governance circles lies in their close 'fit' with the prevailing neoliberal ideology. But although both ideas of justice have initial attractive features, such as attempting to give people considerable liberty to live their lives in accordance with their own conceptions of the good, they ultimately fail upon closer scrutiny to provide a promising basis for the pursuit of global sustainability. The reasons are that, although the concept of sustainable development emphasizes politics of the common good, a strong commitment to the meeting of basic needs and common resource management, the two ideas of justice emphasize heterogeneity in the conception of the good, minimal state, moral pluralism and inalienable property rights.

For the most part, proponents of neoliberalism are aware that the radical normative prescriptions embodied in the Brundtland conception of sustainability are extremely difficult to reconcile with the values that underpin neoliberal philosophy. At the same time they are aware of the urgent need to articulate some form of coherent response to global environmental problems as well as the distributive questions integral to these problems. This in part explains the increasing debates over environmental issues in Western democracies and the questions of fairness in international regime development circles. In the next and concluding chapter I aim to review some of the processes and key discursive tools with which advocates of neoliberalism have attempted to co-opt the ideas of distributive equity inherent in the concept of global sustainability and especially as it relates to the operation of environmental regimes. Principally, I will argue that the 'neoliberal consensus' has come to dominance in specific discourses of environmental governance of which the notion of ecological modernization is the core narrative. The key function of the ecological modernization narrative has been to reconcile the 'radical normative aspirations of global sustainability' (Benton 1999: 199), such as the demand for distributive equity, with the core ideals of neoliberalism, which are market rationality and economic growth. However, I will argue that, to the extent that this project succeeds, the quest for global sustainable development and environmental equity by the South within the context of environmental regimes will remain elusive.

9 Global justice and neoliberal environmental governance

So far, it has been demonstrated that ethical ideas and moral values form integral aspects of regime development and international co-operation for sustainability. In fact, it would appear, at least from the perspective of North–South relations, that distributive bargaining rather than environmental protection is the defining feature of international regime efforts. The empirical analysis provides insights into the shifts and tensions that occur in both policy and discursive terms as a result of the increasing contentions for distributive justice in the operation of multilateral environmental regimes. It transpires, however, that, although equity aspirations and concepts exert a significant impact on the rule content and normative structure of international regimes, it is the policies and programmes that 'fit' neoliberal interpretations of justice which ultimately prevail in the design of the core rules of global environmental regimes. The confrontation of these neoliberal ideas of justice with the ethical prescriptions of sustainable development as articulated by the Brundtland Report nonetheless suggests that the neoliberal ideas of justice do not provide a hopeful base for the pursuit of global sustainability or the ideas of justice inherent in the concept. In this last chapter I explore some of the implications of the attempt to co-opt the ideal of global sustainability and the radical distributional demands inherent in it for neoliberal ends. The chapter starts with a brief commentary on the concept of neoliberalism, focusing on its relationship with the prevailing ideas of justice in multilateral environmental regimes. Next, I discuss how the hegemony of the neoliberal political economic doctrine translates to the dominance of specific discourses on environmental governance of which the notion of ecological modernization is the key narrative. The main function of this key narrative has been to weaken the radical normative elements of the concept of sustainability, especially the emphasis on global egalitarian distribution, and, ultimately, to reconcile the ideal of sustainable development with the neoliberal values. In the final section I highlight some of the implications of this value contest (between ideas of sustainability and neoliberalism) on the study of international environmental regimes.

The hegemony of neoliberalism

Neoliberalism is the most important political economic agenda of our time. It is the set of ideas that form the basis of the current political economic system, to which many of the industrialized countries and, indeed, most of the globe have signed up to (Chomsky 1999: 2). In fact, given its pervasiveness and critical influence in our everyday lives, it is simply said that 'we live in the age of neoliberalism' (Saad-Filho and Johnston 2005: 1).

But despite its pervasiveness and critical importance, the concept still defies a purely theoretical and concise definition. According to Campbell and Pedersen (2001: ix), the concept posits 'a very complex multidimensional project that involves changes in a plethora of institutional arena: substantive and discursive, formal and informal, economic and political; public and private; global, national and local' (Campbell and Pedersen 2001: ix). For Jessop (2002: 453), the concept connotes a 'polyvalent conceptual assemblage in economic, political and ideological discourse ... with many disputes over its scope, application and limitations'. Peck (2004: 394) describes it as a 'perplexingly amorphous political economic phenomena', so difficult to define with great precision. The reason for this according to Filho and Johnston (2005) is that, unlike capitalism, neoliberalism does not define a specific mode of production but rather 'straddles a wide range of social, political and economic' experiences, some of which are abstract rather than concrete. They cite the 'growing power of finance' as one of the abstract dimensions of neoliberalism and the increasing privatization of public service utilities as one of its more concrete manifestations.

In general, despite its polyvalence and amorphousness, the effect of neoliberalism is well recognized and its key features are both well studied and increasingly documented in the literature (Jessop 2002, McCarthy and Prudham 2004, Harvey and Peck 2002; Saad-Filho and Johnston 2005). According to Susan George the main ideas are 'that the market should be allowed to make major social and political decisions; that the State should voluntarily reduce its role in the economy; that corporations should be given total freedom; that trade unions should be curbed; and that citizens should be given less rather than more social protection' (George 1999: 1). Neoliberalism 'at its core entails a commitment to extending the competitive relations of the market as far as possible, keeping state intervention to a minimum' (Holifield 2004: 286). According to Mansfield (2004: 314) it involves 'the emphasis of a particular perspective that links property rights specifically to profit maximization with the underlying assumption that market rationality is natural, universal and inevitably leads to the greater good'. 'The whole point of neoliberalism', for George (1999: 2), is 'that the market should be allowed to determine the fate of human beings and that the economy should dictate its rule to the society and not the other way round'. In international relations and the political economy it demands the dismantling of trade barriers, global economic integration, free capital mobility and export-led growth. For Paterson (1996b: 168), neoliberalism has 'three main roots', which include 'supply side economics, monetarism and public choice theory', all of which are geared to cut inflation, encourage enterprise and minimize state intervention.

Overall, the emerging consensus, which is reflected in the statement of Saad-Filho and Johnston noted above, is that neoliberalism can be conceptualized both as a thought abstraction and as a distinct phenomenon with substantive content, technique and causal processes (Peck and Tickell 2002; Jessop 2002; Castree 2006). The former speaks to the ideology of neoliberalism, which in its pure form entails a utopian vision of market forces completely liberated worldwide with the state altogether ceding its socio-economic and resource-allocating roles to the market (Brenner and Theodore 2000; Castree 2006: 2). 'Actually existing neoliberalism' (Brenner and Theodore 2002), on the other hand, speaks of the myriads of restructuring projects and the hybrids of contemporary policies and programmes designed to realize this vision. The value in drawing this distinction is that one can expect 'actually existing neoliberalism' to exhibit specific issue-area and spatiotemporal characteristics, which result from the interaction between particular sets of neoliberal policies and existing institutional and socio-economic contexts. The essence, then, is that variations in the outworkings of neoliberal ideology can be expected, even when the root ideas of the political economic philosophy remain unchanged.

Of course, depending on one's orientation, one might have problems with this rather broad and somewhat fuzzy characterization. Accordingly there are some who doubt the analytical usefulness of the concept, contending that, in the absence of a concise description, the concept of neoliberalism is a non-starter in the analysis of the present character of the prevailing socio-political system. Clive Barnett, for example, contends that 'there is no such thing as neoliberalism' (Barnett 2005: 9). He argues that the extreme amorphousness of the phenomenon means that neoliberal policies, however they are defined, produce a set of unique institutional and socio-economic configurations, which make it inappropriate to speak of the concept in plenary terms. For Barnett, therefore, the vocabulary is at best a consolation for the aspatially-minded leftists, perpetually preoccupied with identifying and criticizing so-called hegemonic ideologies. As he puts it:

> The vocabulary of 'neoliberalism' and 'neoliberalization' in fact provides a double consolation for leftist academics: it supplies us with plentiful opportunities for unveiling the real workings of hegemonic ideologies in a characteristic gesture of revelation. In so doing, it invites us to align our professional roles with the activities of various actors 'out there', who are always framed as engaging in resistance and contestation.

Drawing from Barnett, Noel Castree equally calls to question the bourgeoning research agenda on neoliberalism, describing it as 'traveling down a road to nowhere' (Castree 2006: 2). His case, similar to that of Barnett, is that neoliberalism is 'impure' on all scales – global, regional and local. And given, therefore, the highly contextual nature of the phenomenon, it implies, he says, that 'neoliberalism depicted over and above context is a pure archetype; something that has no consequence or existence in itself' (Castree 2006: 4). He argues that the historically specific and spatiotemporal variations that characterize different projects of neoliberalization entail that what emerges on the ground is not variants of neoliberalism but 'rather a qualitatively distinct phenomenon in its own right: namely, an articulation between certain neoliberal policies and a raft of other social and natural phenomena' (ibid.: 4).

In response, one can say that these concerns – which understandably emanate mainly from political geographers concerned mainly with spatially specific analysis – are helpful insofar as they serve to highlight the multivariate nature of neoliberalism. They remind us that we are not looking for a specific and non-variant system of production or political economic tools (cf. Saad-Filho and Johnston 2005: 2) but a certain family resemblance of ideas, which, as Castree himself crucially recognizes, engineers 'substantial commonalities of processes and outcomes' (Castree 2006: 5). The concern against totalizing claims from these geographers is therefore largely misplaced when posited as a denial that neoliberalism has a set of core ideas which are identifiable across space and scale or that these policy ideas are not hegemonic in today's political economic system. A possible reason why one may wish to contest the global hegemonic status of neoliberalism could reside in a narrow understanding of the concept of hegemony. For if understood in the Gramscian sense, the complexity associated with 'actually existing neoliberalism' serves to underscore rather than raise doubts over its hegemonic status. Gramsci is clear that the successful establishment of hegemony involves a series of compromises and conciliations (which unavoidably confers complexity upon the hegemonic idea). His argument is that these compromises and conciliations are designed to normalize and integrate institutions and societies into an orbit that is nonetheless controlled by a set of identifiable core ideas which are mostly cast in universal terms (cf. Cox 1983; Lee 1995; Levy and Newell 2005). Complexity is an important feature because, contrary to more traditional understandings, the principal means of dominance is consensus rather than coercion. Hegemony is thus established when the leading class (read states) has managed to embed its interests in institutions and civil societies such that the spontaneous workings of these institutions serve the core interests of the leading class while simultaneously appearing to be gainful to the consenting subalterns. This process ostensibly involves a series of non-core threatening 'concessions to subordinate classes in return to acquiescence in bourgeois leadership' (Cox 1983: 163). What eventually emerges, then, is a set of core ideas overlaid by a highly complex structure of policies and practices, which can sometimes seem 'perplexingly amorphous' and indeterminate. The hegemonism resides in the fact that this set of ideas has 'won legitimacy' over alternative ways of looking at the world and, to the more powerful, represents the existing reality and only way of analysing the global system. It is equally ideological because it helps to create in people certain modes of behaviours and expectations consistent with a given social order (Cox 1983: 135).

Neoliberalization of global environmental governance

An overwhelming majority of the scholarship on neoliberalism focuses on the concept mainly as an economic project. Accordingly, much of the emphasis has been on the implications of the neoliberal project for capital and labour relations and the monetary policies of states, although a large number of studies have also looked at its implications for state and civil society relationships (Chomsky 1999; Brenner and Theodore 2002; Lapavitsas 2005). Often neglected in the scholarship is the fact that the neoliberal project also has very distinctive environmental and normative dimensions. Indeed, as McCarthy and Prudham (2004: 276–278) recently observed, it is very logical to claim that neoliberalism is first and foremost an 'environmental project' to the extent that its key defining features are found in the articulation of new social relations to nature and the reconfigurations of property relations via the legitimization of commons enclosure, the intensification of specific dimensions of primitive accumulation and the comodification of nature (cf. McCarthy 2004: 327; Jessop 2004; Liverman 2006). Of course, there are numerous studies that focus on the impact of neoliberal reforms on the environment but, as McCarthy and Prudham (2004: 275) observe, there has been comparatively little analysis on the various 'tensions and parallels between neoliberalism and environmentalism as ideologies' and on 'the manifestation of neoliberalism as environmental governance per se'. Levy and Newell (2005: 5) largely corroborate this point when they note that initial environmental politics scholarship tended to portray most economic reforms directed at environmental protection as mere 'green-washing' *ad hoc* programmes designed by corporate actors for public relations purposes, whereas in reality what is happening is a much deeper and strategic attempt to co-opt environmental questions and patterns of environmental governance into the dominant modes of the political economic system.

At the same time, the ubiquity and pervasiveness of neoliberalism sometimes creates the impression that it is an immutable, inviolable divine order handed down to govern economic relations within and between states in the twenty-first century and beyond (Chomsky 1999). Many proponents of neoliberalism believe that it is the only realistic alternative to poverty, misery and global economic disaster. Yet ethical analysis, such as has been conducted in previous sections, clearly reveals that neoliberalism draws upon only one set of values and norms among many possible alternatives. Furthermore, they point to the fact that neoliberal environmentalism, that is environmental governance predicated upon neoliberal values, has specific historical and spatiotemporal dimensions.

Weale (1992), Eckersley (1995), Hajer (1995) and McCarthy (2004) among others have presented thorough accounts indicating how a commitment to the neoliberal political ideology by the dominant sections of the globe translated into a systematic and sustained attack on traditional tools of environmental policy. The efficiency and legitimacy of regulatory mechanisms were questioned and the new discourse centred on the preference for market-based and voluntary approaches (Weale 1992; Eckersley 1995: 8–10; Meadowcroft 2005; Christoff 2005). However, much scholarship has shown that, although the argument of efficiency provided 'the rhetorical veneer' (Eckersley 1995: 10) for the promotion of the market-based approaches to environmental protection, the core reason lay in the desire to normalize the radical strains in environmentalism and bring it into the ideological framework of neoliberalism.

A critical plank in this project came in the form of the ecological modernization discourse, which essentially involved the attempt to reconstruct the relationship between environmentalism and the neoliberal political economic philosophy to make them seem more harmonious (Weale 1992; Hajer 1995; Mol 2000). John Barry captures this point well when he argues that the starting point of ecological modernization theory is an outright denial of the notion that environmental protection and the neoliberal economic model are incompatible and an expression of faith in the possibility of equilibrating the apparently opposing demands of both philosophies. The narrative, he says, 'marks a new environmental policy discourse from within the existing institutions of the liberal state . . . [with its] strength as an ideology lying mainly in its capacity to render the imperative for economic growth compatible with the imperative to protect environmental quality' (Barry B 1999: 114). In the bid to achieve this 'reconciliation' the theory relies on three key meso-narratives. These include an emphasis on (i) science and technology, (ii) economic instruments and market rationality, and (iii) governmentality and voluntarism, that is the promotion of individuals and voluntary organizations' activities as a means for national and environmental protection (Weale 1992; Eckersley 1995; Mol 2000; McCarthy 2004; Betsill and Bulkeley 2006; Sending and Newmann 2006; Paterson and Barry 2005).[1] Ecological modernization in general 'stresses the importance of economic and market dynamics in ecological reform and the role of innovators, entrepreneurs, and other economic agents as social carriers of ecological restructuring' (Mol 2000: 313).

For Weale (1992), ecological modernization does not simply aim to achieve reconciliation between environmental protection and economic growth, it equally 'sees the possibility of achieving economic growth by attending to environmental quality' (p. 76; cf. Bernstein 2001: 3). According to this view, environmental protection is actually seen as a basis for future growth. The core premise for this optimism according to Mol (2000) is faith in the roles of science and technology. The hope lies in the expectation that there will be 'changes towards more advanced environmental technologies which not only redirect production processes and products into more environmentally sound ones, but also the engagement in the selective contraction of large technological systems that can no longer fulfil stringent ecological requirements' (p. 313). In modern Western societies, 'technocentrism' or 'technological environmentalism' (Pepper 1996: 37) represents the official dominant set of attitudes to nature at both the national and the international level.

The manifestation of this mindset was frequently encountered in the empirical chapters. The USA has up till now refused to ratify the Basel Convention on the Transboundary Movements of Hazardous Wastes and their Disposal, arguing that what is needed is not a ban on the shipment of wastes to poor developing countries but a convention that concentrates its efforts on promoting the development of

174 *Normative critique*

technologies that minimize waste production. A similar argument also marks its position on the climate change issue. The US government maintains that it is against the Kyoto accord mostly because the agreement does not give priority to the role of technology in combating global climate change. It is against this background that the US government in July 2005 signed the so-called Asia-Pacific climate pact (with Australia, China, India, Japan and South Korea), which focuses almost exclusively on how to develop, deploy and transfer clean technologies as a means to address climate change.

In terms of market rationality, ecological modernization vigorously promotes the idea that it is possible to achieve a win–win situation between ecological integrity and economic development. The starting point in this regard is usually the observation that developed countries generally have higher environmental standards and more sophisticated environmental regulations than developing countries. This condition is directly linked to the high material production and economic growth in the Western democracies, which is intimately connected with technological innovations. Accordingly, it is admitted that free market capitalism might initially lead to environmental degradation but that it simultaneously provides the sorts of resources that are required to maintain a high standard of environmental protection (Anderson and Leal 1997; Bhagwati 1993). McCarthy (2004: 327–328) expresses the point very succinctly:

> The argument, in essence, is that industrialization does cause rapid environmental degradation, but that as economies mature towards a more post-industrial sectoral mix and wealth increases to the point where people can worry about more than bare survival and reproduction, production becomes more efficient and people choose to direct a growing share of surplus towards environmental protection leading to rapid improvement in environmental quality and better conditions than if people were trapped in pre-industrial economies.

Although this argument on the surface seems appealing, it does contain the implication that priority must be accorded to policies that secure economic growth in the event of any conflict between such policies and those pressing for more environmental protection. The empirical analysis provides much evidence on the manifestation of this logic in the design of international environmental policies. The rejection of Part IX of the Third United Nations Conference on the Law of the Sea (UNCLOS III) as well as the emphasis on emission trading, voluntary offset schemes and the clean development mechanism in the Climate Change Convention are all notable examples. In fact, although industrialization and the pursuit of economic growth are the root causes of anthropogenic climate change, corporate actors continue to retain a 'sacred cow status' in the global effort to tackle climate change. Indeed, in some quarters, the perception is not so much that these actors are the cause of climate change but that they are the only hope for solving the problem of climate change (Watson 2006; Walhain 2006). Similarly, many ordinary citizens in the West, despite expressing positive sentiments towards environmentalism (as conceived in the Brundtland sense), are extremely antagonistic to any environmental policy that is perceived as retarding economic growth. Sarah Hendry, the Head of the Global Atmosphere Division in the UK Department for Environment, alluded to this point when she said that any government that neglects economic growth in the pursuit of climate mitigation will not live long to implement its decision.[2]

Governance-wise, there has been an unprecedented use of market instruments in the pursuit of environmental protection at the international level in the last decade. Jordan *et al.* (2003), for example, report that there has been up to a 50 per cent increase in the use of instruments such as eco-labels, eco-taxes and eco-management and auditing systems (EMAS) as a means of addressing environmental problems in Western industrialized countries between 1989 and 1995 (Jordan *et al* 2003: 3). According to Dobson (1998: 488) the philosophy of these instruments lies in the 'idea that we could buy our way to sustainability while producers of goods invented even more exotic ways of enabling us to do so'.

The last major element in the environmental modernization discourse comes in the form of the emphasis on public–private partnerships (PPPs), non-governmental organizations (NGOs) and other such voluntary non-state actors as vanguards for environmental governance at national and global levels. There exists a huge amount of literature focusing on the role of non-state actors in the steering of the wheel of global environmental governance; these include NGOs, transnational networks, businesses and PPPs and hybrid networks (Wapner 1997; Newell 2000; Higgott *et al.* 2000; Josselin and Wallace 2001; Betsil and Bulkeley 2006; Ole and Newman 2006). Although there are a few voices of caution (see McCarthy 2004; Holifield 2004; Christoff 2005; Barry and Eckersley 2005), the majority of these analyses seem to assume that we are witnessing the emergence of a global civil society capable and united in its aim of wresting power from the state or at least generating the sustained pressure needed to keep states on the path of ecologically sound and equitable global development. This literature has diverse theoretical underpinnings, from Foucault's governmentality theory to James Rosenau's notion of governance and Polanyi's 'dual movement', but, on an empirical level, it mostly seems to draw inspiration from the US environmental justice movement, which centres on the putatively successful campaign against the disproportionate siting of waste factories in black neighbourhoods.

Now, I do not think that it is reasonable to suggest that these neoliberal options and approaches have no merit whatsoever. But it remains the case that their underlying philosophy is such that it cannot be wholly reconciled with that of global sustainability as articulated in the Brundtland Report. Ted Benton makes this point in asserting that, 'while neoliberalism has proved extremely flexible and capable of adapting to most unlikely contexts, some of its key features remain wholly irreconcilable with the radical normative aspirations' of global sustainability (Benton, 1999: 199). These radical normative aspirations, according to Benton, most notably include the requirement for global redistribution of wealth along egalitarian principles. McCarthy (2004) puts the point equally succinctly. He says:

Advocates of ecological modernization theory too seldom recognize the parallel between their prescriptions and the received wisdom of neoliberalism: faith in markets and civil society over state; faith in capital to regulate itself voluntarily; and a firm conviction that economic growth can overcome nearly any obstacle, while questions of distribution and equity must wait on the back burner.

It has already been noted in several places in the previous sections that it is essentially the fundamental mismatch between the distributional demands of sustainability and the policy space available to states on the basis of a wider commitment to the neoliberal doctrine which is mostly responsible for the tensions and contradictions in the language and policies of regimes. In the next section I attempt to unpack the key meso-narratives that form the nexus of neoliberal governance with the aim of revealing the extent to which they ignore questions of distributive equity.

Environmental justice and neoliberal environmental governance

The central philosophy of neoliberal environmental governance boils down to the assumption that 'the on-going, internal dynamics of capitalist modernity can be harnessed to improve environmental quality' (McCarthy 2004: 328). As a conciliatory philosophy, ecological modernization seeks out the possibility of preserving the basic structure of the capitalist society while permitting marginal adjustments in current technical, economic and institutional arrangements. Hence, Weale (1992: 89) describes it in terms of searching out the 'point of equilibrium between the imperatives of capital accumulation, political legitimacy and environmental protection'. The faith is that 'structural design in the modern industrial society can be rectified up to the point that environmental problem is perfectly solved' (Mol 2000: 313). Therefore, the philosophy underpinning neoliberal environmental governance has little or nothing to say about power, about the political economy source of scarcity and about distributional politics. While emphasizing a simple faith in technocratic solutions to the environment and in modest 'eco-social restructuring of the basic institutions of the techno-system' (Huber 1985: 56, cited in Mol 1996: 313), it remains dangerously silent on the wider distributional import of enclosure and the other transformations in the social relations with nature that neoliberalism as an environmental project entails. Indeed, the empirical materials covered in this work and the foregoing discussions would suggest that the most significant inadequacy of neoliberal environmental patterns of governance is their inability to countenance questions of distributive equity inherent in the concept of global sustainability.

Benton (1999) has briefly considered the implications of the pervasive norms of neoliberalism on aspirations for distributive justice in international institutions for sustainability. He emphasizes that these institutions have evolved and continue to function in a capitalist context so that, although notions of justice informed by the Brundtland Report tend to serve as regulative ideals, intense tensions remain between these normative aspirations and the tendencies and 'practicalities of contemporary capitalism' (ibid.: 209). For Benton, capitalism's problematic relationship with environmental justice issues will not be resolved by simply trying to offset or correct 'market failures', as the dynamic tendency in market systems for overexploitation is not a consequence of market failure but the very form of calculation that constitutes the market. Benton puts it very succinctly:

> Given the current institutional forms, power relations and economic norms which govern patterns of growth in the world systems, the proposal to target growth at meeting the needs of the poorest whilst preserving the environmental needs of future generations is simply not a feasible option. The prevailing institutional forms are such as to favour the subsumption of residual normative commitments to justice and environmental protection into an economist reading of sustainability as a project aimed at preserving the future resource base for future capital accumulation on a global scale.
>
> (Ibid.: 225)

For Benton, this situation, as for Hayward (2002), is not the same thing as saying that sustainable development is a smoke screen for business as usual or for masking a more fundamental conflict between the interests of the rich North and the poor South, not least because the concept of global sustainability has resulted in an increase and not a decrease in the number of debates on North–South equity. Rather, it suggests that, although sustainable development was originally formulated with a view to striking a balance between capitalist exploitation and distributive justice, the implementation has been difficult in institutions for global environmental governance because of the appeal of neoliberalism and the ways in which important segments in the North and South have subscribed to it.

Julie Davidson (2000: 25–37) corroborates this point. She argues that the core problems encountered in designing intuitively just and equitable environmental policies at the global level arise mainly from the fact that the prevailing ideas of justice stem out of 'a particular set of politico-economic components, in which the pursuit of individual freedom and welfare defined solely in material utilitarian terms have been elevated to an ethical and political ideal'. Continuing, she notes that these politico-economic components conflict with 'the strong normative dimensions embodied in the radical version of sustainability', and so represent the major obstacle in 'addressing concerns about ecological integrity and global social justice'. Barry (Barry B 1999: 117) equally alludes to this point when he argues that neoliberal environmental governance is a highly disciplinary approach to global environmental questions in that the process of ecological management remains heavily weighted in 'favor of dominant industrial interests'. For Barry, the approach is insistently 'concerned with finding means to specific ends and is unable to articulate the full range of normative issues relating to social–environmental affairs' (ibid.: 117).

Many other scholars have provided very useful insights into the inherent

178 *Normative critique*

contradictions between the dominant modes of neoliberal governance and the ideal of global environmental justice (Daly 1996; Sachs 1999; Redclift 2000; Holland 2000; Bernstein 2001; Martinez-Alier 2002). Herman Daly stresses the point that much of the perception that the dominant neoliberal approaches to environmental governance can secure global sustainability resides in the fact that the imperative of distributional politics implied in the notion of sustainable development is either often completely neglected or conflated with the concept of allocation. He argues, however, that allocation is concerned only with supply and demand, based on income, wealth or capacity to pay. This implies that an allocation is said to be efficient insofar as what is demanded matches what is produced. Distributive equity, on the other hand, is concerned with the underlying institutional structure and power relations, which influence how income, wealth and the capacity to pay are allocated within and between countries. It follows, he says, that whereas a given allocation is either efficient or inefficient, a given distribution is either just or unjust. Moreover, whereas the market can ensure efficient allocation, it cannot ensure just distribution (Daly 1996: 158–60; Okereke 2006a).

Daly's argument is very important because it makes clear that, even if it is accepted that market rationality can lead to greater environmental protection, it does not necessarily follow that the various segments of the global community will be well placed to enjoy comparable levels of ecosystemic integrity and material well-being arising from a consistent application of market approaches to environmental management. This in part was the basis of the argument of the developing countries against the principle of prior informed consent (PIC) during the elaboration of the Basel Convention. They pointed out that it was dubious to rely on market forces to determine the terms of the distribution of an environmental bad (in this case hazardous wastes) under the condition of immense economic asymmetry between the South and the North. The general position is that, unless there is first a fundamental restructuring of the global economic infrastructure, which currently works in favour of the dominant North, it would be extremely unreasonable to expect that the unseen hand of the market can guarantee a just distribution of environmental goods or bads between the North and the South (Okereke 2006a). Indeed, the injustices that characterize the siting of hazardous waste plants in the USA and other industrialized countries attest to the fact that the market rationality argument is equally untenable even within countries that have the benefit of advanced environmental regulations and effective political authorities. It is against this background that Low and Gleeson (2001: 3) argue that the only condition which can guarantee a just distribution of environmental goods, both within and between states, is viable political struggle and democratic politics:

> There is no alternative to political struggle, deliberation and action to arrive at a just distribution. Just as the market is needed for allocative efficiency, so some form of democratic politics is needed for just distribution. . . . To solve the problems of distribution and scale, the world would need all the

political and ethical creativity and skill it can muster to develop new political methods.

(Low and Gleeson 2001: 3–4)

But herein lies another problem of the efforts to reconcile neoliberal environmental governance with the distributive aspirations embedded in the ideal of global sustainability. For, as noted earlier, one of the cardinal features of neoliberal environmental governance is the reliance on science and so-called expert knowledge groups for the definition of and solution to environmental problems. However, as Barry very well notes, 'technological environmentalism' remains intimately connected 'with the environmental discourse of policy elites and scientists close to the corridor of power' (Barry 1999: 113). Its key component is the belief that 'the objective scientific "experts" are those in whom trust should be placed when it comes to decision-making about the environment. Because of their relative ignorance the general public are disqualified from participation in this process at any level but the most general' (Pepper 1986: 37). This explains the sharp rise in the profile of international epistemic communities and the reliance continually placed upon them as credible sources of international environmental decision-making (see Haas 1992).

'The increasingly scientized veneer of modern environmentalism' (Hawkins 1993: 223) has created a dynamic in which those who are able to position themselves as 'experts' gain leverage over the 'lay people' in setting the agenda and deciding options for global response strategies. At the same time, the elevation of certain methods and prescriptions in our epistemologies (Breyman 1993) also means that environmentalism, according to Hawkins, 'has been rapidly transformed into depoliticized, managerialist discourse, in which neoclassical resource economics and national environmental accounting are being merged into frameworks that serve to limit public discourse' (Hawkins 1993: 223). It follows that, if Low and Gleeson are right in asserting that deliberation and political struggle are indispensable conditions for achieving distributional justice, one would be hard pressed to expect that the marginalized South could ever hope to secure just policies in global environmental regimes. David Schlosberg has this scenario in view when making the argument that participation and recognition should be given increased emphasis in the discourse of global environmental justice (Schlosberg 2005: 102–107, 2006). And yet the point has to be made that there is a difference between participation and quality participation. At present, most accounts of the process of environmental decision-making tend to conflate attendance with participation. But frequently, the impression that one gets from observing negotiation processes is that developed country parties operate from the mindset that developing country parties lack necessary information and would thus likely come to an 'informed' conclusion if they were sufficiently educated with respect to the issues at stake. For example, during the elaboration of UNCLOS III, one US negotiator came with charts and figures calculated in some cases to three decimal places. His aim was to convince representatives of Southern states that they would gain more

180 *Normative critique*

in financial terms if they allowed the seabed regime to be designed in ways that ran solely on a free market basis (Friedheim 1993).

Another key element in the neoliberal environmental governance philosophy that requires close examination is the argument that Western-style industrialization and capitalist economies are merely necessary stages that must be passed on the road to an ecologically stable society. The logic, as noted, is that capitalist economies provide both the wealth and the technological know-how that are required to maintain a high standard of living, enforce advanced environmental regulations and secure sound ecological integrity. According to this view, it is better to concentrate on pursuing industrial economic growth worldwide as this would provide a share of surplus that could be plugged back to improve environmental standards globally. Again, the fact that the environmental quality of the industrialized countries is generally better is used to buttress this argument.

Now, there is no doubt that a certain degree of poverty leads to a greater despoliation of the environment. For example, a considerable amount of energy could be saved if the millions of people in developing countries who currently depend on woodburning for their daily cooking and heating needs were to have access to more energy-efficient heating systems. As the Brundtland Report clearly admits, poverty can lead to more environmental destruction under some circumstances. However, it is very difficult to stretch this argument to say that Western-style capitalism is an inevitable prerequisite for achieving global environmental sustainability. First, as many empirical studies show, about 10 times more resources would be needed if the whole of the global population was to consume as many resources as those in the industrialized countries. Studies deploying the concept of the 'ecological footprint' and 'ecological space' make it clear that the economic prosperity achieved by the developed countries was, and still is, heavily 'dependent on extra territorial productive capacity through trade or appropriated natural flows' (Nijkamp *et al.* 2004: 751; cf. Wackernagel and Silverstein 2000). In many cases these studies indicate that the developed countries have already exceeded their share of the world's resources and are feeding on those of the developing countries (Wackernagel and Rees 1996; Haberl *et al.* 2004, Monfreda 2004). These data show, as Wackernagel and Silverstein (2000: 393) put it, that 'their footprint has grown larger than their actual territories can sustain, such that they now run an "ecological deficit"'. In fact, those who 'emphasize the positive potentials' (McCarthy 2004: 328) between capitalist growth and environmental justice are wont to neglect the extent to which the material prosperity enjoyed in the North is directly related to the environmental degradation and economic poverty that is experienced in the South (Gokay 2006; Okereke 2006b). For example, to the same extent that industrialized countries have built their development on cheap oil, oil-producing developing countries have been deprived of valuable income and opportunities for improved well-being (Gokay 2006; Fouskas 2006; Mofford 2006). Even now, developed countries, which comprise 25 per cent of the world's population, consume 70 per cent of the world's energy, 85 per cent of its timber and 78 per cent of its metals. The degree of inequity is so glaring that even an EU White Paper on Growth, Competitiveness and Employment (cited in Carley and Spapens 1998: 29) has had to admit that:

Global justice and neoliberal environmental governance 181

Extrapolating current industrial consumption and production patterns to the entire world would require ten times the existing resources, which illustrates the scope for possible distribution tensions and ecological problems at a global level if current tendencies are not curbed.

Sachs (1999) argues that, prior to the rise of the notion of sustainable development, established thinking favoured the reasoning that there are no limits to growth. The concept of limitless growth, he says, went hand in hand with the notion of the superabundance of environmental resources. For Sachs, the establishment of dominant thinking in favour of limitless growth created an atmosphere under which the justice discourses became effectively marginalized in international economic arrangements, with discussions on development and economic growth dominating the arena (Sachs 1999). The process (oversimplified) is as follows. With the notion of well-being firmly entrenched in economic prosperity, international justice came to be seen not so much as concerning itself with (re)distributing wealth among nations but as increasing the total 'pie' that is available and creating more opportunities for more nations to share in the unending resources through free trade, export stimulation and economic aid. This perception was supported by the hegemonic idea that there is no alterative to the market, nor indeed is any alternative desirable, as the market is seen as providing the best means of increasing wealth, spreading development and reducing injustices (Bhagwati 1993: 42–49). This is the logic behind the flurry of international development aid and related activities, which are mostly presented as acts of international justice (Okereke 2006a).

Before concluding this section it remains to say something, albeit briefly, about the relationship between the increasing reliance on non-state actors and PPPs as a means of addressing global environmental challenges – a trend that in a sense can be regarded as one of the most rapidly expanding phenomenon in global environmental governance circles (Rosenau 1997; 1999; Wapner 1997; Young 1997; Newell 2000; Paterson et al. 2003; Collingwood 2006; Betsil and Bulkeley 2006; Dingwerth and Patterberg 2006). As noted, there are many theoretical perspectives from which scholars have sought to explain this phenomenon, but what seems to unite all of them is the belief that these actors have become a lot more influential in the management of global environmental affairs. The general impression is that globalization has led to the 'dilution of government authority' (Low and Gleeson 2001: 2) and that these agents have become insatiable because of the changes in the nature and function of states. Interestingly, some scholars perceive this development in the light of an emerging global civil society capable of curbing the accumulations and exploitative impulses of both states and corporations (Risse-Kappen 1995; Wapner 1997; cf. Hunold and Dryzek 2005: 77).

But although sharing the vision of a strong global civil society expressed in this body of work, it is important to recognize as well that voluntarism can actually be the most subtle of the three dimensions of neoliberal environmental governance. This is because the phenomenon can create a very powerful sense of commonality while masking underlying politics of interest. At the same time, the impression that there has been 'a proliferation and diffusion of state power

182 *Normative critique*

through institutional forms' (McCarthy and Prudham 2004: 280), while not entirely untrue, also tempts us to overstate how far these actors really upset existing structures of power and how effective they are in performing the act of governance. It is not entirely surprising then that, despite the proliferation of literature on governmentality and voluntarism, little scholarship exists that has considered in detail how the orientation of states towards these actors define their approaches or what Barry and Eckersley (2005: xvii) call 'the critical independence of the public sphere' (cf. Hunold and Dryzek 2005: 77). Equally poorly understood is the extent to which these actors contribute to decisive changes in the lives of the marginalized sections of the world. Indeed, it is all too easy even for otherwise critical scholars to forget, as McCarthy and Prudham (2004: 280) put it, that 'faith in corporate cultural shifts and direct citizen pressure to "green" capitalism is suspiciously coterminous with the self-regulation and neo-corporatism characteristic of neoliberalism more broadly' (cf. Cox 1983; Jessop 2002). For instance, Ryan Holifield's work on neoliberalism and environmental justice in the USA shed light on how what he calls 'a special kind of neoliberalism' by the Clinton administration served to 'normalize' the aggrieved and restive approach to environmental justice of non-white and poor communities by developing '"neocommunitarian" programmes to support political empowerment and economic self-efficiency in marginalized communities' (Holifield 2004: 285). In reality, though, these programmes were actually designed to skirt the more radical collectivist approach to environmental justice proposed by these communities, which challenges the power structures of the USA. In the end, the government converted a radical movement for justice with a broad progressive agenda into a community co-operative scheme that now focuses on building trust and self-help economic empowerment. It is reasonable to suggest that much of the private governance and voluntarism, which are encouraged and promoted as 'new' instruments of global environmental governance, have different degrees of foundation in this 'roll out' neoliberalism (Jessop 2002), the aim of which is to preoccupy and pacify aggrieved sections of the international community while leaving the fundamental structural causes of environmental injustice unchanged.

We can deduce from the foregoing that, despite the force of the arguments upon which neoliberal environmental governance is premised, the approach contradicts the distributive equity element of global sustainable development. There are doubts that, even in industrialized countries that boast well-informed civil societies and strong political authorities, neoliberal approaches to environmental governance can secure a just distribution of environmental goods. Given, therefore, the well-known massive economic, power and technological asymmetry between the developed North and the poor South in the context of the added problem of scale and anarchy associated with international relations, it is extremely difficult to imagine how neoliberal approaches to environmental governance can be implemented without compromising the demands of global environmental justice.

Global environmental justice and regime analysis

What then are the implications of the foregoing discussions for the ways that international environmental regimes are studied? The basic answer is self-evident from both the analysis and the critique that were developed in the preceding sections of this work. It has to be quickly stated, however, that any attempt to provide a comprehensive discussion on this issue would require a separate volume given the extremely large and diverse scholarship that has been devoted to the regime analytical research agenda over the past 20 years (Ruggie 1975; Keohane and Nye 1977; Young 1980; Krasner 1983b; Keohane 1984; Haas 1989; Vogler 1995; Hansenclever *et al.* 1996; Arts 2000). But the few remarks that follow should be enough to establish the basic point.

The starting point is to note that the study of international regimes arose principally out of the dissatisfaction with what Haggard and Simmons call the 'sharp contrast between the competitive, zero sum "anarchy" of interstate relations and the "authority" of the domestic politics' (Haggard and Simmons 1987: 491). In other words, the regime analytical research agenda emerged as a counterpoint to the zero-sum 'realist' approaches of the international system in which international politics is characterized solely in terms of power and the contest for relative gains by state actors in an essentially anarchical international environment. The popularity of the regime theory also resides in its departure from the once dominant concept of international organizations with its focus on elaborate institutional structures and international bureaucratic politics (Krasner 1983b). The regime approach offered an alternative to these other two approaches because it placed emphasis on norms as well as both implicit and explicit rules governing the behaviour of states in a defined issue-area. In doing so, room was made for comprehending the roles of informal practices and implicit understandings that underpin international co-operation. John Ruggie, widely credited with first employing the concept of regimes in the study of international co-operation, clearly meant it as a way of capturing the multitude of discernable and fairly regularized patterns in states' behaviours that are not explicitly prompted or dictated by the existence of international organizations or codified rules. In making the simple and profound statement that 'international behavior is institutionalized', Ruggie (1975: 559) meant to underscore what he calls the 'intersubjective quality' (Ruggie 1982: 196) of international co-operation. This entails that the character of international co-operation is not only discernible from the clearly stated conventions found in the policies of the rule-making bodies but also 'that there are underlying principles of order and meaning that shape the manner of their formation and transformations' (ibid.: 196). These underlying principles provide the 'critical tacit understanding that make the bare bones of legal text both comprehensible and workable' (Vogler 2000: 21). This, in turn, speaks to the existence, albeit vaguely, of a given social purpose or teleology to which institutionalized behaviour is directed (Vogler 2003: 27).

But the scholarship of regimes did not eventually mature along this line. Rather, the concept was cleverly hijacked by liberal 'functionalists' who began to use the concept of regimes more narrowly as a way of technically explaining interstate co-operation. The focus then turned to modelling the strategic behaviour of states and predicting the type and strength of regime that might result from such game-theoretic constructs (Keohane and Nye 1977; Snidal 1985; Grieco 1988b). The notion of collective purpose was abandoned as emphasis turned to understating the variables (and later, in response to criticism, the mix of variables) that either enhance or inhibit the interactions of rational state actors (Haas *et al*. 1993; Young 1994, 1997). Although many analysts operating from this rational choice model were quick to admit that patterns of state behaviour are influenced by underlying norms, they maintained that such norms are altogether consistent with the pursuit of national self-interests and therefore could not be understood in the moral sense. For example, in reference to Krasner's definition of regimes as 'sets of implicit or explicit principles, norms, rules and decision-making procedures around which actors expectations converge in any given issue-area' (Krasner 1983b: 2), Keohane (1984: 57) cautions that norms, alongside rules and procedures, must be understood in a deontological sense such that the terms are not taken as being capable of generating obligations that 'are morally binding regardless of considerations of narrowly defined interests'. For, as he says, 'to include norms [defined in the sense of morality] in a definition of necessary regime characteristics would be to make the conception of regimes based strictly on self-interests, a contradiction in terms' (ibid.: 57).

Indeed, it is fair to say that by the time the regime research agenda captured the imagination of international relations scholars, it had come to be firmly associated with neoliberal institutionalism. According to this view, states were not only conceived as rational egoists incapable of appreciating moral arguments but also depicted as unitary actors, meaning that states were regarded as homogenous entities with well-ordered preferences and utility functions. Furthermore, and despite wide acknowledgement that this is not the case in reality, all states according to the liberal institutionalists' approach were seen as equal units. By entrenching these assumptions, neoliberal institutionalists succeeded in endorsing positivism as the dominant epistemological approach to regime analysis (Waltz 1979; Keohane 1984; cf. Viotti and Kauppi 1987: 519; Mansbach and Ferguson 1987: 558; Mantle 1999: 89; Buzan and Little 2001: 3; Vogler 2003: 25–27). Regimes then became conceptualized merely 'as intervening variables standing between basic causal factors on the one hand and outcomes and behavior on the other hand' (Krasner 1983b: 1). This 'contractual' perspective of regimes (Hansenclever *et al*. 1997: 45) implied that institutional arrangements merely provide the means for interest seeking agents to search for optimal solutions to international issues when individual action fails to 'secure Pareto-optimal outcomes' (Krasner 1983b: 2).

The general impact of this approach on the study of environmental regimes was that the overriding concern became that of the effectiveness of regimes, promoted, as Bernstein (2001: 3) puts it, on the 'quest to design better institutions to manage the Earth's resources or to respond to immediate and pressing problems'. The concern, then, was the search for order and how to avoid suboptimal outcomes as questions of justice became completely relegated to the background (Vogler 2000: 22).

More recently, however, a body of works (usually gathered under the broad banner of constructivism) has emerged to challenge the dominant neoliberal institutionalists' assumptions and approaches to regime analysis, spurred on, as it were, by a series of observable phenomena in the development and operation of multilateral environmental regimes (Kratochwil 1989; Onuf 1989; Franck 1990, 1995; Young 1994; Ruggie 1993; Litfin 1993; Vogler 2003). The main project was to recapture the sociological dimension of regimes, that is to show that regimes are social phenomena characterized not only by self-interested actions but also by genuine efforts to organize the planet on the basis of shared intuitions and intentionality. It was also to emphasize the 'intersubjective quality' of regimes, which refers to the fact that regimes are not simply intervening variables, standing 'out there' between the otherwise normal activities of states and outcomes, but they form part of the social life – both shaping and being shaped by the identity of the actors. This understanding is clearly possible only by according a special place to the role and influence of ideas, norms and values in regimes.

But although constructivist approaches represented an important corrective to the rationalistic and positivistic approaches to regimes, they failed to concern themselves more directly with moral and ethical issues in regimes. At the same time, while generating an ample understanding of the ways in which different norms and ideas are constructed and contested in the process of regime development (e.g. Litfin 1993), they failed, in the words of Steven Bernstein, 'to address the prior question of which norms get promoted or prevail in the first place' (Bernstein 2001: 3; cf. Dyer 1989; Bernstein 2000: 465). Constructivist accounts of international regime development provide important insights into how language and discourse are used to construct social reality but they cannot, or at least do not, tell us much about the content of regimes in terms of which set of norms prevails, why they do and what sublime interest they serve. Helpful as the approach is in emphasizing the sociological and normative dimension of regimes, it runs the significant risk of deprecating the role of power and material structure. Further, because constructivism does not concern itself with the underlying order, the crucial point about teleology raised by Vogler is largely sidestepped. The risk is that plenty of effort is devoted to explaining concepts and deconstructing texts while precious little effort is devoted to an assessment of the goal that co-operation is, or ought to be, pursuing.

The foregoing analysis and discussions suggest that international environmental regime development is significantly characterized by a complex interplay between different sets of norms, ideas and values (contra rationalism). The most significant are, on the one hand, the norm of distributive equity, which draws its force from the critical tacit understanding among international actors and the more explicit recognition accorded to it in the paradigm of global sustainability and, on the other hand, the economic norms associated with the hegemonic neoliberal philosophy. The analysis equally indicates that, although this value conflict is not without serious impact, it is the norms associated with the political economic hegemonic doctrine that are mostly favoured to come out on top. The insights gained from Gramscian accounts of the nature and mode of the operation of hegemonic ideology are important in that they help us to transcend the determinism associated with historic materialism and the utopianism that sometimes characterizes normative and idealistic accounts of the international system. We see that international politics, contrary to what realists would have us believe, are not beyond the pale of moral arguments, even though the forces of these arguments remain seriously circumscribed. A combination of Gramscian and constructivist perspectives performs well because we can at once appreciate the crucial role of structure and the ways in which power can be implicated in social relations without losing sight of the role of agency and the ability of well-articulated moral discourses to challenge and sometimes upset the dominant order.

Conclusion

Neoliberalism is not only a political economic concept but also an environmental project. It is an environmental project to the extent that many of its core features have direct implications for human relations with nature. These include distinctive modes of resource appropriation and property rights. Although neoliberalism has proved very resilient and highly adaptable, the philosophy remains unable to countenance the radical normative prescriptions embedded in the concept of global environmental sustainability. In particular, neoliberalism cannot deliver on the distributive demand of sustainability especially within the context of the developed and the developing countries. The ecological modernization discourse represents a very powerful handmaiden of the neoliberal project. Its appeal is closely connected to the promise to simultaneously deliver on both economic growth and environmental protection. It transpires, however, on a closer reading, that the ecological modernization discourse rests on three narratives, all of which operate on questionable assumptions. It is not reasonable to expect that the long-term goals of sustainability can be achieved by the means of neoliberal environmental governance.

10 Conclusions

I have attempted to examine the way that ideas of justice feature both implicitly and explicitly in the course of the development and operation of global environmental regimes. The project was prompted by a noticeable rhetorical inflation of justice in international environmental governance circles and relevant academic literature. The broad aim, therefore, was to understand the nature of the global environmental justice discourse that has developed steadily since the first United Nations Conference on the Law of the Sea and to indicate the impacts, prospects and limitations of this discourse on general interstate relations, but especially within the context of international co-operation for global environmental management and North–South equity. The specific aims were: (i) to identify the particular notions of justice that underlie core environmental policies and the interests they privilege, and to assess the degree of compatibility between such prevailing notions of justice and the concept of sustainable development; and (ii) to highlight the inadequacies of the main approaches to regime analysis as a means of accounting for the ethical dimensions of institutions for global environmental governance.

Demands for justice in international relations are not in themselves new. One need only think of the anti-colonial movements of the early and mid-twentieth century, the debates surrounding the UN Universal Declaration of Human Rights and the aspirations for just and equitable international economic relations canonized in the formal proposal for a New International Economic Order (NIEO) by the group of developing nations (G-77) in 1973. However, this work demonstrates that it is contemporary concern over drastic changes in the global environment that has provided the impetus for the most recent intense and widespread academic engagement with intragenerational equity and the wider ethical issues associated with interstate relations and global institutional governance (Low and Gleeson 2001: 2). This concern for justice in the international relations of the environment has been fuelled by a number of other developments, including socio-economic globalization, deepening levels of independence among states, an increase in disparities of wealth and the awareness of these disparities, a general rise in the appreciation of the concept of a global community, and the peculiar nature of

188 *Normative critique*

environmental problems, which, among others, demand an unusual degree of collective action.

This work finds that demands for global environmental justice arise at various points but mainly take the shape of: (i) contestations for equal access to common property resources; (ii) demands for equitable and fairer representation in global environmental decision-making circles; (iii) clamour for a fairer international economic structure and policies; (iv) claims of rights to certain basic environmental goods such as land and clean water; and (v) demands for compensation arising from historical injustices, especially in relation to the past use of commonly owned resources. For the most part, the demands for greater justice in international co-operation for global environmental management arise from the political South who believe that 'the current concern with environmental issues has emerged out of the problems experienced by the industrially advanced countries whereas the most important aspect of the problems which afflict the environment of the majority of mankind is that of under development' (Founex Report 1971: 1). An increasingly important dimension of the global environmental justice discourse is the protests by indigenous communities against violent removals from their ancestral lands and the attendant denial of access to contiguous and proximate natural resources. However, this book equally demonstrates that the political North also appeals to the need for justice. They question the fairness of the demand that they should take responsibility for historical injustices and also attempt to show how the revision of international policies in the ways suggested by the developing countries could harm their own development or force them to bear a disproportionate burden of international environmental co-operation.

A major result of these contestations over justice is that regime texts and policies are characterized by a contradictory dialectic corresponding to different visions of a just and equitable international society. The nature of the tension arising from these contestations was seen to be particularly intractable for at least four main reasons. The first is that there are no overarching theories of international distributive justice to which actors may readily appeal. Although the theorization of international justice is one of the fastest growing aspects of moral and political philosophy, there remains much to be done in terms of identifying how proposed principles of justice might be adapted to overcome the peculiar challenges associated with the sovereignty-based structure of the international system. This undertheorization of the concept of international distributive justice not only means that parties usually rely on bits and pieces of 'local' theories of justice in their arguments but also results in a situation in which the ideas of justice as canvassed by parties are mostly *ad hoc*, contingent and fragmented. Accordingly, although parties often commit to pursue justice in the text of regimes, the negotiations of the substantive policies are usually marked by a clash of competing principles arising from varying ideas of justice. The second is that, although the commitment to the pursuit of global sustainable development is fairly well established, there are still dissensions on what represents the best approach to solving the problem of global poverty. The third point is that, in the absence of a global government or supranational authority, there is no global distributor of resources who has the power to determine or impose a particular distribution of rights and benefits. The fourth and related point is that, despite growing levels of political and socio-economic interdependence, there remain varying visions of the international community and different senses of solidarity and the common good. Despite these difficulties, the analysis strongly indicates, as is already evident from what has been said so far, that questions of justice have become a prominent part of the attempts by the international community to respond to the drastic changes in the global environment and the general issues that have arisen at the junction between global environmental protection and the economic development of states. Further, with concepts like per capita emissions and the statistical value of life becoming regular terminologies in international decision-making circles, there is little doubt that questions of justice will become even more critical and central in international co-operative efforts towards sustainability in the twenty-first century.

There is a certain hazard in generalization, but the empirical materials covered in this work indicate that, for the most part, the developing countries prefer and seek to promote a more solidarist conception of the international community along with egalitarian ideas of justice in the policies of environmental regimes, whereas the developed industrialized countries tend to promote sovereign-based approaches to global environmental problems along with economic (neoliberal) ideas of justice. A study of the convention texts and policies of three contemporary global environmental agreements shows that both approaches exert some influence on the character and functions of regimes.

The aspirations for global equity and distributional justice by the poor developing countries have given rise to concepts such as the common heritage of mankind (Third United Nations Conference on the Law of the Sea; UNCLOS III), the non-discrimination principle (Basel Convention) and the common but differentiated responsibility principle (United Nations Framework Convention on Climate Change; UNFCCC) in regime texts. In addition, the analysis demonstrates that there have been some significant procedural changes aimed at accommodating the desire for a more equitable representation by the South in global environmental decision-making circles. These adjustments were particularly noticeable with respect to the Law of the Sea treaty and the Convention on Climate Change. At the same time, texts of regimes frequently contain explicit commitments to distributional justice and the necessity of giving attention to the needs of the poor and vulnerable groups, as well as the notion that individuals have certain rights and privileges with respect to environmental quality and access to global environmental resources.

However, this research demonstrates that, for the most part, it is the libertarian ideas of justice advocated by the rich industrialized countries that underpin the core policies of most of the global environmental regimes studied. For example, the need for equitable international economic relations, and even the need to use the 1982 Law of the Sea as a means of addressing wider issues of international justice, were both stressed in the preamble of UNCLOS III. But after more than 10 years of negotiation, the Law of the Sea treaty approved the nationalization and 'enclosure' of over 36 per cent of the ocean space, about 90 per cent of the living resources it contains and about an equivalent percentage of its extractable mineral resources (Sanger 1986: 64; Pontercorvo 1988: 229; Friedheim 1993: 113). Moreover, key players in industrialized countries, led by the USA and the UK, repudiated the common heritage of mankind principle and the seabed regime in which it was designed to apply. For all of its intuitive appeal, they saw the common heritage of mankind principle as another attempt to legitimize socialism in the international economic order, in some quarters describing the concept as nothing but 'declaring a right to steal' (US Senate, Subcommittee on 1982 Law of the Sea).

In the wake of the scandalous dumping of hazardous wastes on the poor developing countries by waste brokers from the industrialized countries, the developing countries sought to highlight the link between these scandalous deals and the endemic inequities in the international political economy. Accordingly, they sought a regime that would ban all such waste trade deals, introduce fairer rules of trade and impose relevant restrictions on the manufacturers of toxic wastes globally. But the developed countries saw the proposal for a ban on toxic waste dumping in developing countries as a violation of free trade and an incursion on personal liberties and freedom. They argued that toxic wastes are products whose value and movement should be determined on the basis of supply and demand. It eventually took the threat of mass voting in subsequent Conference of Parties meetings to secure a ban, which is yet to come into force.

The issue of climate change resurrected age-old problems of international justice, including the issue of historical domination. The character of the problem was widely acknowledged as one in which 'the central ethical issue ... involves the rich imposing risks upon the poorer and more vulnerable' (Grubb 1995: 467–468). Further, the scope of the problem was admitted as having the potential to 'intensify and alter existing disparities of power and wealth both between and within countries' (Paterson 1996b: 11). But despite the fact that parties to the Climate Change Convention recognized the need to make international equity the touchstone of response strategies [Article 3 (1)], the core policies of the Convention, at the insistence of the developed country parties, ended up as a complicated set of programmes that gave the rich states and the big corporations rights to buy and sell emission units even in the developing countries. Not satisfied with this, the USA has continued to insist that international justice demands that the developing countries, in the midst of their poverty, must commit to 'meaningful' emission reduction programmes.

These points reveal a great deal about the lineaments of the interpretations of justice that prevail in global environmental regimes. The rich industrialized countries often favour the idea of justice as property rights or justice as self-interested reciprocity, both of which consider people to be *entitled* to their market-allocated share of wealth irrespective of the degree of want or poverty surrounding them (Nozick 1974: 238; Gauthier 1986). According to these libertarian interpretations of justice, the market is regarded as inherently just and capable of efficiently distributing costs and benefits such that state interventions are viewed not only as unnecessary but also, in fact, as violations of people's individual rights to liberty

(Nozick 1974: ix; Hayek 1976: 68–71). It was shown that, although these ideas of justice were not designed in their original formulations to apply between states, they are nevertheless promoted in environmental regimes by the North mainly because of their close 'fit' with the dominant neoliberal politico-economic ideology. This book demonstrates that the rich industrialized countries, who have commanding roles in the international political economy, tend to favour these neoliberal ideas of justice because they help them retain their leverage over the developing countries and ensure that global co-operation towards sustainability does not radically upset some of the core values to which the ruling blocs in these societies are committed.

The developed countries often defend these ideas of justice by arguing that they ultimately ensure prosperity for all states, even if, initially, some states might have to struggle (Bhagwati 1993). They propose that there is no alternative to the free market but rather that the free market brings about economic prosperity, which in turn enables states to take good care of the environment such that the free market is positively linked with environmental sustainability (GATT 1992b; Bhagwati 1993). It was not within the scope of this research to investigate these claims in detail but the book calls attention to figures from the United Nations Human Development Report (2004) which clearly indicate that the forceful integration of the majority of states into a single global economy has not produced the kind of prosperity prophesied by Western economists and international financial institutions such as the International Monetary Fund and the World Bank. For example, this report reveals, among other provoking figures, that the industrialized countries, with 25 per cent of the world's population, consume about 78 per cent of the global natural resources and account for over 76 per cent of the global consumption expenditure, whilst the degree of poverty has increased in the developing countries in the last 5 years. There is therefore a serious doubt about the validity of the reasons advanced for the promotion of these ideas of justice in regime policies.

In fact, by confronting the core ideas of the two neoliberal ideas of justice with the normative essence of sustainable development as articulated in the 1987 World Commission on Environment and Development (the Brundtland Report, *Our Common Future*; WCED 1987), this book finds that it is extremely difficult to achieve global sustainable development on the basis of these ideas of justice. The analysis revealed four major areas of incompatibility between the neoliberal interpretations of justice and the ethical requirements of sustainable development. First, whereas the concept of sustainable development requires the establishment of rules and institutions 'that seek to embody some notions of common good for the planet as a whole' (Hurrell and Kingsbury 1992: 6), the neoliberal interpretations of justice build on heterogeneity in the conceptions of the good life. Second, whereas the concept of sustainable development entails 'changes in the legal and institutional frameworks [that will enable states] to enforce the common interest' (WCED 1987: 63), the neoliberal ideas of justice sanction the neutrality of states and *laissez-faire* politics. Third, although the Brundtland Report is clear that the concept of sustainable development requires the use of redistributive taxes and the

192 *Normative critique*

direct transfer of resources from the North to the South to meet the needs of the majority of the global population (WCED 1987: 3, 6, 47), the neoliberal conceptions of justice prohibit such transfers on the basis that they violate the rights that people have to their property (Nozick 1974: 238). And fourth, neoliberal ideas of justice approve of the enclosure of commonly owned natural recourses, conceiving of such acts of enclosure as the only way to avoid the ultimate degradation of the commons, whereas the concept of sustainable development entails faith in collective ownership and management of global resources. Overall, the research demonstrates that neither the Southern quest for greater economic parity with the North nor the wider objective of global environmental sustainability can be readily achieved under the prevailing approaches to sustainable development and international environmental co-operation.

The greatest curiosity of these contestations over justice in regime development, however, is the fact that mainstream approaches to regime analysis continue to underappreciate their import as well as the general consequences of the normative dimensions of institutions for global environmental governance. The research demonstrates that proponents of the neorealist and the neoliberal institutionalist approaches to regime analysis continue to debate the question of whether moral values are applicable or inapplicable to interstate institutions – a question that for all intents and purposes has become redundant and anachronistic. Accordingly, the book ends with a normative critique of the orthodox approaches to regime analysis and finds their positivist methods and epistemologies to be grossly inadequate as a means of capturing the prospects and limitations of the increasing aspirations for international distributive justice within the context of sustainability in general and in the operation of multilateral environmental regimes in particular.

Policy debates

The most prominent implication of this work in terms of the study of international relations is that it underscores the importance of values and norms in regime development. The analysis demonstrates that a great deal of the dynamics of regime construction can be accounted for by focusing on the contestations for environmental justice, that is the distribution of environmental benefits and burdens within the global community. These contestations were shown as already exerting significant effects on the language of state actors and other entities in the international arena, especially in terms of how they justify their positions on given environmental issues and policies. It has also been shown that these contestations for justice affect parties' bargaining postures, the rules of procedure, the choice of bargaining environment and the acceptability of substantive policies.

Despite the fact that parties often take different views of what constitutes justice, and notwithstanding the ample evidence regarding the role of the balance of power and self-interests in the rules and operation of regimes, the current position nevertheless represents an enormous improvement on orthodox conceptions and frameworks in which interstate relations were held as being beyond the limits of morality (Morgenthau 1956; Waltz 1979; Keohane 1984). As most of the controversies arise more from how justice or sustainability may be operationalized rather than from the denial of their significance, the strongest impression one gets is that explicit debates are required to build a stronger international consensus regarding the notion of global distributional justice. This implies that the current situation in which little or nothing exists in terms of comprehensive and robust theories of international justice needs to be urgently addressed. There is a need for political philosophers to theorize the concept of international distributional justice more extensively and, in particular, to address the specific question of how the concern over development and global environmental protection can be equitably addressed, taking care to balance the arguments and views of the different sections. At the same time, international relations scholars need to begin to de-emphasize the domestic/international split by giving more attention to the opportunities and challenges inherent in the increasingly dynamic socio-economic globalization.

Regimes are by no means epiphenomena, as scholars within the realist school are wont to suggest (Gilpin 1987; Grieco 1988a, 1988b); however, they also do not lead to mutually satisfying co-operation, as neoliberal institutionalists often suggest (Young 1989a: 199). For example, although the influence of the USA and the superior bargaining power of the developed countries are not in doubt, the ability of the South to extract important concessions, especially when they act as a strong coalition, is equally remarkable (Vogler 2000). Also remarkable is the fact that, in extracting these concessions, the South often relies mainly on pure moral arguments. This suggests that regimes have a constitutive dimension and are better conceived as being part of the efforts by the international community to organize underlying shared values to enhance human welfare and preserve the global environment (Ruggie 1993; Vogler 2003). But given that these co-operative efforts take place under an ethico-political and economic climate that predicates sustainability 'on the promotion and maintenance of liberal economic order' (Bernstein 2001: 4), states often find themselves fighting to secure justice and environmental protection from a rather difficult angle. Hence, apart from explicit debates on the concept of international justice, there is also the need to encourage a more rigorous discourse on the value structure and norm context within which regimes are developed. In the absence of these debates and possible increased international consensus, there is little to suggest that the concept of 'equity' will ultimately prove to be a useful strategic resource for the political South in the counter-hegemonic project of securing global environmental justice.

Notes

1 Introduction

1 The other three preconditions identified by Rowlands are 'economic cost, scientific consensus and presence of commonalities'.
2 Scholars of international politics of the environment frequently make use of the typology that differentiates global environmental problems into three areas: (i) management of global commons (e.g. UNCLOS); (ii) transboundary pollution (e.g. Basel); and (iii) local issues with cumulative impact on the global environment (e.g. climate change) (Haas *et al.* 1993; Young 1994; O'Neill 1998).

2 Regimes as a medium for international distributive justice

1 Although the concept of unlimited sovereignty over natural resources remains the cornerstone of international customary law, there are still many cases in which the policies of international regimes place some limitation on this jurisdiction. The Convention on the International Trading on Endangered Species (CITES) and the Convention on Biological Diversity (CBD) are but two examples.
2 There is no space to discuss the several hundreds of bilateral and regional environmental agreements that fall under this category. The discussion focuses on a few prominent global regimes.
3 Most states made several property rights claims during UNCLOS III on the basis of the argument that securing such exclusive rights is crucial in helping them to meet their responsibilities for providing for the welfare of their citizens. One notable example was the intense debates that occurred between the coastal states and neighbouring landlocked and 'geographically disadvantaged states' about property rights over living marine resources in the exclusive economic zone (EEZ). UNCLOS III eventually legislated that geographically disadvantaged or landlocked states should be granted the right to share the living marine resources within the EEZ of neighbouring coastal states on the basis of equity and sustainable utilization (UNCLOS III, Article 65).
4 It was formerly proclaimed that these resources were the common heritage of mankind – a proclamation that put them in the same category as the seabed, beyond the jurisdiction of states. The developed countries, however, rejected this wording, choosing instead the concept of common concern for humankind.
5 These figures represent the average amount of waste dumped annually in the sea by contracting parties to the Convention. Figures taken from the official web page of MARPOL.
6 The Convention recognizes these arguments and demands as valid. Accordingly, it grants in Article 13.5 of the 1996 London Protocol that the interests and capabilities of developing states be taken into consideration. The Convention subsequently makes

provision for access to and transfer of environmentally sound technology to developing countries on 'favourable terms, including on concessional and preferential terms, as mutually agreed'.
7 The USA continues to oppose the right to sustainable development. It entered a reservation to this right before signing the Rio Declaration saying that it needed more clarification on its meaning.

3 Towards a theory of global environmental justice

1 The task of evaluating how the dominant ideas of justice in regimes fit with the basic understanding of sustainability is reserved until Chapter 8 (after the empirical analysis).
2 A lot of works have been devoted to developing conceptions of global justice in recent times (cf. Sen 1999; Pogge 1998, 2001; Caney 2001, 2005). However, most of these works still take the ideas of justice discussed in this chapter as their basic starting point.
3 For the most part, Dobson does not address the issue of international environmental justice. His focus, rather, is on justice within state boundaries. Also, although Dobson is interested in providing an account of the relationship between the various dimensions of the environmental sustainability discourse and the principles of social justice, my account is far more circumscribed as I focus mainly on North–South justice within negotiated regimes.
4 Not all environmentalists are excited about the notion of global community. There are many environmentalists who express a preference for bioregionalism or what Woodin and Lucas (2004: 3) call 'economic localization'; however, even these environmentalists do not oppose, at least explicitly, the notion of international justice, at least not on conceptual grounds as communitarians do.
5 Frost (2001) articulates seven key points for and against the notion of international justice but I have discussed five main points here, choosing to combine some distinct categories into one.
6 Again, it is worth bearing in mind that this book is clearly based on the assumption that issues of justice are already an important aspect of global environmental institutions and that regime policies currently affect the degree of inequity both between and within countries. I have presented arguments in the previous sections that I feel sufficiently justify this assertion. But although descriptive arguments occupy an important place in the case for justice in global regimes, conceptual arguments are by no means less important.

4 Managing a global commons

1 This was the way that Tommy T. B. Koh of Singapore, the President of UNCLOS III, described the Convention at the final session of the conference in Montego Bay, Jamaica, on 11 December 1982.
2 Active negotiations for UNCLOS III started in December 1973 in Caracas, Venezuela. The Convention was eventually opened for signature in Jamaica in September 1982. However, the build-up to the conference began in 1968 with the setting up of the Committee for the Peaceful Uses of the Ocean Floor and High Sea Beyond National Jurisdictions, which eventually acted as the Preparatory Commission for UNCLOS III (UN Doc. SEA/MB/2).
3 Some of these issues had been addressed with varying degrees of success in UNCLOS I and II. However, in the light of the equity issues that gave rise to UNCLOS III and the context under which it was negotiated, almost all agreements in the previous conventions were radically revised so that the view expressed in some quarters that UNCLOS III was merely a codification of existing practices in international relations

remains factually incorrect (for details on this argument see Zuleta 1983; Koh 1983; Amerasinghe 1985).
4   On 25 February 2004 the US Senate Foreign Relations Committee voted unanimously (19:0) in favour of US ratification but the entire Senate is yet to vote on this treaty.
5   This is not a proposal to account for the development of the complex processes that led to the ocean regime – a task that would call for a separate volume. There are many rich accounts on the origin and development of the law of the sea, which are far too numerous to list here. But, although some background knowledge is assumed, serious attempts have equally been made to present core issues in an accessible manner. This of course carries the risk of oversimplification but seems to me the only way to negotiate the tension.
6   UNGA Res (XXIV) 1967; UNGA Res 2749 (XXV) of 17 December 1970; UNGA Res 2750 (XXV) (C and B); UNGA Res 3067 (XXVIII) 1973.
7   Some authors emphasize the use of informal negotiating committees and issue-specific negotiating groups; the informal institution of the President's 'collegium', the body of principal officers of the conference that acted in an advisory capacity to the President; and the use of Informal Composite Negotiating Text (ICNT) rather than a text drafted by a select team of 'experts' as the basis of negotiations.
8   Conference Chairman Hamilton Shirley Amerasinghe (Sri Lanka), who upon his death on 4 December 1980 was replaced by Tommy T. B. Koh (Singapore). First Committee Chairman: P. B. Engo (United Republic of Cameroon). Vice-Chairmen: the representatives of Brazil, the German Democratic Republic and Japan. Second Committee Chairman: Andres Aguilar (Venezuela). Vice-Chairmen: the representatives of Czechoslovakia, Kenya and Turkey. Third Committee Chairman: Alexander Yaankov (Bulgaria). Vice-Chairmen: the representatives of Colombia, Cyprus and the Federal Republic of Germany.
9   See Law of the Sea hearings before the Subcommittee on Oceanography and the Committee on Merchant Marine and Fisheries on the status of the Law of the Sea treaty negotiations, 97th Congress, 1st and 2nd Sess. 20–21; Garry Knight statement (1982).
10 The United Nations, through various research commissions, attempted to investigate some of these issues in detail prior to the Conference so as to reduce speculations and disagreements. (See, for example, UN Doc. A/CONF.62/25, 'Economic Implications of Seabed Mineral Development in the International Area' and Project CCSP-1/TG.1, 'Seabed Investigations for Manganese Nodules on the Deep Submarine Shelf on East of Tonga Platform'). However, it appears that states took their positions without much reference to these findings. When they were used, states focused on different sections and drew different conclusions to suit their preferred positions.
11 One outstanding achievement of UNCLOS III was the settlement of the question of the breadth of the territorial seas, which had been attempted without success in UNCLOS I and II (Churchill and Lowe 1988: 66–67). Parts II to IV of the Convention text are devoted to the limits of the territorial sea together with closely related issues such as rights of passage and the status of the archipelagic waters.
12 Early claims included the length of a cannon shot; the range that a ship could travel in a relatively short time; 4 nautical miles (proposed by the Scandinavian League in 1598); and the ability to control, which simply states that a coastal state can maintain rights over as much sea as it is able to control. (For details see, among others, Buck 1998 and Churchill and Lowe 1988).
13 The USSR had consistently rejected the 3-nautical mile limit and insisted instead that it would continue to enforce its sovereignty up to 12 nautical miles from its coast. Norway and Spain equally continued to assert 4 and 6 nautical miles, respectively, as the limits of their territorial seas (Buck 1998).
14 Proclamation by President Truman of 28 September 1945 on the 'Policy of the United States with Respect to the Natural Resources of the Subsoil and Seabed of the Continental Shelf', *Department of State Bulletin* 13: 327.

15 Sanger (1986: 64–65) observes that it was the rich countries that benefited the most from the EEZ. Of the 14 countries with the largest EEZ, 11 are developed countries. For statistics and a view of how African countries fare in terms of benefiting from the EEZ and CS regimes, see Egede (2004).
16 It is difficult to see the gesture made in the protection of the marine environment as anything other than a rudimentary framework. Committee III, which dealt with sea pollution, was the first to announce that it had achieved agreement over all of the issues allocated to it. This ease betrayed as cogent the fears entertained from the beginning that 'the protection and preservation of the marine environment was of peripheral interest to the negotiating states' (Ramakrishna 1990: 432). In the end, as a gesture of equity, Part XII legitimized differential pollution standards for the developing countries, it set no clear enforcement procedures and admitted that states could pollute the ocean in line with 'their social and economic needs' [Article 207 (4)].

5 The global waste management regime

1 The Basel Convention is not the only global treaty concerned with the regulation of movement and disposal of wastes and dangerous goods. The International Maritime Organization (IMO) and The International Programme on Chemical Safety are only two of the other regimes whose objectives overlap with those of Basel. But the Basel Convention is generally regarded as the most elaborate and comprehensive at dealing with hazardous and other wastes. For detailed arguments on why the Basel Convention acts as an umbrella for the global waste management regime, see Kummer (1995).
2 There are a lot of assumptions made concerning the reader's knowledge about the Basel Convention. The aim here is not to 'tell every story' of Basel, although key events are presented. The ethical analysis concentrates mainly on key policies and texts. An overview of the Convention can be obtained by consulting many excellent basic texts too numerous to cite here.
3 www.basel.int/meetings/sbc/workdoc.manual.html.Introductions.
4 These meetings were attended by representatives from about 80 countries and about 50 non-governmental organizations, who also participated in the debates.
5 This analysis is not based on the original Basel text alone. The text of the Basel Protocol on Liability and Compensation for Damage Resulting from Transboundary Movements of Hazardous Wastes and their Disposal is also utilized. The decision to focus on this text stems from the prominent role it played in establishing environmental rights for victims of transboundary waste movements.
6 OAU Council of Ministers Resolution on Dumping of Nuclear and Industrial Waste in Africa, 23 May 1988, [CM/Re. 1153(XLVIII], reproduced in *International Legal Materials* 28, 567 (1989).
7 UNCHR resolution 1989/42 of 6 March 1989.
8 The other channels advocated in Article 20 of the Convention include 'through negotiation or any other means of their own choice' and through an arbitration panel.
9 There have been some changes in this regard as the regime has started to focus on the concept of environmentally sound management (ESM) of waste. This concept emphasizes waste reduction at the point of production.
10 This view is not entirely novel. It already has a relatively strong place in the concepts of integrated product approach (IPA), life cycle assessment (LCA), and product-oriented environmental management systems (POEMS). These terms emphasize 'system thinking', a belief that the true assessment of the environmental impact of a product must include what happens at the extraction, transportation of raw materials, production, use and disposal stages of its 'life span'. This logic is hardly noticeable in political analyses of international environmental regimes.
11 The Cairo Guidelines were adopted in the 14th Session of UNEP's Governing Council Meeting through decision 14/30 of 17 June 1987. The guidelines were articulated by the *ad hoc* working group of experts on the environmentally sound management

198   *Notes*

of hazardous wastes set up by the Governing Council through decision 10/24 of May 1982. The Cairo Guidelines set out in broad terms the principles of good waste management, stressing careful handling and minimization of waste production, clean technology and a critical approach to consumption. The Cairo Guidelines are thus the most related works of UNEP on hazardous waste. I have mentioned that other efforts towards a more effective hazardous waste management regime (including Basel) would have built upon these guidelines were it not for the political circumstances surrounding their emergence. The Cairo Guidelines did not get a single mention in all of the Basel texts.

12 Paragraph 4 reads 'convinced that parties should take necessary measures to ensure that the management of hazardous wastes and other wastes including their transboundary movement and deposal is consistent with the protection of human health and the environment whatever the place of disposal'.

13 This is the language used in many mega-environmental treaties in which all humans are lumped together and abstracted from states in ways that roughly correspond to a global community affirming a set of underlying values and 'rights' which they expect to be dispensed by states acting in close co-operation with one another and through appropriate international regimes. See for a few examples the Johannesburg Declaration on Sustainable Development; UNGA resolution A/RES/43/212 of 20 December 1988 on the Responsibility of States for the Protection of the Environment; UN resolution on the Prevention of the Illegal International Traffic in, and Dumping and Resulting Accumulation of, Toxic and Dangerous Products and Wastes Affecting Developing Countries in Particular; and UNGA resolution A/RES/44/224 of 22 December 1989 on International Co-operation in the Field of the Environment.

14 Montgomery actually differentiates between what he calls the perfunctory and the substantive rules. The perfunctory rules touch on subjects such as accession, ratification, entry into force, right to vote, convention of COPs, amendments, establishment of other agencies and *ad hoc* committees. In their third COP, parties to the Basel Convention amended the Convention to include a ban on the movement of hazardous wastes from the OECD to the non-OECD countries. Although this ban is yet to come into force, it qualifies as one of the substantive rules of the Basel Convention according to Montgomery's model.

15 Even up to the present date, a Japanese bilateral aid agency called 2KR continues to ship several tonnes of outdated pesticides to different African countries on a yearly basis. A key feature of this scheme is that recipient countries are required to accumulate a counterpart fund through the sales of 2KR products [2KR Monitoring Network, Tokyo, Japan (www.paw.hi-ho.ne.jp/kr2-net/)].

16 The FAO and WHO estimate that 30 per cent of pesticides sold annually to developing countries – worth US$900 million in the year 2000 – fail to meet international standards and are often mislabelled or entirely unmarked. The same report also indicates that it will take about US$250 million to clean up the contaminated sites in Africa, some of which are in people's backyards or within walking distances of homes and pastures (UN Africa Recovery from FAO data, 2001, reprinted in *Africa Recovery*, 15, 9–14, 2001).

17 Section 34 (3) of the Environmental Protection Act 1990, Section 5 (3) of the Waste and Contaminated Land (Northern Ireland) Order 1997 and Section 54 of the Environmental Protection Act 1990 in Scotland.

18 What has been said should not be read to mean that the doctrine of the intrinsic value of nature is reductively one and the same as the ethic of care as expounded by eco-feminists. Indeed, I am deeply aware that there are many areas of intense disagreement between these two approaches. However, I consider that quite a number of these aspects are simply overdrawn (as some of the leading eco-feminists admit). In particular, it is also important to note that they do not necessarily promote radically

opposing policies in terms of distributional justice at the global level. Indeed, either or both can lead to the compromise of legitimate human needs when pursued to the extreme. For a constructive connection between the two narratives see Shiva (1988). For accounts that seek to portray these two narratives as irreconcilably different, see, among others, Plumwood (1993).
19 Strategic Plan for the Implementation of the Basel Convention: Introduction. Can be accessed by visiting the official website and following the links. www.basel.int/meetings/cop/cop6/StPlan.doc.
20 Article 11 stated that all such bilateral, multilateral or regional agreements should be at least equal to or stronger than the provisions of the Basel Convention.

6 Protecting the global atmosphere

1 The First International Meteorological Conference was held on 23 August 1853 in Brussels (Weiss 1975: 809; Paterson 1996b: 18).
2 Statistics show that over 60 per cent of the anthropogenic greenhouse gas emissions that states are concerned with emanate from the industrialized countries. The gap is such that an average US citizen emits about 6 tonnes of carbon per year compared with an average Indian citizen who emits less than 0.4 tonnes per year (Grubb 1989; Grubler and Nakicenovic 1991; Agarwal and Narain 1991; Banuri et al. 1996).
3 Joint Paper from the AOSIS at the end of the fifth INC session in New York, February 1992 (paper in file with author).
4 There has been an increased emphasis on adaptation both in academic and in policy circles. The UNFCCC in its seventh COP in 2001 approved the preparation of the National Adaptation Program of Action (NAPA). The programme, which is funded by the UNFCCC, contains a raft of guidelines and criteria for selecting measures for enhancing the adaptive capacity of countries.
5 Principles 6, 7 and 11 of the Rio Declaration (1992), Article 4 (2.a) of the Basel Convention (1989), Article 207 of UNCLOS (1982), Article 2(2) of the Vienna Convention (1985), etc.
6 The closest analogies would be the Montreal Protocol and the 1996 Protocol to the IMO London Convention on Waste Dumping, which allows developing country parties some years of grace and the exemption of complying with specific provisions of the protocol respectively.
7 Paragraph 6 of the preambular chapter, Articles 3 (1), 4 (1), 7 (2.b) and 7 (2.c) of the Convention. Articles 10, 13 (4.c) and 13 (4) of the Kyoto Protocol.
8 The situation was initially chaotic, especially with the disintegration of the former USSR. It was not clear what the status of the countries within the former Soviet empire should be. Although some thought that these countries should be classified as developed countries, others thought that they should be grouped with the developing countries instead. In the end, the Convention adopted the phrase 'developed country parties and other parties included in annex I'. Because these countries in transition are included with the developed countries in the emission reduction commitments and following the classification that exists in the Basel Convention and the Montreal Protocol, it seems safe to suggest that a two-part classification has been adopted by the international community, the phraseology notwithstanding (Djoghlaf 1994). In addition, some people feel that China should have a separate status from the developing countries on the basis of its impressive economic growth and population. The classification in the Basel Convention, the Montreal Protocol and most recently the UNFCCC has put paid to these questions even though they are likely to be re-opened in the not-so-distant future.
9 Paragraphs 3, 8, 9, 10, 16, 17, 20, 21 and 22 of the preamble (UNFCCC, 1992).

7 Establishing the core ideas of justice in eco-regimes

1 Neoliberalism is a term that is very commonly used in contemporary scholarly writings but rarely defined. This is partly because its meaning is commonly assumed and partly because it is presented in far too many varied and complex forms to be effectively captured by a semiotic definition. I will have more to say on this in Chapter 9.
2 We have already noted that a general conception of rights does not exist. When Nozick talks about individuals having 'rights' he obviously relies on a particular version of rights, a version of which he is the most vocal proponent. According to Waldron, Nozick 'conceives of rights as *side constraints* – limits on the actions that are morally available to agents. They are essentially negative in character requiring each agent to refrain from performing actions of the specified type. They never require anything other than omission' (Waldron 1993: 204, italics in the original).
3 This is the assertion, according to Cohen (1986: 326), that 'I own myself. I am the owner of myself, my own master'. Cohen explains that this self-ownership assertion applies here in the 'reflexive' sense, i.e. that what owns and what is owned are one and the same thing, namely the whole person.

8 Ethics of global sustainability and neoliberal ideas of justice

1 It is common to run into extended and torturous arguments on the level of commensurability or substitutability between natural capital and man-made capital (this has in fact proved a favourable pastime for most ecological economists) or on the exact limits of growth in the face of technological innovations, which are dangerously silent about the very spirit of sustainability as it is identified here.
2 This is somewhat an oversimplification as the Brundtland Report both relates to and differs from the communitarian positions in more complex ways. For example, like communitarians, the report also emphasizes social relations, and yet it believes in international justice in a way that communitarians do not.
3 It is important to note that the report does not construe development as economic growth or 'what poor nations should do to get richer'. It defines development in very broad terms as 'what we all do in attempting to improve our lot within our abode' (WCED 1987: xi). It is to this extent that development approximates to what philosophers would encapsulate as the quest for a meaningful life.
4 Libertarians of course do talk about the right to life but only in terms of a right not to be bullied by others. In general, they claim that only negative obligations are justified. That is to say, as Luper-Foy (1992: 84) puts it, 'that just behaviour is a matter of not hindering people in the effort to accomplish their ends, not a matter of helping them to accomplish their ends'.
5 Nozick further weakens this proviso in two ways: (i) he says that the proviso is satisfied if someone is made worse off in a particular way provided that their position is improved in another way to counterbalance this worsening; (ii) he later limits his definition of worse off to mainly material terms. Therefore, ultimately, Nozick's proviso on acquisition is not as demanding as that of Locke's. (cf. Cohen 1986: 324).
6 Buchanan (1990: 228–240) distinguishes between these two sorts of co-operation using the ability to contribute as the key variable. In communal schemes, a person's entitlement to a piece of land, say, is not dependent on the fact that he has worked the land. It suffices that he is a member of the community in which the land is located. On the free-standing scheme, however, a person's claim to the land or its proceeds depends on his voluntary involvement in and contributions to the production of the gains to be shared.
7 Some other libertarians have attempted to offer Nozick a lifeline. In seeing insuperable obstacles in the way of laying a concrete claim to the external world, they

propose that natural resources be nationalized and that individual nations may then use such nationalized resources in ways that promote the maximum liberty and well-being of individual nationals. In this quasi-Nozickian theory of justice, nations would control resources within their areas of jurisdiction, but property regimes would still be constructed to provide maximum opportunities for nationals to engage in property acquisition in ways that reflect their talents, choices and power differentials. They also attempt to factor in the welfare of future generations by recommending that rights over natural resources be rented (as opposed to purchased) at the current competitive value and the funds generated allocated to promoting effective equal opportunities for a good life for future generations (cf. Vallentyne and Hillel 2000).

8 Here they raise options such as having a ground rule that equalizes the chances of appropriation for all members; joint management involving the use of trustees; and bequeathing lapsible and non-transferable property rights, etc.

9 Global justice and neoliberal environmental governance

1 Hajer (1995) actually identifies six core elements of ecological modernization theory, including: (i) a move from cure to preventive approaches to environmental protection; (ii) a renewed faith in the role of science and technology; (iii) change from the notion that environmental protection and economic growth is a zero-sum game to the notion that it is a positive-sum game; (iv) change from conceptualizing nature as a free good to conceptualizing it as a public good; (v) shifting the burden of proof to polluters; and (vi) an increase in public participation.

2 Statement made at the conference on Climate Change in a Post-2012 World held at Chatham House in June 2006.

References

Achterberg, W. (2001). 'Environmental Justice And Global Democracy', in B. Gleeson and N. Low (eds), *Governing for the Environment: Global Problems, Ethics and Democracy*. Basingstoke: Palgrave.

Ackerman, B. (1980). *Social Justice in the Liberal State*. New Haven: Yale University Press.

Adger W. N., Paavola, J. Huq, S. and Mace, M. J. (eds) (2006). *Fairness in Adaptation to Climate Change*. Cambridge, MA: MIT Press.

Africa Recovery (2001). 14 (4): Brief Papers.

Agarwal, A. and Narain, S. (1991). *Global Warming in an Unequal World*. New Delhi: Centre for Science and Environment.

Agarwal, A., Narain, S., Sharma, A. and Imchen, A. (eds) (2001). *Global Environmental Negotiations: Poles Apart*. New Delhi: Centre for Science and Environment.

Alder, J. and Wilkinson, D. (1999). *Environmental Law And Ethics*. Basingstoke: Macmillan.

Allott, P. (1983). 'Power Sharing in the Law of the Sea', *American Journal of International Law* 77, 1–30.

Almond, B. (1995). 'Rights and Justice in the Environment Debate', in D. E. Cooper and J. A. Palmer (eds), *Just Environments; Intergenerational, International and Interspecies Issues*. London: Routledge.

Alter, L. (1997). 'Industrial Recycling and Basel Convention', *Resources, Conservation and Recycling* 19, 24–39.

Amerasinghe, H. S. (1985). 'The Third United Nations Conference on the Law of the Sea', in M. H. Nordquist (ed.), *United Nations Convention on the Law of the Sea 1982. A Commentary, Vol. 1*. Boston, Lancaster: Martinus Nijhoff.

Anand, R. (2004). *International Environmental Justice: A North South Dimension*. Aldershot: Ashgate Publishing.

Anand, R. P. (1982). 'Freedom of the Seas: Past Present and Future', in. R. Girardot *et al.* (eds), *New Directions in International Law*. New York: Campus Verlag.

Anand, R. P. (1985). 'Odd Man Out: The United States and the UN Convention on the Law of the Sea', in J. M. Van Dyke (ed.), *Consensuses and Confrontation: The United States and the Law of the Sea Convention*. Hawaii: The Law of the Sea Institute.

Anderson, D. H. (1996). 'The Straddling Stock Agreement: An Initial Assessment', *International and Comparative Law Quarterly* 45, 463–475.

Anderson, T. L. and Leal, D. R. (1991). *Free Market Environmentalism*. Oxford/San Francisco: Westview Press.

Anderson, T. L. and Leal, D. R. (1997). *Enviro-capitalists: Doing Good While Doing Well*. place: Rowman & Littlefield.
Aristotle (1847/1998). *Nicomachean Ethics Book IV*. Translated by J. A. K. Thompson. Harmondsworth: Penguin.
Arrow, K. J. and Fischer, A. C. (1974). 'Environmental Preservation, Uncertainty and Irreversibility', *Quarterly Journal of Economics*, 88 (2), 312–319.
Arrow, K. J., Cline, W. R., Maler, K.-G., Munasinghe, M., Squitieri, R. and Stiglitz, J. E. (1996). 'Intertemporal Equity, Discounting and Economic Efficiency', in IPCC, *Climate Change 1995: Economic and Social Dimensions of Climate Change, Contribution of Working Group III to the Second Assessment Report of the IPCC*. Cambridge: Cambridge University Press.
Arts, B. (2000). 'Regimes, Non-State Actors, and the State system: A "Structurational" Regime Model', *European Journal of International Relations* 6 (4), 513–542.
Athanasiou, T. and Baer, P. (2002). *Dead Heat: Global Justice and Global Warming*. New York: Seven Stories Press.
Attard, D. (1987). *The Exclusive Economic Zone in International Law*. Oxford: Oxford University Press.
Attfield, R. (1999). *The Ethics of the Global Environment*. Edinburgh: Edinburgh University Press.
Attfield, R. (2003). *Environmental Ethics: An Overview for the 21st Century*. Cambridge: Polity Press.
Attfield, R. and Wilkins, B. (eds) (1992). *International Justice and the Third World*. Routledge: London.
Auer, M. (2000). 'Who participates in global environmental governance? Partial answers from international relations theory', *Policy Sciences* 33:155-180.
Augustine, St (1984). *The City of God*. Translated by J. Healey. Harmondsworth: Penguin.
Avineri, S. and de-Shalit A. (1992). *Communitarianism and Individualism*. Oxford: Oxford University Press.
Axerold, R. and Keohane, R. (1986). 'Achieving Co-operation under Anarchy. Strategies and Institutions', in K. Oye (ed.), *Co-operation under Anarchy*. Princeton, NJ: Princeton University Press.
Bachram, H. (2005). 'Climate Fraud and Carbon Colonialism: The New Trade in Greenhouse Gases', *Capitalism Nature and Socialism* 15 (4), 5–20.
Baden, J. and Doughlas, N. (eds) (1998). *Managing the Commons*. Indiana: Indiana University Press.
Baer, P. (2006). 'Adaptation: Who Pays Whom?', in W. N. Adger, J. Paavola, S. Huq and M. J. Mace (eds), *Fairness in Adaptation to Climate Change*. Cambridge, MA: MIT Press.
Banuri, T., Goran-Maler, K. Grubb, M., Jacobson, H.K. and Yamin, F. (1996). 'Equity and Social Considerations', in J. P. Bruce, H. Lee and E. Haites (eds), *Climate Change: Economic and Social Dimensions of Climate Change*. Cambridge: Cambridge University Press.
Barnett, C. (2005). 'The Consolation of "Neoliberalism"', *Geoforum* 36, 7–12.
Barry, B. (1965). *Political Argument*. London: Routledge and Kegan Paul.
Barry, B. (1989). *Theories of Justice*. London: Havester Wheatsheaf.
Barry, B. (1995). *Justice as Impartiality*. Oxford: Calderon Press.
Barry, B. (1999). 'Sustainability and Intergenerational Equity', in A. Dobson (ed.), *Fairness and Futurity: Essays on Environmental Sustainability and Social Justice*. Oxford: Oxford University Press.

Barry, B. and Matravers, M. (1997). 'Justice', in E. Craig (ed.) *Routledge Encyclopaedia of Philosophy*. London: Routledge.
Barry, J. (1999). *Rethinking Green Politics*. London: Sage Publications.
Barry, J. and Eckersley R. (eds) (2005). *The State and the Global Ecological Crisis*. Cambridge, MA: MIT Press.
Baslar, K. (1998). *The Concept of the Common Heritage of Mankind in International Law*. Cambridge: Cambridge University Press.
Beckerman, W. (1994). 'Sustainable Development: Is it a Useful Concept?', *Environmental Values* 3 (3), 191–210.
Beckerman, W. and Pasek, J. (2001). *Justice Posterity and the Environment*. Oxford: Oxford University Press.
Beitz, C. R. (1979). *Political Theory and International Relations*. Princeton, NJ: Princeton University Press.
Beitz, C. (1999). 'Social and Cosmopolitan Liberalism', *International Affairs* 75 (3), 515–529.
Benedick, R. E. (1989). 'Ozone Diplomacy', *Issues in Science and Technology* (Fall), 43–50.
Benedick, R. E. (1991). *Ozone Diplomacy: New Directions in Safeguarding the Planet*. Cambridge, MA: Harvard University Press.
Bentham J. (1948). *The Principles of Morals and Legislation*. New York: Hafner (first published 1789).
Bentham, J. (1970). *An Introduction to the Principles of Morals and Legislation*, ed. by J. H. Burns and H. L .A. Hart. London: Athlone Press.
Benton, T. (1997). 'Ecology, Community and Justice', in T. Hayward and J. O'Neill (eds), *Justice, Property and the Environment: Social and Legal Perspectives*. Sydney, Aldershot: Ashgate.
Benton, T. (1999). 'Sustainable Development and Accumulation of Capital; Reconciling the Irreconcilable', in A. Dobson (ed.), *Fairness and Futurity: Essay on Environmental Sustainability and Social Justice*. Oxford: Oxford University Press.
Bernstein, S. (2000). 'Ideas, Social Structure and the Compromise of Liberal Environmentalism', *European Journal of International Relations* 6 (4), 464–512.
Bernstein, S. (2001). *The Compromise of Liberal Environmentalism*. New York: Columbia University Press.
Betsill, M. and Bulkeley, H. (2006) 'Cities and the Multilevel Governance of Global Climate Change', *Global Governance* 12 (2), 141–159.
Bhagwati, J. (1991). *The World Trading System in Risk*. Hemel Hempstead: Harvester Wheatsheaf.
Bhagwati, J. (1993). 'The Case for Free Trade', *Scientific American* 269 (November), 42–49.
Birnie, P. and Boyle, A. (1992). *International Law and the Environment*. Oxford: Clarendon Press.
Birnie, P. and Boyle, A. (2002). *International Law and the Environment*, 2nd edn. Oxford: Oxford University Press.
Blake, J. (1996). 'The Protection of the Underwater Cultural Heritage', *International and Comparative Law Quarterly* 45, 819–843.
Bodansky, D. (1993). 'The United Nations Framework Convention on Climate Change: A Commentary', *Yale Journal of International Law* 18 (2), 451–558.
Bodansky, D. (2001). 'International Law and the Design of a Climate Change Regime',

in U. Luterbacher and D. Sprinz (eds), *International Relations and Global Climate Change*. Cambridge, MA: MIT Press.

Boezek, B. A. (1984). 'Ideology and the Law of the Sea: The Challenge of the New International Economic Order', *Boston College International and Comparative Law Review* 7 (1), 34–53.

Bogart, J. H. (1985). 'Lockean Provisos and State of Nature Theories', *Ethics* 95 (4), 828–836.

Borgese, E. M. (1986). *The Future of the Oceans: A Report to the Club of Rome*. Montreal: Harvest House.

Borione, D. and Ripert, J. (1994). 'Exercising Common but Differentiated Responsibility', in I. Mintzer and J. A. Leonard (eds), *Negotiating Climate Change: The Inside Story of the Rio Convention*. Cambridge: Cambridge University Press.

Bourne, C. B. (1997). 'The Primacy of the Principle of Equitable Utilisation in the 1997 Watercourses Convention', *Canadian Yearbook of International Law* 35, 215.

Bowler, J. P. (1992). *The Environmental Sciences*. London: Fontana Press.

Bradshaw, J. (1972). 'The Concept of Social Need', *New Society* 2, 640.

Brenner, N. and Theodore, N. (2000). 'Preface: From "New Localism" to the Spaces of Neoliberalism', *Antipode* 34 (3), 341–347.

Breyman, S. (1993). 'Knowledge as Power: Ecology Movements and Global Environmental Problems', in R. D. Lipschutz and K. Conca (eds), *The State and Social Power in Global Environmental Politics*. New York: Columbia University Press.

Brighouse, H. (2004). *Justice*. Cambridge: Polity Press.

Bromley, D. (1998). 'Searching for Sustainability: The Poverty of Spontaneous Order', *Ecological Economics* 24, 31–40.

Brown, C. (1992). *International Relations Theory: New Normative Approaches*. Hemel Hempstead: Harvester Wheatsheaf.

Brown, D. A. (2004). 'Environmental Ethics and Public Policy', *Environmental Ethics* 26, 110–112.

Buchanan, A. (1990). 'Justice and Reciprocity Versus Subject Centred Justice', *Philosophy and Public Affairs* 19 (3), 227–252.

Buck, J. S. (1998). *The Global Commons: An Introduction*. Washington: Island Press.

Bull, H. (1977). *The Anarchical Society: A Study of Order in World Politics*. London: Macmillan.

Bull, H. (1983). 'Justice in International Relations', in A. Hurrell and K. Alderson (eds), *Hedley Bull on International Society*. Basingstoke: Macmillan.

Burke, W. T. (1994). *The New International Law of Fisheries: UNCLOS 1992 and Beyond*. Oxford: Claredon Press.

Butraw, D. and Toman, M. A. (1992). 'Equity and International Agreements for CO_2 Constraint', *Journal of Energy Engineering* 118, 2.

Buzan, B and Little, R. (2001). 'Why International Relations has Failed as an Intellectual Project and What to do About it', *Millennium Journal of International Studies* 30 (1), 19–39.

Calvert, P. and Calvert, S. (1999). *The South, The North and the Environment*. London and New York: Pinter.

Campbell, J. L. and Pedersen, O. K. (2001). *The Rise of Neoliberalism and Institutional Analysis*. Princeton, NJ: Princeton University Press.

Caney, S. (2001). 'Review Article: International Distributive Justice', *Political Studies* 49 (5), 974–981.

Caney, S. (2005). *Justice Beyond Borders: A Global Political Theory*. Oxford: Oxford University Press.
Carley, M. and Spapens, P. (1998). *Sharing the World: Sustainable Living and Global Equity in the 21st Century*. London: Earthscan.
Carroz, J. E. (1984). 'International Aspects of Fishery Management Under the New Regimes of the Oceans', *San Diego Law Review* 21, 513–540.
Castree, N. (2006). 'From Neoliberalism to Neoliberalisation: Consolations, Confusions and Necessary Illusions', *Environment and Planning A* 38, 1–6.
Chatterjee, P. and Finger, M. (1994). *The Earth Brokers: Power, Politics and World Development*. London: Routledge.
Chomsky, N. (1999). *Profit over People: Neoliberalism and Global Order*. London: Turnaround Press.
Christoff, P. (2005) 'Out of Chaos, a Shinning Start? Towards a Typology of Green States', in J. Barry and R. Eckersley (eds), *The State and Global Ecological Crisis*. Cambridge: MIT Press.
Churchill, R. R. and Lowe, A. V. (1983). *The Law of the Sea*. Manchester: Juris.
Churchill, R. R. and Lowe, A. V. (1988). *The Law of the Sea*, 2nd edn. Manchester: Manchester University Press.
Clapp, J. (1994). 'Africa, NGOs and the International Toxic Waste Trade', *Journal of Environment and Development* 3 (2), 17–46.
Clapp, J. (2001). *Toxic Exports. The Transfer of Hazardous Wastes from Rich to Poor Countries*. Ithaca and London: Cornell University Press.
Clement, G. (1996). *Care, Autonomy and Justice: Feminism and the Ethic of Care*. Oxford: Westview Press.
Cline, W. R. (1992). *The Economics of Global Warming*. Washington, DC: Institute for International Economics.
Cohen, G. A. (1986). 'Self-Ownership, World Ownership and Equality Part II', *Social Philosophy and Policy* 3, 320–339.
Coll, S. (1994). 'Free Market Intensifies Waste Problem: Rich Nations Dumping on Poorer Ones', *Washington Post*, March 23, A1.
Collingwood, V. (2006). 'Non-governmental Organisations, Power and Legitimacy in International Society', *Review of International Studies* 32 (3), 439–454.
Colson, D. A. (1985). 'The United States, The Law of the Sea and the Pacific', in J. M. Van Dyke (ed.), *Consensuses and Confrontation: The United States and the Law of the Sea Convention*. Hawaii: The Law of the Sea Institute.
Conca, K., Alberty, M. and Dabelko, G. (1995). 'Ecological Justice', in K. Conca, M. Alberty and G. Dabelko (eds), *Green Planet Blues: Environmental Politics from Stockholm to Rio*. Boulder, CO: Westview Press.
Cooper, R. N. (1998). 'Towards a Real Global Warming Treaty', *Foreign Affairs* 77 (2), 66–79.
Cox, R. W. (1983). 'Gramsci, Hegemony and International Relations: An Essay in Methods', *Millennium* 12, 162–175.
Cox, R. W. (1992). 'Multilateralism and World Order', *Review of International Studies* 18, 161–180.
Daly, H. (1994). 'Fostering Environmentally Sustainable Development: Four Parting Suggestions for the World Bank', *Ecological Economics* 10, 183–187.
Daly, H. (1995).'On Wilfred Beckerman's Critique of Sustainable Development', *Environmental Values* 4 (1), 49–56.

Daly, H. (1996). *Beyond Growth: The Economics of Sustainable Development*. Boston, MA: Beacon Press.

Daly, H. and Goodland, R. (1994). 'An Ecological-Economic Assessment of Deregulation of International Commerce under GATT', *Ecological Economics* 9, 73–79.

Dasgupta, C. (1994). 'The Climate Change Negotiations', in I. Mintzer and J. A. Leonard (eds), *Negotiating Climate Change: The Inside Story of the Rio Convention*. Cambridge: Cambridge University Press.

Davidson, J. (2000). 'Sustainable Development: Business as Usual or a New Way of Living?', *Environmental Ethics* 22, 25–42.

Dingwerth K. and Pattberg P. (2006). 'Global Governance as a Perspective on World Politics', *Global Governance* 12 (2), 185–203.

Djalal, H. (1980). 'The Developing Countries and the Law of the Sea Conference', *Columbia Journal of World Business* 15, 18–34.

Djalal, H. (1985). 'The Effect of the Law of the Sea Convention on the Norms that Now Govern Ocean Activities', in J. M. Van Dyke (ed.), *Consensuses and Confrontation: The United States and the Law of the Sea Convention*. Hawaii: The Law of the Sea Institute.

Djoghlaf, A. (1994). 'The Beginning of International Climate Law', in I. Mintzer and J. A. Leonard (eds), *Negotiating Climate Change: The Inside Story of the Rio Convention*. Cambridge: Cambridge University Press.

Dobson, A. (1990). *Green Political Thought. An Introduction*. London: Routledge.

Dobson, A. (1994). 'Environmentalism', in M. Foley (ed.), *Ideas that Shape Politics*. Manchester: Manchester University Press.

Dobson A. (1998). *Justice and the Environment: Conceptions of Environmental Sustainability and Dimensions of Social Justice*. Oxford: Oxford University Press.

Dobson, A. (ed.) (1999). *Fairness and Futurity: Essays on Environmental Sustainability and Social Justice*. Oxford: Oxford University Press.

Dobson, A. (2000). 'Sustainable Development and the Defence of the Natural World', in K. Lee, M. Desmond and A. Holland (eds), *Global Sustainable Development in the 21st Century*. Edinburgh: Edinburgh University Press.

Dobson, A. (2004). 'Ecological Citizenship and Global Justice: Two Paths Converging?', in A. K. Haugestad and J. D. Wulfhorst (eds), *Future as Fairness: Ecological Justice and Global Citizenship*. Amsterdam: Rodopi.

Dow, K., Kasperson, R. E. and Bohn, M. (2006). 'Exploring the Social Justice Implications of Adaptations', in W. N. Adger, J. Paavola and S. Huq (eds), *Fairness in Adaptation to Climate Change*. Cambridge, MA: MIT Press.

Dowdeswell, E. and Kinley, R. J. (1994). 'Constructive Damage to the Status Quo', in I. Mintzer and J. A. Leonard (eds), *Negotiating Climate Change: The Inside Story of the Rio Convention*. Cambridge: Cambridge University Press.

Dower, N. (1994). 'The Idea of the Environment', in R. Attfield and A. Belsey (eds), *Philosophy and the Natural Environment*. Cambridge: Cambridge University Press.

Dower, N. (1998). 'Sustainability ands the Right to Development,' in R. Attfield and B. Wilkins (eds), *International Justice and the Third World*. London: Routledge.

Drydyk, J. (2001). *Towards Ethical Guidelines for Displacement-Inducing Developments: Filling the Gaps*, Shastri Indo-Canadian Institute and Canadian International Development Agency. Ottawa: Carleton University.

Duff, J. A. (2004). 'A Note on the United States and the Law of the Sea: Looking Back and Moving Forward', *Ocean Development and International Law* 35, 195–219.

Dupuy, R. (1983). 'The Convention on the Law of the Sea and the New International Economic Order', *Impact of Science on Society* 3 (4), 313–324.
Dupuy, P. (1999). 'The Danger of Fragmentation or Unification of the International Legal System and the International Court of Justice', *Journal of International Law and Politics* 31 (4), 791–807.
Dworkin, R. (1977). *Taking Rights Seriously*. London: Duckworth.
Dworkin, R. (1985). *A Matter of Principle*. London: Harvard University Press.
Dyer, H. (1989). 'Normative Theory and International Relations', in H. C. Dyer and L. Mangasarian (eds), *The Study of International Relations: The State of the Art*. London: Macmillan.
Dyer, H. (1993). 'EcoCultures: Global Culture in the Age of Ecology', *Millennium: Journal of International Studies* 22 (3), 483–504.
Dyer, H. (2001). 'The Environment in International Relations', *British Journal of Politics and International Relations* 3 (1), 105–114.
Eckersley, R. (1992). *Environmentalism and Political Theory: Towards an Ecocentric Approach*. London: UCL Press.
Eckersley, R. (1995). *Markets, the State and the Environment: Towards Integration*. Basingstoke: Macmillan.
Eckersley, R. (2005). 'Greening the Nation-State: From Exclusive to Inclusive Sovereignty', in J. Barry and R. Eckersley (eds), *The State and Global Ecological Crisis*. Cambridge: MIT Press.
The Ecologist (1993). *Whose Common Future: Reclaiming the Commons*. London: Earthscan.
Egede, E. (2004). 'The Outer Limits of the Continental Shelf: African States and the 1982 Law of the Sea Convention', *Ocean Development and International Law* 35 (2): 157–178.
Elliott, L. (1998). *The Global Politics of the Environment*. London: Macmillan Press.
Engel, J. R. (1990). Introduction: The Ethics of Sustainable Development', in J. R. Engel and J. G. Engel (eds), *Ethics of Environment and Development: Global Challenge, International Response*. London: Belhaven Press.
Epicurus (1987). 'Kuriai Doxai', in *The Hellenistic Philosophers*, trans. A. A. Long and D. N. Sedley. Cambridge: Cambridge University Press.
Epstein, J. and Gupta, R. (1990). *Controlling the Greenhouse Effect: Five Regimes Compared*. Washington, DC: The Brookings Institute.
Epstein, L.S. (1980), 'Decision-Making and the Temporal Resolution of Uncertainty', *International Economic Review* 21 (2), 269–283.
Erickson, J. (1990). *Greenhouse Earth: Tomorrow's Disaster Today*. USA: Tad Books.
Falk, R. (1971). *This Endangered Planet: Prospects and Proposals for Human Survival*. New York: Vintage Books.
Falk, R. (2001). 'Humane Governance and the Environment: Overcoming Neo-Liberalism', in B. Gleeson and N. Low (eds), *Governing for the Environment: Global Problems, Ethics and Democracy*. Basingstoke: Palgrave.
Fankhauser, S. (1995). *Valuing Climate Change. The Economics of the Greenhouse*. London: Earthscan.
Fankhauser, S. and Tol, R. S. J. (1996). 'Recent Advancements in the Economic Assessment of Climate Change Costs', *Energy Policy* 24 (7), 665–673.
Fankhauser, S. and Tol, R. S. J. (1997). 'The Social Costs of Climate Change: The IPCC Second Assessment Report and Beyond', *Mitigation and Adaptation Strategies for Global Change*, 1, 385–403.

Faucheux, S., Streeten J. and O'Connor, M. (eds) (1998). *Sustainable Development; Concepts, Rationalities and Strategies*. Dordrecht Kluwer Academic Publishers.
Fermann, G. (1993). 'Climate Change, Burden-Sharing Criteria, and Competing Conceptions of Responsibility', *International Challenges* 13 (4), 28–34.
Finnemore, M. and Sikkink, K. (1998). 'International Norm Dynamics and Political Change', *International Organization* 52 (4), 887–917.
Ford, L. H. (2003). 'Challenging Global Governance: Social Movement Agency and Global Civil Society', *Global Environmental Politics* 3 (2), 120–134.
Forder, A. (1974). *Concepts in Social Administration*. London: Routledge.
Forest Principles (1992) *Report of the United Nations Conference on Environment and Human Development* (Rio de Janeiro, 3–14 June 1992).
Forste, W. E. (1988). 'Review of Morals by Agreements', *Extropy: The Journal of Transhumanist Thought*, 14, 63.
The Founex Report on Development and Environment (1971). Geneva: Southcentre Publications.
Fouskas, V. K. (2006). 'Oil in Flames: Production Sharing Agreements (PSAs) and the Issue of Petroleum Nationalism in Iraq', in B. Gokay (ed.), *The Politics of Oil: A Survey*. London: Routledge.
Franck, T. M. (1990). *The Power of Legitimacy Among Nations*. New York: Oxford University Press.
Franck, T. M. (1995). *Fairness in International Law and Institutions*. Oxford: Oxford University Press.
Freeden, M. (1991). *Rights*. Milton Keynes: Open University Press.
French, D. (1998). '1997 Kyoto Protocol to the 1992 UN Framework Convention on Climate Change', *Journal of Environmental Law* 10 (2), 227–239.
Friedheim, R. L. (1993). *Negotiating the New Ocean Regime*. Columbia, SC: South Carolina Press.
Friedheim R. (2000). 'Designing the Ocean Policy Future: An Essay on How I Am Going To Do That,' *Ocean Development and International Law*, 31, 183–195.
Friedman, M. (1962). *Price Theory: A Provisional Text*. Chicago: Aldine.
Frost, R. (2001). 'Towards a Critical Theory of Transnational Justice', *Metaphilosophy* 32 (1/2), 161–179.
Gale, F. (1998). *The Tropical Timber Trade Regime*. Houndmills: Macmillan Press.
Galli, C. D. (1987). 'Hazardous Exports to the Third World: The Need to Abolish The Double Standard', *Columbia Journal of Environmental Law* 12 (39), 70–89.
GATT (1992). 'News Release: Expanding Trade can Help Solve Environmental Problems', 3 February.
Gauthier, D. (1974). 'Justice and Natural Endowment: Towards a Critique of Rawls' Ideological Framework', *Social Theory and Practice* 3, 3–26.
Gauthier, D. (1986). *Morals by Agreements*. Oxford: Oxford University Press.
George, S. (1990). 'Managing the Global House Redefining Economics in a Greenhouse World', in J. Leggett (ed.), *Global Warming: The Greenpeace Report*. Oxford: Oxford University Press.
George, S. (1999). 'A Short History of Neoliberalism', paper presented at the Conference on Economic Sovereignty in a Globalizing World, March 24–26.
de Geus, M. (2001). 'Sustainability, Liberal Democracy, Liberalism', in J. Barry and M. Wissenburg (eds), *Sustaining Liberal Democracy. Ecological Challenges and Opportunities*. London: Routledge.

Ghosh, S. (1980). 'The Legal Regime of Innocent Passage through the Territorial Sea', reprinted in C. Hugo (ed.) (2001), *The Law of the Sea*. Aldershot: Ashgate.
Gilpin, R. (1987). *The Political Economy of International Relations*. Princeton, NJ: Princeton University Press.
Global Commons Institute (1994). Letter, *The Guardian*, 4 July.
Godrej, D. (2001). *The No-Nonsense Guide to Climate Change*. London: Verso.
Gokay, B. (ed.) (2006). *The Politics of Oil: A Survey*. London: Routledge.
Gollier, C., Jullien, B. and Treich, N. (2000), 'Scientific Progress and Irreversibility: An Economic Interpretation of the "Precautionary Principle"', *Journal of Public Economics* 75 (2), 229–253.
Goodin, R. E. (1992). *Green Political Theory*. Cambridge: Polity Press.
Goodland, R. and Daly, H. (1996). 'Environmental Sustainability: Universal and Non-Negotiable', *Ecological Applications* 6 (4), 1002–1017.
Goodwin, B. (1987). *Using Political Ideas*. Chichester: Wiley.
Greenpeace International. (1994). *Database of Known Hazardous Waste Export from OECD to Non-OECD Countries, 1989–March 1994*. Amsterdam: Greenpeace International.
Grieco, J. (1988a). 'Anarchy and the Limits of Co-operation: A Realist Critique of the Newest Liberal Institutionalism', *International Organization* 42, 485–507.
Grieco, J. (1988b). 'Realist Theory and the Problems of International Co-operation: Analysis with an Amended Prisoners Dilemma Model', *Journal of Politics* 50, 600–624.
Grotius, H. (1608). 'The Freedom of the Sea', in J. B. Scott (ed.), *Classics of Law*, (1916), trans. Ralph Van Deman Magoffin. New York: Oxford University Press.
Grubb, M. (1989). *The Greenhouse Effect: Negotiating Targets*. London: Royal Institute of International Affairs.
Grubb, M. (1995). 'Seeking Fair Weather? Ethics and the International Debate on Climate Change', *International Affairs* 71 (3), 462–496.
Grubb, M. and Yamin, F. (2001). 'Climatic Collapse at The Hague: What Happened, Why, and Where do we go From Here?', *International Affairs* 77 (2), 261–276.
Grubb, M., Sebenius, J., Magalhaes, A. and Subak I. M. (1992). 'Sharing the Burden', in I. Mintzer (ed.) *Confronting Climate Change: Risks, Implications and Responses*. Cambridge: Cambridge University Press.
Grubler, A. and Nakicenovic, N. (1991). *International Burden Sharing in Greenhouse Reduction*. New York: Environmental Policy Division, World Bank.
Guha, R. and Martinez-Alier, J. (1997). *Varieties of Environmentalism*. London: Earthscan.
Haas, P. (1989). 'Do Regimes Matter? Epistemic Communities and the Mediterranean Pollution Control', *International Organization* 43, 377–403.
Haas, P. (1992). 'Introduction: Epistemic Communities and International Policy' in P. Haas (ed.), *International Organization* 46 (1), 1–35.
Haas, P. M., Keohane, R. O. and Levy, M. A. (1993). *Institutions for the Earth: Sources of Effective Environmental Protection*. Cambridge, MA: MIT Press.
Haberl, H., Wacknergel, M., Krausmann, F. and Erb, K. H. (2004). 'Ecological Footprint and Human Appropriation of Net Primary Production: A Comparison', *Land Use Policy* 21, 279–288.
Habermas, J. (1981). *Theory of Communicative Action*. Boston, MA: Beacon Press.
Haggard, S. and Simmons, B. A. (1987). 'Theories of International Regime', *International Organization* 41 (3), 491–597.
Hailwood, S. (2004). *Nature, Value and Liberal Philosophy*. London: Acumen.

Hajer, M. (1995). *The Politics of Environmental Discourse: Ecological Modernization and Policy Process*. Oxford: Claderon Press.
Hall, C. (1998). 'Institutional Solutions for Governing the Global Commons: Design Factors And Effectiveness', *Journal of Environment and Development* 7 (2), 86–114.
Hangrove, E. (2003). 'What's Wrong? Who is To Blame?', *Environmental Ethics* 25, 3–4.
Hansenclever, A., Mayer, P. and Rittberger, V. (1996). 'Interests, Power, Knowledge: The Study of International Regimes', *Mershon International Studies Review* 40 (2), 117–228.
Hansenclever, A., Mayer, P. and Rittberger, V. (1997). *Theories of International Regimes*. Cambridge: Cambridge University Press.
Hardin, G. (1968). 'The Tragedy of the Commons', *Science* 162, 38–58.
Hardin, G. (1972). *Exploring New Ethics for Survival: The Voyage of the Spaceship Beagle*. New York: Beagle.
Hare, R. M. (1981). *Moral Thinking*. Oxford: Oxford University Press.
Harman, G. (1983), 'Justice and Moral Bargaining', *Social Philosophy and Policy* 1 (1), 114–131.
Harvey, D. (2000). *Spaces of Hope*. Edinburgh: Edinburgh University Press.
Hatch, M. (1993). 'Domestic Politics and International Negotiations: The Politics of Global Warming in the United States', *Journal of Environment and Development* 2 (2), 1–39.
Hawkins, A. (1993). 'Contested Ground: International Environmentalism and Global Climate Change', in R. D. Lipschutz and K. Conca (eds), *The State and Social Power in Global Environmental Politics*. New York: Columbia University Press.
Hayek, F. (1960). *The Constitution of Liberty*. London: Routledge and Kegan Paul.
Hayek, F. A. (1976). *Law, Legislation and Liberty Vol. 2*. London: Routledge.
Hayes, P. (1993). 'North–South Transfer', in P. Hayes and K. Smith (eds), *The Global Greenhouse Regime: Who Pays?* London: Earthscan.
Hayward T. (1998). *Political Theory and Ecological Values*. Cambridge: Polity Press.
Hayward T. (2000). 'Constitutional Environmental Rights: A Case for Political Analysis', *Political Studies* 48 (3), 558–572.
Hayward, T. (2002). 'Fairness and Futurity: Essays on Sustainability and Social Justice (book review)', *Environmental Values* 11(4), 511–513.
Hayward, T. (2005). *Constitutional Environmental Rights*. Oxford; Oxford University Press.
Heltberg, R. (2002). 'Property Rights and Natural Resource Management in Developing Countries', *Journal of Economic Surveys* 16 (2), 189–214.
Hey, E. (1992). 'The Precautionary Concept in International Environmental Policy and Law', *Georgetown International Environmental Law Review* 4 (2), 303–318.
Higgott, R. A., Underhill, R. D. G. and Bieler, A. (2000). *Non-State Actors and Authority in the Global System*. London: Routledge.
Hilz C. (1992). *The International Toxic Waste Trade*. New York: VanNostrand Reinhold.
Hobbes, T. (1968). *Leviathan*, ed, with an introduction by C. B. Macpherson. Harmondsworth: Penguin.
Hoffmann, S. (1987). 'Super Power Ethics: The Rules of The Game', *Ethics and International Affairs* 1, 37–51.
Holifield, R. (2004). 'Neoliberalism and Environmental Justice in the United States Environmental Protection Agency: Translating Policy into Managerial Practice in Hazardous Waste Remediation', *Geoforum*, 35, 285–297.
Holland, A. (2000). 'Sustainable Development: The Contested Vision', in K. Lee, M.

Desmond and A. Holland (eds), *Global Sustainable Development in the 21st Century*. Edinburgh: Edinburgh University Press.
Hollick, A. L. (1981). *U.S Foreign Policy and the Law of the Sea*. Princeton, NJ: Princeton University Press.
Homer-Dixon, T. F. (1994). 'Environmental Scarcities and Violent Conflict: Evidence from Cases', *International Security* 19 (2), 5–40.
Homer-Dixon, T. F. (1999). *Environment, Scarcity and Violence*. Princeton, NJ: Princeton University Press.
Homer-Dixon, T. F. (2001). *Environment, Scarcity and Violence*. Second edition. Princeton, NJ: Princeton University Press.
Huber, J. (1985). *Die Regenbogengesellschaft Ökologie und Sozialpolitik*. Frankfurt am Main: Fisher Verlag.
Hume, D. (1975). 'An Enquiry Concerning Principles of Moral', in A. Ryan (ed.), *Justice*. Oxford: Oxford University Press.
Humphreys, D. (1996). 'Hegemonic Ideology and The International Tropical Timber Organisation', in J. Vogler and M. F. Imber (eds), *The Environment and International Relations*. London: Routledge.
Hunold, C. and Dryzek, J. (2006). 'Green Political Strategy and the State: Combining Political and Comparative History', in J. Barry and R. Eckersley (eds), *The State and the Global Ecological Crisis*. Cambridge, MA: MIT Press.
Hunt, G. (1998). 'Is There a Conflict Between Environmental Protection and the Development of the Third World?', in R. Attfield and B. Wilkins (eds), *International Justice and the Third World*. London: Routledge.
Hunter, R. (1996). 'Good Intentions Foolish Policy', *Chemistry and Industry* 2, 68.
Huq, S. (2001). 'Climate Change and Bangladesh', *Science* 294, 1617.
Hurrell, A. (2001). 'Global Inequality and International Institutions', *Metaphilosophy* 32 (1/2), 34–57.
Hurrell, A. and Kingsbury, B. (1992). 'The International Politics of the Environment: An Introduction', in A. Hurrell and B. Kingsbury (eds), *The International Politics of the Environment*. Oxford: Clarendon Press.
Hurrell, A. and Woods, N. (ed.) (1999). *Globalization and World Politics*. Oxford: Oxford University Press.
Hyder, T. O. (1994). 'Looking Back to See Forward', in I. Mintzer and J. A. Leonard (eds), *Negotiating Climate Change: The Inside Story of the Rio Convention*. Cambridge: Cambridge University Press.
Illich, I. (1983). 'Silence is a Commons', *CoEvolutionary Quarterly* 22, 5–9.
Independent World Commission on the Oceans (1998). *The Ocean: Our Future*. Cambridge: Cambridge University Press.
Intergovernmental Negotiation Committee (INC) (1991). *Report of the Intergovernmental Negotiating Committee for a Framework Convention on Climate Change on the work of its First Session, held at Washington, D.C. from 4 to 14 February 1991*. UN Doc. A/AC.237/6.
Intergovernmental Panel on Climate Change (IPCC). (1995). *IPCC Second Assessment: Climate Change 1995. A Report of the Intergovernmental Panel on Climate Change*. Cambridge: Cambridge University Press.
Intergovernmental Panel on Climate Change (IPCC). (1996). *Climate Change 1995: Economic and Social Dimensions of Climate Change, Contribution of Working Group III to the Second Assessment Report of the IPCC*. Cambridge: Cambridge University Press.

Intergovernmental Panel on Climate Change (IPCC). (2001). *Climate Change 2001: Impacts, Adaptation and Vulnerability*. Cambridge: Cambridge University Press.

Intergovernmental Panel on Climate Change (IPCC). (2007a). *The Physical Science Basis: Working Group 1 Contribution to the Fourth Assessment Report of the IPCC (Climate Change 2007)*. Cambridge: Cambridge University Press.

Intergovernmental Panel on Climate Change (IPCC). (2007b). *Climate Change 2007 – Impacts, Adaptation and Vulnerability: Working Group II Contribution to the Fourth Assessment Report of the IPCC (Climate Change 2007)*. Cambridge: Cambridge University Press.

International Arbitration Awards (1898) I, 811. Reproduced in *International Environmental Law Reports* 1, 43.

International Tropical Timber Organization (ITTO) (1994). International Tropical Timber Agreement (ITTA). www.itto.or.jp/

Isaac, J. (1987). *Power and the Marxist Theory: A Realist View*. Ithaca, NY: Cornell University Press.

Jacobs, M. (1995). 'Sustainable Development, Capital Substitution and Economic Humility: A Response to Beckerman', *Environmental Values* 4 (1), 50–57.

Jacobs, M. (1999). 'Sustainable Development as a Contested Concept', in A. Dobson (ed.), *Fairness and Futurity: Essays on Environmental Sustainability and Social Justice*. Oxford: Oxford University Press.

Jamieson, D. (1994). 'Global Environmental Justice', in R. Attfield and A. Belsey (eds). *Philosophy and the Natural Environment*. Cambridge: Cambridge University Press.

Jasanoff, S. and Wynne, B. (1998). 'Science and Decision Making', in S. Rayner and E. Malone (eds), *Human Choices and Climate Change: Ten Suggestions for Policy Makers*. Washington, DC: Battelle Memorial Institute.

Jessop, B. (2002). 'Liberalism, Neoliberalism, and Urban Governance: A State-Theoretical Perspective', *Antipode* 34 (3), 452–472.

Johns, D. (2003). 'The IR/Relevance of Environmental Ethics', *Environmental Ethics* 25, 223–224.

Johnston, D. M. (1981). *The Environmental Law of the Sea*. Berlin: Erich Schmidt.

Jordan, A., Wurzel, R. K. W. and Zito, A.R. (2003). ' "New" Instruments of Environmental Governance? National Experiences and Prospects', *Environmental Politics* 12 (1), 1–8.

Josselin, D. and Williams, W. (2001) 'Non-State Actors in World Politics: A Framework,' in D. Josselin and W. Williams (eds), *Non-State Actors in World Politics: A Framework*. New York: Palgrave.

Kasperson, R. and Dow, K. (1991). 'Development and geographical equity in global environmental change: a framework for analysis', *Evaluation Review* 15 (1), 149–171.

Kelly, P. (1990). 'The Need for Eco-Justice', *Fletcher Forum of World Affairs* 14, 327–331.

Keneese, A. and Bower, B. (1979). *Environmental Quality and Residual Management*. Baltimore, MD: Johns Hopkins University Press.

Keohane, R. (1984). *After Hegemony: Co-operation and Discord in the World Political Economy*. Princeton, NJ: Princeton University Press.

Keohane, R. O. and Levy, M. (ed.) (1996). *Institutions for Environmental Aid: Pitfalls and Promise*. Cambridge, MA: MIT Press.

Keohane, R. and Nye, J. (1977). *Power and Interdependence – World Politics in Transition*. Boston, MA: Little Brown.

Keohane R., Haas, P. and Levy M. (1993) 'The Effectiveness of International Environmental Institutions', in P. M. Haas R. Keohane and M. Levy (eds), *Institutions for the Earth: Sources of Effective International Environmental Protection.* Cambridge, MA: MIT Press.

Kersting, W. (1996). 'Weltfriedensordnung und globale Verteilungs-gerechtigkeit', in R. Merkel and R. Wittman (eds), *Zum ewigen Frieden, Grndlagen, Aktualitat und Ausschten einer Idee von Immanuel Kant.* Frankfirt am Main: Suhrkamp.

Khanna, J. and Harford, J. (1996). 'The Ivory Trade Ban: Is It Effective?', *Ecological Economics* 19 (2): 147–155.

Kiss, A. (1985). 'The Common Heritage of Mankind: Utopia or Reality?', *International Journal* 40, 423–441.

Kiss, A. (1991). 'The International Control of Transboundary Movement of Hazardous Wastes', *Texas International Law Journal* 26, 521–539.

Kjellen, B. (2006). 'Foreword', in W. N. Adger, J. Paavola, S. Huq, and M. J. Mace (eds), *Fairness in Adaptation to Climate Change.* Cambridge, MA: MIT Press.

Knox, T. (1938) *Plato's Republic.* Interpreter Series Vol. 7. London: Penguin.

Koh, T. B. (1983). 'A Constitution for the Oceans: A Statement by the President of the Third United Nations Conference on the Law of the Sea', in *The Law of the Sea: United Nations Conference on the Law of the Sea.* New York: The United Nations.

Koh, T. B. (1988). 'The Exclusive Economic Zone', reprinted in C. Hugo (ed.) (2001), *The Law of the Sea.* Aldershot Ashgate.

Kokott, J. (1999). 'Equity in International Law', in F. L. Toth (ed.), *Fair Weather? Equity Concerns in Climate Change.* London: Earthscan.

Korten, D. (1996). *When Corporations Rule the World.* London: Earthscan.

Krasner, S. D. (ed.) (1983a). *International Regimes.* Ithaca, NY: Cornell University Press.

Krasner, S. D. (1983b). 'Structural Causes and Regime Consequences: Regimes as Intervening Variables', in S. D. Krasner (ed.), *International Regimes.* Ithaca, NY: Cornell University Press.

Kratochwil, F. V. (1989). *Rules, Norms and Decisions: On the Conditions of Practical and Legal Reasoning in International Relations and Domestic Affairs.* Cambridge: Cambridge University Press.

Kratochwil, F. and Ruggie, J. G. (1986). 'A State of the Art on an Art of the State', *International Organization* 40, 753–775.

Krueger, J. (1998). 'Prior Informed Consent and the Basel Convention: The Hazards of What Isn't Known', *Journal of Environment and Development* 7 (2), 115–137.

Krueger, J. (1999). *International Trade and Basel Convention.* London: Earthscan.

Kummer, K. (1995). *International Management of Hazardous Wastes: The Basel Convention and Related Legal Rules.* Oxford: Claderon Press.

Kwiatkowska, B. (1988). 'Equitable Marine Boundary Delimitation – A legal Perspective', *International Journal of Estuarine and Costal Law* 3, 287–304.

Kymlicka, W. (2002). *Contemporary Political Philosophy: An Introduction*, 2nd edn. Oxford: Oxford University Press.

Laferriere, E. and Stoett, P. J. (1999). *International Relations Theory and Ecological Thought: Towards a Synthesis.* London: Routledge.

Langhelle, O. (1999). 'Sustainable Development: Exploring the Ethics of Our Common Future', *International Political Science Review* 20 (2), 129–149.

Langhelle, O. (2000). 'Sustainable Development and Social Justice: Expanding the Rawlsian Framework of Global Justice', *Environmental Values* 9 (3), 295–324.

Lapavitsas, C. (2005). 'Mainstream Economics in the Neoliberal Era', in A. Saad-Filho and D. Johnston (eds), *Neoliberalism: A Critical Reader*. London: Pluto Press.

Lee, K. (1995). 'A Neo-Gramscian Approach to International Organization: An Expanded Analysis of Current Reforms to UN Development Activities', in J. Macmillan and A. Linklater (eds), *Boundaries and Questions: New Directions in International Relations*. London and New York: Pinter Press.

Lee, K. (2000). 'Global Sustainable Development: Its Intellectual and Historical Roots', in K. Lee, M. Desmond and A. Holland (eds), *Global Sustainable Development in the 21st Century*. Edinburgh: Edinburgh University Press.

Leff, E. (1996). 'From Ecological Economics to Productive Ecology: Perspectives on Sustainable Development from the South', in R. Costanza, J. Martinez-Alier and O. Segura (eds), *Getting Down to Earth: Practical Applications of Ecological Economics*. Washington: Washington Bland.

Leggett, J. (2000). *The Carbon War: Global Warming at the End of the Oil Era*. London: Penguin Books.

Lele, S. (1991). 'Sustainable Development: A Critical Review', *World Development* 9 (6), 607–621.

Lemos, M. C. and Agarwal, A. (2006). 'Environmental Governance', *Annual Review of Environmental Resources* 37, 295–327.

Levy, D. L and Newell P.J. (eds) (2005). *The Business of Global Environmental Governance*. London: MIT Press.

Lipschutz, R. D. and Conca, K. (eds) (1993). *The State and Social Power in Global Environmental Politics*. New York: Columbia University Press.

Lipschutz, R. D. and Mayer, J. (1993). ' Not Seeing Trees: Rights, Rules, and the Renegotiation of Resources Management Regimes', in R. D. Lipschutz and K. Conca (eds), *The State and Social Power in Global Environmental Politics*. New York: Columbia University Press.

Litfin, T. K. (1993). 'Playing Tug of War with the Nation-State', in R. D. Lipschutz and K. Conca (eds), *The State and Social Power in Global Environmental Politics*. New York: Columbia University Press.

Litfin, T. K. (1994). *Ozone Discourses: Science and Politics in Global Environmental Cooperation*. New York: Columbia University Press.

Liverman, D. (2006). 'Conventions of Climate Change: Constructions of Danger and the Dispossession of the Atmosphere', Presentation paper in the Narratives of Climate Change Plenary Session, RGS-IBG, London, 31 August 2006.

Locke, J. (1690/1924). *Two Treatises on Government*. London: Dent.

Lomasky, L. (1987). *Persons, Rights, and the Moral Community*. Oxford: Oxford University Press.

Loske, R. and Oberthur (1994) 'Joint Implementation Under the Climate Change Convention', *International Environmental Affairs* 6 (1).

Low, N. and Gleeson, B. (1998). *Justice Society and Nature: An Exploration of Political Ecology*. New York: Routledge.

Low, N. and Gleeson, B. (2001). 'The Challenge of Ethical Environmental Governance', in B. Gleeson and N. Low (eds), *Governing for the Environment: Global Problems Ethics and Democracy*. Wiltshire: Palgrave.

Lunde, L. (1991). 'Global Warming and a System of Tradable Emission Permits –A Review of the Current Debate', *International Challenges* 11 (3), 15–31.

Luper-Foy, S. (1992). 'Justice and Natural Resources', *Environmental Values* 1 (1), 47–64.

Bibliography

Luterbacher, U. and Sprinz, D. F. (2001). 'Problems of Global Environmental Co-operation', in U. Luterbacher and D. F. Sprinz (eds), *International Relations and Global Climate Change*. Cambridge, MA: MIT Press.

Lyons, D. (1981). 'The New Indian Claims and Original Rights to Land', in E. Paul (ed.), *Reading Nozick*. Totowa, NJ: Rowman Littlefield.

McCarthy, J. (2004). 'Privatizing Conditions of Production: Trade Agreements as Neoliberal Environmental Governance', *Geoforum* 35 (1), 327–341.

McCarthy, J. and Prudham, S. (2004). 'Neoliberal Nature and the Nature of Neoliberalism', *Geoforum* 35 (1), 275–283.

McCorriston, J. and Hole, F. (1991). 'The Ecology of Seasonal Stress and the Origin of Agriculture in the Near East', *American Anthropologist* 93 (1), 46–69.

MacIntyre, A. (1981). *After Virtue: A Study in Moral Theory*. Duckworth Publishers: London.

McNeill, D. (2000). 'The Concept of Sustainable Development' in K. Lee, M. Desmond and A. Holland (eds), *Global Sustainable Development in the 21st Century*. Edinburgh: Edinburgh University Press.

Mansbach, R. W. and Ferguson, Y. H. (1987). 'Values and Paradigm Change: The Elusive Quest for International Relations Theory', reprinted in P. R. Viotti and M. V. Kauppi (1987), *International Relations Theory: Realism, Pluralism and Globalism*. New York: Macmillan.

Mansfield, B. (2004). 'Neoliberalism in the Oceans: "Rationalisation", Property Rights, and the Commons Question', *Geoforum* 25 (1), 313–326.

Mantle, D. J. (1999). *Critical Political Theory and International Relations Theory*. Unpublished Ph.D. Thesis, Keele University, UK.

Markandya, A. (1991). 'Global Warming: The Economics of Tradable Permits', in D. Pearce (ed.), *Greening the World Economy*. London: Earthscan Publications.

Martinez-Alier, J. (2002). *Environmentalism of the Poor: A Study of Ecological Conflicts and Valuation*. Cheltenham: Edward Elgar.

Marx, K. (1969) 'Critique of the Gotha Programme', in L. Feuer (ed.) *Marx and Engels: Basic Writings on Politics and Philosophy*. London: Fontana.

Maslow, A. (1968). *Towards a Psychology of Being*, 2nd edn. Princeton, NJ: Van Nostrand.

Meadowcroft, J. (2006). 'From Welfare State to Ecostate', in J. Barry and R. Eckersley (eds), *The State and the Global Ecological Crisis*. Cambridge, MA: MIT Press.

Meadows, D. H., Meadows, D. L. and Randers, J. (1972). *The Limits To Growth*. London: Pan.

Meadows, D. H., Meadows, D. L. and Randers, J. (1992). *Beyond The Limits*. London: Earthscan.

Metz, B., Berk, M., den Elzen, M. and de Vries, B. (2002). 'Towards an Equitable Global Climate Change Regime: Compatibility with Article 2 of the Climate Change Convention and the Link with Sustainable Development', *Science Direct* 2 (2/3), 211–232.

Meyer J. (2005). Global Liberalism, Environmentalism and the Changing Boundaries of the Political: Karl Polanyi's Insights', in J. Paavola and I. Lowe (eds), *Environmental Values in a Globalizing World: Nature, Justice and Governance*. London: Routledge.

Mgbeoji, I. (2004). 'Beyond Rhetoric: State Sovereignty, Common Concern, and the Inapplicability of the Common Heritage Concept to Plant Genetic Resources', *Leiden Journal of International Law*, 16: 821–837.

Mill, J. S. (1893). *The Utilitarians*, reprinted 1973. New York: Dent.

Miller, D. (1995). *On Nationality*. Oxford: Oxford University Press.

Miller, D. (1999). 'Justice and Global Inequality', in A. Hurrell and N. Woods (eds), *Inequality, Globalization and World Politics*. Oxford: Oxford University Press.

Miller, D. (2000). *In Defence of Nationality in Citizenship and National Identity*. Cambridge: Polity Press.

Miller, M. A. L. (1995). *The Third World in Global Environmental Politics*. Buckingham: Open University Press.

Mintzer, I. and Leonard J. A. (1994). *Negotiating Climate Change: The Inside Story of the Rio Convention*. Cambridge: Cambridge University Press.

Mofford, E. K. (2006). 'Oil and Power in the Caspian Sea Region: Supermajor Oil Companies and Geopolitics', in B. Gokay (ed.), *The Politics of Oil: A Survey*. London: Routledge.

Mol, A. P. J. (1996). 'Ecological Modernization and Institutional Reflexivity: Environmental Reform in the Late Modern Age', *Environmental Politics* 5 (2), 302–323.

Mol, A. P. (ed.) (2000). *Ecological Modernization Around the World: Perspectives and Critical Debates*. Ilford: Frank Cass.

Monfreda, C. (2004). 'Establishing National Natural Capital Accounts Based on Detailed Ecological Footprint and Biological Capacity Assessments', *Land Use Policy* 21, 231–246.

Montgomery, M. A. (1990). 'Travelling Toxic Trash: An Analysis of the 1989 Basel Convention', *Fletcher Forum of World Affairs* 14, 312–326.

Montgomery, M. A. (1995). 'Reassessing the Waste Trade Crisis: What do we Really Know?', *Journal of Environment and Development* 4 (1), 1–28.

Morgenthau, H. J. (1965). *Scientific Man Versus Power Politics*. Chicago: Chicago University Press.

Morgenthau, J. H. (1956). *Politics among Nations: The Struggle for Power and Peace*. New York: Knopf.

Moyers, B. (1991). *Global Dumping Ground: The International Traffic in Hazardous Wastes*. Cambridge, UL: Lutterworth.

Munda, G. (1997). 'Environmental Economics, Ecological Economics and the Concept of Sustainable Development', *Environmental Values* 6 (2), 213–234.

Naess, A. (1973). 'The Shallow and the Deep, Long Range Ecology Movement. A Summary'. *Inquiry* 16, 95–99.

Newell, P. (2000). *Climate for Change: Non-state Actors and the Global Politics of the Greenhouse*. Cambridge: Cambridge University Press.

Nielsen, K. (1995). 'Global Justice, Capitalism and the Third World', in R. Attfield and B. Wilkins (eds), *International Justice and the Third World*. London: Routledge.

Nijkamp, P., Rossi, E. and Vindigini, G. (2004). 'Ecological Footprint in Plural: Meta-analytic Comparison of Empirical Results', *Regional Studies* 38 (7), 747–765.

Nitze, W. A. (1994). 'A Failure of Presidential Leadership', in I. Mintzer and J. A. Leonard (eds), *Negotiating Climate Change: The Inside Story of the Rio Convention*. Cambridge: Cambridge University Press.

Nordhaus, W. (1991). 'To Slow or Not to Slow: The Economics of the Greenhouse Effect', *Energy Journal* 6, 920–937.

Nozick, R. (1974). *Anarchy, State, and Utopia*. New York: Basic Books.

Nozick, R. (1981). *Political Explanations*. Cambridge, MA: Harvard University Press.

Nussbaum, M. (1990). 'Aristotelian Social Democracy', in R. Doughlas, G. Mara and H. Richardson (eds), *Liberalism and the Good*. New York and London: Routledge.

Nussbaum, M. (2000). *Women and Human Development: The Capability Approach*. Cambridge: Cambridge University Press.

218 Bibliography

OAU (1989). OAU/CM/Res.1225 (L) Resolution on the Control of Transboundary Movement of Hazardous Wastes and their Disposal in Africa. July 17–22.
O'Connell, D. P. (1984). *The International Law of the Sea*, 2 Vols. Oxford: Oxford University Press.
OECD. (1994). *Transboundary Movements of Hazardous Wastes 1992–93 Statistics*. Paris: OECD.
OECD. (1998). *Trade Measures in the Basel Convention on the Control of Transboundary Movements of Hazardous Wastes and their Disposal*, COM/ENV/TD (97)41/FINAL. Paris: OECD.
Ogley, R. C. (1984). *Internationalizing the Seabed*. Aldershot: Gower.
Okereke, C. (2006a). 'Global Environmental Sustainability: Intragenerational Equity and Conceptions of Justice in Multilateral Environmental Regimes', *Geoforum* 37: 725–738.
Okereke, C. (2006b). 'Oil Politics and Environmental Conflict: The Case of Niger Delta Nigeria', in B. Gokay (ed.), *The Politics of Oil: A Survey*. London: Routledge.
O'Neill, J. (1997). *Ecology, Policy and Politics: Human Well-being and the Natural World*. London: Routledge.
O'Neill, K. (1998). 'Out of the Backyard: The Problems of Hazardous Waste Management at a Global Level', *Journal of Environment and Development* 7(2), 138–161.
O'Neill, O. (1980). 'The Most Extensive Liberty', *Proceedings of Aristotelian Society*, 85, 45–59.
O'Neill, O. (1986). *Faces of Hunger*. London: Allen and Unwin.
O'Neill, O. (1989). *Constructions of Reason: Explorations of Kant's Practical Philosophy*. Cambridge: Cambridge University Press.
O'Neill, O. (1991). 'Transnational Justice', in D. Held (ed.), *Political Theory Today*. Cambridge: Polity Press.
O'Neill, O. (2000). *Bounds of Justice*. Cambridge. Cambridge University Press
O'Neill, O (2001). 'Agents of Justice', *Metaphilosophy* 32 (1 /2), 180–185.
Onuf, N. G. (1989). *World of Our Making: Rules and Rule in Social Theory and International Relations*. Columbia: University of South Carolina Press.
O'Riordan, T. and Cameron, J. (1994). *Interpreting the Precautionary Principle*. London: Cameron and May.
Ostrom, E. (1985). 'The Rudiments of a Revised Theory of the Origins, Survival and Performance of Institutions for Collective Action', Working Paper No. 32, Workshop in Political Theory and Policy Analysis, Indiana University, Bloomington, IN.
Ostrom, E. (1990). *Governing the Commons: The Evolution of Institutions for Collective Action*. Cambridge: Cambridge University Press.
Oxman, B. H. (1985). 'Customary International Law and the Exclusive Economic Zone', in J. M. Van Dyke (ed.), *Consensuses and Confrontation: The United States and the Law of the Sea Convention*. Hawaii: The Law of the Sea Institute.
Oxman, B. H. (1994). 'Law of the Sea Forum: The 1994 Agreement and the Convention', *American Journal of International Law* 88, 687–697.
Oye, K. A. (1986). 'Explaining Co-operation under Anarchy: Hypothesis and Strategies,' in K. A. Oye (ed.) *Co-operation Under Anarchy*. Princeton: Princeton University Press.
Ozkaynak, B., Divine, P. and Rigby, D. (2004). 'Operationalizing Strong Sustainability: Definitions, Methodologies and Outcomes', *Environmental Values* 13 (3), 279–303.
Paavola, J. (2005). Interdependence, Pluralism and Globalization: Implications for Environmental Governance', in J. Paavola and I. Lowe (eds). *Environmental Values in a Globalizing World: Nature, Justice and Governance*. London: Routledge.

Paavola, J. (2006). 'Justice in Adaptation to Climate Change in Tanzania', in W. N. Adger et al. (eds), *Fairness in Adaptation to Climate Change*. Cambridge, MA: MIT Press.

Paavola, J. and Lowe, I. (eds) (2005). *Environmental Values in a Globalizing World: Nature, Justice and Governance*. London: Routledge.

Pachauri, R. K. (1992). 'The Climate Change Convention: What it May Mean for the Poor', *Network* 19, 14–15.

Palmer, J. (1995). 'Just Ecological Principles?', in D. Cooper and J. Palmer (eds), *Just Environments: Intergenerational, International and Interspecies Issues*. London: Routledge.

Panjabi, R. K. L. (1993). 'Can International Law Improve the Climate? An Analysis of the United Nations Climate Change Signed at the Rio Summit in 1992', *North Carolina Journal of International Law*, 18, 491–549.

Pardo, A. (1975). *The Common Heritage: Selected Papers on Oceans and the World Order 1967–74*. Valletta, Malta: University of Malta.

Paterson, M. (1996a). 'International Justice and Global Warming', in B. Holden (ed.), *The Ethical Dimensions of Global Change*. London: Macmillan.

Paterson, M. (1996b). *Global Warming and Global Politics*. London: Routledge.

Paterson, M. (2000). *Understanding Global Environmental Politics: Domination, Accumulation and Resistance*. Houndmills: Macmillan.

Paterson, M. (2001). 'Principles of Justice in the Context of Global Climate Change', in U. Luterbacher and D. Sprinz (eds), *International Relations and Global Climate Change*. Cambridge, MA: MIT Press.

Paterson, M. and Barry, J. (2005). 'Modernizing the British State: Ecological Contradictions in the New Labour's Economic Strategy', in J. Barry and R. Eckersley (eds), *The State and Global Ecological Crisis*. Cambridge, MA: MIT Press.

Paterson, M. and Grubb, M. (1992). 'The International Politics of Climate Change', *International Affairs* 68 (2), 293–313.

Paterson, M., Humphreys, D. and Pettiford, L. (2003). 'Conceptualizing Global Environmental Governance: From Interstate Regimes to Counter Hegemonic Struggles', *Global Environmental Politics* 3 (2), 1–9.

Pearce, D. W. (1995).' Valuing Climate Change', *Chemistry and Industry* December, 1024.

Pearce, D. W., Cline, W. R., Achanta, A. N., Frankhauser, S., Pachauri, R.K., Tol, R.S J. and Vellinga, P. (1996). 'The Social Cost of Climate Change', in *The Second Assessment Report of IPCC Working Group III*. Cambridge: Cambridge University Press.

Peck, J. (2004). 'Geography and Public Policy: Constructions of Neoliberalism', *Progress in Human Geography* 28 (3), 392–405.

Peck, J. and Tickell, A. (2002). 'Neoliberalizing Space', *Antipode* 34 (3), 380–404.

Pepper, D. (1984). *The Roots of Modern Environmentalism*. London: Routledge.

Pepper, D. (1993). *Eco-socialism: From Deep Ecology to Social Justice*. London: Routeldge.

Pepper, D. (1996). *Modern Environmentalism: An Introduction*. London, New York: Routledge.

Perez de Cuellar, J. (1983). 'International Law is Irrevocably Transformed: Statement by the Secretary General of the United Nations', reprinted in *The Law of the Sea: United Nations Convention on the Law of the Sea*. New York: The United Nations.

Pinchot, G. (1910). *The Fight for Conservation*. Washington: Double Day Page and Company, University of Washington.

Plant, R. (1997). *Modern Political Thought*. Oxford: Basil Blackwell.

Bibliography

Plumwood, V. (1993). *Feminism and the Mastery of Nature.* London: Routledge.
Pogge, T. (1988). 'Rawls and Global Justice', *Canadian Journal of Political Philosophy* 18 (2), 227–256.
Pogge, T. (1989). *Realizing Rawls.* Ithaca, NY: Cornell University Press.
Pogge, T. (1992). 'Cosmopolitanism and Sovereignty', *Ethics* 103, 48–75.
Pogge, T. (1994). 'An Egalitarian Law of Peoples', *Philosophy and Public Affairs* 23 (3), 195–224.
Pogge, T. (1998). 'A Global Resource Dividend', in D. Crocker and T. Linden (eds.), *Ethics of Consumption: The Good Life, Justice and Global Stewardship.* Lanham, MD: Rowman and Littlefield.
Pogge, T. (2001). 'Priorities of Global Justice', *Metaphilosophy* 32 (1/2), 6–24.
Pogge, T. (2002). *World Poverty and Human Rights.* Cambridge: Polity Press.
Pontecorvo, G. (1987). 'The Impact of the Law of the Sea Treaty on the Organisation of World Fisheries: Some Preliminary Observations on Production', in E. D. Brown and R. R. Churchill (eds), *The UN Convention of the Law of the Sea: Impact and Implementation.* Honolulu: Law of the Sea Institute.
Pontecorvo, G. (1988). 'The Enclosure of the Marine Commons: Adjustments and Redistribution in World Fisheries', *Marine Policy* 12 (4), 361–372.
Porter, G. and Brown, J. W. (1995). *Global Environmental Politics*, 2nd edn. Boulder, CO: Westview Press.
Puckett J. (1992). 'Dumping on our World Neighbours: The International Trade in Hazardous Wastes, and the Case for an Immediate Ban on All Hazardous Waste Exports from Industrialised to Less-Industrialised Countries', in H. O. Bergesen, M. Norderhaug and J. P. Lester (eds), *Green Globe Yearbook.* Oxford: Oxford University Press.
Puckett, J. (1994). 'Disposing of the Waste Trade: Closing the Recycling Loophole', *The Ecologist* 24 (2), 53–58.
Rahman, A. and Rocerel, A. (1994). 'A View From the Ground Up', in I. Mintzer and J. A. Leonard (eds), *Negotiating Climate Change: The Inside Story of the Rio Convention.* Cambridge: Cambridge University Press.
Raiffa, H. (1982). *The Art and Science of Negotiation.* Cambridge, MA: Harvard University Press.
Ramakrishna, K. (1990). 'North South Issues, Common Heritage of Mankind and Global Climate Change', *Millennium Journal of International Studies* 19 (3), 429–445.
Rawls, J. (1971). *A Theory of Justice.* Oxford: Oxford University Press.
Rawls, J. (1980). 'Kantian Constructivism in Moral Theory', *Journal of Philosophy* 77 (9), 515–572.
Rawls, J. (1993). *Political Liberalism.* New York: Columbia University Press.
Rawls, J. (1999). *The Law of Peoples.* Cambridge: Harvard University Press.
Rayner, S. and Malone, E. (1998). *Human Choices and Climate Change: Ten Suggestions for Policy Makers.* Washington, DC: Battelle Memorial Institute.
Rayner, S., Malone, E. and Thompson, M. (1999). 'Equity Issues and Integrated Assessment', in F. Toth (ed.), *Fair Weather: Equity Concerns in Climate Change.* London: Earthscan.
Redclift, M. (1987). *Sustainable Development: Exploring the Contradictions.* London: Methuen.
Redclift, M. (2000). 'Global Equity: The Environment and Development', in K. Lee, M. Desmond and A. Holland (eds), *Global Sustainable Development in the 21st Century.* Edinburgh: Edinburgh University Press.

Ridley, M. and Low, B. (1993). 'Can Selfishness Save the Environment?', *Human Ecology Review* 1 (1), 1–13.
Roe D., Miliken, T., Millidge, S., Mremi, J., Mosha, S. and Grieg-Gran, M. (2002). *Making a Killing or Making a Living: Wildlife Trade, Trade Controls and Rural Livelihoods*. London: IIED Press.
Rosenau, J. (1997) *Along the Domestic Foreign Frontier: Exploring Governance in a Turbulent World*. Cambridge: Cambridge University Press.
Rosendal, G. K. (1995). 'The Convention on Biological Diversity: A Viable Instrument for Conservation and Sustainable Use?', in H. Gleckman (ed.), *Green Globe Yearbook*. Oxford: Oford University Press.
Rowlands, I. H. (1991). 'Ozone Layer Depletion and Global Warming: New Sources of Environmental Disputes', *Peace and Change* 16 (3), 260–284.
Rowlands, I. H. (1995). *The Politics of Global Atmospheric Change*. Manchester: Manchester University Press.
Rowlands, I. H. (1997).'International Fairness and Justice in Addressing Global Climate Change', *Environmental Politics*, 6 (3), 1–19.
Royal Society (2006). Climate Change: what we know and what we need to know, Policy document 22/02: 9.
Ruggie, J. G. (1975). 'International Responses to Technology: Concepts and Trends', *International Organization* 29, 557–583.
Ruggie, J. G. (1982). 'International Regimes, Transactions, and Change: Embedded Liberalism in the Postwar Economic Order', *International Organization* 36 (2), 195–231.
Ruggie, J. G. (1993). Multilateralism: The Anatomy of an Institution', in J. G. Ruggie (ed.), *Multilateralism Matters: The Theory and Praxis of an Institutional Form*. New York: Columbia University Press.
Rummel-Bulska, I. (1994). 'The Basel Convention. A Global Approach for the Management of Hazardous Waste', *Environmental Policy and Law* 24 (1), 13–18.
Saad-Filho, A. and Johnston, D. (eds) (2005). *Neoliberalism: A Critical Reader*. England: Pluto Press.
Sachs, W. (1993). 'Global Ecology and Shadow of "Development"', in W. Sachs (ed.), *Global Ecology – A New Arena of Political Conflict*. London: Zed Books.
Sachs, W. (1999). *Planet Dialectics: Exploration in Environment and Development*. London: Zed Books.
Sagoff, M. (1995). 'Can Environmentalists be Liberals', in R. Elliot (ed.), *Environmental Ethics: Oxford Readings in Philosophy*. Oxford: Oxford University Press.
Sahlins, M. (1996). 'The Sadness of Sweetness: The Native Anthropology of Western Cosmology', *Current Anthropology* 37, 397–498.
Sandel, M. (1982). *Liberalism and the Limits of Justice*. Cambridge: Cambridge University Press.
Sandel, M. (1984). 'Procedural Republic and the Unencumbered Self', *Political Theory* 12, 81–96.
Sands, P. (ed.) (1992a). *The Antarctic Environment and International Law* (International Environmental Law and Policy Series). London: Springer.
Sands, P. (ed.) (1992b). *The Effectiveness of International Environmental Agreements: A Survey of Existing Legal Instruments*. Cambridge: Grotuis Publications.
Sands, P. (1995). *Principles of International Environmental Law, Vol. 1*. Manchester; Manchester University Press.
Sanger, C. (1986). *Ordering the Oceans: The Making of the Law of the Sea*. London: Zed Books.

Sax, J. L. (1990). 'The Search for Environmental Rights', *Journal of Land Use and Environmental Law* 6, 93–105.
Scalon, T. M. (1982). 'Contractualism and Utilitarianism', in S. Amartya and B. Williams (eds), *Utilitarianism and Beyond*. Cambridge: Cambridge University Press.
Schlosberg, D. (2005). 'Reconceiving Environmental Justice: Global Movements and Political Theory,' in J. Paavola and I. Lowe (eds), *Environmental Values in a Globalizing World: Nature, Justice and Governance*. London: Routledge.
Schlosberg, D. (2006). 'Environmental and Ecological Justice: Theory and Practice in the United States', in J. Barry and R. Eckersley (eds), *The State and the Global Ecological Crisis*. Cambridge, MA: MIT Press.
Schneider, H. S. and Lane, J. (2006). 'Dangers and Thresholds in Climate Change and the Implications for Justice', in W. N. Adger, J. Paavola, S. Huq and M. J. Mace (eds), *Fairness in Adaptation to Climate Change*. Cambridge, MA: MIT Press.
Scully, R.T. and Kimbal, L. A. (1989). 'Antarctica: Is there Life after Minerals: The Mineral Treaty and Beyond', *Marine Policy* 13 (22), 87–98.
Semmens, A. (2001). 'Maximizing Justice for Environmental Refuges: A Transnational Institution on Behalf of the Deterritorialized', in. B. Glesson and N. Low (eds), *Governing for the Environment: Global Problems, Ethics and Democracy*. Wiltshire: Palgrave.
Sen, A. (1999). *Development as Freedom*. New York: Knopf.
Sending, J. O. and Newmann, B. I. (2006). 'Governance to Governmentality: Analysing NGOs, States, and Power', *International Studies Quarterly* 50, 651–672.
Shiva, V. (1988). *Staying Alive: Women, Ecology and Development*. London: Zed Books.
Shiva, V. (2006). *Earth Democracy: Justice, Sustainability and Peace*. London: Zed Books.
Shue, H. (1983). 'The Burden of Justice', *The Journal of Philosophy* 80 (10), 600–608.
Shue, H. (1992) 'The Unavoidability of Justice', in A. Hurrell and B. Kingsbury (eds), *International Politics of the Environment: Actors Interests and Institutions*. Oxford: Clarendon Press.
Shue, H. (1993). 'Subsistence Emissions and Luxury Emissions', *Law and Policy* 15 (1), 39–59.
Shue, H. (1994). 'Avoidable Necessity: Global Warming, International Fairness, and Alternative Energy', in I. Shapiro and J. W. DeCew (eds), *Theory and Practice*. New York: New York University Press.
Shukla, P. R. (1999). 'Justice, Equity and Efficiency in Climate Change: A Developing Country Perspective', in F. L. Toth (ed.), *Fair Weather? Equity Concerns in Climate Change*. London: Earthscan.
Smith, K. J. and Ahuja, D. (1993). 'Who Pays to Solve the Problem and by How Much?', in P. Hayes and K. Smith (eds), *The Global Greenhouse Regime: Who Pays? Science, Economics and Global Politics in the North–South Convention*. London: Earthscan.
Smith, R. (2003). 'Place and Chips: Virtual Communities, Governance and the Environment', in M. Paterson *et al.* (eds), special issue of *Global Environmental Politics* 3 (2), 88–102.
Snidal, D. (1985). 'Coordination Versus Prisoners Dilemma: Implications for International Co-operation and Regimes', *American Political Science Review* 79, 923–942.
Song, Y. (2005). 'Declarations and Statements with Respect to the 1982 UNCLOS: Potential Legal Disputes between the United States and China after U.S. Accession to the Convention,' *Ocean Development and International Law*, 36, 261–289.
Soper, K. (1997). 'Human Needs and Natural Relations', in T. Hayward and J. O'Neill

(eds), *Justice, Property and the Environment: Social and Legal Perspectives*. Sydney, Aldershot: Ashgate.

Soper K. (2005). 'The Enchantments and Disenchantments of Nature: Implications for Consumption in a Globalized World', in J. Paavola and I. Lowe (eds), *Environmental Values in a Globalizing World: Nature, Justice and Governance*. London: Routledge.

Soroos, M. (1997). *The Endangered Atmosphere: Preserving the Global Commons*. Columbia, SC: University of South Carolina Press.

Spangenberg, J. (2001). 'Towards Sustainability', in B. Gleeson and N. Low (eds), *Governing for the Environment: Global Problems Ethics and Democracy*. Wiltshire: Palgrave.

Steiner, H. (1977). 'The Natural Rights to the Means of Production', *Philosophical Quarterly* 27 (106), 41–49.

Steiner, H. (1994). *An Essay on Rights*. Oxford and Cambridge: Blackwell.

Sterba, J. (1980). *Justice: Alternative Perspectives*. Belmont, CA: Wadsworth Publishing Company.

Sterba, J. (1986). 'Recent Works in Alternative Conceptions of Justice', *American Philosophical Quarterly* 23 (1), 1–22.

Stern, N. (2007). *The Economics of Climate Change: The Stern Review*. Cambridge: Cambridge University Press.

Stevenson, J. R. and Oxman, B. H. (1974). 'The Preparations for the Law of the Sea Conference', *American Journal of International Law* 68 (1), 9–13.

Stoett, J. P. (1997). *The International Politics of Whaling*. Vancouver: Vancouver University of British Columbia.

Stokke, O. S. and Thommessen, O. B. (2003). *Yearbook of International Co-operation*. London: Earthscan.

Strange, S. (1983). 'Cave! Hic Dragones: A Critique of Regime Analysis', in D. S. Krasner (ed.), *International Regimes*. Ithaca, NY: Cornell University Press.

Strange, S. (1987). 'The Persistent Myth of Lost Hegemony', *International Organization* 41, 551–574.

Stavropoulos, C. A. (1985). 'Procedural Problems on the Third Conference on the Law of the Sea', in M. H. Nordquist (ed.), *United Nations Convention on the Law of the Sea 1982. A Commentary, Vol 1*. Boston, Lancaster: Martinus Nijhoff.

Strohm, L. (1993). 'The Environmental Politics on International Waste Trade', *Journal of Environment and Development* 2 (2), 129–153.

Strong, M. (1999). 'Hunger, Poverty, Population and Environment', The Hunger Project Millennium Lecture, Madras, India.

Susskind, L. and Ozawa, C. (1992). 'Negotiating More Effective International Environmental Agreements', in Hurrell and Kingsbury (eds), *International Politics of the Environment: Actors Interests and Institutions*. Oxford: Clarendon Press.

Susskind, L. E. (1994). *Environmental Diplomacy: Negotiating More Effective Global Agreements*. New York: Oxford University Press.

Swanson, T. M. (1992) 'The Evolving Trade Mechanisms in CITES', *Review of European Community & International Environmental Law* 1 (1), 57–63.

Tasioulas, J. (1989). 'Justice Equity and Law', in E. Craig (ed.) *Routledge Encyclopaedia of Philosophy*. London: Routledge.

Taylor, C. (1989). *Sources of Self: The Making of the Modern Identity*. Cambridge: Cambridge University Press.

Third United Nations Conference on the Law of the Sea (UNCLOS III) (1979). *Official Records: Summary Records of Meetings, Vol. II*. New York: United Nations.

Bibliography

Third United Nations Conference on the Law of the Sea (UNCLOS III) (1982). 'Third United Nations Conference on the Law of the Sea'. Reprinted in *The Law of the Sea: United Nations Convention on the Law of the Sea*. New York: The United Nations.

Thomas S. D. and Twyman, C. (2006). 'Adaptation and Equity in Resource Dependent Societies', in W. N. Adger *et al*. (eds), *Fairness in Adaptation to Climate Change*. Cambridge, MA: MIT Press.

Thompson, J. (1992). *Justice and the World Order: A Philosophical Inquiry*. London: Routledge.

Thompson, M. and Rayner, S. (1998). 'Cultural Discourses', in S. Rayner and E. Malone (eds), *Human Choice and Climate Change*. Columbus, OH: Battelle Press.

Tol, F., Fankhauser, R. and Pearce, D. (1999). 'Empirical and Ethical Arguments in Climate Change: Impact Evaluation and Aggregation', in L. F. Toth (ed), *Fair Weather? Equity Concerns in Climate Change*. London: Earthscan.

Tol, R. S. J., Downing, T. E., Kuik, O. J. and Smith, J. B. (2004). 'Distributional Aspects of Climate Change Impacts', *Global Environmental Change* 14, 259–272.

Tolba, M. (1990). 'The Global Agenda and the Hazardous Waste Challenge', *Marine Policy* 14 (3), 205–209.

Tooze, R. (1990). 'Regimes and International Co-operation', in A. J. R. Groom and P. Taylor (eds), *Frameworks for International Co-operation*. London: Pinter Press.

Toth, F. L. (ed.) (1999). *Fair Weather? Equity Concerns in Climate Change*. London: Earthscan.

Trainer, T. (1985). *Abandon Affluence*. London: Zed Books.

United Nations Conference on Environment and Development (UNCED). (1992). *Agenda 21: Programme of Action for Sustainable Development*. Rio Declaration on Environment and Development, Rio de Janeiro.

United Nations Conference on the Human Environment (UNCHE). (1972). Stockholm.

United Nations Environment Programme (UNEP). (1982) Governing Council Decision 10/24, 31 May.

United Nations Environment Programme (UNEP). (1987). Governing Council Decision 14/30, June 17.

United Nations Human Development Report (2004). Human Development Report 2004.

United Nations Resolutions 1802 (XVII) (1962). International Co-operation in the peaceful use of the outer space. New York: United Nations.

Vallentyne, P. and Hillel, S. (eds) (2000). *The Origins of Left-Libertarianism: An Anthology of Historical Writing*. London: Palgrave.

Vallentyne, P. and Steiner, H. (eds) (2000). *Left-Libertarianism and its Critics: The Contemporary Debate*. London: Palgrave.

Vallette, J. and Spalding, H. (1990). *The International Trade in Hazardous Waste: A Greenpeace Inventory*, 5th edn. Washington, DC: Greenpeace International Waste Trade Project.

Van Korten, G. C. and Bulte E. H. (2002). *The Economics of Nature: Managing Biological Assets*. Edinburgh: Blackwell Publishing.

Viotti, P. and Kauppi, M. V. (1987). *International Relations Theory: Realism, Pluralism and Globalism*. New York: Macmillan.

Vogler, J. (1995). *The Global Commons: A Regime Analysis*. Chichester: John Wiley.

Vogler, J. (1996). 'The Environment in International Relations, Legacies and Contention', in Vogler J. and Imber M. (eds), *The Environment and International Relations*. London: Routeldge.

Vogler, J. (2000). *The Global Commons: Environmental and Technological Governance*, 2nd edn. Chichester: John Wiley.

Vogler, J. (2003). 'Taking Institutions Seriously: How Regimes can be Relevant to Multi-level Environmental Governance', *Global Environmental Politics* 3 (2), 25–39.

Vogler, J. and Imber, M. (eds) (1996). *The Environment and International Relations*. London: Routledge.

Wackernagel, M and Rees, W. (1996). *Our Ecological Footprint. Reducing Human Impact on the Earth*. Gabriola Island: New Society

Wackernagel, M. and Silverstein, J. (2000). 'Big Things First: Focusing on the Scale Imperative with the Ecological Footprint', *Ecological Economics* 32, 341–394.

Waldron, J. (1993). *Liberal Rights, Collected Papers 1981-1991*. Cambridge: Cambridge University Press.

Walhain, S. (2006) 'Trading Opportunities under the EU ETS'. Paper delivered at 'Climate Change in a Post 2012 World' organized by the Chatham Conference, 26 June. http://www.chathamhouse.org.uk/

Walker, G. and Bulkeley, H. (eds) (2006). 'Geographies of Environmental Justice', *Geoforum* 37, 655–659.

Walker, R. B. J. (1989). 'History and Structure in the Theory of International Relations', *Millennium* 18 (2), 163–184.

Waltz, K. (1979). *Theory of International Politics*. Reading, MA: Adison Wesley.

Walzer, M. (1977). *Just and Unjust Wars: A Moral Argument with Historical Illustrations*. New York: Basic Books.

Wapner, P. (1997). 'Governance in Global Civil Society', in O. Young (ed.), *Global Governance: Drawing Insight from Environmental Experience*. Cambridge, MA: MIT Press.

Weale, A. (1992). *The New Politics of Pollution*. Manchester: Manchester University Press.

Weber, M. (1946). 'Politics as Vocation', in H. H. Gerth and C. W. Mills (eds), *From Max Weber: Essays in Sociology*. New York: Oxford University Press.

Wenar, L. (2001). 'Contractualism and Global Economic Justice', *Metaphilosophy* 32 (1/2), 79–94.

Weiss, E. B. (1975). 'International Responses to Weather Modification', *International Organization* 29, 805–826.

Weiss, E. B., McCaffrey, C. Margraw, D. B. and Tarlock, A. D. (eds) (1998). *International Environmental Law and Policy*. New York: Aspen Publishers.

Weissman, R. (2005). 'Taking on Corporate Power – and Winning', *National Monitor* (Winter), 25–43.

von Weizsäcker, E. U. (1994). *Earth Politics*. London: Zed Books.

Wendt, A. (1987). 'The Agent-Structure Problem in International Relations Theory', *International Organization* 41, 335–370.

Wendt, A. (1995). 'Constructing International Politics', *International Security* 20, 71–81.

Wettestad, J. (1991). 'Verifications of International Greenhouse Agreements: A Mismatch Between Technical and Political Feasibility', *International Challenges* 11 (1), 41–47.

Wijkman, P. M. (1982) 'Managing the Global Commons', *International Organization* 36 (3), 511–536.

Williams, B. (1981). *Moral Luck*. Cambridge: Cambridge University Press.

Williams, B. (1995). 'Ethics', in A. C. Grayling (ed.), *Philosophy: A Guide Through the Subject*. Oxford: Oxford University Press.

Williams, G. and Mawdsley, E. (2006). 'Postcolonial Environmental Justice: Government and Governance in India', *Geoforum* 37, 660–670.

Wingenbach, E. (1999). 'Unjust Context: The Priority of Stability in Rawls's Contextualised Theory of Justice', *American Journal of Political Sciences* 43 (1), 213–232.

Wissenburg, M. (2001). 'Sustainability and the Limits of Liberalism', in J. Barry and M. Wissenburg (eds), *Sustaining Liberal Democracy: Ecological Challenges and Opportunities*. Houndmills: Palgrave.

Woodin, M. and Lucas, C. (2004). *Green Alternatives to Globalization: A Manifesto*. London: Pluto Press.

World Bank (2000). Technical Annex for a proposed credit of $72 million to the Republic of Kenya for an emergency power supply project. Report T-7388-KE.

World Bank (2001). Action Plan for the Reduction of Poverty (2001–2005) (PARPA). Strategy Document for Reduction of Poverty and Promotion of Economic Growth.

World Commission on the Environment and Development (WCED). (1987). *Our Common Future*. Oxford: Oxford University Press.

Worster, D. (1982). *Nature's Economy: The Roots of Ecology*. New York: Random House

Wynne, B. (1989). 'The Toxic Waste Trade: International Regulatory Issues and Options', *Third World Quarterly* 11 (3), 120–146.

Yamin F. (1995) 'Biodiversity, Ethics and International Law', *International Affairs* 71 (3), 529–546.

Young, H. P. (1991). *Sharing the Burden of Global Warming*. College Park: University of Maryland.

Young, O. (1980). 'International Regimes: Problems of Concept Formation', *World Politics* 32, 331–356.

Young, O. (1989a). *International Co-operation: Building Regimes for Natural Resources and the Environment*. Ithaca, NY: Cornell University Press.

Young, O. (1989b). 'The Politics of International Regimes Formation: Managing Natural Resources and the Environment', *International Organization* 43, 349–375.

Young, O. (1992). 'The Effectiveness of International Institutions: Hard Cases and Critical Variables', in J. Rosenau and E. Czempiel (eds), *Governance without Government: Order and Change in World Politics*. Cambridge: Cambridge University Press.

Young O. (1994). *International Governance: Protecting the Environment in a Stateless Society*. Ithaca, NY: Cornell University Press.

Young O. (1997). 'Rights Rules and Resources in World Affairs', in O. Young (ed.), *Global Governance: Drawing Insight from the Environmental Experience*. Cambridge, MA: MIT Press.

Young, O. (1998). 'The Effectiveness of International Environmental Regimes', *International Environmental Affairs* 10 (4), 267–289.

Young. O. (1999). *The Effectiveness of International Environmental Regimes; Causal Connections and Behavioural Mechanisms*. Cambridge, MA: MIT Press.

Zartman, W. I. and Berman, R. M. (1982). *The Practical Negotiator*. New Haven,, CT: Yale University Press.

Zuleta, B. (1983). 'Introduction', in *The Law of the Sea: United Nations Convention on the Law of the Sea*. New York: The United Nations.

Index

accumulation 149, 176, 177; and institutions 177; as nature commodification 172; capital 176; primitive 172; in relation to sustainability 149; and the state 181
Ackerman, B. 150, 155
adaptation 26, 105, 106,108; concern for developing countries 105; funding for projects 108; and justice 26; National Program of Action 199n4; valuation and ethics of 106; view of AOSIS 105; and vulnerability 105
Adger, W. N. 8, 25, 105, 109
Africa: debt and waste trade 96, 137–8; dumping of DDT 91–2, 198n15; EEZ 197n15; *see also* OAU
African elephants 23, 31, 38
Agarwal, A. 5, 8, 18, 84, 87, 88, 97, 111, 113, 137
Agenda 21(Earth Summit) 30, 62, 94 118
altruism 145
anarchy: feature of international relations 16, 182, 183
Anderson, T. 76, 136, 138, 174
animus revertendi 77
Antarctica: as a global common 18, 153, 163; conservation 38; resources 20; role of science 103; Treaty 19, 20
anthropogenic emissions 104, 106, 118, 126–7
AOSIS (Association of Small Island States) 105, 106
Area, the, as the seabed 67, 65, 79, 144
Aristotle: on duty of care 93; on equity and justice 4; on justice as virtue 8, 33, on particular justice 33; on the primacy of justice 8; on universal justice 33
Arvid Pardo 60, 63, 64, 137

atmosphere: equal ownership 114; as a global common 112; not a common heritage of mankind 137, 163
atomism 126
Attfield, R. 5, 47, 53, 114, 156, 160
Augustine, St 33
Australia 66, 174

Bamako Convention 95
bargaining, the use of power in 61, 63, 132, 140, 165; *see* Hobbes; Nozick
Barry, B. 38, 43, 114, 132, 140, 152, 155
Basel Convention: conceptions of justice in 81–3, 98; and globalisation 13, 56, 80; and individual environmental rights 86; and international trade 13, 22; parties to 80–2; role of Greenpeace 96; substantive rules 88; weakness 96
Basel Ban 95, 98; as a tool of international justice 97
Bentham, J. 8, 35, 36
Benton, T. 50, 147, 162, 167, 175, 176, 177
Bering Sea Fur seals, arbitration 77
Bhagwati, S. 136, 138, 174, 181, 191
biotechnology, sharing profits of 30
Bogart, J. 128, 140, 164; on Nozick 132–3
bourgeois 171
Brazil 21, 120
Bretton Woods 115
Brundtland Report: and communitarianism 200n2; conceptions of justice in 146–9, 151–9, 162; ethics of 146–9, 177; on human needs 50; against neoliberalism 149–62, 167–8, 175, 191; on planet's inequality 7
bubbles 119; *see also* flexible mechanism
Byrd, Senator Robert 134

228   Index

Cairo Guidelines 80, 83, 198n11
Canada 16, 17, 66
capacity building 95
capacity to pay: as a criterion for justice 102; different from justice 178; in relation to common but differentiated responsibility 112
capitalism: different from neoliberalism 169; dominance 158; good for the environment 174, 180; and minimum state 41; and property rights 160; and state welfare 49
categorical imperative 49
Catharina, Dutch ship 58
China 24, 105, 111, 113, 114, 157, 174, 199n8; the value of life 108
Chomsky, N. 169, 172
civic fraternity 40
class 14, 39, 171
clean development mechanism 99, 117, 119; as flexible mechanism 119; as an idea of international justice 117, 119, 122; as instrument of colonialism 129; how useful is 119–20
Clinton, President Bill 70, 134, 182
collective ownership of global resources 19, 111, 164, 194; *see also* Ostrom
collective utility 38
colonialism 28, 53, 82, 120, 154
Colson, D. 70, 71
command and control 118, 139
common but differentiated responsibility: ambiguity of meaning 111, 112; based on culpability 111, 112; as capacity to act 111; idea of international justice 10, 99, 109; origin of 109–10, norm of climate regime 110, 111; philosophy 110; relationship with polluter pays principle 111
common concern for mankind 21, 113, 114; biodiversity convention 21; climate change 113; leading to equal management rights 114
common heritage of mankind: applied to the seabed regime 63–8; attempt to apply to Brazilian Amazon 21; attempt to apply to global atmosphere 137; branded as a right to steal 66, 134, 190; branded as socialism 190; as cosmopolitanism 143; as egalitarian justice 57, 136 189; as an equity concept 10, 62, 162; implying common ownership 67; in relation to NIEO 133; opposed to libertarian justice 162; rejected by the US 133, 134, 190; *see also* Pardo; US Senate
common pool resources 21, 75, 76
common property resources 14, 77, 162, 188; examples of 18, regimes 25, 18, 161 subject of dispute 19, 21, 25, 77, 161
communal property management 135, 200n6
communitarianism 32, 36, 46
community: ethical 46, 94, 132, 136, 144, 159, 193, 198n13, 200; feminist idea of 94; and justice 46–8, 114, 162; and Marxism 49
comparative burden 102
compensatory justice 19, 101
Competent Authority 89
comprehensive approach to greenhouse emission reduction 117, 141
conception: different from concept 34, 147; of the good 43, 45, 132, 150–5, 167, 191; of international community 80, 144; of justice 32, 34–7; of sovereignty 93
consensus: and bargaining 63, 103; condition for accepting regimes 194n1; as an idea of justice 63; a means of dominance 171; the rule of 61–3
consequentialist ethic 36
conservation: different from sustainability 14–17, 23; in the EEZ 78; function of regimes 18, 76–8; of the marine resources 19, 58, 76; some harms local communities 23–4, 38
constitutional environmentalism 84, 87; *see also* Hayward
constrained maximiser 130, 131
constructivism 184,185
consumptive utilization 23
continental shelf 21, 58, 72, 135; example of common property resource 21; oil reserves in 71; property rights in 135; regime as enclosure 162; the regime of 72–5
contractarian justice 44,126
cosmopolitan rights, in Basel Convention 84–7
cosmopolitanism 40, 46, 53; argument against 46; main tenet 53
counter-hegemonic resistance 79, 98, 193
Cox, R. 38, 63, 171, 182; *see also* Gramsci

Daly, H. 138, 147, 152, 153, 156, 178
Dasgupta, C. 102, 103, 111, 112, 141, 115

Davidson, J. 148, 149, 152, 153, 158, 177
DDT, pesticide 91
debt for nature swap 23
deep seabed 17, 18, 58, 68; as common heritage of mankind 64,66; equity concerns in 63–9; mining in 66, 69, 166n10; Pioneer Investors 66, 67, 68, 70
democracy 52, 147
dependence 53, 66, 160
deontology 150, 184
discrimination 28, 68, 86
Dobson, A.: on conceptions of sustainability 35; on global citizenship 47; on the good life 152; on justice as meeting needs 47, 50, 147, 149; on liberal environmentalism 175
duty of care 93,94,95
duty to co-operate 95
duty to re-import waste 10,92,98,144

ecological footprint 180
ecological modernization 167, 168, 173, 174, 186
ecological space 138, 180
Ecomar, Italian waste company 89
economic rationality 94; see also market rationality
Ecuador 74
enclosure: CDM as 120; Grotius on 63, 64; of commons 77, 79, 120, 150, 161–4; of EEZ 75; of the high sea 74, 78; of international straits 71; neoliberal instrument 172; role of President Truman 136; against sustainability 161–4, 165, 176, 189, 192
end of the pipe 97
Enterprise, the 68, 70, 137, 144, 170
environmental racism 82, 98
environmentalism 84, 158, 152, 172; constitutional 84, 87; liberal 152, 172; as political ideology 172, 173; technological 158, 179
Epicurus 44
epistemic communities 179
equal entitlements and emission allocation 114
ethic of care 198n18
ethnocentrism 36, 51, 53
Exclusive Economic Zone (EEZ) 72–5, 78, 79, 135, 162

FAO (Food and Agricultural Organization) 92, 198n16

flexible mechanisms 119
Forest Principles 22, 30
Foucault, M. 175, 182
Founex Report 109, 188
free market 66, 67, 69, 77, 121, 129, 132, 134, 137–40, 143, 161, 174
Franck , T. 34, 47, 185
free riding 24
freedom: defined as utilitarianism 177, 190; and justice 33, 90, 158; of the sea 59, 60, 64, 70, 77; and self-determination 150; the state and individual 48, 151, 152, 158

G-77 65, 103, 105, 118, 141, 187
garbage imperialism 82, 89, 90
GATT 22, 191
Gauthier, D. 44, 45, 72, 126, 129, 130, 140, 150, 152, 159, 165, 166, 190
gentleman's agreement 62
geostationary orbit 53
Germany 69, 77, 162, 165, 196n8
global citizenship 84, 97
global commons 18–20; 31, 40, 57, 162; enclosure of 150; the institute of 108; overuse of 101
Global Environmental Facility (GEF) 115, 116, 121
global resource dividend 40; *see also* Pogge
global sink 25
globalists 50, 52, 53
Gramsci, A. 171
grandfathering 102
green capitalism 182
green fund scheme 106
Greenpeace International 90, 96, 97, 98
Grieco, J. 183, 193
Grotius, H. 58
Guha, M. 15, 16
Guinea Bissau 90

Haas, P. M. 179, 183, 184
Hagel, Senator Chuck 134
Haiti 81, 166
Harman, G. 44, 45, 126, 130, 131, 140, 150, 159
Hayek, F. A. 41, 42, 136, 137, 155, 191
Hayward, T. 9, 27, 28, 84, 88, 177
hazardous wastes 22, 23, 27, 30, 137, 142, 144, 155; ban on trade in 95, 97, 98; conceptions of justice in 81–99; elaboration of regime on 80–1; scope of convention 83–4

230 *Index*

hedonism 37
hegemony 169, 171
historical emissions 113, 145
Hobbes, T. 44, 45, 63, 130; on justice as mutual advantage 44, 45, 63; on state of nature 130; on the use of threat in bargaining 63, 140, 166
Hugh, D. 31
human needs: a requirement of justice 46, 48, 50, 148, 151; as theory of justice 48–50
human rights 28, 29, 40, 82, 114, 187

Iceland 77
ideal speech situation 103
ideology: economic 45, 106, 123, 126, 136, 155; free market 77, 78, 121, 134, neoliberal 167, 172, 185; political 40, 134, 137, 139, 141
Illich, I. 163
incinerator ash 90
India 24, 111, 113, 114, 120, 157, 174
indigenous peoples 22, 30, 143
individual rights 84, 86, 88, 95, 142, 190
individual talents, and ideas of justice 43, 46, 128, 138
individualism 47
industrialization 15, 16, 174, 179
inherent morality, disputed 45, 130
initial acquisition, the principle of 161
innocent passage, right of 70, 71, 72, 73, 135
intellectual property rights 137
intergenerational equity 4
international aid 129
International Court of Justice (ICJ) 19, 77, 82, 101
international straits 71, 72, 74
interspecies justice 4
intragenerational equity 12, 121, 187
IPCC 25, 26, 107, 108, 113, 139
irreversibility, of nature 37, 153
IUCN 15

Jamaica 57, 195n1
Jelly Wax, Italian waste firm 89
justice: as communitarianism 46–8; concept and conceptions 33–49; contrasted with equity 4; as egalitarianism 38–40; as entitlement 127–9; primacy of 33; as property rights 41–3; as self-interested reciprocity 129–31; as utility maximization 35–8

Kant, I. 39, 114
Kenya 196n8
Khian Sea, the voyage of 90
Koh, T. B. 57, 61, 62, 135, 195n1, 196n8
Koko, Nigeria 89
Kyoto Protocol 118, 119, 120, 121, 134, 139, 144, 157

labour principle, of John Locke 41
laissez-faire 155, 157, 191; conflict with sustainability 157; supported by neoliberalism 190
landlocked states 72, 74, 194
landmass, criterion for burden sharing 102
land use 22, 23, 64, 66, 71, 90, 120, 131, 161; developing countries demand rights to 188; enclosure 120, 161–4; justice of initial appropriation 41–2, 127–9, 161
LDCF (Least Developed Countries Fund) 108
Leff, E. 138, 158
Leggett, J. 8, 62, 100, 106, 118, 157
Liability Protocol, of Basel Convention 87
liberal democracy 38, 40, 52, 152; effect on justice formulation 38, 40, 52; in relation to sustainability 52, 152
liberal environmentalism 150, 152, 175
liberal equality 46
liberal neutrality 40, 155, 158; leading to state neutrality 40, 154, 155; countered by environmentalists 157, 158
liberalism 41, 44, 46, 73, 77, 125, 136, 166; on community 46; and free market 136; and individual liberty 41; relation to libertarianism 125; and tolerance 166; underwrites enclosure of commons 73, 77
libertarianism 42, 43, 125, 127, 132; criticized by communitarians 46; individual liberty 42, 43; on property rights 132–9; relation to liberalism 125–6; on the role of the state 154–6; on self-ownership, 41, 134, 150, 200n3; on welfare state 45, 127, 132
liberty: on conceptions of the good 167; deeper problems 164–6, 200n7; definition 49, 150, 151, 161; as freedom of trade 90; fundamental value 38, 40, 41, 42, 43, 190; national 84, 90; opposed by communitarians 151, 152, 153; in relation to rights 48; and self-ownership 165; and social goods 38; and social equality 46, 159; versus

community welfare 132
limits to growth 101, 138, 146, 181
Locke, J. 38, 41, 127, 162; on the justice of initial appropriation 41, 127, 161; labour principle of, 41; on self-sovereignty 132–3; on social contract 38; supporting commons enclosure 161–2
Lockean proviso 161

manganese nodules 66, 69, 196n10
mare clausum 58, 70
mare liberum 58, 70
marine resources 19, 76, 77, 79
maritime states 65, 72
market rationality 13, 121, 167, 173, 174, 178
Marshall Islands 89
Marx, K. 8, 48, 160
materialism, historic 187
middle class, Western 14, 15
migratory stock, fish 19, 76
Mill, J. S. 8, 33, 35, 36
minimal state 4, 41, 132, 154–60; defined 41, 132; environmental critique of 158–60
minimum justice 80, 98
mitigation, of climate change 25, 26, 105, 106–8, 110, 122, 175
modus vivendi 43
Moi, A. 82
Montego Bay 57, 195n1
Montreal Protocol 22, 24, 30, 111, 112, 118, 199n6
moral elitism 36
moral pluralism 152, 153, 154, 167
moral relativism 47
moral subjectivism 44
morality 33, 41, 75, 129; based on human needs 48, 49; constructed from game theories 129; end result of justice 35; of God and natural rights 41; inherent in man 126; instrumental 44; as mere conventions 45, 75, 129–31, 165; unity with justice 33
mutual advantage 43, 52, 126, 129, 140, 142, 159, 160; as a theory of justice 43–5, 129–31

NAPA (National Adaptation Programme of Action) 199n4
national prerogative 142
national resources 18, 21

natural limits 101; *see also* limits to growth
nautical miles 70, 71, 72, 73, 74, 135, 196n12, 196n13
needs 46, 47, 48, 50, 59, 61, 65, 95, 114, 144, 148, 149, 151; communitarians on 46; libertarians on 49, 158; the philosophy of 48–50, 158–60
neoliberalism 125, 168–9, 170, 172–4, 176, 177; contrasted with capitalism 169; defined 169–70; and ecological modernization 173; and environmental economic 139; as an environmental project 172–4; meaning contested 170, 171, 196; opposed to global sustainability 175–6, 177
neorealism 10, 183, 184, 193
neutrality, of states 155, 191
New England 165
NGOs 22, 23, 96, 103, 121, 142, 175
NIEO (New International Economic Order) 133, 134, 187
Nitze, W. A. 105, 139, 141, 157
non-discrimination, the principle of 92, 95, 97, 98, 189
North–South equity 18, 24, 35, 60, 65, 72, 109, 119, 125, 146, 168, 177, 187
Nozick, R. 41, 42, 127, 150, 158, 161; against redistribution 42, 159; endorses minimum state 155; on justice as entitlement 127–9; on justice as property rights 41–3; on negative rights 127; on self-ownership 133, 150; in support of enclosure 161; on tracking 'bestness' 151

OAU (Organisation for African Unity) 74, 82, 154, 197n6
OECD (Organisation for Economic Co-operation and Development) 82, 91, 106, 117, 122, 140, 141, 198n14
oil 20, 27, 71, 72, 73, 180; in the EEZ 75; in the seabed 73
outer space 17, 18, 53, 163

package deal 61, 62, 79
parallel system, in seabed exploitation 68
Pardo, A. 59, 63, 64, 137
Paterson, M. 8, 16, 100, 104, 113, 117, 139, 169, 173, 181, 190
per capita 99, 111, 113–14, 121, 142, 189
Peru 73
pesticides 92, 198n15; *see also* DDT

232 *Index*

Philadelphia 90
PIC (prior informed consent) 88–90, 96, 97, 98, 138, 141, 142, 144, 178
pioneer investors, in seabed mining 66, 67, 68, 70
planet protection fund 118
Pogge, T. 4, 40, 49, 52, 53, 114, 132, 195n2
Polanyi, K. 175
polar bear 17
polluter pays principle 86, 102, 106, 107, 111, 112
pollution: air 22; atmospheric 111; equal rights to 113, 114; land-based 71; of local rivers 120; industrial 121; marine 24, 25, 29; oil 27
positivism 184
power 30, 43, 63, 131, 155, 176, 185, 190, 193; aided by structure 153, 176, 183; definition 63; determined by talent and resources 43; in international relations 45; and justice 44, 64; as norm determinant 30; use in bargaining 44, 63, 131, 133, 140–3
precautionary principle 37, 105
preferential rights, in resource allocation 77, 78
preservation 17, 75, 84, 94, 151, 158
primitive accumulation 172
property rights 21, 41, 65, 71, 72, 77, 135, 161, 196; dominance of 135–7; justice as 41–4, 127–9; and profit maximisation 196; in regime allocation 21–2; over EEZ 71; over sea resources 72, 77; versus sustainability 160–1
prudence 94
Puckett, J. 81, 89, 141, 153

rational bargaining 79, 116, 166
rational choice theory 10, 31, 130, 131, 184
Rawls, J. 4, 8, 33, 34, 35, 38, 39, 40, 41, 42, 44, 52, 63, 114, 126, 128, 147, 150, 155; on the basic structure of justice 39; contrasted with libertarianism 38, 39, 40, 126; on cosmopolitanism 40; difference principle of 40; on distinction between concept and conceptions 34, 147; the environmental critique of 150, 155; the libertarian critique of 42; main ideas of justice 39; on the primacy of justice 33, 34; the socialist critique of 49; on utility 41
rectification 127

redistribution 7, 42, 51, 128, 132, 133, 134, 175, 143, 154, 156, 158, 159, 165, 175
regime analysis 4, 10, 11, 12, 31, 182, 184, 187, 192
res communes 65, 73, 76, 77
res nullius 58, 65, 73
rights: ad hoc 78; civic 29; environmental 10, 14, 29, 84; of equal entitlements 114; and ethic of care 97; of indigenous people 22, 30; of national independence 16; natural 41; navigational 71, 86; negative versus positive 41, 48, 65; over common pool resources 21; of permanent sovereignty over resources 18; social 29
right to steal, and the common heritage of mankind 66, 134, 190
Rio Summit 28, 30, 62, 100, 118, 141, 159, 195n7, 199n5
risk 37, 141, 185
Ruggie, J. 10, 38, 183, 185, 193
Russia 118

scarcity 21, 33, 52, 76, 176
SCCF (Special Climate Change Fund) 108
seabed: the Authority 62, 66, 67, 106, 133; as common heritage of mankind 64, 65, 67, 133, 136; as common property resource 18, 53, 67; mining in 66, 67; property rights over 135; the regime 63–9; resources in 66; Truman declaration 73
Selden J. 58, 59
self-denial 37
self-ownership 41, 134, 151, 150, 200n3
self-sovereignty 133; *see also* self-ownership
sequestration 106
Shue, H. 8, 10, 25, 26, 34, 52, 102, 111, 116, 166
Sierra Club 15
slave trade 53, 58, 165
social compromise 130
social contract 38, 39, 41, 130
social equality 38, 46, 159
social goods 38, 39, 47
social identity 63
social solidarity 40
sociology 83
sovereignty 9, 15, 16, 21, 41, 65, 98, 137, 143; economic 65, 98, 143; permanent 21, 137, 194n1; and equality of states 68; over self 41, 98, 133; principle in

IR 16, 18, 88
state of nature 39, 42, 130, 132
state: homogenous 47, 184; rational egoists 184
status quo rights 102
Sterba, J. 33, 34, 36, 38, 41, 127, 154
Stockholm Declaration 6, 28, 110
Strong, M. 7
Subjectivism, moral 44
sustainable development: and the enclosure of commons 161–4; and the good life 150–4; and the neutral state 154–8; and subsistence rights 158–60; difference between concept and conception 148–9; in compatibility with neoliberal governance 172–82; incompatibility with neoliberal justice 149–64
tax, international 118
technology transfer 95, 144
temperance 33
territorial sea, the regime of 70–2
tipping point 29
toxic imperialism 98
tracking 'bestness' 151
tragedy of the commons 20, 21, 161, 163
transit passage, right of 71, 72
trustee rights 77

Uganda 120
utilitarianism 32, 36, 38, 40, 41, 43, 50, 76; justice as 35, 37; Rawls against 40; *see also* Rawls
UNCED 7, 16, 30, 57, 118, 137, 138, 159
UNCLOS III, the regime 57–79
UNEP 19, 22, 80, 81, 83, 102
universalism 35
USA (United Sates of America): against right to sustainable development 195n7; against the seabed regime 68, 69, 162; against subsistence rights 159; bullying in international negotiations 140, 141, 155; on the common heritage of mankind 133, 134, 137, 190; on the extension of the territorial sea 71; on minimal state 155; on offshore drilling 71, 74, 75; opposed to the Basel ban 96, 138, 139; on quantified emission reduction targets 117; on the ratification of the new seabed regime 70; refusal to ratify Basel Treaty 81, 173; on rights over living marine resources 73, 74, 77; on the Seabed Authority 68; on transit passage rights 71, 72
US Senate 66, 70, 134, 157, 190, 196n4
utility 36, 37, 38, 43, 130, 166, 184
utility function 38
utility maximization 43, 166
utopia 41, 125

value of life 45, 114, 189
veil of ignorance 39
veto 63, 103, 139
violence 16
virtue 33
Vogler, J. 9, 11, 16, 20, 52, 53, 57, 58, 61, 64, 65, 71, 163, 183, 185
voluntarism 171, 181, 182

Walker, R. B. J. 126
waste brokers 87, 89, 90, 96, 97, 190
waste cycle 83, 97
WCED 7, 148, 151, 156, 159, 162, 192
Wendt, A. 10
White House effect 106
willingness to pay 102
WTO 22

Yellowstone Park 15, 152
Yosemite Valley 15
Young, O. 7, 10, 18, 25, 30, 83, 102, 181, 183, 184, 185, 193

Zimbabwe 89
Zuleta, B. 57, 61, 62, 65

For Product Safety Concerns and Information please contact our EU
representative GPSR@taylorandfrancis.com
Taylor & Francis Verlag GmbH, Kaufingerstraße 24, 80331 München, Germany

www.ingramcontent.com/pod-product-compliance
Lightning Source LLC
Chambersburg PA
CBHW062148300426
44115CB00012BA/2042